Before
Jane Austen

Original water color of Thomas Rowlandson's "Battle of Upton."

Before Jane Austen

The Shaping of the English Novel
in the Eighteenth Century

BY HARRISON R. STEEVES

With Contemporary Eighteenth-Century

Illustrations

HOLT,
RINEHART AND WINSTON
NEW YORK CHICAGO
SAN FRANCISCO

Designer: Ernst Reichl
88105—0115
Printed in the
United States of America

To Edna

I Render Thanks . . .

. . . to the many institutions and individuals who have contributed to the making of this book. My greatest debts, both literary and iconographic, have been to the New York Public Library and the library of Yale University. I am under less massive but no less significant obligation to the British Museum, the Library of Congress, the Royal Academy of Arts, and the libraries of Columbia, Dartmouth, Harvard, Dickinson College, and the Shippensburg (Pennsylvania) State College. It need scarcely be added that even the best of collections, without the attention and aid of librarians and curators, is, so to speak, food without drink. For that kind of knowledgeable and willing help, I must record a particular debt to those in charge of special collections in the New York Public Library— Miss Elizabeth Roth, First Assistant Curator of the Print Room; Dr. John D. Gordon, Curator of the Berg Collection; and Mr. Joseph T. Rankin, of the Fine Arts Library. I am under similar obligation to Miss Linda Lutz, of the Baker Library of Dartmouth College, Mrs. Joyce Steerman of the Rare Book Room at Yale, and Miss Helen Moyer, of Shippensburg.

My personal contacts in the writing of this book have been few but greatly helpful. Perhaps I owe most to three scholars who have recently contributed to our better knowledge of Godwin and his circle: Professor Burton R. Pollin and Professor Jack W. Marken, both of whom have been kind enough to read and offer judgment upon the chapter on "Social Justice," and Dr. David V. Erdman. Professor John Crossett has done the same friendly service for the chapters on Richardson and "Sex in the Eighteenth-Century Perspective," and Professor John H. Sutherland for that on Robert Bage.

Two permissions granted me lie quite outside the order of customary privilege. The first is Dr. Kenneth Garlick's, the owner's, permission to use the crayon and pencil drawing by Sir Thomas Lawrence of Godwin and Holcroft at the State Trials of 1794, which to the best of our knowledge has never before been published. The other is the permission of the library of Yale University for use of the original Rowlandson water color which serves as frontispiece. Etchings, both black and white and hand-colored, were made from this in 1791, but the original water color is probably reproduced here for the first time.

For highly valued services in connection with the publication of the volume I have to thank Mrs. Mary Squire Abbot, of Mmes. McIntosh and Otis, New York, and Mr. Thomas C. Wallace, editor for Holt, Rinehart, and Winston.

My wife, Dr. Edna L. Steeves, takes the last, and therefore the most honored place, in this more or less academic procession. In the intervals of her own professorial work she has hunted, read, noted, and, most importantly, listened patiently and judged.

HARRISON R. STEEVES
PROFESSOR EMERITUS, COLUMBIA UNIVERSITY

Contents

Illustrations

Before
Jane Austen

CHAPTER I

View from Pisgah

FEW OF even the faithful readers of English fiction—those to whom Jane Austen, Dickens, Thackeray, Trollope, Hardy, and James are more than names—have read widely in the fiction before Jane Austen's time. Even the great fictions of the early eighteenth century, *Robinson Crusoe* and *Gulliver's Travels,* are better known in versions that have reduced them to children's stories; and it is a fairly safe guess that most readers brought up on these tales cannot say who wrote them. Two other novels, of the mid-century, seem to have withstood the abrasion of time, Fielding's *Tom Jones,* read more or less surreptitiously during the nineteenth century as a book that could not be procured from the Sunday-school libraries, and Goldsmith's *Vicar of Wakefield,* green in the memories of high-school students as recently as a generation ago as a book both entertaining and safe for young explorers of life. Sterne's *Tristram Shandy* and perhaps his *Sentimental Journey*—if we consent to call them novels—are no doubt still read and properly appreciated. But who of us today have memories, either favorable or adverse, of *Clarissa, Humphry Clinker, Rasselas, Evelina, Vathek,* or the once incredibly popular florid Gothic romances of Ann Radcliffe?

This volume is to deal with the years in which the novel was still an experiment. At the beginning of the eighteenth century there was no novel. By the end, novels of every description were being published, not in dozens but in hundreds. The badness of the product was universally recognized, but perhaps fifty had emerged out of the ruck of mediocrity, some tolerable, some good, and some great. But even the best of them— remember, they were still experiments—were likely to be too long, too didactic, a little too stiff in style, a little too puritanical, a little too commonplace, or in a word, a little too uninteresting, to people who had come to know something better because it was more highly developed.

The history of any art has its significance, despite the few modernists who think kindergarten practice in finger-painting more important than what can be learned from Velasquez and Vermeer. For even esthetic revolt is revolt against something, and the nature of that something needs to be fairly apprehended; it may even reveal an unexpected and exhilarating interest. The history of the novel, we have noted, is a history of quick growth, quick because in some respects it is no more than the adaptation and fusion of other and well-matured literary forms. There are no primitives among the novelists; for plot-making had been studied and elaborated in the drama and in shorter narrative forms like the novella; character portraiture had reached the level of accomplished art in the seventeenth-century writers of "characters" and in periodicals like *The Spectator*; situation and incident had been competently handled in long narratives of the romantic type, even as far back as Malory's *Morte d'Arthur*—or for that matter the Homeric epics and the Northern sagas, with striking sharpness in the domestic sagas of Iceland. The novel, then, can be regarded as an assembled rather than an invented artistic form. But once discovered and identified, its importance became immediately clear, and its perfecting in methods and techniques made rapid progress.

That is going to be the area of our study; and the justification of the study is intrinsic interest, which we assert without reservation or apology. The score or more of novels to which we shall give particular attention "date." It is *because* they date that we are to consider them. All of them have some anticipatory touch of modernity, but in most of them we shall find incompleteness and ineptitude—matters of interest in any study of development. Even awkwardness will be found to have its quaint or its amusing side.

We are to be concerned with the novel of the eighteenth century as first of all (to quote Matthew Arnold's phrase in another connection) a "criticism of life." But a criticism, of course, of contemporary life—or rather, a criticism of life in its contemporary setting. For life can be viewed accurately only in connection with the social context of the period. We are going to try to find out how the more significant novels of the period impressed and influenced the readers of the time. And we shall be necessarily very much concerned with the slow progress of the form in penetration, circumference, social truth, and dignity.

The eighteenth century was one of the long steps in what was once confidently called "the liberation of man." Today we are less certain that liberation is anything more than the changing horizon of history in the making. But we do know that so far as progress may mean at least advance from worse to better in social institutions and social relations, that century did accomplish a great deal toward a fairer appraisal of human worth and for the equalization of opportunity.

On the political side, the mileposts of liberation are more conspicuous, though no more memorable, than on the social side. That is principally because of the two great political overturns of the century, the American and the French Revolutions. Yet even the antagonisms and the doubts that followed the loss of the American colonies had by the end of the century accomplished little in England toward the moderation of autocracy and the neutralizing of political amateurism and corruption. The very word "democracy" was accompanied usually by appropriate profanity, and the struggle between tory and liberal (on the whole a struggle for power rather than social betterment) at the close of the period seemed to be a stalemate. Over this long interval, the influence of imaginative literature upon political opinion was very slight.

On the social side, however, literature, and notably fiction, played a more effectual part. Before the eighteenth century, polite literature had been addressed principally to the upper classes, who all but monopolized the privileges of wealth, fashion, education, and indeed general literacy, all combining to give them the tremendous social leverage known as influence. This prestige had less support, however, than political power had, and it could be challenged or even attacked openly and vocally. It was the fiction, and also the discursive writing, of Bunyan, Defoe, and Swift that started sympathetic understanding of the poverty, limited lives, vulgar pleasures, and cheap emotional refuges of the underprivileged; even more, of their exposure to crime and a brutalizing criminal law.

By the end of the century the iniquities arising from privilege had been repeatedly canvassed in fiction. The most conspicuous one, and perhaps the most censurable, had been presented in numberless stories of honest but socially disadvantaged young women exposed to the appetites of wealthy libertines, with their tempting ways of life, legal immunities, and cavalier and often boastful inhumanity. But apart from its abuses, privilege had begun to be questioned as a just measure of moral and social worth; and by the end of the century the rival philosophies of aristocracy and democracy—in their social rather than their political aspects— had been submitted in fiction to a good deal of interested scrutiny. There was no decision rendered, nor could there be; but at least the claims of the plain man had been presented and argued.

For all that, it was difficult to overcome the distaste of "nice" people for the vulgarities of the plain man—his illiteracy, his obligation to work, his uncleanliness, his perspiration, his antipathies, and his increasing clamor for equality. At the very end of the century, Henry James Pye, then poet laureate, argued the rival claims of class in two incredibly dull novels, *The Aristocrat* and *The Democrat,* to a conclusion quite acceptable to the opinions of George IV. Yet social prejudices were entertained also by less prejudiced minds. Jane Austen was inclined to look without interest upon the unvarnished plain citizen, except in his proper place—in the tenant farmer's cottage or in a footman's livery.

While we shall use a few pages for surveying English fiction before the eighteenth century, we shall really begin with Daniel Defoe. Plenty of prose fiction had been written before his time, some of it pleasant, some deadly. But almost all of it missed what we recognize today as the essential purpose of the novel—if not to create the impression of downright and uncompromising reality, at any rate to deal with what seem to be real people, in situations which have the tang of the life of the time and which pose significant problems related to that life. That is as near as we are going to come to a preliminary definition of the novel, adding to it, of course, the fact that its vehicle is conventionally prose narrative.

We are going to quote a great deal, in accord with our view that much of the essential and the interesting in our earlier fiction can be conveyed without our being lost in its wastes or drowned in its profusion. Adequate, even generous, quotation will save us too from the frivolity of trying to discuss literature in a vacuum of knowledge of the thing discussed. Quotation is meant to furnish the core of the book.

Jane Austen is the terminus of our discussion principally for two reasons. First, that she comes exactly at the end of a century highly important in intellectual and cultural history, and at the beginning of another century equally epoch-making. And the line of demarcation between these two centuries is not merely an accident of measured time but a turning point in social and cultural tradition. Miss Austen can properly be called the first *modern* English novelist, the earliest to be read with the feeling that she depicts *our* life, and not a life placed back somewhere in history, or off somewhere in imagined space.

Miss Austen was also the first novelist to free herself from conventions that had limited the novel in both matter and form and dressed it in what we feel today to have been a heavy and pretentious prose. She assimilated most of what the eighteenth century had learned of the novel through experiment. She discarded theatrical situations, took the primary virtues for granted, introduced upper-middle-class characters without aristocratic arrogance and equally without a proletarian axe to grind, made her characters flexible and amenable to reason, made a virtue of social intelligence, and wrote in a langue close to everyday use. No one before her had accomplished all of these things; few had accomplished many of them; many had accomplished none.

This is not a chronology of our early fiction, or a survey, or a catalogue raisonné, or any other of those lengthy short cuts to a speaking acquaintance with names and dates, but an ignorance of literature itself—the true written word. I know no way of honestly extending one's knowledge of literature other than by reading it—not reading *about* it. Yet there is a sanction for sampling the better writing of a period which does not on the whole offer remunerative reading, except as it looks forward to better things. Fiction in the eighteenth century presents just that sort of interest. The novels, or near-novels, of the period which every cultivated reader ought to know at first hand can easily be numbered on the fingers, almost on the fingers of one hand. But so limited an acquaintance cannot give us the literary feeling of the period as expressed in its fiction. For that, we need to know not merely more in quantity but more variety. A conspectus of the more memorable fiction of the times must inevitably trace the course of development of the novel, but our interest is not to be limited by that narrow and technical approach to fiction. We are really to be concerned with what interested readers of fiction in this formative period, and with why they were interested. The fact that contemporary judgments were transient and faulty, simply because they lacked the perspective of time, is a matter of interest in itself, and one which we shall try to examine under the light not only of prevailing taste, but of social history.

Obviously, we shall be considering primarily the greater names, but a few also of the second magnitude; and where literary relations are indisputably important, a rare one with limited or merely contemporary interest, or one that seems to have been overlooked. For this book has been written not to increase the erudition of scholars, and not for young persons who have to pass examinations, but for people who read novels, who are fond of them as a genre, and who are not averse to knowing something about the earlier development of the great tradition.

CHAPTER II

From Arcadia to Mount Zion

STORY TELLING is as old as civilization, and today there is no tribal folk so primitive that they lack a body of traditional stories which are recited on occasion by their wise men, their magic workers, their old men and women, or their young warriors and lovers. Over the course of time primitive stories settle into forms and modes, which scholars (who have a fondness for classification) name and define for us as types. Among the shorter forms we have beast fables, fertility tales, ballads, fabliaux, (which are piquant tales in verse), and novelle (which are more finished prose fabliaux). The most familiar longer narratives of traditional form are romances of various sorts in either verse or prose, and epic poems. Speaking generally, shorter forms tend to amalgamate with one another and to stretch out into longer forms. In the various tales of Chaucer alone we can find a gathering of most of the story types familiar down to his time except the actually primitive ballad, such as the Robin Hood cycle, and the primitive epic like *The Iliad* and *Beowulf*.

All this we can note and pass; for our concern is with a narrative form which emerges late in literary history, which shows residues and influences from many earlier story forms, and which can develop only where high social organization and studied manners have replaced primitive folkways, education has become fairly general, individuality has called for recognition, and literary art itself has passed through many experimental hands to reach a point at which it can be recognized and talked about. The novel is, in other words, a latter-day form, voicing the ways and interests of an advanced society, and developing rapidly in range and effectiveness as achievement succeeds experiment.

If the novel were no more than a long story in prose, then its history would stretch back the greater part of the Christian era; for long prose narratives were widely known in the later stages of ancient Greek civilization. Were they novels? The answer can be found in the briefest glance at one of them, probably the best of the lot—the *Aethiopica* (otherwise known as *Theagenes and Chariclea*) of Heliodorus, written about A.D. 400.

It is the story of the romantic attachment of two young people discovered at the scene of a battle between Mediterranean pirates. Their identities are unknown, and their unprotected situation makes them, during the greater part of the action, slaves to a succession of owners. Land and naval battles are frequent, the contestants including Phoenicians, Greeks, Persians, Egyptians, and Ethiopians; friends and foes change in quick succession; the scene shifts constantly from country to country over a large part of the Mediterranean littoral. The lovers are separated, rejoined, and separated again, Theagenes seeming at times to be engaged in an unending pursuit race after Chariclea. Their lives—and Chariclea's chastity—are exposed to an almost unbroken succession of threats. Death hovers over them almost continuously. The end is a recognition scene— Chariclea is the daughter of the Queen of Ethiopia—and true and constant love ends in their marriage.

It is a readable story, with more ingenious plot than the scramble of incident would seem to imply. The incidents themselves, although not highly varied, carry some amount of story interest, and the theme of romantic love is handled with a spirituality and tenderness that might surprise the modern reader.

But it is not a novel. Its action is too violent, too diverse to be convincing; its principals are devoted but conventional lovers who might have been taken bodily out of Roman comedy; the course of the narrative is a succession of episodes which have little relation to its fragmented plot, and which could be detached and fitted into almost any other story of the same time and type; finally, these distinct episodes are usually brought to an end through chance intervention and even outright miracles. In a word, the basis of this story is not realistic; it gives no broad view of the life of the time; its characters are dim and difficult to realize except in their roles as lovers; and their actions are simply physical responses to new situations which raise problems of immediate action, but rarely of conduct. It is simply one of the many forms of "romance," which tends to idealize, to exalt, and to excite, rather than to transcribe, to analyze, and to judge.

If we take a long jump—almost nine hundred years—to Chaucer's lengthy poetical story of *Troilus and Criseyde,* we find a straightforward narrative of pseudo-historical setting—the Trojan War—which introduces us to characters of modern type, consciously and even sophisticatedly motivated, carrying forward a consistent and well-organized plot, which, in spite of the highly romantic setting, is built brick by brick out of credible actions and happenings. There is little to prevent our considering as a novel this fascinating adaptation of old story material, except that it is in verse (why shouldn't a novel take verse form?), that its indebtedness to romantic legend gives it the atmosphere of romance, and that it is diluted with mythic and supernatural elements.

It is hard to identify exactly the period within which the novel first appears in characteristic form, simply because the approach to a norm is gradual. It is furthermore a matter of controversy what ultimate form embodies, and it would be absurd to think that it would not continue to develop—that is, to change—so long as it continues to be written. So instead of trying to place a finger upon a point in time at which we can say, "Here is the first English novel," we shall begin with the period in which the melting pot of narrative types began to show—in England, at least— the good metal that we call the novel. We need go no farther back for this than the Elizabethan period, which is almost identical with the life of Shakespeare. Much prose fiction had been written before the Elizabethan age, but it would be unprofitable for us to grope around in the mass of fictive material which anticipated only vaguely and incompletely the purpose and methods of the novel. Suffice it to say that by the time Shakespeare had taken possession of the English stage, stories of length which had something of the appearance of novels also were coming into vogue.

In England it was a great—a *very* great—period for literature, as well as for the social and political integration of the nation. Drama burst into almost explosive splendor during the ten years prior to 1600. Poetry found a new and widely diffused glory after two generally uninspired centuries. The literary essay came into being. Books were written upon history, exploration, geography, antiquities, and even literary criticism.

But prose fiction languished. Probably the chief reason was that in a still largely illiterate age the spoken word of the stage had wider appeal than the printed word. Also, no doubt, the brilliance of the drama tended to blast the other literary types. It is worth noting that the very moderate achievement in fiction came in an important part from the hands of young men writing for the stage. Apparently they found the theatre more interesting, and perhaps more remunerative, than story-writing. None of the Elizabethan fiction shows an art much in advance of that seen in the *Aethiopica*; and comparison with *Troilus and Criseyde* shows a falling off in almost every aspect of power.

Elizabethan fiction appealed to a wide variety of interests and tastes, from the politest and most literate, to the illiterate and uncultivated. We can stop briefly to examine a few of these romances (so far as they seem to anticipate the later novel in any very definite way), which for the purposes of discussion are often classified into distinct and recognized types.

The earliest is John Lyly's *Euphues,* published in 1579, almost at the dawn of the English literary renaissance. It is a piece of pure literary

snobbery, fashionably affected and read only by the fastidious and the pretentious. Much learning has been expended upon the sources and stylistic
models for Lyly's romance, but they are of no close concern for us, since
we are interested mainly in what Elizabethan romances did for the novel
still-to-be. The meager and indistinct story in *Euphues* is so diluted with
pose and mannerism that the work is only to be noted in passing as one of
the things that Elizabethan society might read. But we shall sample it,
though as little more than a literary curiosity.

> Ah, fond wench, dost thou think Euphues will deem thee constant to
> him when thou hast been inconstant to his friend? Weenest thou that
> he will have no mistrust of thy faithfulness when he hath had trial of
> thy fickleness? Will he have no doubt of thine honor when thou thy-
> self callest thine honesty in question? Yes, yes, Lucilla, well doth
> he know that the glass once crazed will with the least clap be cracked;
> that the cloth which staineth with milk will soon lose his color with
> vinegar; that the eagle's wing will waste the feather as well of the
> phoenix as of the pheasant; that she that hath been faithless to one
> will never be faithful to any.
>
> But can Euphues convince me of fleeting, seeing that for his sake I
> break my fidelity? Can he condemn me of disloyalty when he is the
> only cause of my disliking? May he justly condemn me of treachery
> who hath this testimony as trial of my good will? Doth not he re-
> member that the broken bone, once set together, is stronger than ever
> it was? That the greatest blot is taken off with the pumice? That
> though the spider poison the fly, she cannot infect the bee? That al-
> though I have been light to Philautus, yet I may be lovely to Euphues?
> It is not my desire but his deserts that moveth my mind to this choice,
> neither the want of the like good will in Philautus, but the lack of the
> like good qualities that removeth my fancy from the one to the other.*

The finickiness of style seems self-evident—alliteration, sustained
parallelism, pairing of phrases, rhetorical questions, pairing up of meta-
phors and similes (some of which fall in the category of "unnatural natural history"), repetition of idea in changes of phrase. But these things
have no importance for the longer future of the novel, except so far as
some of these false elegancies of style continued to contaminate English
prose—and therefore the prose of fiction—for years after the fad of euphuism had passed.

A later piece of somewhat similar texture and fashion is Sir Philip
Sidney's *Arcadia,* written for Sidney's sister, the Countess of Pembroke,

---

*Spelling and punctuation have been somewhat modernized in all the quotations from
Elizabethan fiction.

and circulated privately for some years before its publication in 1590 under the title of *The Countess of Pembroke's Arcadia.* This too is a story for gentlemen and ladies, a study in elevated manners and conduct, gathering up a large number of diverse story materials, and fusing them within an artificially complicated plot which depicts a group of noble men and women posing as shepherds and shepherdesses. Motive and materials are prevailingly romantic. As a story for the élite, it is highly styled, but not, as is *Euphues,* offensively so.

Thus Dorus, having delivered his hands of his three tormentors, took speedily the benefit of his device, and mounting the gracious Pamela upon a fair horse he had provided for her, he thrust himself forthwith into the wildest part of the desert, where he had left marks to guide him from place to place to the next seaport, disguising her very fitly with scarves, although he rested assured that he should meet with nobody til he came to his bark, into which he meant to enter by night. But Pamela, who all this time transported with desire and troubled with fear, had never free scope of judgment to look with perfect consideration into her own enterprise, but even by the laws of love had laid the care of herself upon him to whom she had given herself, now that the pang of desire with evident hope was quieted, and most part of the fear passed, reason began to renew his shining in her heart, and make her see herself in herself, and weigh with what wings she flew out of her native country and upon what ground she built her determination. But love, fortified with her lover's presence, kept still his own in her heart, so that as they [rode] together with her hand upon her faithful servant's shoulder, suddenly, casting her bashful eyes to the ground, and yet bending herself towards him (like the client that commits the cause of all his worth to a well-trusted advocate) from a mild spirit said unto him these sweetly delivered words. "Prince Musidorous, (for so my assured hope is I may justly call you) since with no other my heart could ever have yielded to go, and if so I do not rightly term you, all other words are as bootless as my deed miserable, and I as unfortunate as you wicked—my Prince Musidorus, I say now that the vehement shows of your faithful love towards me have brought my mind to answer it in so due a proportion that contrary to all rules of reason I have laid in you my state, my life, my honor. It is now your part to double your former care and make me see your virtue no less in preserving than in obtaining, and your faith to be a faith as much in freedom as in bondage. Tender now your own workmanship, and so govern your love towards me, as I may still remain worthy to be loved; your promise you remember which here by the eternal givers of virtue I conjure you to observe. Let me be your own, as I am, by no unjust conquest; let not our joys, which ought ever to last, be stained in our own consciences; let no shadow of repentance steal into the sweet consideration of our mutual happiness! I have yielded to be your wife; stay then til the time that I may rightly be so; let no other defiled name burden my heart! What should I more say? If I have chosen well, all doubt is past, since your action only must determine whether I shall have done virtuously or shamefully in following you."

It is clear that the *Arcadia* is not going to further importantly development in the novel; for it looks back to conventional romantic traditions : chivalry, idealized pastoralism, and exaggerative incident, and is written in a language that is artificial and unfamiliar. No other judgment could be pronounced upon the handful of similar romances that appeared before 1600. Perhaps the only other one of them that we are under obligation to note is Thomas Lodge's *Rosalynde* (1590), which is memorable at least for having furnished the story for Shakespeare's *As You Like It*.

But we are within sight of more promising things, not in absolute literary merit, but for what they are to furnish and suggest for future fiction.

A notable one is Thomas Nashe's *The Unfortunate Traveler, or the Life of Jack Wilton* (1594). The title itself breathes suggestions of common doings by common people. It is the first English picaresque romance, or "romance of roguery." The earlier Spanish picaresques had shown little respect for good taste in the handling of either character or incident, but *The Unfortunate Traveler* outdoes its predecessors in sheer brutalism. There is the usual succession of offensive but harmless practical jokes, but there are also major incidents related not only with gusto but with heartless and sometimes sickening detail. Anyone interested in what Elizabethan judicial torture and execution looked like to the curious spectator will discover the complete answer here, in two separate accounts of the public killing of a criminal. Nashe's showy nonchalance in the handling of such incidents may be less vicious than faithful to the conventions of the type. Apart from these harrowing episodes, the tale is articulate, racy, and intrinsically entertaining beyond almost anything that the English narrative forms had produced since the time of Chaucer. The excerpt following is quite characteristic. It recounts the escape of the hero and his mistress from the house of an accomplished Italian she-criminal.

Oars nor wind could not stir nor blow faster than we toiled out of Tiber; a number of good fellows would give sice-ace and the dice* that with so little toil they could leave Tyburn† behind them. Out of ken we were before the Countess came from the feast. When she returned and found her house not so much pestered as it was wont, her chests,

---

*Gambler's terms.
†The hill in London where public executions took place.

her closets, and her cupboards broke open to take air, and that both I
and my keeper was missing; oh, then she fared like a frantic bac-
chanal; she stamped, she stared, she beat her head against the walls,
scratched her face, bit her fingers, and strewed all the chamber with
her hair. None of her servants durst stay in her sight, but she beat them
out in heaps and bade them go seek, search they knew not where, and
hang themselves, and never look her in the face more if they did not
hunt us out. After her fury had reasonably spent itself, her breast
began to swell with the mother* caused by her former fretting and
chafing, and she grew very ill at ease. Whereupon she knocked for one
of her maids, and bade her run into her closet and fetch her a little
glass that stood on the upper shelf, wherein there was *spiritus vini*.†
The maid went, and mistaking, took the glass of poison which Dia-
mante had given her and she kept in store for me. Coming with it as
fast as her legs could carry her, her mistress at her return was in a
swoon, and lay for dead on the floor; whereat she shrieked out, and fell
to rubbing and chafing her very busily. When that would not serve, she
took a key and opened her mouth, and having heard that *spiritus vini*
was a thing of mighty operation, able to call a man from death to life,
she took the poison, and verily thinking it to be *spiritus vini* (such as
she was sent for) poured a large quantity of it into her throat, and
jogged on her back to digest it. It revived her with a very vengeance,
for it killed her outright; only she awakened and lifted up her hands,
but spake ne'er a word. Then was the maid in my granddame's beans,
and knew not what should become of her. I heard the Pope took pity
on her, and because her trespass was not voluntary, but chance medley,
he assigned her no other punishment but this, to drink out the rest of
the poison in the glass that was left and so go scot-free.

This is the language of every day, simple, easy, communicative, and,
although slangy, put together without airs or false literary grace. Its fitness
for plain narrative is evident in almost every phrase—though Nashe
could, on occasion, adopt some of the empty tricks of euphuism.

Yet in spite of the fact that *The Unfortunate Traveler* has molded its
material into a continuity, it is after all only the sort of continuity that
derives from the attachment to a single life of all the events recorded. It
is a long story, but a merely episodic long story; not a novel. It must be
noted, however, that Nashe has improved upon the narrative of slight and
detachable happenings; for the "container" of all these incidents is Wilton's military career on the Continent (with a slight background of
historical fact), relieved by a long adventure in Rome during an interval
in his service as a mercenary in various European armies. There is enough

*Stomach trouble.
†Brandy.

here to oblige us to concede Nashe's story a modicum of intended unity, and that is what the novel-to-be still stands most in need of. For the rest, it can be said without reservation that fiction of ponderable length had not suffered in Nashe's hands in characterization, in humor, in effective irony, in narrative travel, nor in the use of sufficiently articulate and unaffected prose. *Euphues* and the *Arcadia* are frankly not readable by anyone lacking the urge of scholarly interests. *The Unfortunate Traveler* can be read without too great a strain upon the patience of the uninitiated.

The last Elizabethan for our purposes is Thomas Deloney. He was a traveling weaver, later a maker and singer of popular ballads; and it is his familiarity in both these characters with wayside anecdotes and ballad themes that probably accounts for a mind stored with innumerable odds and ends of story matter. His "novels" are, somewhat like Nashe's, collections of jests, frisky tales, moral tales, and scraps of romances and chronicles. But they show, again like Nashe's picaresque story, a tendency to concentrate about certain major incidents. The first of his novels, known under the title of *Jack of Newbury,* was licensed for publication in March, 1596/7, and was no doubt published within the year, but no copy is known of any imprint before that of 1626—the tenth edition. Evidently all the earlier issues were widely read and handed about until they were worn to shreds and thrown away. This was true also of early printings of his other two novels, *The Gentle Craft,* in two parts, written for the greater glory of the shoemaker's trade, and *Thomas of Reading,* a largely fictitious narrative of the cloth-weaving trade in the time of Henry I. All three novels may quite possibly have been written within a single year; none of them, at all events, later than 1600.

There is another kind of unity in Deloney's narratives than that found in Nashe's *Unfortunate Traveler.* They have biographical continuity (though *The Gentle Craft* takes up in succession the lives of *three* different legendary shoemakers), but their episodic structure is held together also by the fact that each deals with a single phase of the expanding industrial and mercantile life of England. But too much cannot be made of this binding theme, for Deloney finds occasion, in *Jack of Newbury,* for instance, to introduce anecdotes only remotely related to the concerns of its principal, John Winchcombe, the master weaver. In general, Deloney borrows such incident freely from currently familiar sources, and any sort of story can be grist for his mill. How little he is bothered by the problem of fitting it into his general design can be gathered from the fact that three out of the eleven chapters of *Jack of Newbury* relate tricks perpetrated by Jack's servants upon outsiders, and two tell of his taking a hand in solving his maids' problems of the heart. Yet even in these instances there is a kind of environmental unity in the picture of well-treated journeyman and apprentices, strongly attached to their master but having their bit of fun when he is not watching too closely.

What has been said of *Jack of Newbury* applies equally to the other two narratives. There are good spots in both—for example, the racy story of Long Meg of Westminster in *The Gentle Craft* and of the murder of Thomas Cole in the bedchamber of his inn in *Thomas of Reading,* the latter incredible in detail, but circumstantially complete and convincing—a fair example of the "probable impossible." Deloney's merit, like Nashe's, is that he finds his material in the familiar and even commonplace concerns of unpretending people, and clothes his narrative in their everyday language. But Deloney's stories are not picaresque, and in their general avoidance of picaresque themes they depict with greater realism the life and interests of the masses.

The comfortable commonplaceness of Deloney's narrative can be felt in the quotation we give from *Jack of Newbury.* The situation here was not uncommon in the industrial history of the time—the skillful journeyman as a candidate for the hand of his late master's widow, the lady in this case taking the initiative.

When Jack found the favor to be his dame's secretary,* he thought it an extraordinary kindness; and guessing by the yarn it would prove a good web, began to question with his dame in this sort. "Although it becometh not me your servant to pry into your secrets, nor to be busy about matters of your love, yet for so much as it hath pleased you to use conference with me in those causes, I pray you let me intreat you to know their names that be your suitors, and of what profession they be."

"Marry, John," (saith she) "that you shall, and I pray thee take a cushion and sit down by me."

"Dame," (quoth he) "I thank you, but there is no reason I should sit on a cushion till I have deserved it."

"If thou hast not, thou mightest have done" (said she) "but some soldiers never find favour."

John replied, "That maketh me indeed to want favor; for I never durst try maidens because they seem coy, nor wives for fear of their husbands, nor widows, doubting their disdainfulness."

"Tush, John" (quoth she) "he that fears and doubts womankind cannot be counted mankind; and take this for a principle: all things are not as they seem. But let us leave this, and proceed to our former matter."

The widow has three suitors, it appears: a tanner, a tailor, and a par-

---

*To share in her secrets.

son. The merits of each she recites to Jack, likewise the reason that she finds none of them acceptable. And at last she comes to the point, after he has commended each of her suitors to her, one after the other.

"I perceive thy consent is quickly got to any, having no care how I am matched, so I be matched. I wis, I wis, I could not let thee go so lightly, being loath that anyone should have thee, except I could love her as well as myself."

Jack thanks her, but he is schooled in marital casuistry, and he sees many reasons of both prudence and policy for declining the invitation. He has a matter-of-fact reply for her—at least for the time. She answers him in turn.

"Well said, John" (quoth she) "thy song is not so sure, but thy voice is as sweet; but seeing the time agrees with our stomachs, though loath, yet will we give over for this time and betake ourselves to our suppers." Then calling the rest of her servants, they fell to their meat merrily, and after their supper, the good-wife went abroad for her recreation, to walk awhile with one of her neighbors. And in the mean space John got himself up into his chamber, and there began to meditate upon this matter, bethinking with himself what he were best to do; for well he perceived that his dame's affection was great towards him. Knowing therefore the woman's disposition, and withal that her estate was reasonable good, and considering beside that he should find a house ready furnished, he thought it best not to let slip that good occasion, lest he should never come to the like. But again, when he considered her years to be unfitting to his youth, and that she that sometime had been his dame would perhaps disdain to be governed by him that had been her poor servant, and that it would prove but a bad bargain, doubting many inconveniences that might grow thereby, he therefore resolved to be silent rather than to proceed further. Therefore he got him straight to bed and the next morning settled himself close to his business.

But the widow is intent upon her purpose and clever enough to attain it, through a not altogether innocent but amusing stratagem. The two are married, have their little difficulties, in themselves diverting, and settle down to domesticity. This is the start of Jack's rise in the world. The episode is simply one passage in a success story.

Perhaps we can discern here an improvement upon Nashe's achievement; for Deloney's narrative shows ease and naturalness in his dialogue and in Jack's little moment of rumination. Style is appropriate, the characters fairly convincing, the situation credible, and fitted skillfully into the mass of the story. These are serviceable contributions to the novel; so there is no great impropriety in using the word "novel" at this point where all its constituents seem to have been recognized and assembled. But much remains to be done.

To all appearances, the novel was in a sufficiently developed state by 1600 to go on to further and rapid advance. Instead, it remained dormant for almost a century. Looking back upon it from the point of view of its later development, nothing appeared during the seventeenth century that could be thought to enlarge its possibilities much beyond the modest attainment of Deloney. Perhaps the one writer of the period (apart from Bunyan) who measurably advanced the art of the novel was Mrs. Aphra Behn, generally credited with having been the first professional woman of letters. She had learned the writer's trade in the theater, for which she had written during the 1680's comedies which even her not-at-all finicky contemporaries thought rather daring—for a woman. Her best remembered novel—she used the term herself, although it barely applies—*Oroonoko* (1680), gives us the earliest treatment of a theme which was to become popular during the next century—the nobility of character of the uncivilized "natural" man. *Oroonoko* draws additional interest from the fact that Mrs. Behn wrote with first-hand knowledge of the unfamiliar scene of her story—the Caribbean coast of South America—of which she offers agreeable glimpses in more or less formal description. Much has been made of *Oroonoko* as the precursor of a new type; but as something resembling a novel, it has less interest than her other little novels—*The Fair Jilt* (1688), *Agnes de Castro* (1688), a conventional tragic fiction with a modest touch of art, and *The Nun* (1689). *The Fair Jilt* and *The Nun* are sprightly departures from the proprieties. All, however, are novels of incident; character is not fluid but fixed, gay, disreputable, and sometimes vicious; her conclusions have little rational connection with the course of her narrative; and in spite of her experience in writing for the stage, she ties herself up in stiffly framed and interminable sentences. Yet there is the flavor of the easygoing life of the period—or what the men and women of her time liked to think of as that life. In that respect, Mrs. Behn has actually contributed something to what was finally to be called the novels of manners. But even at their best, her novels are no more than tastelessly smart, and to the average reader of today they must inevitably seem limited and dull.

The one work of prose fiction in this period which demands attention, not really as a novel but as a sustained story in its own domain of romance, and unquestionably a great book, is John Bunyan's *Pilgrim's Progress* (1678).

No book in our literature, probably in all the world's literature, has proved more completely that reputation is the plaything of time. Next to the Bible, it was for two centuries after its publication thought to be the most widely read book in Western Europe. Today it is a rare reader who can find edification in its obstinate didacticism. The change in attitudes is less one of literary taste than in the spirit of religion. If we could read it with the same detachment that we bring to the pagan *Odyssey* or the Moslem *Arabian Nights,* its theology could not detract much from its interest. But there is no great place in the world today for a contentious and parochial puritanism, and that, unfortunately, is what animates the entire action of *The Pilgrim's Progress.* But let us look at Bunyan's writing before we discuss his sectarianism. First, the very opening sentences of the book :

> As I walked through the wilderness of this world, I lighted on a certain place where there was a den, and I laid me down in that place to sleep, and as I slept, I dreamed a dream. I dreamed, and behold, I saw a man clothed with rags, standing in a certain place, with his face from his own house, a book in his hand, and a great burden upon his back. I looked, and saw him open the book and read therein, and as he read, he wept and trembled, and not being able longer to contain, he brake out with a lamentable cry, saying, "What shall I do?"
>
> In this plight therefore he went home, and refrained himself as long as he could, that his wife and children should not perceive his distress, but he could not be silent long, because that his trouble increased; wherefore at length he brake his mind to his wife and children and thus he began to talk to them. "Oh, my dear Wife," said he, "and you the children of my bowels, I your dear friend am in myself undone, by reason of a burden that lieth hard upon me."

The burden is the burden of sin; the book is the Bible; the man is the sinner under conviction. We shall soon know him as the pilgrim Christian and we shall find him shortly upon his way to the holy city of Zion, his Heaven. But on the way he is to encounter hindrances and opposition, to meet with the fiend Apollyon and Giant Despair, to pass through Vanity Fair and the Valley of the Shadow of Death, and to encounter and talk with pilgrims like himself not so well confirmed in the faith, and falling by the wayside through their weakness or perversity. There are also moments of peace and friendly talk and encouragement, in which he recruits his strength and his faith. And at last with his friend and companion Hopeful, he crosses the River of Death and walks with him up to the gate of the Holy City :

> Now when they were come up to the gate, there were written over it in letters of gold, Blessed are they that do his commandments, that they may enter into the city.
>
> Then I saw in my dream that the shining men bid them call at the

gate; the which when they did, some from above looked over the gate, to wit, Enoch, Moses, and Elijah, etc., to whom it was said, "These pilgrims are come from the City of Destruction, for the love that they bare to the King of this place;" and then the pilgrims gave in unto them each man his certificate which they had received in the beginning. Those therefore were carried in to the King, who when he had read them said, "Where are the men?" To whom it was answered, "They are standing without the gate." The King then commanded to open the gate, "that the righteous nation," said He, "that keepeth truth may enter in."

Now I saw in my dream that these two men went in at the gate; and lo, as they entered, they were transfigured, and they had raiment put on that shone like gold. There was also that met them with harps and crowns, and gave them to them; the harps to praise withal, and the crowns in token of honor. Then I heard in my dream that all the bells of the city rang again for joy, and that it was said unto them, "Enter ye into the joy of our Lord." I also heard the men themselves, that they sang with a loud voice, saying, "Blessing, honor, glory, and power be to him that sitteth upon the throne, and to the Lamb forever and ever."

Now just as the gates were opened to let in the men, I looked in after them, and behold, the city shone like the sun; the streets also were paved with gold, and in them walked many men with crowns on their heads, palms in their hands, and golden harps to sing praises withal. There were also of them that had wings, and they answered one another without intermission, saying, "Holy, holy, holy is the Lord." And after that they shut up the gates, which when I had seen, I wished myself among them.

What is there in between the fine simplicity of that opening and the lyric splendor of the conclusion, embellished with its familiar scriptural imagery? The intervening story is actually a story of the road, in design not too unlike others of its type, but differing in the extreme from them in its elevated purpose, its sober and dignified characters, its symbolic incident, and its intense spiritual seriousness.

The story is one of the great allegories, and also one of the most lucid, its allegory following in the main St. Paul's conception of Christianity as an unending conflict with the forces of the world as well as with those of Hell itself. Many of its places and scenes exemplify the disturbances of mind which from time to time may beset the believer—Doubting Castle, the Slough of Despond, Vanity Fair, The Hill called Error, and the Valley of the Shadow of Death; others represent the brighter spots in his experience—what Christian himself calls his "golden hours"—such as the House of the Interpreter, the path along the River of the Water of Life, the Delectable Mountains, and the Land of Beulah. There are encounters with characters personifying evil and temptation, including Apollyon, Demas, Giant Despair, and the Flatterer. These would stop his progress toward the Holy City or draw him from the true way, and they are embodied opposition to the moral as well as the strictly spiritual conceptions of Christianity.

There are other meetings with other wayfarers or casual strangers, such as Pliable, Mr. Worldly Wiseman, Talkative, and Ignorance; and with these Christian enters into debate on questions of conduct, sincerity, and, above all, points of doctrine. These debates usually open as invitations to edifying talk, but they usually end as acrimonious contentions in which Christian, and his successive companions, Faithful and Hopeful, repudiate and even abuse their adversaries in arguments which they themselves have started. But to Bunyan perhaps they were the passages of greatest significance in his entire work, since they deal with the insidious rather than the patent hindrances to the religious life. And to him and his fellow believers the exact articles of one's faith, even to their very minutiae, were as determinative a test of his claim upon the bounty of God as was the record of his good works. Indeed, in the puritan outlook of that time one's title to salvation *was grace* (the assurance that one's sins were forgiven and that he was the child of God) *and not good works.**

It is unhappy that a writer with so keen a sense of the power of the written word should ultimately suffer so greatly in reputation because of his dogmatic intolerance. For the passages of greatest effect in *Pilgrim's Progress* are those which apply to Christianity the conceptions and the imagery of knightly romance, and which introduce conflicts like that with Apollyon, the dungeons of Doubting Castle, and the superstitious terrors of the Valley of the Shadow of Death. But it is simply a fact that Bunyan wanted no one in his Heaven who was not entirely of his own mind. The average modern reader is satisfied to let him have his Heaven; for it would be a solemn and depressing place for most of us. Few people of today would dissent from the final word of Ignorance in one of these overbearing diatribes of Christian's :

> *Ign.* "Sir, I was born in the country that lieth off there, a little on the left hand, and am going to the Celestial City."
>
> *Chr.* "But how do you think to get in at the gate, for you may find some difficulty there?"
>
> *Ign.* "As other good people doth," said he.

---

*The doctrine is still held by some sectarian groups. Fielding has the temerity to ridicule it in the person of Parson Williams in *Shamela*, his parody of Richardson's *Pamela*.

Chr. "But what have you to show at that gate, that may cause that the gate shall be opened to you?"

Ign. "I know my Lord's will, and have been a good liver; I pay every man his own; I pray, fast, pay tithes, and give alms, and have left my country for whither I am going."

Chr. "But thou camest not in at the wicket gate that is at the head of this way; thou camest in hither through that same crooked lane, and therefore I fear that however thou mayst think of thyself, when the reckoning day shall come, thou wilt have laid to thy charge that thou art a thief and a robber, instead of getting admittance into the city."

Ign. "Gentlemen, ye be utter strangers to me; I know you not. Be content to follow the religion of your country, and I will follow the religion of mine. I hope all will be well."

Perhaps we might even approve Talkative's farewell to Faithful, after the latter has followed up an inquisitorial gambit by upbraiding him because he looks upon conversation as entertainment : "I cannot but conclude you are some peevish or melancholic man, not fit to be discoursed with; and so adieu."

It would be impossible to say that *Pilgrim's Progress* had given any important impulse to the fiction of its time. It is both fanciful and realistic—fanciful in its effective use of the machinery of the older romances; realistic in characterization and dialogue. But its persistent disputation carries it almost outside the realm of fiction. And its once great popularity is scarcely to be credited to appreciation of its merits as narrative, but to its uncompromisingly puritan interpretation of Christian beliefs. When puritanism as a view of life as well as of faith had had its day, then the work which had been regarded almost as a supplement to the Bible began to weary instead of inspiring its readers.

The popularity of *Pilgrim's Progress* remained undiminished until well on into the nineteenth century. It is noteworthy that the book occupied so important a place in the literature of Protestantism for so long a time, for the evangelical sects were inclined in Bunyan's day to discountenance fiction not only because it was felt to reflect the thinking and the doings of a corrupt society, but because it was regarded as in its very nature a form of lying, and was therefore one of the devices of the Father of Lies to delude true believers.

Yet with the Restoration, in 1660, the theater had revived. Comedy, particularly the comedy of manners, once more became fashionable, and reflected faithfully, perhaps over-faithfully, down to the end of this century the social effects of the gaiety and improbity of the court. Poetry again flourished; prose improved for literary purposes; but fiction remained for some time the homelier sister of the kindred arts. In the last quarter of the century there was a passing taste for esoteric romance, principally French, but it need not detain us, for it was almost undiluted affectation, and it appealed to few who were not infected with preciosity.

But reading had become more widely diffused among the middle classes. Money was coming into their hands, principally through trade. Their day of power under Cromwell's regime had done a good deal for their confidence and their spirit; and the moderate improvement in their social status had naturally raised the level of their literacy. As we have seen, there had been a more or less proletarian literature before this period, but proletarian fiction had exerted little influence upon literary taste, except in so far as it tended to encourage the "realistic" outlook and to discredit the highly colored romances which had been produced largely for loftier tastes. That trend to realism, however, meant an enlargement of the field of fiction, but even more importantly, the gradual replacement of an artificial and now antiquated medium by rational and more acceptable themes and motives. From this time on, the distinction between romantic and realistic fiction was clearly recognized, and felt in the more intelligent preferences of readers of the novel.

But looking back over the entire seventeenth century, we can find little that would supply the place which the novel now holds for the vast number of readers, not only literate but educated, who form its present following. And even after 1700, awareness of the novel as a new and effective literary type crept only slowly into the consciousness of readers. It was not until almost the middle of the century that the novel came into clear perspective, and was produced in fairly large numbers, and finally achieved the literary eminence which it still holds.

CHAPTER III

𝕸𝖆𝖓 𝖔𝖓 𝖆𝖓 𝕴𝖘𝖑𝖆𝖓𝖉

Daniel Defoe

PROBABLY NOT one reader in a score knows the name of Daniel Defoe* in any other connection than as the author of *Robinson Crusoe,* and most of us have known that peerless story only as children. Yet Defoe gave the world at least a half-dozen longer works of fiction sufficiently interesting for a grown-up whose taste had not been vitiated by radio and TV. Furthermore, Defoe is the first writer of fiction to whom the title "father of the English novel" might be applied without radical misjudgment—although on this point there is room for debate. However, few of our scholars or critics of fiction would hesitate to name him the father of modern realism.

The most important of Defoe's longer fictions were all published within the five years following the appearance of *Robinson Crusoe* in 1719. For Defoe, as a completely professional writer, made the most of the sudden and almost unparalleled popularity of that great tale of the solitary man on an island. These stories have a common likeness. They portray utter plebeians—often social outcasts—for Defoe was by birth, training, occupation, religion, and sympathies a man of the people. He was contemptuous of everything that belonged to high life, and he had no patience with the prim indignation of the upper classes over the vulgarities, the shifts, and the depravities almost inevitably linked to ignorance and poverty. His humanity and moral convictions, combined with his experience and skill as a journalist, made him the annalist of contemporary crime, in minutely detailed "lives" of prostitutes, fancy women, pirates, pickpockets, housebreakers, stool pigeons, quacks, and youthful delinquents. Their stories are usually set forth with frank first-person direct-

---

*Daniel Defoe (1659?-1731). *Robinson Crusoe,* 1719; *Captain Singleton,* 1720; *Memoirs of a Cavalier,* 1720; *Moll Flanders,* 1722; *A Journal of the Plague Year,* 1722; *Colonel Jacque,* 1722; *The Fortunate Mistress (Roxana),* 1724; *A New Voyage Round the World,* 1724. These are all abbreviated titles, but the ones by which the narratives are best known. Full titles of *Robinson Crusoe* and *Moll Flanders* are given in the text.

Frontispiece to the first edition of Defoe's *Robinson Crusoe*, 1719; engraved by Clark and John Pine.

ness and generally motivated by late, though honest, repentance. Many of them, in particular the pirate stories, have to do with more or less historic characters. Others, including *Robinson Crusoe,* may build upon a fragment of actual history. Still others, notably his two lives of "fallen women," *Moll Flanders* and *Roxana,* were so far as we know entirely his own.

Robinson Crusoe, plainly his greatest work, and his first long narrative, laid the foundation for his reputation. Its full and quite adequate title was *The Life and Strange Surprising Adventures of Robinson Crusoe of York, Mariner, Who Lived Eight and Twenty Years All Alone, on the Coast of America, near the Mouth of the Great River Oroonoque; Having Been Cast on Shore by Shipwreck, wherein All the Men Perished but Himself. With an Account How He Was at Last Strangely Delivered by Pirates. Written by Himself.* A sequel, *The Farther Adventures of Robinson Crusoe,* was published later in the same year, 1719.

Here are the narratives —in addition to *Robinson Crusoe*—which came from the press in those five years of headlong composition. And they were but a part, though a major part, of his entire activity as a writer. Simultaneously he produced in rapid succession shorter narratives, tracts, and pamphlets on economic and political matters. He was, indeed, one of the historic marvels of creative activity, like Mozart, Michelangelo, and Lope de Vega.

First, and perhaps most characteristic, are the stories, more or less of the picaresque type. But in no case did these show the jaunty picaresque unconcern for moral sentiment. All, in fact, were on Defoe's own statement written with definite moral aims. The best of them are *Colonel Jacque,* the story of a juvenile outcast and criminal-in-training, and the two female rogue stories, *Moll Flanders* and *The Fortunate Mistress,* the latter generally known as *Roxana.*

Moll Flanders is almost pure rogue-romance. Like *Robinson Crusoe* and *Colonel Jacque,* it carries a ponderous but diverting and even seductive title: *The Fortunes and Misfortunes of the Famous Moll Flanders, Who Was Born in Newgate, and during a Life of Continued Variety for Three-score Years besides Her Childhood, Was Twelve years a Whore, Five Times a Wife (whereof Once to her Own Brother), Twelve Years a Thief, Eight Years a Transported Felon in Virginia, at Last Grew Rich, Lived Honest, and Died a Penitent. Written from Her Own Memorandums.* It is a remarkable mirror of contemporary life, and we shall have more to say of it further on.

Roxana, the far from exemplary heroine of *The Fortunate Mistress,* is Moll Flanders in gold brocade and pearls. At first more or less the victim of circumstances, she becomes the clever merchant of her own beauty and graces, and reaps one fortune after another. In spite of Roxana's tears of regret, and Defoe's unremitted moralizing, this is, if there ever was one, a glamor story. Curiously enough, the customary finale of repentance and reform is cut down to the very last brief paragraph. After a long succession of lovers, and a career as fashionable prostitute in London, she tells us simply that "after some years of flourishing and outwardly happy circumstances, I fell into a dreadful course of calamities, . . . the very reverse of our former days. . . . I was brought so low again that my repentance seemed to be only the consequence of my misery, as my misery was of my crime." This casual and unenlightening conclusion almost obliges us to think that Defoe was pressed for publication before the book was actually ready for the press. Conclusions have been supplied by other ambitious hands, but they add no interest to the narrative as Defoe left it.

Colonel Jacque is no better story than either *Moll Flanders* or *Roxana*, and it lacks the sprightly interest of the more unconventional theme of the woman reprobate. One thing, however, makes it memorable. Its early chapters provide one of the most graphic, and therefore one of the most pitiful, pictures we have of the life of a boy of the London streets who was born to crime as he was born to poverty and homelessness.

The next important category of Defoe's fiction is his stories of sea-adventure and exploration, inspired, no doubt, by his known fondness for books on discovery, travel, and geography. As a class, these fictions are not as challenging as his lives of thieves and prostitutes, for they show less interest in people than in movement and, at times, vivid action.

The earliest of them was *The Life, Adventures, and Piracies of the Famous Captain Singleton* (1720). The wide scene of this narrative is the three great oceans, or the parts of them that were then known. In spite of its breadth, at least geographically, the story is minutely circumstantial, descending even to prosaic records of the number of pieces of eight and the ships' stores taken from their captures. In fact, a character of rather exceptional interest in the tale is a Quaker taken off one of Singleton's captures who chooses to become Singleton's business manager and bookkeeper in preference to walking the plank; for piracy then, as now, prospered best when conducted on strictly business principles. Perhaps the most remarkable part of the book describes the crossing of central Africa from west to east by a band of stranded pirates—something not achieved, needless to say, for a century and a half to come. It is a tribute to the vigor of Defoe's imagination that, working from a few known facts as to the northern and coastal regions of the continent, he made some very shrewd guesses as to what the interior was like—even to placing with some accuracy the desert and great lake regions, then completely unknown.

A New Voyage Round the World is a sort of companion piece to *Captain Singleton*. Here again Defoe's gift of geographical divination comes into play, for a substantial part of the narrative is taken up with the crossing of the Andes—at that time unthinkable—from what today would be Chile to Argentina.

One major fiction remains, in its own way almost as notable as *Robinson Crusoe*. This was *A Journal of the Plague Year* (1722). The *Journal* professes to be an eyewitness' account of the disastrous epidemic of 1665 in London. It is one of the purest and most convincing examples of realism of the cumulative sort, pounding out unremittingly little incident after little incident to overwhelm incredulity by the mere mass of manufactured evidence. It was drawn in substantial part from known and reliable historical sources, but these serve only as a foundation for the sort of personal narrative in which Defoe is fully aware of his own powers. The work is crammed with week-to-week mortality statistics, exact notations of time and place, sanitary and preventive suggestions (some sane and practical, others uninspired guesswork); and while these gratuitous supplements to the ascertainable facts are unreliable in detail, they no doubt approximate the conditions they pretend to describe. But the power of the work—its interest as a story—resides in Defoe's own contribution. This comprises anecdotes of sickness and death, of mass panic, of the daily collection and burial of bodies in enormous open graves, of deserted streets and homes, opportunistic crime, negligent and often corrupt policing, and the long and ceaseless exodus from the city, obstructed in terror on every roadway by the frightened countryside. These things are brought home to us through the running narrative of the principal. And there is in addition the patience and wisdom, often quaint, often humorous, of this compassionate and intelligent narrator. In its very nature the book is highly repetitious, but repetition is an important part of Defoe's realistic mechanics. And his method carried such conviction that for a century and a half after its publication, the *Journal* was accepted as an entirely authentic record.

This cursory view of the area of Defoe's work in fiction, and of his approach to the writer's problems, is probably sufficient to place him as a writer familiar and sympathetic with the common life of his time, and skilled in the use of his materials. For a closer look at his methods and his literary manner, we shall take his two most popular stories—*Robinson Crusoe,* because it is still one of the best examples—if not the best—of circumstantial realism; and *Moll Flanders,* because it conforms so closely to the general view of what goes to the making of a novel that many scholars and critics have called it, without reservation, the first English novel.

There are those who question whether Defoe was really an artist, and who take his literalism and his plainness of style as proofs of mediocrity. But isn't artlessness a form of art? It is upon Defoe's simplicity, simpli-

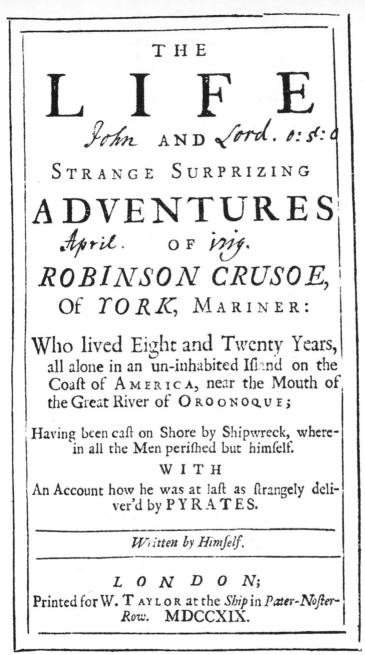

THE
L I F E

John AND *Lord. o: s: 0*

STRANGE SURPRIZING

ADVENTURES

April. OF *vij.*

ROBINSON CRUSOE,

Of YORK, MARINER:

Who lived Eight and Twenty Years,
all alone in an un-inhabited Island on the
Coast of AMERICA, near the Mouth of
the Great River of OROONOQUE;

Having been cast on Shore by Shipwreck, wherein all the Men perished but himself.

WITH

An Account how he was at last as strangely deliver'd by PYRATES.

Written by Himself.

L O N D O N;

Printed for W. TAYLOR at the *Ship* in *Pater-Noster-
Row.* MDCCXIX.

A typical early eighteenth-century descriptive title page, from the first
edition of Defoe's *Robinson Crusoe*, 1719. The written signature is
probably the original owner's, with the date of acquisition (1719),
the actual year of publication.

city even to commonplaceness, that his realism hinges. His technique is more than anything else the ingenious concealment of conscious technique, and the deliberate adoption of narrative devices and expedients that sometimes seem to mark him as a blundering and fumbling anecdotist. Let us look more closely at his curious and at times perhaps devious ways of getting the best of the average reader's will to disbelieve.

All his narratives, we have said, are, with insignificant exceptions, told in the first person. But that simple sort of objectivity is bolstered by a number of artifices that confirm the personal outlook of the narrator. They appear characteristically in this passage from *Robinson Crusoe*.

Having now brought my mind a little to relish my condition, and given over looking out to sea, to see if I could spy a ship; I say, giving over these things, I began to apply myself to accommodate my way of living, and to make things as easy to me as I could.

I have already described my habitation, which was a tent under the side of a rock, surrounded with a strong pale of posts and cables; but I might now rather call it a wall, for I raised a kind of wall up against it of turfs, about two feet thick on the outside, and after some time—I think it was a year and a half—I raised rafters from it leading to the rock, and thatched or covered it with boughs of trees and such things as I could get to keep out the rain, which I found at some times of the year very violent.

I have already observed how I brought all my goods into this pale, and into the cave which I had made behind me. But I must observe, too, that at first this was a confused heap of goods, which as they lay in no order, so they took up all my place; I had no room to turn myself. So I set myself to enlarge my cave and works farther into the earth, for it was a loose, sandy rock which yielded easily to the labor I bestowed on it. And so, when I found I was pretty safe as to beasts of prey, I worked sideways to the right hand into the rock; and then, turning to the right again, worked quite out, and made me a door to come out on the outside of my pale or fortification. This gave me not only egress and regress, as it were a back way to my tent and to my storehouse, but gave me room to stow my goods.

And now I began to apply myself to make such necessary things as I found I most wanted, as particularly a chair and a table; for without these I was not able to enjoy the few comforts I had in the world. I could not write nor eat, or do several things with so much pleasure without a table.

So I went to work; and here I must needs observe, that as reason is the substance and original of the mathematics, so by stating and squaring everything by reason, and by making the most rational judgment of things, every man may be in time master of every mechanical art. I had never handled a tool in my life; and yet in time, by labor, application and contrivance, I found at last that I wanted nothing but I could have made it, especially if I had had tools. However, I made abundance of things even without tools, and some with no more tools than an adze and a hatchet, which perhaps, were never made that way before, and that with infinite labor. For example, if I wanted a board, I had no other way but to cut down a tree, set it on an edge before me, and hew it flat on either side with my axe, till I had brought it to be thin as a plank, and then dub it smooth with my adze. It is true, by this method I could make but one board out of a whole tree, but this I had no remedy for but patience, any more than I had for the prodigious deal of time and labor which it took me to make a plank or board. But my time or labor was little worth, and so it was as well employed one way as another.

However, I made me a table and a chair, as I observed before, in the first place, and this I did out of the short pieces of boards that I brought on my raft from the ship. But when I had wrought out some boards, as above, I made large shelves of the breadth of a foot and a half one over another, all along one side of my cave, to lay all my tools, nails, and iron-work; and, in a word, to separate everything at large in their places, that I might come easily at them. I knocked pieces into the wall of the rock to hang my guns and all things that would hang up; so that had my cave been to be seen, it looked like a magazine of all necessary things; and I had everything so ready at my hand, that it was a great pleasure to me to see all my goods in such order, and especially to find my stock of all necessaries so great.

The style is not only plain to severity; it is inexpert and labored. Defoe's prose is by no orthodox standard literary prose—not even for his own time; for Donne and Sir Thomas Browne, Dryden and Swift, had made English prose a more flexible instrument than it is in his hands. His prose is wasteful of words; it is repetitious; it is involved, and sometimes hopelessly tangled; it is careless of the reasonable limits to the length of a sentence; and it is sown with mannerisms that make it safely possible to identify a narrative piece of his on no other grounds of evidence.*

We need not be fussy about this question of style. In fact, we can afford to neglect it, unless style is a purposed part of the narrative method. In Defoe's case, it is that. "Style," we have been told, "is the man." But in narrative art that may or may not be wholly true. Where the writer poses, as Defoe commonly does, as the principal in his own narrative, then style

---

*These mannerisms are largely informal turns of phrase more common in everyday speech than in writing. Examples are: *in short; as I have said or I say*, with a repetition; *as above; says he; be that as is may; that is to say. Viz* is common. There are departures from conventional syntax, such as *neither-or* and *in order to this*, and not infrequent instances of what today we should call bad grammar, such as *you was*, and *between him and I.*

becomes no more than a usable mechanism, expressive of social place, education, and any other environmental factors. Since Defoe's interest is generally in the ordinary concerns of very ordinary people, style denotes the cultural limitations of men and women who, by their circumstances, are neither sure of themselves nor overly articulate. Further, it is quite probable that Defoe, who had a taint of puritanism, would have thought a "cultivated" style at least pretentious, and perhaps hypocritical. This prose is precisely the right prose for Defoe's purposes; for it meets the understandings and the social placement of most of his readers.

Apart from this appropriateness of style, there are narrative expedients equally important, and often equally distinctive. First of all, there is the vast spread of detail, often incidental, sometimes extraneous. Nothing whatever seems immaterial to Defoe's principals. They appraise their day-to-day experiences only in relation to their own egos and their affairs, and with the minuteness of conscientious diarists. The inventory, for example, of what Crusoe took from the wreck of his ship is pretty much like a catalogue of the ship's entire movable lading. Some of it is invaluable, some doubtfully useful, some of it worthless for any immediate purpose. And what Crusoe left behind is almost as meticulously noted as what he was able to take away. But the lavishness of detail is not wasted. We follow Crusoe's search for everything of possible value because we share his anxiety to escape an untimely and perhaps hideous death; and when his first raft-load is pushed off from the side of the vessel, we are fully alert to the importance of the scrambled cargo for his very existence.

Detail in *Robinson Crusoe* is, in the nature of his situation, largely material—what Crusoe retrieved from the wreck; what he found on the island (the habitable cave, foods, materials for tools and utensils); what he made (a defensive palisade, pottery, a dug-out canoe), and how he made it. From the first, his life is wholly one of happenings—at least for the many years before Friday crosses his path. The fascination of the story depends so much on what he sees, what he has, and what he does, all by his solitary self, that for many readers interest sags from the moment that human beings are reintroduced into his world.

Not the least of the challenges to Crusoe's ingenuity arise from his need of things with which his generally good luck has failed to supply him, as well as from his fumbling attempts to provide them himself. This we have seen in the last passage quoted. But sometimes Crusoe's best efforts result in flat failure. He can, by hard work, produce usable furniture, and by a long course of trial and error he makes both pots and baskets. But when he conceives the notion of building a boat, he is defeated not by the conditions of the problem, but by his want of foresight when he attacks it.

I went to work upon this boat the most like a fool that ever man did who had any of his senses awake. I pleased myself with the design without determining whether I was ever able to undertake it. Not but that the difficulty of launching my boat came often into my head; but I put a stop to my own inquiries into it by the foolish answer which I gave myself, "Let's first make it; I'll warrant I'll find some way or other to get it along when 'tis done."

This was a most preposterous method; but the eagerness of my fancy prevailed, and to work I went. I felled a cedar tree; I question much whether Solomon ever had such a one for the building of the temple at Jerusalem. It was five feet ten inches diameter at the lowest part next the stump, and four feet eleven inches diameter at the end of twenty-two feet, after which it lessened for a while, and then parted into branches. It was not without infinite labor that I felled this tree. I was twenty days hacking and hewing at it at the bottom; I was fourteen more getting the branches and limbs and the vast spreading head of it cut off, which I hacked and hewed through with axe and hatchet, and inexpressible labor. After this, it cost me a month to shape it and dub it to a proportion, and to something like the bottom of a boat, that it might swim upright as it ought to do. It cost me near three months more to clear the inside, and work it so as to make an exact boat of it. This I did, indeed, without fire, by mere mallet and chisel, and by the dint of hard labor, till I had brought it to be a very handsome *periagua,* and big enough to have carried me and all my cargo.

When I had gone through all this work, I was extremely delighted with it. The boat was really much bigger than I ever saw a *periagua* that was made of one tree, in my life. Many a weary stroke it had cost, you may be sure; and there remained nothing but to get it into the water; and had I got it into the water, I made no question but I should have begun the maddest voyage, and the most unlikely to be performed, that ever was undertaken.

But all my devices to get it into the water failed me, though they cost me infinite labor too. It lay about one hundred yards from the water, and not more; but the first inconvenience was, it was uphill towards the creek. Well, to take away this discouragement, I resolved to dig into the surface of the earth, and so make the declivity. This I began, and it cost me a prodigious deal of pains; but who grudges pains, that have their deliverance in view? But when this was worked through, and this difficulty managed, it was still much at one; for I could no more stir the canoe than I could the other boat.

Then I measured the distance of ground, and resolved to cut a dock or canal, to bring the water up to the canoe, seeing I could not bring the canoe down to the water. Well, I began this work; and when I began to enter into it and calculate how deep it was to be dug, how broad, how the stuff to be thrown out, I found that by the number of hands I had, being none but my own, it must have been ten or twelve years before I should have gone through with it; for the shore lay high, so that at the upper end it must have been at least twenty feet deep; so at length, though with great reluctancy, I gave this attempt over also.

This grieved me heartily; and now I saw, though too late, the folly of beginning a work before we count the cost, and before we judge rightly of our own strength to go through with it.

The insurmountable difficulty here, and the ineptitude in dealing with it, is a sensible departure from monotonous lụck and unfailing invention. In the many imitations of *Robinson Crusoe* (*The Hermit,* for example, and *The Swiss Family Robinson*), Providence seems to take too unfailingly helpful a hand in the castaway's welfare. But in *Robinson Crusoe,* nature is niggardly and the human being fallible. It is worth remembering that there are no breadfruit trees and no cocoanut palms on Crusoe's island. And his handy-man resourcefulness, notable as it is, carries no suggestion of omniscience or omnipotence. That is good art. It respects the probabilities, and at the same time increases suspense and heightens our interest in the hero's varying fortunes.

This artful restraint of Defoe's in the handling of incident is supplemented by occasional solemn doubts as to the truth or the accuracy of incidents or rumors actually brought into the story. This is not specially apparent in *Robinson Crusoe,* since Crusoe is the sole witness and recorder of what happens on his island, but it permeates *The Journal of the Plague Year,* which in its nature gathers up much hearsay and current gossip.

They did tell me, indeed, of a nurse in one place that laid a wet cloth upon the face of a dying patient whom she tended, and so put an end to his life, who was just expiring before; and another that smothered a young woman she was looking to when she was in a fainting fit and would have come to herself; some that killed them by giving them one thing, some another, and some starved them by giving them nothing at all. But these stories had two marks of suspicion that always attended them, which caused me always to slight them, and to look on them as mere stories that people continually frightened one another with. First, that wherever it was that we heard it, they always placed the scene at the farther end of the the town, opposite or most remote from where you were to hear it. If you heard it in Whitechapel, it had happened at St. Giles's, or at Westminster, or Holborn, or that end of the town. If you heard of it at that end of the town, then it was done in Whitechapel, or the Minories, or about Cripplegate parish. If you heard of it in the City, why, then it happened in Southwark; and if you heard of it in Southwark, then it was done in the City, and the like.

In the next place, of what part soever that you heard the story, the particulars were always the same, especially that of laying a wet double clout on a dying man's face, and that of smothering a young gentlewoman; so that it was apparent, at least in my judgment, that there was more of tale than of truth in those things.

None of Defoe's fictions is without a steady insistence upon its moral lesson. All are built upon a single formula—the depiction in detail of a life of social remissness, vice, or crime, accompanied by a running confession of the narrator's consciousness of his wickedness, his penitence, and his reiterated advice to the reader to avoid following in his footsteps. Some form of obvious punishment is a part of these narratives—public whipping, transportation, imprisonment, business reverses, social exile, and frequently the shadow of the gallows—to make repentance effective.

This insistence upon a clear relation between transgression and retribution applies somewhat less to *Robinson Crusoe, The Fortunate Mistress,* and *The Journal of the Plague Year* than to *Moll Flanders, Colonel Jacque,* and *Captain Singleton.* But the differences are in Defoe's view merely in degree. Robinson Crusoe shows no markedly vicious propensity; his tragic error is the wasted and discontented life that preceded his shipwreck. Roxana would seem to be innocent of active crime, for her life of sexual freedom is nevertheless one of conscientious loyalty to her protectors, and she practices none of the attendant vices of the common prostitute. But she is vain, avaricious, hypocritical, and a ruinous influence upon her best and most constant friend, her servant Amy. In the *Journal* the narrator is a man of great character and sympathies; but the plague itself Defoe represents as a judgment of God upon the wickedness of the city; and the story is a running indictment of ignorance, superstition, improvidence, and the wretched weaknesses of human nature that come to the surface under heavy visitations. All of the fictions, then, are treatises upon sin and retributive justice, even when punishment lies within the conscience of the offender.

No knowledgeable student of Defoe has failed to bring into focus the question of how much of his professed morality was actually inherent in his character, and how much just literary pretense. It is scarcely possible to dodge the question, not because pious professions must be called into doubt, but because there is much in Defoe's background that forces the problem of his personality upon our attention. He was beyond doubt a venal writer and a devious politician, and probably a sort of political stool pigeon. But he was also an open foe of tyranny and privilege, and a purveyor of social enlightenment—witness his advocacy of a broader education for women, reasonable bankruptcy laws, the organization of insurance upon a statistical instead of a gambling basis,* penal reform, and above all, liberty of conscience and opinion. Perhaps the question of his true character narrows down to the strong contrast of his intelligence as a student of men and affairs with his opportunism as journalist, pamphleteer, and political servant.

This question comes sharply forward in all of his "crime stories." At a time when crime as a business—so it is estimated—attracted a tenth of the London populace; when the public execution of a "big" criminal brought out thousands of spectators; when something like a hundred and fifty offenses were punishable by death; and when the King's highways could be traveled safely by carriages only with the protection of a private armed guard, it is not remarkable that crime stories found a large market, and were produced in quantities by writers with a reportorial flair, whether or not their "reporting" was what it pretended to be. Defoe himself wrote a few of these ostensibly "true" stories of notorious criminals, which would appear in numbers on the streets after a particularly sensational hanging. When he came to the writing of clearly invented crime stories, he modeled them upon the shorter type which sometimes carried the sanction of at least a little basic truth. In his *Serious Reflections of Robinson Crusoe,* a sequel to the two earlier Crusoe stories, he takes the pains to defend his graphic depiction of crime and waywardness (sometimes, as he acknowledges, more piquant than terrifying) on the plea that these fictions take the form of parables.

> The selling or writing a parable, or an allusive statement . . . is always distinguished from . . . jesting with truth, in that it is designed and effectively turned for instructive and upright ends, and has its moral justly applied.

He takes the position then, of excusing to the moralist what he decries in the disinterested story-teller—the insistence upon the truth of the thing told, when it is not true. That liberty to "invent truth" becomes a cardinal expedient in Defoe's art. The introductions to many of his stories embody solemn declarations of their substantial truth. In *Robinson Crusoe,* for example, "the editor believes the thing to be a just history of fact; neither is there any appearance of fiction in it." The same squinting logic justifies for Defoe the fable itself when it might be charged with unseemly frankness. In the "Author's Preface" to *Moll Flanders* he says :

> Some of the vicious part of her life, which could not be modestly told, is quite left out, and several other parts are very much shortened.

---

*All these in his *Essay on Projects,* 1698.

The Famous ROXANA.

Engraved frontispiece, unsigned, to the first edition of Daniel Defoe's
The Fortunate Mistress, 1724.

What is left 'tis hoped will not offend the chastest reader or the modestest hearer; and as the best use is to be made of even the worst story, the moral, 'tis hoped, will keep the reader serious, even where the story might incline him to be otherwise. To give the history of a wicked life repented of, necessarily requires that the wicked part should be made as wicked as the real history of it will bear, to illustrate and give a beauty to the penitent part, which is certainly the best and brightest, if related with equal spirit and life.

When Defoe goes on to make the point that he writes to enforce the moral lesson, rather than to offer entertainment, we are almost obliged to question his sincerity.

But as this work is chiefly recommended to those who know how to read it, and how to make the good uses of it which the story all along recommends to them, so it is to be hoped that such readers will be much more pleased with the moral than with the fable, with the application than with the relation, and with the end of the writer than with the life of the person written of.

But sincere or insincere, these urgent asseverations of truth and this insistence upon the moral aim had their value for realistic effect, if for no other reason than that they disarmed skepticism; for large numbers of the readers of Defoe's time liked the semblance of truth and distrusted imagination.

Defoe can, however, pose a case of conscience, or of judgment, with all the appearance of impartiality. In *Roxana,* for example, this bold female defends her unwillingness to marry the man whose mistress she has already become :

I told him I had, perhaps, different notions of matrimony from what the received custom had given us of it; that I thought a woman was a free agent as well as a man, and was born free, and could she manage herself suitably, might enjoy that liberty to as much purpose as the men do; that the laws of matrimony were indeed otherwise, and mankind at this time acted quite upon other principles, and those such that a woman gave herself entirely away from herself in marriage, and capitulated, only to be at best but an upper servant; . . . that the very nature of the marriage contract was in short nothing but giving up liberty, estate, authority, and everything to the man, and the woman was indeed a mere woman ever after—that is to say—a slave.

The argument is pursued with warmth; counterargument is ineffectual, because it is largely the plea of custom—from which Roxana has already declared her independence. But the concluding paragraph was strong meat for the masculine diet at the time of Defoe's writing :

> "It is not you," says I, "that I suspect, but the laws of matrimony puts the power into your hands, bids you do it, commands you to command, and binds me, forsooth, to obey. You that are now on even terms with me, and I with you," says I, "are the next hour set up upon the throne, and the humble wife placed as your foot-stool; all the rest, all that you call oneness of interest, mutual affection, and the like, is courtesy and kindness then, and a woman is indeed infinitely obliged where she meets with it, but can't help herself where it fails."

So strongly put, the argument compels us to think that Defoe himself is propounding a view that was not to be even arguable until the very end of his century. But as cleverly urged as it is, it is not Defoe's view; since only a few pages later Roxana tells us that she was merely putting off her lover; for "I aimed at being a kept mistress, and to have a handsome maintenance, and I was still for getting money, and laying it up too, as much as he [a later lover] could desire me, only by a worse way." Yet Roxana's presentment is not necessarily vitiated by the fact that it is proposed in what Defoe would have us regard as the Devil's interest. Perhaps it expresses a conviction, or at least a favorable attitude, that Defoe would prefer not to have to justify. It is one more of the fairly numerous instances in which equivocality in the created character leaves us guessing whether Defoe's character was equivocal.

Defoe is a master of situation, though his command is sometimes obscured by the generally pedestrian program of his story. There are plenty of instances of it, among them Crusoe's discovery of the footprint on the beach, Roxana's announcement of her pregnancy to her Dutch lover after she has declined to marry him, Colonel Jacque's confrontation, after years of separation, with his unfaithful wife, and, again in *Roxana,* the daughter's painful insistence upon claiming Roxana as her mother. Yet we need not deplore too deeply that Defoe seems to neglect "good theater." In some degree he distrusts the dramatic moment, apparently not because it invites emotion and encourages false sentiment, but because it detracts from his kind of truth to life. It also lies somewhat outside his province of moral suasion unless it is closely identified with a moral issue.

But Defoe's merits—and his lasting importance for later writers of the novel—rest less upon his evocation of reality in the single incident, and more upon his exploration of the larger areas of experience with which the novel can deal. For consideration of that more comprehensive aspect of his work, *Moll Flanders* will be most to our purpose; for more than any other of his narratives, it looks like a novel.

Moll is an illegitimate child, born in Newgate prison of a criminal mother. But she is reared under favorable conditions, is industrious and ambitious, and is finally placed as an upper servant in a genteel family. Here she is seduced by the oldest son of the family under a promise of marriage, perhaps seriously intended. But from fear of the opposition of his family, he fails to keep his promise; and a younger brother falling in love with her, she marries him to conceal her lapse and to oblige the elder, whom she really loves. In a single page we are told that this first marriage lasts five years, until the death of her husband, when she is left with two children and £1200. Moll, it might be noted, is careful to cast up the profit and loss account in all her marriages.

She is then deceived into a marriage for money, in which her own attempt to deceive has its part. Her husband is a bankrupt who had counted upon relief by her "fortune," He absconds, and persuades her to take surreptitiously from his business enough movable stock to leave her this time with about £500.

Her next venture for a husband is managed with the wisdom of unhappy experience; she makes certain of the fortune before she marries. She and her husband move to his estates in Virginia, where she meets his mother, from whose gossip about her past Moll discovers shortly that she has married her half-brother. Moll puts an end to the impossible situation by returning to England with a stock of goods which should make her independent, but most of it is lost or damaged at sea, and she finds herself on the verge of poverty. In spite of the fact that her third marriage is not only incestuous but bigamous, and that she has taken no steps to annul either of her earlier marriages, she proceeds to lay plans for a fourth husband. The plans miscarry, and she slips unwarily into a liaison which lasts for some years, produces three children, and when it ends, leaves her once more with a little less than £500. She then maneuvers herself into marriage with a fourth husband, but again there is deception on both sides, and in spite of the fact that they are deeply attached to each other, they part regretfully.

Her worldly stock is now greatly reduced, but after a clever show of reticence, she succeeds in making a fifth marriage, with a man of substance. After "five years of the utmost tranquility" he dies, and she is left in "a dismal and disconsolate case indeed," for her husband's business has fallen off, and at forty-eight she knows that her chances of recouping her fortunes by another marriage are slender.

At the end of three years of widowhood, during which she has made no serious effort to secure her future, she is tempted by dire need into a small theft. This initiates a change for the worse in her whole scheme of life. She becomes a professional thief, learning her trade under a "schoolmistress," who, by assiduous training, makes her an artist in shoplifting and in watch-lifting; that is, detaching watches from the girdles of well-to-do women. At this last pursuit she quickly becomes adept enough to support herself and her instructress amply. From this point her story becomes a chronicle of theft and minor crime, interspersed with paroxysms of grief and repentance, but pursued nevertheless with assurance and skill. At last she is brought to account. She is arrested, tried, and condemned to death, and sent back to Newgate to await execution. Here she meets her fourth husband again, who, as a highwayman even when he married Moll, has lived a life of "genteel" crime, and now awaits his own fate. Through chicane, influence, and bribery, they succeed in having their sentences commuted to transportation to the American colonies as convict servants and, when on shipboard, in escaping servitude to become landholders and planters. In America they live on the solid material fruits of repentance until their return to England when their period of sentence has expired, to live a respectable and religious life together.

We have skipped the detail of Moll's criminal life, not because it is dull, for emphatically it is not, but because it is the stuff of the book, and cannot be curtailed without losing its spice. Incident is cleverly contrived, and is varied and circumstantial enough to keep interest going.

Quantitatively, *Moll Flanders* provides enough material for a novel, and as the story of a life, it conforms to what is probably the most familiar pattern of novel. And while its theme is uncommon in the sense that the criminal life is not familiar at first hand to most of us, Defoe gives it all the marks of reality. It is also in some depth a study of character. These are all accepted ingredients of the novel as we have come to know it. Is there an ingredient lacking—something that deprives it not of interest, but of the weight and influence of first-rate biographical novels, such as *Emma, Vanity Fair, Middlemarch,* and *Esther Waters,* all of them comparable studies of feminine mind and character in a specific social setting?

There is an instant answer to the question. *Moll Flanders* did not bring the novel into full and perfect bloom, and it was impossible that it should have. It lacks in the first place amplitude of characterization. Moll's growth in personality, even in her own errant type of personality, is not a calculated and realized progress, but is haphazard and never far advanced. We know from the start—for she tells us—what is lacking in her mental and moral make-up. She is pliant, unresourceful, vain, without moral conviction, and without real foresight. With disillusionment she acquires practical sense very quickly, but it is applied only to the good management of a bad life. From the moment of her seduction she drifts on a sea of more or less extraneous events. She plans and lives her life only as opportunity presents itself from day to day, and she measures its very questionable success only when she casts up accounts in pounds, shillings, and pence after one more marriage or one more "job." In the first half of her story, while she still has beauty, to capitalize, she moves with the same complacency from one parasitic union to another. When her beauty is no longer a working asset, her irresponsible nature thrives upon crime in the same unimaginative fashion. Moments of compunction, shame, and sometimes terror, come and go, but from beginning to end of her career all she does conforms to the "tragic fault" with which Defoe endows her at the outset. That conformity to preconceived character, which Fielding later calls "conservation of character," is characteristic of an inheritance from classical tragedy. It is acceptable when character is represented, as it is in the Greek drama, in a compact episode without a lengthy time sequence. But in a fictive work which traverses any great part of the life of an individual, as the novel generally does, it commits the character to a kind of spiritual inertia, and allows events rather than initiative to determine for better or worse the course of development. In the modern novel, character is commonly presented as a problem, not as a *fixe*. In Defoe's mind that conception is scarcely adumbrated.

Moll's moral inertia is accounted for in part by her social placement. It is not easy to realize the bleakness of the alternative in Defoe's day between having the wherewithal to live and not having it. Moll constantly stresses this point, yet her defense is to an important degree rationalization.* She admits it, and reiterates it. For her easy fatalism is not a philosophy; it is the slow enervation of a lazy mind. And Defoe himself would have been the last to excuse a deficiency of character upon a deterministic prescript.

The aesthetic deficiency, however, is not that Moll is weak willed, but that her want of mind is the unconscious omission of her creator. That she should not face her problems intelligently is one thing, but that Defoe should not pose those problems clearly and reveal to us a mind operating upon them for good or bad is another. Moll seems to lack an activated mental life, and that is one thing that the modern novel attempts to give us.

But Defoe's projection of her emotional life too is inadequate. And

---

*Perhaps it should be noted that in the period in which Defoe sets Moll's story there was a considerably sounder *economic* sanction for a life of skillful crime—always disregarding, of course, an almost certain windup on the gallows tree. Moll herself estimates that she can live "very easy" on fifteen pounds a year. But a successful coup with a good watch or a bolt of silk could bring in upwards of twenty pounds. When every article of luxury was the product of highly skilled handwork, a sharp practitioner of the thieving arts could live well even after the fence or the pawn-broker had taken his share. Colonel Jacque regarded the theft of a silk handkerchief as a passable day's work.

again, the fault is not that Moll is emotionally deficient (lacking even the stir of an energetic egotism), but that Defoe fails to picture satisfactorily an aspect of mind so interesting to any reader that it becomes an artistic essential. Perhaps it was beyond Defoe's power to do justice to the sentiments. Yet when a woman is given a succession of five husbands (not to mention "informal" marriages), we are fairly entitled to some moving sense of her feelings toward at least some of them. But while Defoe will give pages to the strategy and the profit and loss calculations of Moll when she is angling for a new husband, he generally dismisses the emotional experience in a paragraph or two—not that that experience is wanting. The exceptions are her attachment to the young man who seduced her, and her sustained affection, even after years of separation, for her fourth husband. Even these are treated descriptively rather than movingly. It may be doubtful whether Defoe's reserve in this respect reflects incapacity or deliberate reticence. But here again is a lack of creative imagination that remains to be supplied and fully explored by later novelists.

In still another aspect Defoe's imagination fails to take in a function of the modern novel. Moll seems to accept her social environment almost without consciousness of its meaning for her and her kind. She is not a social rebel, for she lacks the moral force that might make her one. She is sensible not merely of the unspeakable nastiness of the eighteenth-century prisons, but of their demoralizing effects. Yet she seems to regard the cruelties and injustices of the penal system as part of the order of things. She is not given to cerebration even when her own welfare is so closely concerned. And of the smaller adjustments of conduct and policy involved in one's consciousness of a social environment, we get very little. This is true also of Roxana and Colonel Jacque, whose beings and doings are set forth in broad enough perspective to permit us to call the literary medium in some sense a novel. In all these cases, however, the relation to the old picaresque tale is too close to permit a detached view of society, or a self-interested view sufficiently reflective.

All of Defoe's narratives tend to emphasize the event, the adventure, the material gain or loss, rather than the personality concerned. Defoe apparently apprehends feeling principally in the form of repentance, but too often his repentance scarcely seems to fit a character who has thoroughly enjoyed a repletion of tainted fun. All of his novels depict action outside the social bounds, so there is little occasion for his characters to face fairly the day-to-day problems of a normal social existence.

But what stories! When one has read *Moll Flanders* or *Robinson Crusoe,* the attempt to distinguish what it is *not* seems like mere mental proliferation. How important is it that Defoe does not think and write like Henry James? What is surprising is that these tales, perceptive, graphic, and entertaining beyond anything to be expected after the vapid romances of the French, should have fallen from the hands of a writer largely unconscious (for all we can gather) of his own stature, and disowned by the literary lords of his own generation. I have no quarrel with the critic who declared *Moll Flanders* "a great novel, if not the greatest," and I see only an amusing ambiguity in his discreet reservation.

As to *Robinson Crusoe,* it is unnecessary to breathe a word of praise about it; for all that can be said about it has already been well said, and many times repeated.

CHAPTER IV

Saeva Indignatio

Jonathan Swift

IT MAY be a question whether Jonathan Swift* should find a place in a conspectus of the eighteenth-century novel; for the one work of his which bears even a resemblance in form to the novel is *Gulliver's Travels,* and that violates most of the articles of the canon. Yet here mere precisianism would be ill-advised, just as in the case of Bunyan. For what could be more to the point in a discussion of the materials and methods of fiction than this story which for well over two centuries has excited the imaginations of readers both keen and dull, and which since the decline of the popularity of *The Pilgrim's Progress* probably shares with *Robinson Crusoe* the distinction of being the most familiar story in our language.

Gulliver's Travels was published in 1726. The name of its author did not appear on the early editions. Swift's authorship was, in fact, known to only a few of his intimates. Even more curiously, in his correspondence with his closest friends, most of whom are known to have been in the secret, the book is usually referred to under cover of elaborate make-believe as to its authorship. This game of anonymity was kept up, no doubt, in part for their amusement, but also because there was actual danger of reprisals for some of the strictures which the work contained upon the favoritism and corruption which permeated British politics in the reign of George I. Swift's *Tale of a Tub,* a tremendous travesty upon sectarianism and ritualism, published in 1704, had already cost him (he himself thought) preferment in the church to which he was entitled. It is not surprising, therefore, that he hesitated to acknowledge the authorship of a work which might have endangered his personal safety.

---

*Jonathan Swift (1667-1745). The chapter title is from the Latin epitaph Swift wrote for himself: "Here lies Jonathan Swift where savage indignation (*saeva indignatio*) no longer can tear his heart." Swift wrote three moderately long fictions—*The Battle of the Books* (published 1704, though written earlier), an episode in a literary controversy; *A Tale of a Tub* (1704), a satire on sectarianism; and *Gulliver's Travels* (1726).

The structure of the book is so familiar that we need scarcely dwell upon it—four sea voyages of Lemuel Gulliver to "remote," but actually non-existent, lands. The geography of the travels, though preposterous in the light of our present knowledge, was not incredible in Swift's time, when the South Seas were still incompletely explored and it was not known whether there was a land connection between North America and Asia.

The design of the first two voyages, to Lilliput and Brobdingnag, is very simply conceived. In Lilliput we find a race of human midgets presented to us with all their buildings, tools, and clothing, on the scale of one inch to a foot. In Brobdingnag the inhabitants are giants on the reverse scale— one foot to the inch. The satiric purpose of the book is achieved with the same simplicity. The Lilliputians are small not only in body but in mind, character, and social outlook. The Brobdingnagians are gross, physically revolting because the coarseness of their features, their skin, their hair, and their bodies generally, are enlarged as under a microscope. But the irony of this section lies rather in the fact that the great-minded King of Brobdingnag sees Gulliver's countrymen, just as Gulliver saw the Lilliputians, as a pretentious but annoying little race, little in every way.

The last two voyages, "A Voyage to Laputa, Balnibarbi, Luggnagg, Glubbdubdrib and Japan," and "A Voyage to the Country of the Houyhnhnms," move into other latitudes of fantasy. The former is a sort of sportive "omnium-gatherum" of human frailties, notably those of the pretentiously learned. The latter book reverses the relations of human beings and horses, horses becoming the living exponents of humanity, good sense, and good manners; and the race of Yahoos—unspeakably degraded human beings—becoming walking symbols of animality and physical vileness.

The explanation of this whole devastating picture of humanity lies in the age which produced it. Contemporaries spoke of "the age of reason" and "the enlightenment," but Kipling (no social historian, but a judge of human values) called it "brutal." Both pronouncements are right; and that appears in almost every word of *Gulliver's Travels*. There was a truly elevated but small minority of the intelligent, in science, in philosophy, and in the arts, trailed by another minority, generally distinct, of the wealthy and socially well-placed, but over-bearing, idle, avaricious, and corrupt. The politicians of the period came largely from the second group; but they were more or less in contact with the "intelligentsia," of whom Swift was one of the most brilliant and distinguished.

On the other hand, there was a proletariat debased beyond almost anything we know in human history, particularly debased because the ruling classes were perfectly aware of their plight and contemptuously indifferent to it. That is what Kipling means by "brutal." If one wishes a glimpse of the depth of their poverty, misery and almost unescapable criminality, he may see it pictured vividly enough in Defoe's *Colonel Jacque.* We tend —and like—to feel that in any phase of civilization, society enjoys a general and conscious well-being. But in Swift's day, British civilization was a spectacle of contrasts; of opportunity with utter hopelessness, of beauty with filth, of privilege with helplessness, and—as Swift himself pictures it—of complacent gentility with cancerous social degradation.

But to Swift, all this was not to be blamed merely upon a system of calculated political and social inequity; it was implicit in the nature of man. He could have agreed with Bernard Shaw that "civilization is a disease produced by the practice of building societies with rotten materials," but he would not have shared Shaw's conviction that better material can be assured if we take thought toward the object. To Shaw the way to improvement was a eugenic program; to Swift there was no way.

The voyage to Lilliput opens with an amusing objectivity; just the simple picture of midgets moving about with the busy preoccupation and consequence of our own kind. It continues with the gradual subservience of Gulliver—this miraculous reservoir of strength and energy—to the ambitious purposes of the diminutive politicians. It moves then into that socially significant area where the superior gifts and powers of a great individual become more and more frightening to the mediocre and the unimaginative.* It ends with Gulliver fleeing for his life from a country which had by this time gone into a dither of fright, envy, and, finally, hatred of its benefactor.

The satire of the "Voyage to Lilliput" is direct, unmistakable, but generally mild in comparison with that of the "Voyage to Brobdingnag." In Lilliput, Gulliver learned contempt for the little people; in Brobdingnag he is faced with the littleness of himself and his contemporaries, a much sterner lesson, and one which, human as he is, he is unable to accept and digest.

A series of conferences with His Brobdingnagian Majesty has disappointed, even angered him, because the King has not appeared to share his views as to the perfection of the British constitution, the disinterestedness of statesmen, the fairness of their laws, or the integrity of their courts. The King's summary opinion of what Gulliver has told him is this :

"My little friend Grildrig, you have made a most admirable panegyric upon your country; you have clearly proved that ignorance, idle-

---

*A recurrent theme in later literature, reappearing in Ibsen's *An Enemy of the People,* Samuel Butler's *Erewhon,* Nietzsche's eruptive philosophy, Shaw's plays generally, and Wells' *Invisible Man, Food of the Gods,* and *Country of the Blind.*

ness, and vice, are the proper ingredients for qualifying a legislator : that laws are best explained, interpreted, and applied by those whose interest and abilities lie in perverting, confounding, and eluding them. I observe among you some lines of an institution, which in its original might have been tolerable, but these half erased, and the rest wholly blurred and blotted by corruptions. It doth not appear from all you have said, how any one virtue is required towards the procurement of any one station among you; much less that men are ennobled on account of their virtue, that priests are advanced for their piety or learning, soldiers for their conduct or valor, judges for their integrity, senators for the love of their country, or counsellors for their wisdom. As for yourself" (continued the King) "who have spent the greatest part of your life in travelling, I am well disposed to hope you may hitherto have escaped many vices of your country. But by what I have gathered by your own relation, and the answers I have with much pains wringed and extorted from you, I cannot but conclude the bulk of your natives to be the most pernicious race of little odious vermin that nature ever suffered to crawl upon the surface of the earth."

But the climax of Gulliver's discomfiture comes when he attempts, a little vaingloriously, to enlighten the King upon the European art of war as an instrument of political policy.

In hopes to ingratiate myself further into his Majesty's favor, I told him of an invention discovered between three and four hundred years ago, to make a certain powder, into an heap of which the smallest spark of fire falling, would kindle the whole in a moment, although it were as big as a mountain, and make it all fly up in the air together, with a noise and agitation greater than thunder. That a proper quantity of this powder rammed into a hollow tube of brass or iron, according to its bigness, would drive a ball of iron or lead with such violence and speed, as nothing was able to sustain its force. That the largest balls thus discharged, would not only destroy whole ranks of an army at once, but batter the strongest walls to the ground, sink down ships with a thousand men in each, to the bottom of the sea; and, when linked together by a chain, would cut through masts and rigging; divide hundreds of bodies in the middle, and lay all waste before them. That we often put this powder into some large hollow balls of iron, and discharged them by an engine into some city we were besieging, which would rip up the pavements, tear the houses to pieces, burst and throw splinters on every side, dashing out the brains of all who came near. That I knew the ingredients very well, which were cheap, and common; I understood the manner of compounding them, and could direct his workmen how to make those tubes, of a size proportionable to all other things in his Majesty's kingdom, and the largest need not be above an hundred feet long; twenty or thirty of which tubes, charged with the proper quantity of powder and balls, would batter down the walls of the strongest town in his dominions in a few hours, or destroy the whole metropolis, if ever it should pretend to dispute his absolute commands. This I humbly offered to his Majesty, as a small tribute of acknowledgment in return of so many marks that I had received of his royal favor and protection.

The King was struck with horror at the description I had given of those terrible engines, and the proposal I had made. He was amazed how so impotent and grovelling an insect as I (these were his expressions) could entertain such inhuman ideas, and in so familiar a manner as to appear wholly unmoved at all the scenes of blood and desolation, which I had painted as the common effects of those destructive machines, whereof he said, some evil genius, enemy to mankind, must have been the first contriver. . . .

A strange effect of narrow principles and short views! that a prince possessed of every quality which procures veneration, love, and esteem; of strong parts, great wisdom, and profound learning, enbued with admirable talents for government, and almost adored by his subjects, should from a nice unnecessary scruple, whereof in Europe we can have no conception, let slip an opportunity put into his hands, that would have made him absolute master of the lives, the liberties, and the fortunes of his people. Neither do I say this with the least intention to detract from the many virtues of that excellent King, whose character I am sensible will on this account be very much lessened in the opinion of an English reader : but I take this defect among them to have risen from their ignorance, they not having hitherto reduced politics into a science, as the more acute wits of Europe have done.

In the "Voyage to Laputa"—and we can skip the rest of the title—the picture is more varied, and perhaps even difficult to understand in detail. For Swift assembles here a large number of more or less private peeves, and ridicules men and manners that are strictly contemporary and characteristically British. Much scholarship has been spent upon the particular points in this attack, but for our purposes it is only necessary to note that he arraigns most persistently what he regarded as the pretensions of scientists and projectors, "projectors" being the current name for men with ideas to sell.* Most of it is at least amusing, however extravagant—the savant who plans to extract sunshine from cucumbers to bottle and use for growing more cucumbers; a scheme for the abolition of spoken words in con-

---

*It might be noted that one scholar, Arthur E. Case, has taken the entire fabric of the travels to be strictly satire of English politics and politicians—a "politico-social treatise" on the extremes of good and bad government.

versation; another for absorbing knowledge by writing instruction on wafers and eating them.

But the most transfixing passage in this part of the work is the account of the Struldbrugs, the immortals on the island of Luggnagg. Swift's treatment of the theme of immortality proceeds from Gulliver's wishful notion of the inestimable advantage of that state. He imagines, quite naturally, an eternal life under all the conditions which would make it desirable—health, physical and mental energy, friends, means—in a word, all that a normal being in an agreeable environment could ask. But Swift traps Gulliver—and the reader—into this quite legitimate expectation, only to destroy Gulliver's happy picture upon quite another supposition—that immortality must lengthen out and intensify all the incapacities, pains, and miseries of extreme old age, from which death gives us mortals a final kindly release.

This is not only a tricky argument; it is illogical. For the successive periods of life—its infancy, prime, and decline—are apportioned to its length. Shaw's assumption in *Back to Methuselah,* that an infinitely lengthened life would include an infinitely lengthened prime, is quite as supportable as Swift's and, of course, considerably more cheerful. But we cannot quibble with Swift's assumptions, for they are meant to serve his own purpose, which is to picture as powerfully as possible the tragedy of age, with its attendant deterioration and helplessness. It is part of the program that he intends to illustrate his frequently quoted remark that he could love individuals, but he hated mankind. Age in itself can scarcely be either admired or loved, except as we may associate it with those to whom we are attached for other reasons. It can be tolerated because we know there is a period to it. Extreme age is pitiable, and it can be appalling. Here is Swift's picture.

> He gave me a particular account of the *struldbrugs* among them. He said they commonly acted like mortals, till about thirty years old, after which by degrees they grew melancholy and dejected, increasing in both till they came to fourscore. This he learned from their own confession : for otherwise there not being above two or three of that species born in an age, they were too few to form a general observation by. When they came to fourscore years, which is reckoned the extremity of living in this country, they had not only all the follies and infirmities of other old men, but many more which arose from the dreadful prospect of never dying. They were not only opinionative, peevish, covetous, morose, vain, talkative, but uncapable of friendship, and dead to all natural affection, which never descended below their grandchildren. Envy and impotent desires are their prevailing passions. But those objects against which their envy seems principally

directed, are the vices of the younger sort, and the deaths of the old. By reflecting on the former, they find themselves cut off from all possibility of pleasure; and whenever they see a funeral, they lament and repine that others have gone to a harbour of rest, to which they themselves never can hope to arrive. They have no remembrance of anything but what they learned and observed in their youth and middle age, and even that is very imperfect. And for the truth or particulars of any fact, it is safer to depend on common traditions than upon their best recollections. The least miserable among them appear to be those who turn to dotage, and entirely lose their memories; these meet with more pity and assistance, because they want many bad qualities which abound in others.

If a *struldbrug* happen to marry one of his own kind, the marriage is dissolved of course by the courtesy of the kingdom, as soon as the younger of the two comes to fourscore. For the law thinks it a reasonable indulgence, that those who are condemned without any fault of their own to a perpetual continuance in the world, should not have their misery doubled by the load of a wife.

As soon as they have completed the term of eighty years, they are looked on as dead in law; their heirs immediately succeed to their estates, only a small pittance is reserved for their support, and the poor ones are maintained at the public charge. After that period they are held incapable of any employment of trust or profit, they cannot purchase lands or take leases, neither are they allowed to be witnesses in any cause, either civil or criminal, not even for the decision of meers and bounds.

At ninety they lose their teeth and hair, they have at that age no distinction of taste, but eat and drink whatever they can get, without relish or appetite. The diseases they were subject to still continue without increasing or diminishing. In talking they forget the common appellation of things, and the names of persons, even of those who are their nearest friends and relations. For the same reason, they never can amuse themselves with reading, because their memory will not serve to carry them from the beginning of a sentence to the end; and by this defect they are deprived of the only entertainment whereof they might otherwise be capable.

The language of this country being always upon the flux, the *struldbrugs* of one age do not understand those of another, neither are they able after two hundred years to hold any conversation (farther than by a few general words) with their neighbors the mortals; and thus they lie under the disadvantage of living like foreigners in their own country.

This was the account given me of the *struldbrugs,* as near as I can remember. I afterwards saw five or six of different ages, the youngest not above two hundred years old, who were brought to me at several times by some of my friends; but although they were told that I was a great traveler, and had seen all the world, they had not the least curisity to ask me a question; only desired I would give them *slumskudask,* or a token of remembrance, which is a modest way of begging, to avoid the law that strictly forbids it, because they are provided for by the public, although indeed with a very scanty allowance.

They are despised and hated by all sorts of people; when one of them is born, it is reckoned ominous, and their birth is recorded very particularly; so that you may know their age by consulting the registry, which however hath not been kept above a thousand years past, or at least hath been destroyed by time or public disturbances. But the usual way of computing how old they are, is by asking them what kings or great persons they can remember, and then consulting history, for infallibly the last prince in their mind did not begin his reign after they were fourscore years old.

They were the most mortifying sight I ever beheld, and the women more horrible than the men. Besides the usual deformities in extreme old age, they acquired an additional ghastliness in proportion to their number of years which is not to be described; and among half a dozen, I soon distinguished which was the eldest, although there was not above a century or two between them.

We have seen a progressively unfavorable view of civilized humanity and human frailties in the voyages to Lilliput, Brobdingnag, and Laputa. The "Voyage to the Country of the Houyhnhnms" is the climax to the impeachment in terms of almost incredible bitterness. Yet it is rather remarkable that children are likely to find this interchange of the places of men and horses not merely amusing but fascinating. It envisages animals as children like to think of them; and it is developed with entertaining circumstantiality, at which Swift is always adept. And the horse is the perfect animal for Swift's purpose—familiar, physically impressive, yet equable and well-behaved. To adults Swift's picture presents itself quite differently, not because horses are exalted to a place which probably most horse lovers would justify in some measure, but because the Yahoo is so devastating a caricature of humanity. On its surface the picture is not too unreasonable or unjust, particularly since our present anthropological knowledge confirms Swift's assumption of a close, if not a derivative, relationship between man and the lower animals.

Perhaps the Yahoo's spiritual and moral debasement is less repulsive to most readers than his physical animality and his filth. The spiritual indictment can be laughed off, but the living and the social habits of the Yahoo are blistering to our collective vanity. Yet it must be remembered that Swift lived in densely overcrowded English and Irish cities when slums, slum life, and slum people were almost inhumanly vile—in the main, mostly because of their appalling poverty. And Swift, like most of his contemporaries, pitied the miserable condition of the impoverished, but blamed it in large part upon indolence and innate criminality. When Swift wrote his daring *Drapier's Letters* against the debasement of the Irish coinage, it was in the interest of a pauper populace—whom he detested.

The Yahoos are beyond debate strong medicine for weak stomachs. Yet their natures and habits, as Swift represents them, are no more meant to represent humanity faithfully than their flat faces, the bristles down their backs, and their long claws. They are caricature, and caricature has its own purposes; even, when it is good, its own kind of dignity. Compared with most of our newspaper comic strips, the portrait of the Yahoo has a rational grotesqueness. Swift's bitterness here is often interpreted as the rancor of personal disappointment; but it is also Swift's kind of amusement—intellectual amusement, understood and enjoyed in an age in which satire was familiar and enjoyable. It also has its corrective function, as comedy at its best should have.

Are Swift's equines any more convincing than his Yahoos? These genteel horses are not themselves meant to image the perfect human being, because they are all but emotionless. Their lives are lived upon a plane of unfailing reason, but their virtues are negative. They are, to be sure, free from improbity, from duplicity, from ambition, from devious wisdom. Money has to be explained to them, as well as foreign trade, statesmanship, and many other civilized human concerns. This innocence is sufficient for them, because they eat hay, and live on a hay economy. But ignorance is not superior wisdom, and freedom from social vices is not affirmative virtue in a society which is after all a comity rather than an organized society. Swift himself, if pressed, would have admitted their lack of certain agreeable frivolities—parties and gab, books to read, not to speak of music and art, political campaigns and newspapers. Their utter unsentimentality, of which Swift makes one of his strongest points, would be depressing in a world of human beings.

The satire in this last book of *Gulliver's Travels*—for that matter in all four books—is not directed against the human race, but against the abuses of a civilization which has overvalued, and therefore debased, the instruments of social control. Swift simply echoes the complaint of all political philosophers from Plato and Aristotle down to De Tocqueville and Maine, that political institutions are only as reliable as the men who control them. It is a rather curious position for a man to take who had his own personal interest in party politics and his own hopes for preferment. Yet his "fierce indignation" is not assumed. He felt deeply the ignominy of contemporary political life, and the shame of an inequitable and pitiless social system. The moral context of *Gulliver's Travels* is almost exclusively politico-social, for reasons self-evident in the work itself.

We have discussed *Gulliver's Travels* principally because it was one of the things that pleased readers before the chemically pure novel came into existence. It also brought into an as yet unmatured fiction some qualities and expedients that could be absorbed into the novel when it came of age. It put vitality, plenty of it, into hitherto humdrum prose narrative. It proved the potential interest of even trivial circumstance and incident, if they were organic. It combined adventure with everyday feeling, thinking, and acting.

But above all, it introduced the spirit of poetic satire into English fiction, and in a medium capable of delicate handling, even though Swift himself had more use for strong effects. In Fielding, Jane Austen, Thackeray, and Trollope, satire is only one voice in an elaborately harmonized score. In Swift, as in Voltaire, Butler, and Anatole France, it is a dominant voice in consonance with the taste of his generation. Perhaps it is too imperative for the over-delicate ear, but it suggested possibilities that have been appropriated, enlarged, and refined by many writers of fiction since Swift's time.

CHAPTER V

Virtue Rewarded

Samuel Richardson

WHATEVER HAS been said about Samuel Richardson,* no one has tried to make him out as personally impressive. Somewhat undersized, somewhat pursy, moderately successful as printer and publisher, fond of himself, fond of his family, fond of women in a quite unimpeachable way, fond of his own talk, faultlessly respectable, aggressively moral, over-sensitive, willing to counsel and inclined to preach, until 1740 he would have struck his contemporaries—and did—as sound, successful, pious, meetable, but by no stretch of imagination important, unless a touch of self-importance would have made him so.

In 1740 he wrote *Pamela*. Within a year he was the most talked-about person from London to the remotest rural backwaters. In the country, sermons were preached with the story of Pamela as their theme. In London, her story was painted, as Eliza Haywood tells us, upon the walls of Vauxhall—which was rather like embellishing the Temple of Baal with the story of Joseph and Potiphar's wife.

The reader's first look at *Pamela* will suffer from the effects of his entire stock of modern prejudices. In this view, the novel is too loquacious, too feminine, too sanctimonious, too melodramatic, too sententious, too prissy; and, it has also been said, too ignorant of the society it professes to depict. But does this comprehensive censure mean much more than that the book is (in our own contemptuous slang) "dated"? There is little likelihood that *Pamela* can be made to appeal to what Saintsbury called the "uncivilized" reader—that is, the reader possessed of neither tolerance nor perspective. But if there is something to be gained in the attempt to make a dated work understandable, *Pamela* is one of the best subjects for the trial. For it is by general acknowledgment the first work, at least in England, to

*Samuel Richardson (1689-1761). *Pamela, or Virtue Rewarded* (1740); *Pamela, the Second Part* (1741); *Clarissa, or the History of a Young Lady* (1748); *History of Sir Charles Grandison* (1753).

mark the completed transition from the prose tale to the modern novel.

Before Richardson's time English fiction was without a clear tradition and without an economy. Defoe had been the one writer of fiction to realize fairly fully the way to tell a long story, but it was his own way, and Richardson did not try to follow it. So in spite of the fact that through his trade as printer and his reading habits, he knew the literature of his time and knew it rather well, Richardson would have found only a thin and intermittent stream of effective prose fiction to serve him not necessarily with models, but for instruction and stimulus.

The genesis of *Pamela* was a plan for Richardson to compose a handbook of letter-writing, which was afterwards published. While he was at work on it, he conceived the idea of a volume of letters as a medium for the discussion of problems of conduct. His breaking into fiction was therefore to some extent an accident, and his purpose in writing was moral instruction. Both facts were somewhat prejudicial to artistic success; for not thinking of his art *as* art, he floundered more or less in his own inexperience, and even at times (on his own admission) found himself wondering where his next step was going to carry him.

His achievement was the product of industry rather than the born story-teller's instinct. He had no great capacity of self-criticism, asked all sorts of friends for all sorts of advice about the work in hand, disrelished altering or rejecting what he had once written, and though he was always, and even obstinately, clear as to the outcome of his narrative, he was often uncertain of the path to be traveled. Writing was for him therefore a process of trial and error without the capacity, or the will, to recognize and cast out the error. There seems little doubt that to his mind a written page was a work of virtue regardless of what was on it. He probably never recognized the processes of writing as different from the processes of conversation—at which, by the way, he was thought to be proficient.

So by the circumstances attending the design of the first work he undertook—the manual of letter-writing—and probably without reflective choice, he was committed from the beginning to the letter form, but less from an understanding of its limitations than from the fact that he had become used to it. Its great hazard for him, in view of his inexperience and his inherent tendency to ramble, was that it encouraged dawdling. And no writer ever dawdled with greater complacency.

The theme of *Pamela* is simplicity itself. A young serving-maid, charming and intelligent, deservedly the favorite of an aristocratic and kindly mistress, is retained after her mistress's death in the household of her son, Mr. B——. Spoiled and willful, as well as rakish, Mr. B—— proceeds to take advantage of her position by attempting to seduce her. Her virtue is fortified by both piety and prudence, but she is under the almost hopeless disadvantage of the poor and unprotected girl in the employment (which then meant the power) of the man of means and social station. Her struggle to prevent disgrace is the substance of the plot, which ends in Mr. B——'s bowing to her virtuous resolution and finally taking her as his wife.

Pamela's correspondence is almost entirely one-sided. There are a few responses from her parents and a few enclosures of other brief letters, but the story is told in the main by her own letters to her parents. Her output, let it be said, is utterly incredible. Two letters written in a single day of great events toward the end of the "First Part" of *Pamela* run to 36,000 words. Regardless of the time consumed in the day's doings, it is impossible for even a highly experienced and very rapid writer to turn out any such amount. Further, the letters involve much needless repetition, profess (notably in the 36,000 word bout) to give word-for-word reports of long exchanges of conversation, and generally dwell inexhaustibly upon minute circumstantial detail and tittle-tattle. The novel, therefore, is lengthy beyond any reasonable warrant, and is blandly indifferent to what is essential and what superfluous.

These things have been said not to condemn the novel before we come to it, but to prepare the reader for a story different in design and intention from the sort to which he is accustomed. We must also expect to find that the literary medium itself is, necessarily, antiquated. Up to this point, we have met no very alarming example of "elegant" eighteenth-century prose—prose that glories in ponderous words and in sentences intricate in construction and Latinate in tone. Dr Johnson, who comes later, is, of course, its famous exemplar. In his faultless hands it has at least dignity, though to our ways of thinking it is pretentious. But in an uncultivated writer it is cumbersome, and may be monstrous.

Mr. B—— and Pamela, then, are the protagonists in a protracted conflict of passions, Mr. B——'s role aggressive, Pamela's defensive. The dying words of Mr. B——'s mother were, "My dear son, remember my poor Pamela," and Mr. B——'s regard for this injunction begins with apparently friendly attentions and gifts in memory of his mother. But interest in the girl grows with familiarity, and since she resists his gentler approaches, he proceeds to frontal attack. She dislikes tousling even more than casual kisses, and hastens to acquaint her parents and Mrs. Jervis, the housekeeper, with her embarrassment, intending to leave Mr. B——'s house and return to her family.

Her master, however, like most of the young members of the landed gentry of the time, feels that his consequence entitles him to certain powers over his female servants which were not stipulated in the statutes of the realm. He is not only surprised but affronted by Pamela's resistance, which he regards as a rebuff to his good will. The attitude seems both fatuous and

vicious, but it reflects the fashionable psychology of the time. It is not
Pamela's virtue that seems ridiculous to Mr. B——, but that a girl of the
laboring classes should pretend to virtue. In the alternation of his feelings
between lively passion and contempt for her "low" condition, he wavers
between casting her out of the house and forcing her to his will. Yet not
surprisingly, he finds procrastination the easy policy, and he keeps her
about him by a half-promise to release her when she has finished certain
domestic duties she has undertaken.

Meanwhile, Pamela prepares cheerfully for her going. She will not take
with her the fine things that were given her from her old mistress's ward-
robe, partly because they were, as she feels, given as a bribe by Mr. B——.
and partly because they will not fit her humble place in her parents' home.

How would they look upon me, thought I to myself, when they
should come to be threadbare and worn out? And how should I look
even if I could purchase home-spun clothes, to dwindle into them one
by one as I got them? Maybe an old silk gown and linsey-woolsey
petticoat and the like. So, thought I, I had better get myself equipped
in the dress that will become my condition. And though it may look
but poor to what I have been used to wear of late days, yet it will
serve me, when I am with you, for a good holiday and Sunday suit, and
what, by a blessing on my industry, I may, perhaps, make a shift to
keep up to. So, as I was saying, unknown to anybody, I bought of
Farmer Nichols' wife and daughters a good sad-colored stuff, of their
own spinning, enough to make me a gown and two petticoats; and I
made robings and facing of a pretty bit of calico I had by me.

I had a pretty good camblet quilted coat that I thought might do
tolerably well; and I bought two flannel undercoats, not so good as my
swan-skin and fine linen ones, but what will keep me warm if any
neighbor should get me to help them to milk, as sometimes I used to do
formerly; for I am resolved to do all your good neighbors what kindness I can, and hope to make myself as much beloved about you as I
am here.

I got some Scots cloth, and made me, at mornings and nights, when
nobody saw me, two shifts. I have enough left for two shirts and two
shifts for you, my dear father and mother. When I come home, I'll
make them for you, and desire your acceptance.

Then I bought of a pedlar two pretty round-eared caps, a little
straw hat, and a pair of knit mittens turned up with white calico, and
two pair of blue worsted hose with white clocks, that make a smartish
appearance, I'll assure you; and two yards of black ribband for my
shift sleeves, and to serve as a necklace. When I had them all come
home, I went and looked at them once in two hours for two days
together. . . .

Pamela exhibits to Mrs. Jarvis "all my store." From the first comprehensively illustrated English novel. Engraved by Hubert Gravelot after Francis Hayman for the first illustrated edition of Richardson's *Pamela,* 1742 (comprising the sixth edition of Volumes 1 and 2, *Pamela, First Part,* and the third edition of Volumes 3 and 4, *Pamela, Second Part*).

In a few days she has finished the work on her clothes, and :

> . . . dressed myself in my new garb; and put on my round-eared or-
> dinary cap, but with a green knot, my home-spun gown and petticoat,
> and plain leather shoes, but yet they are what they call Spanish
> leather, and my ordinary hose, ordinary, I mean, to what I have been
> lately used to, though I should think good yarn may do very well for
> every day when I come home. A plain muslin tucker I put on, and my
> black silk necklace instead of the French necklace my lady gave me.
> And put the ear-rings out of my ears. When I was quite equipped, I
> took my straw hat in my hand, with its two blue strings, and looked in
> the glass, as proud as anything. To say truth, I never liked myself so
> well in my life.
>
> O the pleasure of descending with ease, innocence, and resignation!
> Indeed there is nothing like it! An humble mind, I plainly see, cannot
> meet with any very shocking disappointment, let Fortune's wheel turn
> round as it will.
>
> So I went down to look for Mrs. Jervis, to see how she liked me. . . .

Her efforts are not wasted. Mrs. Jervis insists, against Pamela's modest
protests, on presenting her to Mr. B——.
Of course the mischief has started all over again. Pamela is coquetting,
B—— thinks; while Pamela thinks B—— is both wicked and untruthful;
for he has permitted her—which means commanded her—to remain another fortnight. That very night he makes an attempt upon Pamela by
hiding in the closet of her chamber when she goes to bed. But Mrs. Jervis
will not leave her, and prevents his effecting his purpose; not, however,
before Pamela faints from fright. In the morning Mr. B—— calls Mrs.
Jervis to account for her "interference."

> "Mrs. Jervis," said he, "since I know *you* and you know *me* so well,
> I don't know how we shall live together for the future." . . . "Sir,"
> said she, "I will take the liberty to say what I think is best for both. I
> have so much grief that you should attempt to do any injury to this
> poor girl, and especially in my chamber, that I should think myself
> accessory to the mischief if I was not to take notice of it. Though my
> ruin may depend upon it, I desire not to stay; but pray let poor Pamela
> and me go together." . . . "With all my heart," said he, "and the sooner
> the better." She fell a crying. "I find," said he, "this girl has made a
> party of the whole house in her favor against me." "Her innocence
> deserves it of us all," said she very kindly; "and I never could have
> thought that the son of my dear good lady departed, could have so
> forfeited his honor as to endeavor to destroy a virtue he ought to
> protect. . . As for Pamela, she is at her liberty, I hope, to go away next
> Thursday, as she intends."

Events move slowly in the days remaining. Mrs. Jervis, after proper apologies, is restored to her position in the household, and Pamela and Mr. B—— seem by tacit agreement to stay out of each other's way. But her "wicked master" nurses resentment at his defeat and is outraged by her "impudence" in giving him her opinion of his actions.

Mrs. Jervis, kindly and well-intentioned, but a bit of a bungler, again exposes Pamela to her master by hiding him in her closet during what she knows is to be Pamela's leave-taking of her, in the hope that he will be moved by compassion. The plan has, to Mrs. Jervis' credit, a certain effect. He summons Pamela on the following morning.

> He took me up in a kinder manner than ever I had known, and he said, "Shut the door, Pamela, and come to me in my closet; I want to have a little serious talk with you." . . . "How can I, Sir," said I; "how can I!" and wrung my hands. "O pray Sir, let me go out of your presence, I beseech you." . . . "By the God that made me," said he, "I'll do you no harm. Shut the parlor door and come to me in my library."
>
> I shut the parlor door, as he bid me, but stood at it irresolutely. "Place some confidence in me," said he; "surely you may when I have spoken thus solemnly." So I crept towards him with trembling feet, and my heart throbbing through my handkerchief. "Come in," said he, "when I bid you." I did so. "Pray Sir," said I, "pity and spare me!" "I will," said he, "as I hope to be saved. . . . Don't doubt me, Pamela; from this moment I will no longer consider you as my servant, and I desire you will not use me with ingratitude for the kindness I am going to express towards you. . . . You have too much good sense not to discover that I, in spite of my heart, and all the pride of it, cannot but love you. Look up to me, my sweet-faced girl, I *must* say I love you, and have put on a behaviour to you that was much against my heart, in hopes to frighten you from your reservedness. You see I own it ingenuously; and don't play your sex upon me for it."

The overture leads to a proposal that Mr. B—— shall offer help to Pamela's father, who is, exactly as Pamela states it, "poor but honest." B—— again declares his love for her, but Pamela reads correctly the meaning of both items of the proposal :

> I trembled to find my poor heart giving way. "O good Sir," said I, "spare a poor girl that cannot look up to you and speak. My heart is full; and why should you wish to undo me?" . . . "Only oblige me," said he, "to stay a fortnight longer, and John shall carry word to your father that I will see him in the meantime, either here or at the Swan in the village." . . . "O Sir," said I, "my heart will burst, but, on my bended knees, I beg you to let me go tomorrow, as I designed; and

don't offer to tempt a poor creature whose will would be yours if my virtue would permit." ... "It shall permit it," said he; "for I intend no injury to you, God is my witness!" ... "Impossible," said I; "I cannot, Sir, believe you, after what has passed. How many ways are there to undo poor creatures! Good God, protect me this one time, and send me but to my dear father's cot in safety!" ... "Strange, damned fate," says he, "that when I speak so solemnly, I can't be believed!" ... "What *should* I believe, Sir," said I; "what *can* I believe? What have you said, but that I am to stay a fortnight longer? And what then is to become of me?" ... "My pride of birth and fortune ("damn them both," said he, "since they cannot obtain credit with you, but only add to your suspicions) will not let me descend all at once. I therefore ask you but a fortnight's stay, that after this declaration I may pacify those proud demands upon me." O how my heart throbbed, and I begun (for I did not know what I did) to say the Lord's Prayer. ... "None of your beads to me, Pamela," said he; "thou art a perfect nun." But I said aloud, with my eyes lifted up to Heaven, *"Lead me not into temptation, but deliver me from evil, O my good God!"* He hugged me in his arms and said, "Well, my dear girl, then you stay this fortnight, and you shall see what I shall do for you."

He went out, and I was tortured with twenty different doubts in a minute; sometimes I thought that to stay a week or a fortnight longer in this house, to obey him, while Mrs. Jervis was with me, could do no great harm. But then, thought I, how do I know what I may be *able* to do? I have withstood his *anger,* but may I not relent at his *kindness?*

Mr. B——'s offers become more tempting and more transparent. He will not only make her father independent; he will provide Pamela herself with a life of ease and elegance, and with a husband of his own choosing (a far from unfamiliar eighteenth-century expedient) to screen his reputation and hers! The husband, in fact, is already in hand—his chaplain in Lincolnshire. Pamela asks for an hour for thought—though actually to gain time—and writes him a polite refusal of all his offers, repeating her plea to be sent home promptly.

In the morning Pamela departs for her home. But before she has traveled far, she discovers that her master has sent her not to her parents, but to his Lincolnshire estate, there to await his will under the care of his housekeeper, Mrs. Jewkes. Mrs. Jewkes is an old limb of the devil, and has been, in fact, a competent aid in previous amatory transactions of her master's. She wastes no courtesy on Pamela, shows her no sympathy, and devotes her time to arguing or taming her charge into preparation for Mr. B——'s next move. Mr. B—— remains at his Bedfordshire estate—the one from which Pamela had been sent—while the softening-up process goes on.

Pamela, however, is no docile lamb in Mrs. Jewkes' hands. She opposes her own resourcefulness to Mrs. Jewkes' practised cleverness, but the wily woman is too much for her. Pamela attempts escape, unsuccessfully, appeals to the neighbors in vain, for they are Mr. B——'s friends or dependents, and finally thinks to find refuge in marriage with Mr. Williams, her master's chaplain. This, too, falls through. Her imprisonment, for it is literally that, is tightened as she struggles.

The long and exhausting wait is brought to a crisis when a letter from B—— to Mrs. Jewkes falls by accident into Pamela's hands. The letter opens up B——'s deepened resentment at Pamela's obstinacy, and his fury at his chaplain for having offered to help her out of her plight. Its concluding paragraph reads :

> I think I now hate her perfectly; and, though I will do nothing to her *myself,* yet I can bear for the sake of my revenge, *injured honor,* and *slighted love,* to see anything, even what *she most fears,* be *done to her;* and then she may be turned loose to her evil destiny, to echo to the woods and groves her piteous lamentations for the loss of her fantastical innocence, which the romantic idiot makes such a work about. I shall go to London with my sister Davers; and the moment I can disengage myself, which perhaps may be in three weeks from this time, I will be with you, and decide *her* fate and put an end to your trouble. Meantime, be doubly careful; for this innocent, as I have warned you, is full of contrivances.

The brutality of this letter, and of one addressed to Pamela herself at the same time, leads her to contemplate suicide.

> Then, thought I, (O, that thought was surely of the Devil's instigation, for it was very soothing and powerful with me) these wicked wretches, who now have no remorse, no pity on me, will then be moved to repent their misdoings; and when they see the dead corpse of the unhappy Pamela dragged out on these banks, lying breathless at their feet, they will find that remorse to soften their obdurate hearts, which now has no place there! My master, my angry master, will then forget his resentments, say, "Oh, this is the unhappy Pamela that I have causelessly persecuted and destroyed. Now do I see she preferred her honesty to her life," will he say, "and is no hypocrite nor deceiver, but was the innocent creature she pretended to be." Then, thought I, will he perhaps shed a few tears over the poor corpse of his persecuted servant, ... yet will he be inwardly grieved, and order me a decent funeral, and save me from the dreadful stake, and highway interment. The young men and maidens all around my father's will pity poor Pamela! But O! I hope I shall not be the subject of their ballads and elegies, but that my memory, for the sake of my dear father and mother, may quickly slide into oblivion.

But there is an end even to waiting. From out of the blue comes one brief and panicky note from Pamela :

Good Sirs! good Sirs! What will become of me? Here is my master come in his fine chariot! Indeed he is! What shall I do? Where shall I hide myself? O—what shall I do? Pray for me! But O, you will not see this! Now, good God of Heaven, preserve me, if it is thy blessed will!

Two hours afterwards she hears her master coming up the stairs. Richardson cannot miss the chance to slip in a Richardsonian detail— "I shall choose a boiled chicken [for dinner] with butter and parsley." If the sentence had been written in 1960, we should call it symbolic. In Richardson it is certainly unequivocal.

He put on a stern and majestic air, and he can look very majestic when he pleases. "Well, perverse Pamela, ungrateful runaway," said he, for my first salutation, "you do well, don't you, to give me all this trouble and vexation?" I could not speak, but throwing myself on the floor, hid my face, and was ready to die with grief and apprehension. . . . He said, "Well may you hide your face; well may you be ashamed to see me, vile forward one as you are!" . . . I sobbed and wept, but could not speak. And he let me lie, and went to the door, and called Mrs. Jewkes. "There," said he, "take up that fallen angel; but I have now no patience with her. The little hypocrite prostrated herself thus in hopes to move my weakness in her favor, and that I'll raise her from the floor myself. But I shall not touch her. No," said he, "let such fellows as Williams be taken in by her artful wiles! I know her now, and she is for any fool's turn that will be caught by her."
I sighed as if my heart would break!—and Mrs. Jewkes lifted me up to my knees, for I trembled so I could not stand. "Come," said she, "Mrs. Pamela; learn to know your best friend! Confess your unworthy behavior, and beg his honor's forgiveness of all your faults." . . . I was ready to faint; and he said, "She is mistress of arts, I'll assure you, and will mimic a fit, ten to one, in a minute."
I was struck to the heart with this, and could not speak presently; only lifted my eyes up to Heaven, and at last said, "God forgive you, 'Sir." . . . He seemed in a great passion, and walked up and down the room, casting sometimes an eye upon me, and seeming as if he would have spoken, but checked himself. And at last he said, "When she has *acted* this her *first part* over, perhaps I will see her again, and she will *soon* know what she has to trust to."

Despite his anger and his arrogance, Mr. B—— is still slave enough to his passion to make a final effort to secure her. He offers for her consideration a set of "articles" which would, if she agreed to them, settle upon her all that the haughtiest mistress might exact; and he concludes with a threat that if she is not compliant, "you shall meet with all you fear, without the least benefit arising from it to yourself." Her reply is not only full; it is compendious. And it is, of course, a refusal, with the commitment of her case to God Almighty. The result is, inevitably, that Mr. B—— reaches a new high in anger and humiliation, and he and Mrs. Jewkes set about contriving a plan for her betrayal.

The following night Mr. B—— disguises himself as a maid-servant and conceals his identity until Pamela thinks she is safely in bed with Mrs. Jewkes. The details of the attempt are given with more than necessary clarity, Mrs. Jewkes playing a capable assisting part. But when all seems lost, Pamela faints and is saved. It is probably not a mode of escape that one could recommend with confidence to other young ladies in similar situations; but Mr. B——is thoroughly frightened, and in spite of Mrs. Jewkes' impatient urgings he gives up the attempt. This is the turning point in Pamela's varying fortunes. Her jealousy for her purity, the effectiveness of her resistance, and perhaps most of all, the enhancement of her desirability in the very course of the pursuit, convince B—— that she must be won neither by force nor by guile.

With Pamela safe from further assault, at least for the time being, the interest turns to Mr. B——. He has so far made no claim upon our understanding, much less our sympathy; for we have seen him only as the spoiled and arrogant child of luxury. But in his repentant mood, and with growth of self-knowledge, there is a resurgence of conscience and a willingness to consider upon its own merits this problem of "unequal" love. The claims of personality, of social place, and of reputation, on Pamela's side as well as his, begin to orient themselves in his hitherto passionate and irresponsible mind. There is a long pause in the action of the story, and time for reflection. If he cannot as yet regard Pamela as his equal, he can at least accept her as a woman with a mind as well as feelings. We find him in the entirely new position of pleading for Pamela's aid in the solution of their joint problem. With this approach, he very quickly learns that Pamela's own heart is touched, despite his rascally treatment of her. The change is not surprising to the reader, for Pamela has already suggested as much in her letters home But the barrier of B——'s family pride remains, and his desire for an understanding is still stated upon his own terms :

"But what can I do? Consider the pride of my condition. I cannot endure the thought of marriage, even with a person of equal or superior degree to myself, and have declined several proposals of that kind. How then, with the distance between us in the world's judgment, can I think of making you my wife? Yet I must have you; I cannot bear the thoughts of any other man supplanting me in your affections."

Pamela comments :

It is impossible for me to express the agitations of my mind on this unexpected declaration, so contrary to his former behavior. His manner, too, had something so noble and so sincere, as I thought, that, alas for me! I found I had need of all my poor discretion to ward off the blow which his treatment gave to my most guarded thoughts. I threw myself at his feet; for I trembled and could hardly stand. "O Sir," said I, "spare your poor servant's confusion! O, spare the poor Pamela!" . . . "Speak out," said he, "and tell me what you think I ought to do."

She takes up B——'s question, after some understandable hesitation.

"As to *my* thoughts of what you ought to do, I must needs say that I think you ought to regard the world's opinion, and avoid doing anything disgraceful to your birth and fortune; and therefore if you really honor the poor Pamela with your respect, a little time, absence, and the conversation of worthier persons of my sex will effectually enable you to overcome a regard so unworthy your condition. And this, good Sir, is the best advice I can offer."

If this seems disingenuous, it must be remembered that Pamela, in accord with the general feeling of her time, would have shared without question Mr. B——'s own view of what he owed his position. But as the conversation is pursued, its drift starts Pamela's old doubts once more :

"Ah, Sir," said I, "there my doubt recurs that you may thus graciously use me to take advantage of my credulity."

"Still perverse and doubting," said he. "Cannot you take me as I am at present? and that, I have told you, is sincere and undesigning, whatever I may be hereafter."

"Ah Sir," replied I, "what can I say? I have already said too much if this dreadful *hereafter* should take place. Don't bid me say how well I can—" And then, my face glowing as the fire, I, all abashed, leaned upon his shoulder to hide my confusion.

He clasped me to him with great ardor, and said, "Hide your dear face in my bosom, my beloved Pamela; your innocent freedoms charm me! But then, say how well—what?"

"If you will be good," said I, "to your poor servant, and spare her, I cannot say too much. But if not, I am doubly undone! Undone indeed!"

Said he, "I hope my present temper will hold; for I tell you frankly

Pamela confesses her love to Mr. B ....; engraved by James Heath
after Edward F. Burney. One of the many illustrative plates from
The Novelist's Magazine, 1780-1788. With the conventional rococo
frame used with this entire series of prints. Note the halo effect in
Pamela's hat. 1785.

that I have known in this agreeable hour more sincere pleasure than I have experienced in all the guilty tumults that my desiring soul compelled me into, in the hopes of possessing you on my own terms. And Pamela, you must pray for the continuance of this temper, and I hope your prayers will get the better of my temptations."

This sweet goodness overpowered all my reserves. I threw myself at his feet and embraced his knees. "What pleasure, Sir, you give me at these gracious words is not lent your poor servant to express! I shall be too much rewarded for all my sufferings if this goodness hold! God grant it may, for your own soul's sake as well as mine. And Oh, how happy shall I be if—"

He stopt me and said. "But, my dear girl, what must we do about the world and the world's censure? Indeed I cannot marry."

Now was I again struck all of a heap. However, soon recollecting myself— "Sir," said I, "I have not the presumption to hope such an honor. If I may be permitted to return in peace and safety to my poor parents, to pray for you there, it is all I at present request. This, Sir, after all my apprehensions and dangers, will be a great pleasure to me. And if I know my own poor heart, I shall wish you happy in a lady of a suitable degree, and rejoice most sincerely in every circumstance that shall make for the happiness of my late good lady's most beloved son."

"Well," said he, "this conversation, Pamela, is gone farther than I intended it. You need not be afraid of trusting yourself with *me;* I ought to be doubtful of trusting myself when I am with *you.* But before I say anything further upon this subject, I will take my proud heart to task; and till then, let everything be as if this conversation had never passed."

The moral dilemma which Pamela faces—of meeting B——'s demand that she place her confidence in him, yet accepting some vague status for affection outside of marriage—is heightened by her receiving an anonymous letter warning her that her master is planning a mock marriage. The letter revives her doubts, although it is actually groundless. Meanwhile, there is a long passage in the story concerned with Pamela's "papers"— that is, with the copies she has kept of her letters to her parents. The passage calls for comment only because the letters, when they are finally turned over to B——, add to his understanding of both her good faith and her actual sufferings. He is brought almost to the point of offering her honorable marriage, when Pamela again voices her doubts of his sincerity. She asks again to be sent home.

He was in a fearful passion then. "And is it *thus,*" said he, "in my fond conceding moments, that I am to be answered and despised?

Perverse, unreasonable Pamela! begone from my sight, and know as well how to behave in a hopeful prospect as in a distressful state. Then, and not till then, shall you attract my notice."

I was startled, and going to speak, but he stamped with his foot and said, "Begone, I tell you; I cannot bear this stupid romantic folly."

It is more than a pettish explosion; it is the occasion, at last, for a clear decision. Pamela is to go back to her parents! With Mrs. Jewkes' ill-natured help, she prepares her little belongings for departure the next day. There is a concluding scene with Mr. B——, not of his seeking.

As I passed by the parlor [Mrs. Jewkes] stepped in and said, "Sir, you have nothing to say to this girl before she goes?"—I heard him reply, though I did not see him, "Who bid you say *the girl*, Mrs. Jewkes, in that manner? She has offended only me."

"I beg your honor's pardon," said the wretch; "but if I was your honor, she should not, for all the trouble she has cost you, go away scot-free." "No more of this, as I *told you before*," said he; "what, when I have such proof that her virtue is all her pride, shall I rob her of that? —No," added he, "let her go, perverse and foolish as she is. But she *deserves* to go honest, and she *shall* go so."

I was so transported by this unexpected goodness that I opened the door before I knew what I did, and said, falling on my knees with my hands folded and lifted up, "O thank your honor a million of times! May God bless you for this instance of your goodness to me! I will pray for you as long as I live, and so shall my dear father and mother. And Mrs. Jewkes," said I, "I will pray for you, too, poor wicked wretch that you are."

He turned from me, went into his closet, and shut the door. He need not have done so; for I would not have gone nearer to him. Surely, I did not say *so much*, as to incur all this displeasure.

I think I was loth to leave the house. Can you believe it? What could be the matter with me, I wonder? I felt something so strange at my heart! I wonder what ailed me! But this was so *unexpected*; I believe that was all. Yet I am very strange still. Surely I cannot be like the old murmuring Israelites, to long after the onions and garlic of Egypt, when they had suffered there such heavy bondage?—I'll take thee, O contradictory, ungovernable heart, to severe task for this thy strange impulse, when I get to my dear father and mother's, and if I find anything in thee that should not be, depend upon it, thou shalt be humbled, if strict abstinence, prayer, and mortification will do it."

So we find Pamela on her way home in her master's chariot, a horseman with a pair of pistols accompanying her to protect her against the perils of the highway. They stop in the evening at a little roadside inn,

where a letter is put into her hands by her armed escort; it is from
Mr. B——.

> When these lines are delivered to you, you will be far on your way to
> your father and mother, where you have so long desired to be; and I
> hope I shall forbear thinking of you with the least shadow of that fond-
> ness my foolish heart had entertained for you. I bear you no ill will,
> but the end of my detaining you being over, I would not that you
> should tarry with me an hour after the ungenerous preference you gave
> at a time I was inclined to pass over all other considerations, for an
> honorable address to you. For well I found the tables entirely turned
> upon me, and that I was in far more danger from *you* than you were
> from *me*. For I was just upon resolving to defy all the censures of the
> world, and to make you my wife.

There is more, all reflecting the pain of a deeply disturbed heart. But
Pamela continues with her own reflections:

> This letter, when I expected some new plot, has affected me more
> than anything of *that* sort could have done. His great value for me is
> here confessed, and his rigorous behavior accounted for in such a man-
> ner as tortures me much. . . . My dear parents, forgive me, but I found
> before, to my grief, that my heart was too partial in his favor. But now,
> with so much openness, affection, and *honor* too (which was all I had
> doubted) I am quite overcome. This was a happiness, however, I had no
> reason to expect. But I must own to you that I shall never be able to
> think of anybody in the world but him. "Presumption," you will say,
> and so it is; but love is not a voluntary thing—Love, did I say?—But
> come, it has not, I hope, gone so far as to make me *very* uneasy; for I
> know not *how* it came, nor *when* it began; but it has crept, like a thief,
> upon me, before I knew what was the matter.

It is unnecessary to magnify Pamela's sense of her loss—or to judge it
cynically. She resolves to conquer her "treacherous heart"; and in the
morning the party is again on its way. But at their next stopping-place,
they are overtaken by a messenger "all over in a lather, man and horse,"
from Mr. B——. Again a letter is put into her trembling hand:

> In vain, my Pamela, do I struggle against my affection for you. I
> must needs, after you were gone, venture to entertain myself with your
> journal. When I found Mrs. Jewkes's bad usage of you, after your
> dreadful temptations and hurts, and particularly your generous con-
> cern on hearing how narrowly I escaped drowning (though my death
> would have been your *freedom* and I had made it your *interest* to wish
> it) and your most agreeable confession in another place that notwith-
> standing all my hard usage, you could not *hate* me, expressed in so

sweet, so soft, and innocent a manner that I flatter myself you may be brought to *love* me. . . . I began to repent my parting with you, and, God is my witness, for no unlawful end, as *you* would call it, but the very contrary; as all this was improved in your favor by your behavior at leaving my house; for O, that melodious voice praying for me at your departure, and thanking me for my rebuke to Mrs. Jewkes, still dwells upon my ears and delights my memory.* I went to bed, but could not rest. About two I arose, and made Thomas get one of the best horses ready, in order to overtake you, while I sat down to write.

Now, my dear Pamela, let me beg of you, on receipt of this, to order Robin to drive you back again to my house. I would have set out myself, for the pleasure of bearing you company back in the chariot, but am really indisposed; I believe with vexation that I parted thus with my soul's delight, as I now find you are, and must be, in spite of the pride of my own heart.

You cannot imagine the obligation your return will lay me under to your goodness; and yet, if you will not so far favor me, you will be under no restraint, as my letter enclosed to Colbrand will show. But spare me, my dearest girl, the confusion of following you to your father's, which I must do if you persist to go on; I find I cannot live a day without you.

If you are the generous Pamela I imagine you to be (for hitherto you have been all goodness where it has not been merited) let me then see the further excellence of your disposition that you can forgive the man who loves you more than himself. . . . When I have all my proud and perhaps *punctilious* doubts answered, I shall have nothing to do but to make you happy, and be so myself. *For I must be yours, and only yours.*

We can pass over Pamela's raptures, mixed with concern that Mr. B—— is ill. She decides she will "trust in his generosity." "Upon the whole, I resolved to obey him, and if he uses me ill afterwards, double will be his ungenerous guilt." The chariot takes the road back, and in spite of the tortures of carriage travel on the rough highways of the time, Pamela is back again late that night.

At this point we have followed the course of little more than half the story. The moral problem has been settled and the conventional romantic conclusion reached. But the social problem remains. Mr. B——'s obligations to his class and position are still to be faced, and in the eighteenth-century social philosophy those obligations could not be whimsically repudiated. At the moment of Pamela's return B—— has already heard from his sister, the one remaining member of his family. She berates him for whatever the gossip about his relations with Pamela may imply. "You will

---

*It is almost needless to remark here that at their worst, Richardson's sentences can be simply appalling.

have her either for a kept mistress or a wife. If the former, there are enough to be had without ruining a poor girl my mother loved, who really was a very good one; and of *this* you may be ashamed. As to the *other,* I dare say you don't think of it; but if you *should,* you would be utterly inexcusable."

The conclusion of the story—we are still on the "First Part" of *Pamela*—contains little actual interest, except for a dramatic episode or two. Preparations go forward for the wedding, on the eve of which a surprise visit is received from Pamela's father, Goodman Andrews, who has come down resolved to rescue his daughter from what he is certain is a continuance of Mr. B——'s intrigues. He is slow to convince, but at length persuaded by Pamela herself that she is not traveling the road to ruin. The old man, who, it is hinted, has once seen better days, but has fallen into debt and become a common laborer, is evidently one of Richardson's favorites. My feeling is that he is a boresome footler. He is an unintended caricature of rustic simplicity, standing about worrying about his "mean" attire, afraid that he will embarrass Pamela, raising his hands in admiration at every new evidence of B——'s elegance and liberality, and shedding tears of anxiety, joy, surprise, or piety, whatever the occasion calls for, with a profusion hard to match even among the sentimental ladies of the latter part of the century.

After the wedding, Mr. B—— and his bride settle down to a running discussion of how Pamela is to take her place in the society of the neighborhood. Mr. B—— is full of advice and precepts, all of which seem designed to establish Richardson's conviction of the indispensableness of the hereditary aristocracy and the necessary subjection of the wife's will to the husband's. It is not edifying for a modern reader who may feel tempted to admire Richardson; but Pamela accepts B——'s views and admonitions with all but sublime subservience. Two major episodes stand out from the general paucity of action; one a protracted verbal battle between Pamela and Lady Davers, who visits her during her husband's absence; the other, Pamela's introduction to, and subsequent enchantment by, a "love-child" of Mr. B——'s, who is at school in the neighborhood.

The battle with Lady Davers almost reaches the point of actual fisticuffs, the odds three to one against Pamela, for Lady Davers comes accompanied by her waiting-woman and her nephew, both of whom take part in the skirmish. Pamela is roughly handled, but her moderation and good sense stand off the united attack until her husband's home-coming, and the melee ends with a sound scolding from Mr. B—— which puts his sister and her attendants in their place. Lady Davers' somewhat forced reconciliation with Pamela is the first step in a growing intimacy which makes her in the end one of Pamela's most devoted supporters.

The story of Sally Godfrey, mother of Mr. B——'s natural child, is not an unusual one for the time. In fact, Pamela's interest in it, which leads ultimately to the adoption of the little girl—"Miss Goodwin"—derives in large part from its similarity in all but the outcome to her own earlier experiences with Mr. B——.

The conclusion of *Pamela* can be briefly stated. The household removes to the Bedfordshire estate, Mr. B—— restores to their places the two or three faithful servants whom he had discharged because of their "interference" with his designs upon Pamela, and the couple settles down to a serene life of mutual adoration, admired and respected by their fashionable neighbors, who are soon captivated by Pamela's exemplary character and graces.

We can scarcely note this conclusion without commenting on the fact that by the end of the story Richardson has raised his heroine almost to the level of sainthood. Mr. B——'s worship is echoed in the general devotion of the neighborhood, which Pamela absorbs and passes on word for word in her letters to her family, always with protestations of modesty at having to repeat such very flattering and undeserved praises.

There is no reason for a single serious word upon the "Second Part" of *Pamela,* beyond the fact that it is a continuation of the first part. It was an afterthought, the effect of the importunities of Richardson's admirers, and as fiction (into which category it falls only by grace of the fact that it looks something like a story) it is a deplorable failure.

The Pamela of *Part Two* is, like the Pamela of the original story, a mirror of perfection; not, in this case, a paragon of maidenly chastity, for her marriage to Mr. B—— has settled all that, but a fountainhead of wisdom upon agricultural economy, politics, education, class responsibilities, manners, and what not. Characteristically, she sits as the center of table-talk, all eyes upon her, all ears agog, her judgment deferentially called for upon questions of conduct and conscience. Admiration and compliment attend every spoken word, and she retails this adulation with self-conscious deprecation in her letters home. Richardson asks us to bow with him before this idol of his own making, but the ritual becomes tedious, then ridiculous, and finally downright offensive.

A few things do happen in this second part. Pamela adopts "Miss Goodwin"; she rescues Mr. B—— from what has threatened to become an amatory lapse, and she writes a long, a very long, discourse upon education in the form of a commentary upon Locke's *Thoughts.* But scraps of action cannot save the work from Richardson's fatuous intentness upon making this part of the story a complete manual of respectability and culture.

Discussion of Richardson, and particularly of *Pamela,* has from the very day of the book's appearance been contentious. Controversy has settled principally upon three questions, whether its "morality" is really moral, or despicable; whether Richardson's characters resemble humanity as most of us know it; and whether he writes badly because he didn't know better or because almost nobody wrote well at that time.

Let us take the first question first. Opinion upon it splits wide open : either (it is argued) Pamela was innately good and sincerely pious, or she was just a clever "go-getter," specious and hypocritical. And even those who elect the first alternative may differ as to whether she was honestly clean-minded or just a prude. I have stated these typical reactions baldly because judgments of the book are commonly more violent than critical.

Perhaps we ought to begin our weighing of the moral issue by recalling what amounts to a critical truism—that the *psychological* setting of a work of fiction calls for as much attention as its social or strictly literary setting. How did people *think* about these matters at this time? The answer is by no means difficult to come at. In the eighteenth century people felt in the main that sexual purity was a part of everyday goodness. At the same time, it was fully recognized that there are many, and sometimes quite distinct, sanctions for chastity. The most familiar sanction, then— and to many it was absolute—was religious; and there were few people in Richardson's time who did not profess some form of religion. With Pamela, we are left in no doubt that with her this was the pre-eminent sanction.

Scarcely less significant is the social sanction—the view that social experience establishes a value for purity, in that it implies more stable personal relations, offers some assurance of protection against the invasion of family relations, protects a husband against the chance of having to bring up another man's bastards, and limits the spread of disease. Pamela was not—at least as we know her—a profoundly thoughtful girl; so she has little or nothing to say upon these matters. But they did enter into the thoughts of any literate girl of the time, if for no other reason than that they were thoroughly, if often cynically, canvassed in the plays, the poetry, the periodicals, the fiction, and the tracts of the period.

The third recognized sanction is the prudential—the view that purity has (particularly for the male's appraisal of the female) not only a sentimental, but what might be called a "commodity" value. Most of us pretend, even today, to be shocked or disgusted at this view that a virtuous woman has a trading advantage over the unvirtuous. But we know that it is a fact, that it plays a large part in marital planning, and that common sense argues for an objective attitude toward giving away or throwing away what it may be advantageous to keep. Pamela has not only been credited with this motive; she has been *accused* of it, as though it were a moral offense to place a higher rather than a lower value upon one's personality and attractions.

Here are three sufficient justifications of virtue. Pamela would have recognized and accepted all three. She has much to say about two of them.

It is fair to ask a reader who condemns Pamela's "prudery" what he would have her do. The concrete answer can be taken for granted, but it is usually expressed in evasive abstractions like "the dictates of the heart," or "sexual liberty." As to the dictates of the heart, it is sufficient to say that over the greater part of the story it has little relevance. Pamela feels no serious attachment for Mr. B—— until he is on the point of offering her honorable marriage, when she discovers that he has been growing upon her. But this creates a new situation, and one in which she can no longer act from a single and simple motive.

As to "sexual liberty," it could have meant in Pamela's time only sexual irresponsibility. There was then no intelligent contraceptive practice, and sexual freedom generally meant for a woman satiation, abandonment, probably illegitimate children, and ultimately complete degradation. If these rather serious disadvantages were sometimes offset by generous offers of support, the acceptance of such offers would have placed the relationship upon a money basis, which is still offensive to most of us. Then there was the additional question whether in most cases such offers were carried out in good faith. In numberless cases it is certain that they were not. Any alternative to Pamela's code, therefore, would have been a gamble, with the odds heavily against the taker. Pamela was a wise girl, by any standards, but especially so by the standards of her time. It is to the credit of her good sense that she recognized not only that the wages of sin were death, but also that they could entail a great deal of desperately bad luck.

Probably no other young lady in fiction—or perhaps in actual life—has drawn so much matter for conversation from the simple fact of her virginity. The complaint of the twentieth-century grandmother that "young people today can talk about anything, but they can't talk about anyhing else" seems to touch Pamela as closely as it does our youth. For Pamela's perpetual twitter about her virtue is in its way quite as sexy as the conversancy of our teenagers with all there is to be thought and said about sex. At any rate, however we may judge Pamela's sexual conscience, it is certain that on this question of sex her anxious mind was neither muddled nor diseased. If she were among us today, she would not have to discuss imagined or self-induced sexual problems with a psychiatrist.

Richardson makes his whole case for virtue on pious grounds. Today it would be made more convincingly upon prudential and psychological grounds—yet perfectly valid ones. If Pamela's only motive were to preserve her virginity until she could dispose of it at her own choice and to her best advantage, it would be a sound motive. And if she didn't like to expose her person to a man's embarrassing investigations, that too would justify her acting exactly as she did. But the view that she was poor-spirited because she didn't go to bed with Mr. B—— when he wanted her to, seems to me completely unreflective, even though it *seems* to have been supported by so generally thoughtful a person as Henry Fielding. I emphasize "seems," for it is at least doubtful that Fielding intended his burlesque *Shamela* as condemnation of Pamela's purity. But we can come to that question later.

As to our second question—whether Richardson has given us recognizably human characters—there is more excuse to express an honest doubt. God- and goddess-like characters are not human, any more than Satanic characters; and Richardson had a weakness for both types.

Richardson seems to be nearer life in depicting women than in depicting men. He was brought up by an aunt; he had written love-letters for love-stricken but illiterate young women when he was still in his early teens; he enjoyed women's society and talk more than men's; and when he was blessed with children, they turned out to be all girls. It is simply a fact that Pamela seems to contain more living blood than Mr. B——, and Clarissa, in his novel of that name, more than her seducer Lovelace.

What is unconvincing in Pamela is not her virtue, for even in our derisive day virtue has not become ridiculous. Nor is it her piety, for pious women (in the objectionable eighteenth-century sense) were not necessarily hypocrites. Nor is it hypocrisy—though Richardson's art was not firm enough to make her appear completely sincere—nor priggishness!

In the externals of conduct Pamela is not so very different from the later Sophia Western of Fielding or Fanny Burney's Evelina, but in the things that make a woman interesting as a woman, Pamela is wanting. Sophia and Evelina are still imperfectly conceived, but they do begin to show the complex and not always entertaining traits that make a woman worth trying to understand. Feminine potential, however, in a freer and less artificial society, was to be far more intimately realized and depicted at the end of the century by Jane Austen. We are speaking now of this sort of understanding in the novel only; for after all, there was precisely that kind of knowledge and power in the creation of the characters of Juliet, Rosalind, and Cleopatra two centuries earlier.

Womanliness is not only an attribute; it is an art. A woman without *conscious* femininity is not a convincing woman, whatever else she may be. We cannot imagine Pamela switching her behind as she crossed the room before Mr. B——'s appraising eye, not to encourage his roving thoughts, but to justify her physical authority as a woman. Up to the time he is ready to marry Pamela, Mr. B—— thinks that her reticences and

palpitations are merely artful. B—— is simply ignorant of *her* ignorance
of anything resembling coquetry. But Richardson seems to be unaware
that art is not the antithesis of nature; it is only a way of regarding and
using nature.

Scarcely less objectionable than her sexual colorlessness is Pamela's
vanity. Here again the narrowness of Richardson's moral vision is evident
in the fact that he makes it a virtue. When Pamela herself speaks of it, she
calls it "pride," or "modesty." But it is modesty of the fig-leaf order, gro-
tesquely declaring what it affects to hide. She is vain of her virtue, of her
piety, of her "humble estate," of her prissy truthfulness, of the adulation
showered upon her, which she is at such pains to repeat in her letters, but
above all, she is vain of her freedom from vanity. She is so completely
without perspective of herself—without a sense of humor, if you like—that
it never occurs to her, and never could, that her untiring glorification of
her virtues makes her ridiculous.

Despite Pamela's bookish piety, despite Mr. B——'s worldliness, they
are both innocents. And they are both sentimentalists. Pamela adores Mr.
B—— because he adores her; Mr. B—— adores Pamela because she adores
him. It is the egotism that Meredith describes as the "grandson of the
hoof"; self-love in the guise of love for another. What must one think of
this as a sample of intelligent affection, on either Mr. B——'s part or on
Pamela's?

> As the chariot was returning home from this sweet airing, he said :
> "From all that has now passed between us, my Pamela will see, and be-
> lieve, that the trials of her virtue are all over from me; but perhaps
> there will be some few yet to come of her patience and humility. For,
> importuned by Lady Darnford and her daughters, I promised them
> a sight of my beloved girl; so I intend to have their whole family, and
> Lady Jones' and Mrs. Peters' family, to dine with me once in a few
> days. And as I believe you would hardly choose to grace the table on
> the occasion, until you can do it in your own right, you will not refuse
> coming down to us if I desire it. For I would preface our nuptials," said
> the dear gentleman—O what a sweet word was that!—"with their
> good opinion of your merit; and to see you and your sweet manner
> will be enough for that purpose; and so, by degrees, prepare my neigh-
> bors for what is to follow. They already have your character from me,
> and are disposed to admire you."
>
> "Sir," said I, "after all that has passed I should be unworthy not to
> say that I *can* have no will but yours; and however awkwardly I shall
> behave in such company, weighed down by the sense of your obliga-
> tions on one side, and my own unworthiness with their observations on
> the other, I will not scruple to obey you."

"I am obliged to you, Pamela," said he, "and pray be only dressed as you are; for since they know your condition, and heard the story of your present dress, and how you came by it, one of the young ladies begs it as a favor to see you just as you are. And I am rather pleased it should be so, because they will perceive you owe nothing to dress, but make a much better figure with your own native stock of loveliness than the greatest ladies arrayed in the most splendid attire and adorned with the most glittering jewels."

"O Sir," said I, "your goodness beholds your poor servant in a light greatly beyond her merit! But it must not be expected that others, especially ladies, will look upon me with your favorable eyes. Yet I should be best pleased to wear this humble garb till you, for your own sake, shall order it otherwise; for," said I, "I hope it will be always my pride to glory most in your goodness, to show everyone that as to my happiness in this life, I am entirely the work of your bounty, and to let the world see from what a lowly original you have raised me to honor that the greatest ladies would rejoice in."

"Admirable Pamela," said he; "excellent girl!—Surely thy sentiments are superior to those of all thy sex! I might have *addressed* a hundred fine ladies, but never could have had reason to *admire* one as I do you."

As, my dear father and mother, I repeat these sayings, only because they are the effect of my master's goodness, being far from presuming to think I deserve one of them, so I hope you will not attribute it to my vanity. For I do assure you, I think I ought rather to be more *humble,* as I am more *obliged*; for it must be always a sign of a poor condition to receive obligations one cannot repay, as it is of a rich mind when it can confer them without accepting or needing a return. It is, on one side, the state of the human creature, compared, on the other, to the Creator. And so, with due deference, may his beneficence be said to be god-like, and that is the highest that can be said.

Are these the words of human beings, or is this an exchange of compliments between Olympian Zeus and one of Raphael's Madonnas, holding hands in an eighteenth-century chariot?

We have still to consider the prose in which *Pamela* is given to us. And we can answer without long and learned debate the question we have already raised regarding it. Prose immediately before Richardson's time *had* reached a point of relatively high effectiveness. Richardson does not use it either carefully or artistically. He is capable of clothing a simple and self-contained idea in a well-made sentence, but he is quite as capable of losing himself in hopeless involvements if the idea needs to be expanded or qualified. One sentence will illustrate this floundering at its worst. It is taken not from *Pamela* but from *Clarissa*.

And now, Sir, if I have seemed to show some spirit, not quite foreign to the relation I have the honor to bear to you and to my sister, and which may be deemed not altogether of a piece with part of my character which once, it seems, gained me everyone's love, be pleased to consider to *whom* and to *what* it is owing, and that this part of that character was not dispensed with till it subjected me to that scorn and to those insults which a brother, who has been *so tenacious of an independence voluntarily* given up by me, and who has appeared so *exalted* upon it, ought not to have shown to *anybody,* much less to a *weak* and *defenceless* sister, who is, notwithstanding, an affectionate and respectful one, and would be glad to show herself to be so upon all future occasions, as she has in every action of her past life, although of late she has met with such unkind returns.

It is possible to extricate some sense from this, but it is a rough challenge to even a well-disposed reader.

But this inability to unify and consolidate—or perhaps this indifference to the need of doing so—is not the only defect of Richardson's style. Wordiness is probably the most grievous item in the critical indictment of Richardson. It is simply literary wastage; and if there is no grace of style to redeem it, it can be a formidable barrier to interest. Richardson had little notion of verbal economy. There can be no possible standard of wordage in a novel, but there can be an intelligent sense of what wordage can accomplish. All Richardson's novels are far too long for anything that the reader can get out of them. That does not call for demonstration; it has been the experience of practically every latter-day reader who has had the courage to attempt him.

Our discussion of *Pamela* will seem to have been on the whole disparaging. It has had in view, to be frank, the predilections of the modern reader, rather than the state of fiction before Richardson, and the value of his contributions to the materials and the methods of fiction. After so much attention to the insufficiencies of *Pamela,* we must take fair consideration of what, on the positive side, this novel *was.* We must recognize the fact that Richardson's point of view here, and in all his novels, is true to the creeds and the social habits of a large portion of the British population in a period of social and intellectual transition. There is a social sanction for the views and conduct of Pamela, but equally for Mr. B——'s. Both characters show a well defined and characteristic class-consciousness, viewed with revealing objectivity, even though with didactic purpose and partiality. The social picture is interesting because it is definite, but in many respects it may be strange to us.

The characters, and especially Pamela, once understood in relation to their social setting, have personality, though focused during the greater part of the story upon their problems in a single moral dimension. Pamela herself is revealed to us with a thoroughness probably never before realized. The letter form has a good deal to do with this, for it can probe deeply into the realities of thought and feeling, upon terms of intimacy not easy to equal in novels of the omniscient outlook. Yet letters, helpful as they were to Richardson, were quickly seen to have their disadvantages as well as their advantages. By Jane Austen's time they had fallen into disfavor.

The closeness and assiduity of Richardson's analysis of mind and motive involved him in repetition and often aimless lucubration. Probably no novelist ever expanded a single major incident into a larger area of action, but its diffuseness leaves us with the impression that he plays with his theme rather than working to reduce it to its briefest terms of effectiveness. Yet we can scarcely blame him, for prose fiction before his time had recognized no rational limit to length and made no virtue of compression. When all is said, Richardson gave to unified action the breadth of the later novel, but economy was something still to be discovered and brought into studied practice.

Clarissa, Richardson's second novel, is another story of seduction, with a disastrous instead of a romantic outcome. The heroine in this instance is a young woman of social position and refinement, and the villain—for we can safely call him that—a suitor for the hand of the heroine after he has been rejected by her older sister. The motives involved, however, are not those we might expect in a novel of this type; for Clarissa's affections are not seriously engaged, with Lovelace or with anyone else, and Lovelace's professed love is strongly diluted with a frantic wish for revenge for his jilting. In the background of the action is Clarissa's family—middle-class parvenus whose greed and snobbery are largely responsible for her tragedy

Clarissa, unlike Pamela, is as a character complex enough to be interesting. She is a woman of spirit and independence, and when her family attempts to force her into a marriage with a boor, simply to enlarge the family estates and influence, she refuses to be sacrificed. The result is, in effect, house imprisonment and curtailing of everyday privileges, not to speak of constant subjection to ill-tempered argument and innuendo. As the family pressure tightens, she attempts to gain her freedom by entrusting herself to Lovelace, to be placed, as she thinks, among her friends. On her own declaration, she is not in love with Lovelace, and would not consider marrying him, not alone because she dislikes his vanity and self-

CLARISSA.

The death of Clarissa Harlowe, to illustrate Richardson's *Clarissa,*
engraved by Heath after Thomas Stothard. One of the numerous
plates designed by Stothard to illustrate the novels reprinted in
The Novelist's Magazine from 1780 to 1788. 1784.

sufficiency, but because he is a notorious rake who has accomplished a good deal of damage among ladies both good and bad.*

Lovelace is a well-designed villain as villains go. His character has already been hinted at, but not the Iago-like pride he takes in being the kind of man he is. His interest in Clarissa is quite impersonally sensual, for he can "love" any handsome and agreeable woman, and he is clever enough to see that Clarissa's difficulties may provide his opportunity. His letters to his cronies, which are fairly numerous, make it clear that for him "sex is fun," and a large part of the fun is the glory of the conquest.

The elopement, then, is for Clarissa simply escape from the unendurable coercion of her family. It is Clarissa's last freely taken move. Lovelace removes her promptly to a bordello, where for a time she is deceived into thinking the mistress is a relation of Lovelace's, and the girls of her establishment members of her family. Her simplicity may seem incredible, but it is what Richardson asks us to accept. The sequel is the expected one—Clarissa is drugged and violated by Lovelace. Betrayal is followed by cheap indignity—Clarissa's arrest on a charge of owing money for board and clothing to the keeper of the bawdy house, though this affront is not initiated by Lovelace.

The remainder of the story is taken up with a change of heart in Lovelace, who now pays honorable court to Clarissa, and with the despair and physical decline of Clarissa, who resolutely refuses Lovelace on the ground of his brutality to her. Clarissa's mind is singly devoted to death, which comes to her in time. She appeals to her family for final reconciliation, but they ignore her advances, convinced as they are that she has connived at her own ruin. There is no possible meeting of minds here. Clarissa is indignant that they think her guilty. They are resentful at her refusal to lend herself to the family's ambitions. In the end there is understanding, or partial understanding, on the part of the family, but it can be acknowledged only in self-pitying tears over her coffin. Lovelace's wickedness is expiated in the "gentlemanly" way, in a duel with a cousin of Clarissa's. He welcomes death, though with a fatalism that wavers between boastful cynicism and passionate remorse.

---

*Ian Watt (*The Rise of the Novel*) takes the view that Clarissa is "unconsciously" in love with Lovelace. This seems to me a sophisticated interpretation of what Clarissa actually writes, and what, I am certain, Richardson wished us to think. Psychoanalysis of a *character's* emotions may tell us a good deal of the *author's* mind, but interpretation of the character itself—especially in the case of a writer as transparent as Richardson—can have no more validity than the words of the author can supply. I am sure that Richardson intimates that there is merely the speculative ground for affection that might exist in the early stages of contact of two marriageable young people, and that would be subject to any number of conditioned judgments.

It is remarkable that in a novel so exclusively concerned with sex there is practically no effort made to deal affirmatively with love. In Clarissa's moral conflict the heart is scarcely involved. With both her family and Lovelace she is fighting for her right to possess and govern herself. She *could,* she reiterates, have loved Lovelace if he had not abused her, but only upon the condition of his "reform." It is not surprising that to Lovelace (unlike Mr. B——) that condition is laughable; for as an audacious and talented seducer he is accustomed to regard love as something else than a basis for bargaining.

At its simplest, *Clarissa* is the story of a woman who does not want to marry the man she does not want to marry. Her emotions (which are undeniable and powerful) are those of an individualist willing to pay the uttermost farthing for the preservation of her individuality. The long and dramatic conflict of wills between Clarissa and Lovelace could have been handled with something like greatness if Richardson were not so unsufferably repetitious, but it is never anything but a conflict of wills, not of discrete and complementary feminine and masculine identities.

Beneath that will of Clarissa's there shows at times an actual hardness of character as well as of resolution. During her attempts to re-establish understanding with her family the question is raised—and repeated—whether she is going to have a child. It may not be a considerate question, if the family is possessed of any capacity for pity, yet it is a natural one. It is also one of interest to the reader. Clarissa goes into throes of resentment that the question is asked, but she does not answer it! Again in her farewell letter to Lovelace she shows a vituperative bitterness quite out of harmony with her piety and her long martyrdom after Lovelace's offense. Her bitterness has been well-deserved, and a death-bed letter gives unanswerably the advantage of the last word; but this letter all but belies the high mind and forgiving nature that Richardson has pictured for us.

Clarissa, somewhat like Pamela, seems deficient in essentially feminine intelligence. She has an aptitude for indiscretion, and fails to see through the thinnest of Lovelace's deceptions. Yet she plays a role consistent with her character as we are given to understand it. It is not a part of twentieth-century thinking (or even nineteenth-century) that Lovelace's cruel imposition upon her entails for her the need for martyrdom. Yet it is a resolute and appealing martyrdom. Her friends in her affliction often speak of her as an angel; and she does in these last days show some attributes of the heavenly order. But are angels deficient in common sense?

Wider tolerances in questions of sex have produced a radical change in the average reader's attitude upon the arguable moral issues in *Pamela* and *Clarissa.* The change is apparent not only in a derisive amusement at Pamela's piety and her scruples, but also in contempt for her sexual brinkmanship. It is clever, that is conceded; but is it honest? As to Clarissa, she confronts really no explicit moral issue (apart from the prudential) since her freedom of moral choice is extinguished before she is in a position to exercise it. The twentieth century seems to disrelish Pamela as too shrewd a trader in the sexual commodity, but its judgment of Clarissa seems to be that in her dealings with Lovelace down to the time of her flight, she is simply an unfortunate fool.

It was often said of Richardson in his lifetime that for a critic of high society he did not know enough of either its people or its ways. How much is enough? Except in his last novel, *Sir Charles Grandison,* he pretended to no more than a commoner's acquaintance with élite society; yet his criticism of it shows discrimination. The aplomb of the gentleman, his pride, and in general his education and his wealth, Richardson knew, were admirable only as his character could make them so. If he were a spoiled and over-privileged egoist, his advantages could make him anything from idiot to brute. If he were instinctively fine, and virtuous in the broad old Roman sense, then his example could be, to use Samuel Butler's phrase, "the best of all gospels."

The two earlier novels portray the English aristocrat in his worst role, at a time when dissipation and arrogance were accepted almost as symbols of rank. The truth of the portraits, however, is attested again and again in the fiction of most of Richardson's important successors over the next fifty years.

In *Sir Charles Grandison,* his last novel, Richardson meant to depict the aristocrat at his best, on his own ground and with his own traditions. Here the point of view is no longer external; it must be inwardly informed and familiar. If his purpose was laudatory —and it was—then unfamiliarity would tend to vague idealization. And it did. This novel was, by comparison with the earlier ones, a failure, largely because it was felt that Richardson was out of his social depth. And it is curiously interesting that in spite of the enormous popular affection for Pamela and Clarissa, when he tried to design a woman, Harriet Byron, to meet the specifications of his perfect gentleman, he produced a creature that even his contemporaries thought fleshless and vapid.

Yet it would wrong Richardson to condemn *Grandison* offhand. The novel has, in the first place, breadth. The action is not limited to the concerns of a particular "he" and "she," as both the earlier novels are, but covers a wider social area, and introduces minor characters that have some title to interest in themselves—notably Grandison's sister Charlotte, the adolescent Emily, and the elders of the Selby Family. I am deliberately excluding the Signorina Clementina della Porretta—Richardson's notion of the purest Italian aristocracy—whose backbone contains calcium enough but is unhappily disjointed.

The episodes that attach to the Signorina Clementina, etc., seem to support the view that if Richardson ever achieved something that looked like art, it was not because he meant to. The signorina's story introduces for a time the possibility of the embarrassing third in an amatory triangle. It raises an issue of sentimental casuistry—whether humane sympathy ought to take precedence over love when the two seem to conflict. It creates, without arguing, a case for Anglicanism over Roman Catholicism, and in a minor way for English as against Italian culture, and so offers moral support to the conviction of nine out of ten middle-class Englishmen of the period that English beliefs and ways were God's own plan for perfecting the world he created. But only the first of these is a literary motive, and its effectiveness is vitiated by the complete willingness of the two young ladies whose hearts are bursting with love for Grandison to have him settle the matter in whatever way his wisdom and his sympathies may decide for him. There is no struggle here, beyond the competition of the two in polite self-sacrifice, a magnificent concession to sentimentalism, but not human, and ultimately not honest. I am willing to register a personal opinion that the Porretta story, which takes up large portions of the last two-thirds of the work, is intrusive, pretentious, morally lame, and uncomfortably morbid.

Yet despite the Porretta episodes, which perhaps I take too painfully, *Grandison* shows that Richardson had learned something, and it was a measurable something, from the writing of his first two novels. It is certainly the firmest of the three, and perhaps the most readable. But the latter suggestion is not made with the reader in view whose consumption is a novel a day. *Grandison* is at least five times too long. It is also one of the most aqueous novels ever written. No crude metaphor can convey any sense of the imminence of tears upon every least emotional occasion, the pleasant quite as much as the unpleasant.

It is also one of the most stressfully sentimental novels. Connoisseurs who can detect the nice shadings of quality in the various vintages and growths of sentimentalism have much to say of "delicacy" as one of its phases. Harriet Byron and her friends discourse largely and lengthily of delicacy as the interval before her marriage to Grandison diminishes to weeks, then days, then hours. Her delicacy becomes more and more fretful as the crisis approaches, until one almost gets the impression that friendly and co-operative defloration is as grim as a major operation. There is more to it, of course, than that; for what is really at the bottom of Miss Byron's mind is that all these people standing about at the wedding will be thinking about something—well, about something that it is not at all nice for them all to be thinking about. And even Sir Charles, that model of propriety and consideration, must be thinking about it too. It is all very painful. But one must do one's best not to faint at the altar, and the ordeal will pass, as others have; and Sir Charles is after all, very tender and sympathetic.

If we must call Richardson prurient, this episode, pages and pages of the flutterings of a "delicate" mind about one single "indelicate" idea. seems a piece of primary evidence. One can see why in *Shamela,* Fielding ridiculed the somewhat less prostrating palpitations of Harriet's literary sister Pamela by making Shamela a woman of the boldest and baldest sexuality.

Richardson's insistence upon a substantial reward for virtue and the confounding of vice brings *Grandison* to an oddly tangential conclusion. Within the convention, the reader might expect some sort of joint apotheosis of Sir Charles and Harriet. Instead, Grandison goes on a mission of mercy to the bedside of Sir Hargrave Pollexfen, the villain whose attempt to abduct Harriet ended in her timely rescue by Sir Charles. Richardson has held him in reserve for a stern example of providential justice, presenting him only twice after the last echoes of his wicked attempt have faded away; once when he is thoroughly beaten by some Parisian gentlemen with whose women folk he has been unwisely free, and again when he falls ill of a fatal malady which is not described with pathological minuteness, but which we are given to understand has not resulted from overeating. But Sir Charles hurries at Sir Hargrave's request to "close his eyes"; and there is a large legacy. For whom do you think? For Harriet? For Sir Charles? For each, singly and severally! It is one of the most Christmassy deathbeds that ever graced the doctrine of retribution.

Perhaps we are now in a position to consider with what justice the title of "father of the English novel" has been thrust upon Richardson

The title is a dubious one, for it depends largely upon our definition of the novel. Clearly *Arcadia, The Pilgrim's Progress,* and *Gulliver's Travels,* to which we have already paid our respects, are "out" because none of them attempts to transcribe life in the light of normal experience. But Defoe's *Robinson Crusoe* (still more, his *Moll Flanders*) shows most of the earmarks of the modern novel, together with broad and lasting interest which Richardson's novels scarcely equal.

The claim in Richardson's favor must depend upon whatever differentiates his first novel from, let us say, *Moll Flanders,* both of them lengthy prose pictures from contemporary life and character, resembling the modern novel in external form.

Pamela is different because it is not merely a sequence in time, but a rational sequence, in which will and choice take control of events; and

Grandison to the rescue of Harriet Byron, from the first illustrated edition of *Sir Charles Grandison*, 1778; designed and engraved by Isaac Taylor.

events do not merely follow one another, but follow one another in the main as effect follows cause. Pamela is the arbitress of events; Moll is their victim. The distinction is not principally a moral one; it affects the whole course of the story, for in *Moll Flanders* plot has the effect of rolling down hill once the initial push is given. In *Pamela* one feels that the story moves under power. New events in *Moll Flanders* are in some degree repetitions of old events; in *Pamela* new events are significant turning points in action, and have determinative force. *Moll Flanders* is the very type of episodic novel, although a thin thread of plot runs through it.

On the score of fidelity to life and character, certainly *Pamela* has little or no advantage over *Moll Flanders,* which *is,* whatever it is not, a high spot in the realism of incident. The great superiority of *Pamela* to its predecessors lies in Richardson's intimate and studied portraiture. Perhaps portraiture is the wrong word, since a portrait cannot show its subject in the course of development. Suppose we substitute the standard "characterization." Defoe's characterization is almost static; Moll Flanders is a bad girl and she grows worse. The novel ends on a note of repentance for a great deal of wasted life and opportunity. But as to character, its principal is simply what events have tended to make her.

Pamela, on the other hand, has in her character directive force. Not only that; in spite of the fact that her convictions are doctrinal rather than thoughtful, we see the constant processes of mind and spirit actually at work, altering and determining her prospects as decisions are reached and adaptations made. This is psychological analysis, almost unattempted by Defoe, even at his best. Probably he comes nearest it in his heroine Roxana, who is a great casuist; but she is no Pamela in either fullness or clearness of character.

Lastly, if we regard the novel as a contribution to experience, *Pamela* is again a work of greater power. That fact embodies Richardson's greater breadth of view of the social scene and greater appreciation of the inwardness of character. It also implies greater creative seriousness than is seen in Defoe's reportorial interest in social deviants.

In summary, these points seem to justify dating the end of the old order of realistic episode and the beginning of the new novel of social and personal analysis with the publication of *Pamela.* There are reasons for not classing it among the firsts in fiction, but there seems to be no good reason for refusing it primacy among novels of the modern temper.

Final judgment of Richardson, however, must give consideration to one significant fact. Richardson's reputation for over two centuries has been, for reasons I hope are already clear, more or less a critical football, kicked back and forth between praise and contempt. Yet some undeniably great writers have appreciated, commended, and acknowledged a debt to him. Jane Austen found his later novels absorbing. Sir Leslie Stephen notes that Balzac, George Sand, and even Alfred de Musset admired him. Yet commendation throughout the nineteenth century tended to be also apologetic, even in so favorable a writer as Austin Dobson.

In our century critical and scholarly approval of him has been revived. He is certainly no longer a subject of mere ridicule. Whether this is because nothing is without interest to the historian of literature, or any other area of culture, and will outlast our present epidemic of approval of almost everything eighteenth century, is anybody's guess. But it is at any rate a salutary change from much casual and smart denigration of a writer to whom all later novelists owe a debt of gratitude, and whom any intelligent and well-disposed reader should find rewarding—we might add, *sotto voce,* in the abridged versions.*

---

*It is all but a scholarly obligation to consider in connection with this question of primacy the claims of the French novelist Pierre Marivaux. His *Vie de Marianne* began to appear in 1731 and was continued in parts until 1741. It is possible, but not demonstrable, that Richardson knew the work and may have owed to it the theme of *Pamela.* Marianne is as unmistakably French as Pamela is English, but her story, so long as it remains centered on the heroine herself, is more convincing than *Pamela,* and certainly livelier. Marivaux writes almost without plan, however, digresses freely, and finally loses himself in the long life-story of a nun who has befriended Marianne. In the midst of this digression the narrative stops short. Though he lived a score of years after the appearance of the last part published, Marivaux seems to have lost all interest in the story. Mme. Marie Riccoboni published a conclusion which is said to have satisfied him; but it is difficult to see why he even tolerated it, for it is thin and theatrical and reintroduces the heroine in an all's-well-that-ends-well closing scene in which she wears down her former lover with middle-class sarcasms.

CHAPTER VI

Sex in the Eighteenth-Century Perspective

It is a commonplace that the essential stuff of the novel, whether romantic or realistic, has been the relations of men to women and women to men, and more particularly, the specific concerns of sex. Richardson's novels, as we have seen, are taken up wholly with the interests of sex; furthermore, those interests are represented in a markedly different light from that of novels in the nineteenth and twentieth centuries.

Three salient facts will strike the explorer of eighteenth-century fiction as he enlarges his acquaintance with the field. The first is that it seems to be inordinately concerned with seemingly abnormal aspects of sex—with libertinism, callous intrigue, and even sexual violence. Second, sexual escapades and promiscuity are represented not as diversions of a vulgar and semi-secret sort, but as a large and characteristic part of the amusement of the urban upper classes. Third, the sexual manners of the period have an obviously close relation to marriage and the marital status among the upper classes, particularly to the *mariage de convenance,* or marriage for social and financial position in which free choice and affection are conventionally presumed to play no very important part.

As to what seems distinctive in the eighteenth-century view of sex, at least in its bearings upon literature, questions inevitably arise. Were eighteenth-century people different? Is the fiction itself truthful or theatrically exaggerated? Is there an animus underlying the unfavorable view of the aristocratic rake and his ways? Let us see what we can see.

Many profound things have been said about sex, most of them neither philosophical nor scientific. There seems to be general agreement that it is very popular, also unpredictably disruptive of the quiet and contented life. If it were not so, there would be no modern novel. The ancient epic and pseudo-epic narratives made fighting the prime interest of the male. But when civilization put fighting into its proper place, as an intermission to the politer activities, the novel, a thoroughly civilized literary medium, fell back upon sex as the motive and the activity most productive of the excitement which makes life rewarding for most of us. It is something about which we cannot do very much except think and talk. La Rochefoucauld observed that if there were no literature, there would be no romance. It is equally true that if there were no romance, there would be no literature to speak of—at least not of the sort that most people find interesting.

We are told by psychologists and anthropologists that sexual ideas and customs change. No doubt they do. Yet some ideas about sex seem as firmly rooted in human nature as sex itself. On the whole, however, it is not too far wrong to recognize that sexual urges and habits can be roughly divided into the savage and the civilized. Perhaps the chief difference is that the savage sexual approach is with an instrument of violence, and the civilized approach with persuasive speech.

Yet vestiges of savagery persist; and in the eighteenth century they furnish to a surprising extent the materials of fiction. If the upper-class male of the period were a satisfactory sampling of manhood—which is at least debatable—then it could scarcely be denied that the sexual manners and customs of the aristocratic English society of the period were considerably less civilized than in ancient Athens. The principal reason for this was the imitation by the peerage and the landed gentry of the libertine fashions which the Stuarts had brought back from the French court at the Restoration, and which continued, with perhaps less spirit and imagination, well into the reigns of George I and George II.

The sexual manners of the British aristocracy at that time can well be called bad manners, for their social effects were in many ways injurious and sometimes iniquitous. Both men and women exercised great sexual freedom, though the women, no doubt, with more discretion than the men. In a roistering, gaming, drinking, and whoring age, it was not held seriously against a marriageable man that he had sown successive, and in all probability productive, crops of wild oats. And the young man of fashion who entered upon marriage with virginal innocence was all but unknown in fiction until after the mid-century. Marriageable young women accepted their husbands as they found them, even wasted by dissipation and foul with disease. We are confronted again and again in the fiction of the times with the fact that dissipation was indeed seriously regarded as a contributory part of a young man's education. And the effects upon his health, which were after all a matter of public health, were a standard subject of jest. Severer views of sexual behavior were felt to be middle-class and pietistic.

It may seem surprising that sexual liberty was granted to married women almost as freely as to their spouses. But on the face of things, it takes two to make a liaison, and liaisons had been from time immemorial a recognized part of aristocratic life. In addition, the diagnostic of the aristocratic life was idleness, not only supported by wealth, but proudly cherished as a class distinction. So upper-class women as well as men were put to it to find amusement enough to take up the long hours of the day and night. Education and culture might bave supplied resources, but only for those possessed of character as well as intelligence; for young men of wealth and fashion went to the universities not to become thinkers, but to pursue the youthful vices in an environment of pleasure and with lively companions of their own class. Chesterfield, Gibbon, Mackenzie, Bage and Godwin all make it clear that the universities were turning out fops and spendthrifts as numerously as scholars and divines. But London society was populated also by other gentlemen whose pretensions to fashion were unadulterated by any knowledge of a world outside their own.

Yet if the pursuits of a gentleman's leisure were, when they were not vicious, limited and vague, his wife's were much more so. Any woman instructed in the languages (apart from French, an accepted mark of class), or history, or mathematics beyond household arithmetic, had as a rule to gain her exceptional attainments through sheer force of will, and probably against the opposition of the gentlemen of her family, who would have kept her in "her proper place" at the tambour-frame or the harpsichord. Her "educated innocence," designed to insure her peaceful submission to her lords and masters, was carefully neglectful of any rational knowledge of sex. Yet women from early adolescence were brought up on scandal as the stuff of fashionable conversation; so sophistication, through their contact with gay married women, stimulated their curiosity without diminishing their ignorance.

The arts of idleness, at any rate, were the circumference of woman's accepted culture—those, and dress. Dress itself was a consuming interest, as it always is in a wealthy and over-leisured society. And dress contributed directly to sexual preoccupation and opportunity. Skirts were during most of the period long enough to mop the indescribably filthy streets, with their open sewers; so knees were not commonly supposed to be visible except as a matter of privilege. But the art of managing the skirts was—and had to be, especially when circular hoops came in—developed to a high degree of finesse. What was universally referred to as "the neck" extended to the nipples, but in the early part of the century did not actually expose them. The usually wide and deep décolletage revealed a frontal area which in broad daylight was likely to be covered by a diaphanous bodice or with a lace or frilled handkerchief pinned in place, but perhaps not so firmly as to preclude the chance of accidental disclosures. When a fictional heroine of the time tells us that an enterprising gentleman "put his hand into my bosom," it can be certain that the opportunity was fully advertised in the lady's costume. Toward the end of the century nipples came briefly into full glory in ultra-fashionable dress, although they were regarded as daring and were more widely favored on the continental side of the Channel. Somewhat later, the Empire styling elevated the breasts by tight and high girdling. Mary Wollstonecroft lamented that "protuberances" were emphasized beyond the generous provisions of nature. The extremists in style are said to have dampened thin undergarments to make them cling to the limbs, or to have worn single garments so thin that almost nothing of the lady's superficial anatomy was left to be imagined. On the whole, however, it will have to be admitted that in eighteenth-century dress there was no symbol of natural innocence more expressive than our own Bikini.

Marriage itself would not necessarily alter pre-marital views and habits. The plays and novels of the time reflect the fact that an upper-class marriage was more than likely to be an economic-social status, with full freedom, sometimes stipulated, for husband and wife to pursue their own amours. Assignations were made at routs, assemblies, salons, and particularly at the highly popular masquerades, where the married society women and the women of the town hunted side by side. For the men were not alone in the pursuit of the game. The fiction of the time is well populated with Lady Hardys, Lady Bellastons, and Lady Wantworths* whose mission in life was to prevent young men from becoming bored with virtue, and even in mere mischief to break up promising youthful ventures in romantic love. The competition of the married adventuresses with the young belles was ruthless. With the professionals, the ladies of the streets, it was sportive and cynical. A foot-free married woman, still more, a young widow exempt by her social eminence from attack, could be indifferent to scandal, which was actively circulated, and scandal might even add zest to the enjoyment of a *liaison*.

For the aristocratic classes then, sex was an occupation and an unending subject of conversation. Love-making, in its more aggressive and promiscuous forms, became a conventional part of the diversions open to men and women. So for a married couple intent on "getting the most out of life," acceptable married behavior meant not impeding each other's amours, but keeping out of each other's way.

How liberally the obligations of marriage might be interpreted may be seen in the later novels of Mrs. Eliza Haywood, by general acknowledgment the most graphic chronicler in fiction of the frivolities of high society at the mid-century. Her *Jemmy and Jenny Jessamy* (1753) is not a great

---

*Mrs. Haywood's *Betsy Thoughtless*, Fielding's *Tom Jones*, and Mrs. Robinson's *Angelina*.

novel, though it is still readable, but it can be taken to be both faithful to and sympathetic with contemporary fashionable life.

Jenny Jessamy is a diverting but maturely conceived character of solid womanhood under a gay and casual social manner. She has been engaged since her infancy, through a hopeful parental understanding, to a distant cousin, Jemmy, of the same family name. Oddly enough, as the two young people emerge into adulthood, the engagement actually "takes." When the marriage becomes a near-term prospect, they are quite agreed that they are all for it, not as a mere financial and social status, but as a firm and affectionate life relationship. Yet they stop upon the threshold of marriage to take one more serious look. And it is the woman —not the man—who proposes that they live another year of fashionable life in London, with men and women of every social stamp, to determine whether they will be satisfied to accept the serious concerns of marriage without being bored or irritated by its humdrum responsibilities. Jenny tells Jemmy :

> "It follows then that every one before they engage in marriage should be well vers'd in all those things, whatever they are, which constitute the happiness of it. This town is an ample school, and both of us have acquaintance enough in it to learn, from the mistakes of others, how to regulate our own conduct and passions so as not to be laughed at ourselves for what we laugh at in them."
>
> "Spoke like a philosopheress," rejoined Jemmy; "and upon second thoughts, I agree with you, that as everything is ready for us and we can marry when we will, it will be best for us both to stay till we have got some further lights into the mysterious duties of the conjugal union."

That pact is settled, but to it Jemmy adds another and a rather startling proposal :

> "As learning will not come of itself, and we should be equally perfect in the different parts we are to act together hereafter, suppose we should resolve to communicate to each other all the discoveries we are able to make, among the several families that either of us converse with, and also all the confidences which are reposed in us. By this means I shall be acquainted with all the humors of your sex, and you no stranger to those of mine."

That part of the agreement is not entered upon as a clearing-house for scandal, but as an aid to understanding. They part then, each to live life in his own way, without conditions or restraints, except as these might arise

Mrs. Eliza Haywood at work with her assistants; engraved
by Jacob Bonneau after Samuel Wale; from *The Female
Spectator*, seventh edition, 1771.

from their good will and good intentions. The year's experience will determine whether or not the marriage should take place.

It may be surmised that while the unison of minds in this unusual compact is complete, the two will respond differently to what is entailed. Jemmy is the man of his time, but Jenny is not his mere feminine counterpart, for she has not only the intelligence but the sincerity to play her part soberly and with circumspection.

While he does not drift into an easy libertinism, which he is quite free to do, he does taste a few amorous adventures, and he falls somewhat short of that perfect frankness which he had himself proposed, in not telling Jenny of them. Yet on the whole he reads his responsibility as a responsible man should. He has only one *affaire du corps,* and that merely a passing diversion. His freedom from other entanglements, however, has been due more to opportune accidents than to wise planning.

At any rate, at the end of the year he comes to Jenny with a fairly clean slate. But luck has it that he is caught up through his own inadvertence in the aftermath of one encounter in which, although technically innocent, he had not lived up to the article of frankness. Jenny produces unexpectedly a damning letter, and appearances are much against him.

> "'How would marriage, my dear Jessamy, agree with the promise you made in this of coming to the arms of the kind she to whom you wrote it, with a heart entirely unencumbered with any cares but those of pleasing her?"
>
> "Good God," [he cries] "how justly is my folly punished"—then turning to Jenny—"Yet when known," continued he, "by how odd an accident I was betrayed into this error, you will, I am sure, forgive me."

But mark the dignity of her reply :

> "I will know nothing farther of this matter," reply'd Jenny, "nor shall I ever think of it hereafter. All I desire is that when we marry, you will either have no amours, or be more cautious in concealing them. And in return, I promise never to examine into your conduct, to send no spies to watch your motions, to listen to no tales that might be brought me, nor by any methods whatever endeavor to discover more than you would have me."
>
> "Generous creature," rejoin'd he, kissing her hand, "yet permit me to assure you, by all my hopes of happiness, that the fault I am now detected in was never eagerly pursued by me—that it was only an intention. I did not proceed to swerve even in thought from the fidelity I owe my dear forgiving Jenny."
>
> "Make no vows on this last head, I beseech you," said she. "I have heard people much older and more experienced than ourselves say

that the surest way to do a thing is to resolve against it. Besides, my dear Jemmy," added she with the most engaging sprightliness, "I shall not be so unreasonable to expect more constancy from you than human nature and your constitution will allow; and if you are as good as you can [be], may very well content myself with your endeavors to be better."

This is one of the rare passages in a long story in which Mrs. Haywood manages to surmount the shortcomings of her glib reportorial style.* If a few words of dialogue can give a character substance, this does so. Jenny is neither flirt nor prig. Her morality is pragmatic, too tolerant for the Puritan temper and perhaps too careless of her own deeper interests. But the exchange of views seems to reflect the effect which the *mariage de convenance* exerted upon upper-class family life. At the same time, it is worth noting that it is the woman who in this case implies not only the existence but the acceptableness of differentiated sex standards which favor the man. Jenny will not adopt for herself the behavior in marriage that she is willing to tolerate from her husband.

There is a show of moral judgment in Mrs Haywood's novels; how sincere, may perhaps be questioned. Yet in her *History of Miss Betsy Thoughtless* (1751) she at least propounds a case the moral implications of which seem to be as clear as those of, let us say, Richardson's *Pamela*. Betsy comes up to London, with her fortune, resolved to see life before she settles down to the solemn duties of marriage. Her name, of course, describes her mental temper. She is a girl of honest intentions, but she will not take advice, and she refuses to worry about her reputation. By the end of the year she has gathered a good deal of experience in the hardest way. She has escaped (if my memory holds) four separate attempts at ravishment, all from gentlemen who are her social equals; she has listened to the pathetic stories of young ladies who have followed the same philosophy of finding things out for themselves; she has lost a likable and eligible suitor; and she has married a worthless adventurer. But pure luck comes to her aid. Her husband dies, and the man who has loved her faithfully in spite of her sillinesses is still waiting. *Betsy Thoughtless* is the typical novel of intrigue, about as frivolous as the life it depicts, but better, perhaps, than its reputation would make us think it; for even readers of Mrs. Haywood's own time professed to feel that it advertised too free and easy a morality.

One explanation, and perhaps excuse, for the libertinism of men of

---

*We have not given Mrs. Haywood lengthy consideration as a novelist, though she had gifts as a storyteller. Her novels are scrappy, superficial, peopled with stock characters, fair mirrors of the life of the times, but inferior to those of Richardson, Fielding, and Smollett, whose successes anticipated her later narratives, the only stories of hers that can properly be called novels even in the liberal use of the term.

fashion was the prevalence of opportunity not only from the businesslike women who pulled at the sleeves of young gentlemen as they walked the streets, but from married women of social position. The worldly Earl of Chesterfield, it may be remembered, advised his son to take a mistress, but he insisted upon his making an "arrangement" with a married woman of social place, not a professional, who, he says, would be sure to bring him to profligacy, prodigality, and incurable disease. Chesterfield assures the young man that he will find no lack of wealthy and well-placed women who will think it a pleasure to oblige him.

Women of fashion and consequence naturally enjoyed immunities from both the physical and the social effects of their freedom. Middle-class women owed more to their reputations. The tradesman's wife was likely to be more or less engaged in her husband's business. She did not have time to kill, and if she drifted from the path of virtue, it would probably have been because of her exposure to gentleman-adventurers cruising among the shops. The morality of her class was probably higher than that of her social superiors, and it was likely to be sustained by dissenting, and therefore stricter, principles. In Elizabethan times the citizen's wife was commonly pictured as "easy." In the eighteenth century the presumption had turned in her favor.

The lower-class women of the period were for obvious reasons looked upon as legitimate prey for the sexual sportsman. It is all but impossible for us to appreciate the contrast between the glitter of the privileged classes and the filth and pitiful dependency of the urban poor, or to appraise temptation in terms of that contrast. There was always an over-supply of unskilled and underpaid labor; for the city poor, who were employed in vast numbers in domestic work and as underlings in the shops and the trades, were not only prolific, but were being constantly recruited from the country. Where either men or women could be employed for the same work, men almost naturally had the preference, even in domestic service. Defoe called attention to it in the early part of the century; Mrs. Mary Anne Radcliffe regarded it as the prevailing cause of prostitution, and Mary Wollstonecraft deplored it. All these causes combined with the extreme poverty and degradation of the common workers to create a large floating population of unemployed and unemployables, with women greatly in the majority.* The cliché "poor but honest" had a meaning then, for it was far from easy for the poor to be honest.

---

*Mary Anne Radcliffe, *The Female Advocate, or an Attempt to Recover the Rights of Women from Male Usurpation,* 1799; also her *Memoirs,* 1810. This was not the Mrs. Ann (Ward) Radcliffe of the Gothic romances. "Mrs." Wollstonecraft's presentment—*Thoughts on the Education of Daughters* (1787)—reflects her own grim experience in trying to secure honest employment.

The problems of the *respectable* poor were particularly harassing, for they had not only poverty but social conscience to deal with, and respectability limited instead of increased their chances of decent employment. If a woman had accomplishments,* she might find employment as teacher or governess, but in spoiled and worldly families such positions were exposed and humiliating. In Miss Austen's *Emma,* written after improvement in the situation had got well under way, Jane Fairfax looks upon the prospect with despair. "Companions" were generally enlisted from among the poor connections of the family, and were universally snubbed. Fanny Burney tells us that the word "toad-eater" was the recognized synonym for companion. For almost any position in which respectability could be maintained contacts and influence were all but indispensable. The needle industries would seem an obvious entry to respectable independence, but the milliners' and the mantua-makers' shops were notorious meeting places for upper-class assignations, and their employees were often looked upon as ready partners in amorous adventure. What was generally left was domestic sewing, or just plain household service, and in the latter a pretty and agreeable woman was subjected to the bawdy talk and enterprise of every male in the house. Unless a needy and socially unplaced woman had the luck to find protection among the well-to-do members of her own family, she was truly unfortunate, and generally a mark for imaginative contemplation by males in search of amusement. Mary Wollstonecraft ventures the guess that nine out of ten middle *or upper-class* women thrown on their own resources were sooner or later bound to be seduced.

While the excitement of the chase lent piquancy to the liaisons of upper-class men and women, arrangements between men of fashion and women of the lower classes were common, because they were easier to make, were less costly, and carried less risk. A girl with no pretensions to social place was assumed to be compliant, or at least procurable, if enough promises of clothes, money, an establishment, or, in a pinch, marriage, were brought to bear upon her resistance. If she held out, there was always the possibility of rape, and there was much knowledge in circulation as to how to go about it, with or without the help of bawds, procurers, initiated menials, or drugs. If the fiction of the time is only moderately reliable evidence, rape was not uncommon among men who felt that their position guarded them from prosecution; and some rakes had a reputation for pre-

---

At the end of the century, these might be some small skill in water colors and embroidery, some training in singing and familiarity with harp, harpsichord or lute, and speaking acquaintance with French. In the *first part* of the century, that breadth of "education" for a woman would have been rare.

ferring that approach. In Richardson's *Pamela, Clarissa,* and *Sir Charles Grandison*; Fielding's *Joseph Andrews, Tom Jones,* and *Amelia*; Smollett's *Peregrine Pickle;* Mrs. Haywood's *Jenny and Jemmy Jessamy* and *Betsy Thoughtless*; Frances Burney's *Evelina*; Robert Bage's *Barham Downs*; Thomas Holcroft's *Anna St. Ives*; Mrs. Inchbald's *Simple Story*; many, perhaps most, of the Gothic romances; and dozens of minor novels right down to the close of the century; sexual violence, or an attempt at it, has at least an incidental place. In most of them it provides the actual complication. It is remarkable that in the fiction which treats this theme the offender almost always enjoys immunity from prosecution, through wealth, influence in the city magistrates' or country justices' courts, but above all, the usual unwillingness of the victim to make her predicament public. In only one of the novels mentioned is it apparent that legal redress is to be sought.

The "ruin" of a girl meant generally her becoming ultimately a common prostitute. The typical "harlot's progress," to use Hogarth's title, is illustrated with striking uniformity in the familiar interpolated stories, the so-called "little histories," of abandoned women which appear and reappear in the best-known novels of the time.

The degradation of the prostitute was greater then than it is today, and contempt for her was thoughtlessly and unthinkably cruel. Yet understandably so, for prostitution went hand in hand with pretentious vulgarity, drunkenness, extortion, thievery, perjury, and infanticide. It was rarely prosecuted under its own name, although there were statutes against it. But protection against arrest and imprisonment entailed bribery of officers of the law and what amounted to slavery to bawds and procurers. These could enforce their power over the professional by the threat of lawful imprisonment for debt incurred for clothing, lodging, and business opportunities. How destructive of character and spirit imprisonment was is repeatedly pictured in Defoe's narratives, later and even more forcefully by the humanitarian novelists, notably William Godwin.

Love in the modern sense; that is, sexual interest associated more or less closely with other spiritual and intellectual relations, is, to be sure, the romantic theme of most eighteenth-century fictions, but sinister sexual complication is a characteristic adjunct of the standard theme. In the whole breadth of that fiction we see sex in all its fluctuating lights and shadows, but very commonly as a road to misery of one sort or another. The Hellenic sense of sex as a tragic interference with inward peace is a philosophic view of its effect upon the spirit. In the eighteenth century its material effects could be even more hopelessly tragic. Perhaps with this picture before us we can understand why the moralists of the century spoke of seduction or sexual surrender as "worse than death." In the merely physi-

cal sense it often was. Morally, it might in the end result in the utter anni-
hilation of personality and self-respect. The fears and compunctions of
the heroines of fiction were not illusions and not mere pietistic sentiments; they were practical wisdom.

This survey of the sexual mores of the period has brought under examination some of the gross differences between the eighteenth-century sexual climate and our own. The modern reader of even the most elevated
novels of the period may very well ask why serious novelists, both men
and women, are prone to picture extravagant and often atrocious sex
relationships. Even in their mildest aspect they may seem alien to normal
emotion. Peregrine Pickle's sexual rampages upon the continent while his
heart is sworn to the virtuous and lovely Emilia, to most of us seem to reflect some deficiency of the spirit. That can be said without the suspicion
of Pharisaism. And the contrast of the thoroughly masculine Fielding's
sentimental apotheosis of the politely bred Sophia with his sarcastic contempt for Molly Seagrim (whose pliancy seems to be largely a matter of
social placement) is again an instance of a callousness so ingrained in the
spirit of the times that it could dominate even a notably kindly and just
mind.

On the more normal, or perhaps rather the less sensational, aspect of
marital relationships, it may impress the reader of eighteenth-century fiction that upper-class marriages, even in the novels of writers unaffected
by upper-class prejudices, seem to involve financial arrangements smacking more of trade than of affection. That situation is not as purely mercenary as it may appear. For the eighteenth-century conception of "family" envisaged a head who was responsible for many more relations and
dependents than his wife and children. In addition, estates and social
place were costly to maintain, and they were as much a part of the family
establishment as the individuals who bore its name. So it must not be
thought surprising that a fifty-thousand pound heiress, or an eligible peer
with "ten thousand a year," were taught that they were entitled to partners in marriage whose fortunes had some relation to their own. That not
unreasonable expectation had great influence upon parents in making
marriage contracts that would to some extent insure the welfare of the
future family. If such fortunes were wasted by spendthrift living, as they
often were, it was not for lack of prevision.

Probably more often than not a worldly and ambitious couple would
see eye-to-eye with their elders when the arrangement seemed advantageous. But an apparently acceptable arrangement might be revolting if
the affections were already engaged elsewhere, or if the sentiments found a
mariage de convenance distasteful. This was most likely to be the case if

the prospective bridegroom was a wastrel or roué, or the bride-to-be an uncultivated heiress to the vulgar profits of trade.

Although family opinion carried great weight in these arrangements, especially with the higher aristocracy, coercion was frowned upon. But it was not unknown; and the ability of fully resolved parents or guardians to make life miserable for an entirely dependent young woman, brought up in luxury and literally unable to do anything for herself, could in fact amount to compulsion. That situation provides the theme for some of the most notable novels of the mid-century.

In Richardson's *Clarissa* it creates a complete impasse. Clarissa runs away from her home, not because she is in love, but because her family's candidate for her hand is repulsive to her tastes and her feelings. Sophia Western, in Fielding's *Tom Jones,* escapes from confinement because she will not marry a man she finds contemptible—although she is also in love with Tom Jones. Both Clarissa and Sophia have been shut up on prison fare in order to bring them into line. In two of Fanny Burney's novels, *Cecilia* and *Camilla,* family interests and demands are opposed to sincere and worthy affections, and the family prerogative is not only accepted; it is defended by the lovers who are its victims. Next to the narrower spiritual and physical implications of sex, this problem of financing the upper-class marriage is the commonest source of complication in the fictions of the period. We must not be surprised at its gravity for the young people who had hearts to bestow but who were all but obliged to bow to the urgency of family obligations.

Upon every aspect of this question of the relations of the sexes there is a significant difference in the attitudes of the men and the women novelists. The men (except for Richardson, who has been by some flippant writers classed with the women novelists) incline to take male opportunism and irresponsibility as normal manifestations of male character. But from Mrs. Haywood down to Mrs. Inchbald, Mary Wollstonecraft, and Amelia Opie, at the turn of the century, woman's subservient and often humiliating role is presented by women writers with increasing resentment. At the end of the century even the serious men novelists—Bage and Godwin, for example—contend not only for political and legal equality for women, but for everyday decency in the treatment of wives and daughters—even more, perhaps, of women who lacked the security of marriage and family recognition. Woman's exposure to the brutalities of sex was just one phase of the moral and legal problem. Her legal incapacities, her economic helplessness, her subjection to male opinion and temper, and her lack of means of redress for all these indignities, were forced into recognition and discussion principally through the efforts of women writers. Yet remedies followed slowly, for public opinion on these problems was not greatly altered before the middle of the next century.

We raised three questions at the beginning of our discussion of the literary view of sex within our period which have not been directly answered. Let us review them in the light of what we have seen.

The first question was whether eighteenth-century people were different. In underlying human nature, of course not. But in social nurture and traditions they were, and we have seen the extent to which these differences affected social perspective. To the tradition of the God-given superiority of the well-born, and the declining but still lively respect for their privileges and exemptions, there was added the brute fact of an almost unbelievable economic gulf between the upmost and the lowest classes. A well-placed man of wealth might afford to lose thirty thousand pounds in a night's gambling, yet the clergyman who held a rural living from him might be expected to support a family on thirty pounds a year; and the tenants on his estate might not be able to feed themselves properly.* One social historian tells us that in the early part of the century a fifth of the population of London lived in some degree upon the proceeds of forced crime, and a tenth of its women were prostitutes either professionally or as occasion might help them to eke out uncertain subsistence wages. The implications of that amazing disparity in social place and power go far to explain the sexual absolutism of the upper classes and the sexual subjection of the lower.

Our second question was whether the fiction which presents these problems of sex from so special a point of view is, by and large, "true to life." We are likely to assume that the novel of the period is meant to be truthful, taking it for granted that the aim of reality is its essential point of difference from the romance. Besides, the novelists themselves—Richardson, Fielding, and Burney all take stout stands in the matter—say they mean to depict life as it is. But producing the effect of reality does not mean using materials from life that can be vouched for as matters of common experience. And we must ask the theorists whether realism pretends to depict preponderant experience, or whether anything normally possible is in its nature realistic. The question is important for us not because we have to settle what literary realism implies, but because we are concerned here simply with the question of social truth or untruth. No single work of fiction—despite Zola and Strindberg and Dreiser—has any probative value as social evidence. Yet when the bearing of the *mass* of fiction of a period upon social problems is unmistakable, then presumptions as to its value as social evidence are in order. That value, however,

---

*The instances are from actual fiction at the mid-century,

will depend upon the ethical consensus of the writers as well as upon their ability to sift facts and make judgments. So we seem to be back where we started. At this remove from the scene, it is probably impossible to measure the truth of the fiction to the life depicted, but there is *some* truth in it, and probably a great deal.

Our third question was whether an animus—an obstinately nursed grievance—underlies the unfavorable view of aristocratic morals. I am inclined to say "Yes," if on no other ground than that of the bitter social discontent and agitation that mark the period. Yet the presence of animus does not call into question the justice of a complaint, or of the way in which the complaint is presented. When the greater part of the fiction of a period seems to take the position that a socially aggrandized V.I.P. is more than likely to be an s.o.b.,* and that most of them are in fact just that, then we seem forced to think that there is substantial support for that view, whether prejudiced or not. The case for the defense might have been argued by the writer of a "society" novel, but there was no capable writer of that class in our period. Even Fielding, Fanny Burney, and Mrs. Inchbald, all of them respectful of upper-class culture, held no defensive brief for aristocratic morals; and while that is negative evidence, it has its bearing on the question.

---

*A term with which, spelled out, the eighteenth-century gentleman was perfectly familiar.

CHAPTER VII

𝔄 𝔐𝔞𝔫𝔩𝔶 𝔐𝔞𝔫

Henry Fielding

IF WE could judge an author's ego from the outlook and tone of his works, Richardson and Fielding* would seem a perfect antithesis of characters and personalities—Richardson prissy, petty, unbendingly sober, complacently moral; Fielding good-natured, waggish, with an ethical point of view implicit in his phrase "Morality is prudence." In their views of their art they appear equally opposed. Richardson's narrative is an indefinitely expanded Addisonian essay, coherent, and sharply focused upon a character who exemplifies a principle. Fielding's narrative, in spite of a pretense of classical unity, is not only loose, digressive, and strongly tinctured with his own personality, but makes a virtue of the liberties he takes with form and workmanship. Yet in a very definite sense Richardson accounts for Fielding. What principally induced Fielding to write fiction after a long and fairly successful career as a playwright was his feeling that Richardson and his *Pamela* were ridiculous and his judgment of people and conduct false.

It is not surprising, therefore, that opinions of the two have tended to approve one at the expense of the other. Readers even down to the very end of the century were either Richardsonians or Fieldingites. And this sharp division of opinion was as a rule based not upon their relative literary merits but upon the moral standards inferred from their fictions. If Richardson was a good man, then Fielding must be a wicked one; if Fielding was an honest man, then Richardson must be a hypocrite. And the division of opinion was characteristic not only of sectarian, prejudiced, and uncritical appraisal; it was reflected in the pronouncements of critics of authority. Dr Johnson said of *Tom Jones*, "I scarcely know a

---

*Henry Fielding (1707-1754). *An Apology for the Life of Mrs. Shamela Andrews* (published anonymously, 1741); *The History of the Adventures of Joseph Andrews* (1742); *The History of the Life of the Late Mr. Jonathan Wild the Great* (1743); *The History of Tom Jones, A Foundling* (1749); *The History of Amelia* (1751).

more corrupt work"; while Coleridge declared, "I loathe the cant which can recommend *Pamela* and *Clarissa* as strictly moral, though they poison the imagination of the young with *tinct. lyttae,** while *Tom Jones* is prohibited as loose."

Both Fielding and Richardson had a good deal to say about sex. To Richardson it was a matter of either romantic sentiment or grave and inexcusable guilt. Fielding made normal sexual interests part of the texture of the life of normal people. Perhaps it is doubtful whether either's treatment of sex would ruffle the susceptibilities of a reader if he were not predisposed to take sex either too seriously or too fancifully. At any rate, in approaching Fielding's novels we shall see that he handles the incongruities and the problems arising from sex as he handles all problems of conduct—as matter for either light or sober treatment, depending upon character, circumstances, traditions, or anything else that might be involved in the given situation.

Fielding's first venture in fiction, *Shamela* (1741), was a *tour de force,* incited by amused disgust at the solemn pretentiousness of *Pamela,* which had appeared in the preceding year. It is burlesque rather than parody; that is, ridicule of the whole intention of Richardson's performance rather than a travesty upon its style and tone.† Its animating idea is that Pamela's morality is simply what we would today call "caginess," in itself not a mark of strong character but of astute opportunism, and different from the caginess of an adventuress only because the social setting is different. In *Shamela,* therefore, Fielding, introduces a woman with neither principles nor shame, who counterfeits a virtue with which she has long since parted, and commends herself to the gullible Mr. Booby (Fielding's enlargement of Mr. B——) by constantly, like Pamela, advertising her pride in her purity. Fielding mocks the pious femininity of Mrs. Jarvis by making her a one-time keeper of a "house." Shamela's mother becomes an experienced bawd. Parson Williams, Pamela's confidant, becomes Shamela's paramour, who justifies his carryings-on with Shamela by the Biblical text "Be not righteous over-much." The burlesque is merciless, and it is not surprising that Richardson, who had his full share of self-esteem, was deeply offended by it.

Joseph Andrews was published in the following year, 1742. It is begun, and ends, in the same spirit of ridicule. Joseph is "esteemed to be" Pamela's brother, exposed to temptation by the amorous Lady Booby, Mr. B——'s recently widowed aunt. But Joseph's virtue is as strongly

---

*A drug once used as a sexual excitant.

†But Fielding in his preface to *Joseph Andrews* objects to the word *burlesque* as applying to his fiction.

Published as the Act directs by J. Sibbald 1792.   Rowlandson Inv.t et Fec.t

Joseph Andrews and Lady Booby. Uncolored state of Thomas Rowlandson's etching
to illustrate Fielding's *Joseph Andrews*. 1792.

fortified as Pamela's, and when Lady Booby finds his defense impregnable, she has him paid his wages and turns him off.

With Joseph's escape from Lady Booby, the motive and tempo of the story change. It becomes a novel of the road, admittedly modeled upon Cervantes, in which Joseph, his sweetheart Fanny, and a splendid creation in character, Parson Adams, share in the adventures of the wayside and the country inns. Pamela, Richardson's very own Pamela, is introduced in person in the concluding episodes of the story. She had acquired pride of place through her marriage with Squire B——, so is not excessively pleased with the idea of her brother Joseph marrying an illiterate farm maid; but she is persuaded by Squire B—— to "behave with great decency" toward Fanny.

Fielding in his "Preface" calls *Joseph Andrews* a "comic epic poem in prose," a description which seems to carry more than one contradiction in terms. What Fielding means to say is that its spirit is comic; that is, cheerful in mood and directed to a pleasant ending. Its narrative travel and the number and variety of its characters are epic; for it introduces many people and adventures, and allows free and digressive treatment of a profusion of interspersed incidents. In these respects its obvious relationship is to the *Odyssey*, rather than the *Iliad* or the *Aeneid*, although in the *Journal of a Voyage to Lisbon* Fielding speaks of the *Odyssey* as a distinct "species" from the epic. *Joseph Andrews*, finally, is conceived as a "poem" in everything but meter, a matter, as Fielding sees it, of secondary importance. Fielding, then, has laid out a pattern of performance to which he apparently intends his novels to conform; not only *Joseph Andrews*, but later *Tom Jones* and *Amelia*.

But Fielding does not call any of these works novels; he names them "histories," all of them, including his *Jonathan Wild*. He justifies his use of the word "history" by setting up a parallel with political history, the aim of which is faithful interpretation of recorded occurrences. The parallel seems to fail on that point of truth to fact, yet fiction can show truth to life, as the all-comprehensive fact, by the good faith of the author, who must not exaggerate, idealize, prettify, or degrade it, but show it in its natural colors.

Joseph Andrews outdoes Cervantes in the very things in which Fielding proposes to imitate him. The motive of both is the seeking of adventure— though in *Joseph Andrews* it is found lurking at every stopping-place, rather than sought after. Both are novels of the road—almost of necessity because of the theme. In both, the principal is an idealist, absent-minded, impractical, and ridden with an idea—for Parson Adams is really the principal of the story, not Joseph himself. And this principal is attended by a well-meaning but somewhat slow-minded squire—that is, Sancho

Panza in *Don Quixote,* Joseph in Fielding's narrative. But in action, *Don Quixote* is slow and ponderous—regrettably so to many readers. *Joseph Andrews* is a rapid succession of lively incidents. Above all, Cervantes' diffuseness—what Fielding asserts as his "liberty to digress"—is in Fielding almost the prime interest of the work.

The meager plot of the story can be told in one sentence. Joseph, having lost his place, starts homeward afoot on a journey of some days, picks up Parson Adams on the road, and Fanny, who is on her way to meet him, and they proceed all together to their destination, where sundry problems of identity and relationship are solved and the young people are finally and happily married. It is a diverting story, but only to be read; it cannot be boiled down, for its volatile ingredients would be distilled off in the process.

In both tales the incidents are for the most part breaches of the peace —in *Don Quixote* provoked by the Knight himself, for knightly glory and the honor of his Dulcinea. In *Joseph Andrews* the good parson does not provoke them, but is ready and happy to use his powerful fist or his crab-tree cudgel when provocation is given—for the defense of the weak and the vindication of the Christian virtues.

What gives vitality to *Joseph Andrews* is Parson Adams, this magnanimous and powerful innocent—for Joseph and Fanny are only two engagingly simple and natural lovers. And the vehicle of interest is the succession of road-side meetings, hours in stagecoaches, on horseback, or tramping the roads, incipient crimes overtaken by petty and blundering justice, and above all, noisy and bloody fights originating usually in the kitchens of alehouses and inns, in which the Parson's fortunes vary with the odds against him. There are two major digressions, both "little histories," the stories of Leonora and of Mr. Wilson, but the greater interest attaches to the battles, the highway robberies, the wordy rivalries of gossips, and the abuses of rank and authority under which Adams suffers more or less patiently, all of which hurry past us at the rate of about an episode to a chapter.

Joseph Andrews was followed a year later by *Jonathan Wild,* a singular book and one of an unhappily rare genre. We might copy Fielding's fondness for pigeonholing his works by calling this a moral-satiric picaresque. Its hero was, it is perhaps unnecessary to say, a notorious thief who became "fence" and informer, and died on the gallows at Tyburn. Daniel Defoe had already written a life of Wild, based on fact, certainly, but also in all probability, liberally doctored. Fielding's "history" is almost wholly invention, but it is an achievement in sustained irony unsurpassed by anything in our language, even by Thackeray's *Barry Lyndon,* a story of somewhat the same design and temper.

Jonathan Wild belongs to a literary order to which scholars have given the name of "mock encomium," which means patently praise of something that is notably unpraiseworthy, whether foolish (as in Erasmus' *Praise of Folly*), reprehensible, or downright vicious. In this case the latter category fits, since the subject of condemnation is Wild's cruel and unscrupulous criminality. The tone of treatment is clear in the proposition argued throughout the narrative that "greatness" and "goodness" are opposed terms; and the method and style are sufficiently illustrated in this quotation recounting Wild's behavior on the morning of his execution.

"At length the morning came which Fortune at his birth had resolutely ordained for the consummation of our hero's GREATNESS. He had himself indeed modestly declined the public honor she had intended him, and had taken a quantity of laudanum in order to retire quietly off the stage. But we have already observed in the course of our wonderful history that to struggle against this lady's decrees is vain and impotent; and whether she hath determined you shall be hanged or be a prime minister, it is in either case lost labor to resist. Laudanum, therefore, being unable to stop the breath of our hero, which the fruit of hemp-seed,* and not the spirit of poppy-seed, was to overcome, he was at the usual hour attended by the proper gentleman appointed for that purpose, and acquainted that the cart was ready. On this occasion he asserted that greatness of courage which hath been so much celebrated in other heroes, and knowing it was impossible to resist, he gravely declared he would attend them. . . .

When he came to the tree of glory, he was welcomed with an universal shout of the people, who were there assembled in prodigious numbers to behold a sight much more rare in populous cities than one would reasonably imagine it would be, viz. : the proper catastrophe of a great man.

But though envy was, through fear, obliged to join in the general voice in applause on this occasion, there were not wanting some who maligned this completion of glory which was now about to be fulfilled on our hero, and endeavored to prevent it by knocking him on the head as he stood under the tree, while the ordinary† was performing his last office. They therefore began to batter the cart with stones, brickbats, dirt, and all manner of mischievous weapons, some of which, erroneously playing on the robes of the ecclesiastic, made him so expeditious in his repetition that with wonderful alacrity he had ended in almost an instant, and conveyed himself to a place of safety in a hackney-coach, where he waited the conclusion in a temper of mind described in these verses :

---

*That is, a rope.
†Chaplain.

Suave mari magno, turbantibus aequora ventis,
E terra alterius magnum spectare laborem.*

We must not, however, omit one circumstance, as it serves to show the most admirable conservation of character in our hero to his last moment; which was, that while the ordinary was busy in his ejaculations, Wild, in the midst of a shower of stones, etc., which played upon him, applied his hands to the parson's pocket, and emptied it of his bottle-screw, which he carried out of the world in his hand. . . .

Thus fell Jonathan Wild the GREAT, by a death as glorious as his life had been, and which was so truly agreeable to it that the latter must have been deplorably maimed without the former; a death which hath been alone wanting to complete the characters of several ancient and modern heroes, whose histories would then have been read with much greater pleasure by the wisest of all ages.

Even in these few sentences there are sufficient hints that the satire has political undertones. Wild observes in one of the early chapters that "every prig [thief] might be a statesman if he pleased," and the story as it progresses abounds in shrewd parallels between the politician and the low criminal. It is in fact a kind of running commentary upon the corruptions of the long-lived Walpole government and the abuses of position and privilege in the relations of the upper and the lower classes.

Two great novels followed : *Tom Jones* and *Amelia*. If there is a sacrosanct reputation among eighteenth-century novelists, it is Fielding's, and its sanction is the popularity of *Tom Jones*. That popularity may very well have carried over from the days when *Tom Jones* enjoyed the reputation of a wicked book. But even today it is an interesting question whether it holds its place because it is a good novel or because it is a good story. The distinction has its importance.

For the few who may not have read *Tom Jones* we outline the bare framework of the story.

Tom is a foundling, discovered in the bed of the wholesome and kindly Squire Allworthy upon his return from a protracted absence in London. The child is attributed to, and acknowledged by, a young girl of the village, Jenny Jones, who has earned the envy of her neighbors by a conscious superiority and some pretenses to education. Squire Allworthy, as local justice, has her leave the neighborhood to protect her reputation and allow her a new start. After Jenny's departure, the babe is fathered upon the local schoolmaster Partridge, with no other justification than groundless

---

*To survey the great work from another spot, whether the sea is rough or smooth.
†Fielding's phrase for consistency to character as defined.

rumor, and Partridge also leaves town, as he has lost his good repute and is thrown upon his own resources.

Tom is brought up in Allworthy's house with the same kindness as young Blifil, the son of Allworthy's sister Bridget, now a widow. The characters of the two boys are drawn in strong contrast. Tom is adventurous, impetuous, and indiscreet, but modest, good-natured, and loyal. Blifil is devious, and occupied in studying his own advantage. His character develops quite awry; insincerity becomes hypocrisy, and he cultivates lying by innuendo—much to Tom's disadvantage; for Blifil, brought up to believe himself Allworthy's heir, begrudges Tom any possible share in the estate, and envies him the qualities of nature that are so foreign to his own.

As Tom grows into young manhood, two young women enter the story —Molly Seagrim, daughter of Allworthy's gamekeeper, discovered soon to be something of a trollop, and Sophia Western, daughter of a neighboring squire—gentle, ladylike, and in her susceptible years. Tom is interested in both of them, for understandably different reasons. Molly, a strapping country wench, has thrown herself in Tom's way, and Sophia, not altogether intelligently aware of the promptings of her own heart, has allowed herself to fall in love with this young man who is without acknowledged paternity, fortune, or prospects. This situation is socially impossible, although it has not yet reached an actual impasse. Squire Western, Sophia's father, illiterate, boorish, and interested only in hunting and drinking, has all the pride of the rural squire; so Tom and Sophia, though they see each other constantly with growing intimacy and affection, indulge no vain expectations of a future life together.

Their problem is probably no more than half appreciated by the two until a quick succession of happenings ends it for the time being. Allworthy and Western arrange for Sophia's marriage to Blifil, much against the young lady's inclinations. Finally, a series of indiscretions provides occasion for Blifil to blacken Tom's character in a way peculiarly painful to Allworthy and offensive to his sense of justice. The result is Tom's dismissal from Allworthy's house, and through a sheer accident, his loss of the substantial gift of money with which Allworthy has set him loose in the world.

Jones, meeting a company of recruits on the road, volunteers for military service, but in a disagreement with a boastful ensign is wounded and obliged to leave the company. At an inn he picks up by accident (coincidences are far from rare in Fielding's novels) his reputed father, Partridge, who offers to accompany Jones on his travels. The narrative is broken here by one of Fielding's little histories, the story of the Man of the Hill, encountered by chance and willing to tell Jones the story of his life. This episode concludes with Tom's chance rescue of Mrs. Waters from an at-

Tom Jones to the rescue of Mrs. Waters; from the earliest illustrations of a novel by Fielding—M.D. LaPlace's French translation of *Tom Jones,* Londres (probably Paris), 1750. Engraved by Jan Punt after Hubert Gravelot.

tempt on her life. Of her, more is to be heard in the latter portion of the novel. The meeting with Mrs. Waters is the occasion of another departure by Jones from the path of continence. It is also the occasion of the memorable "battle of Upton," in which the refusal of the landlady of the local inn to open her house to a lady "no better than she should be" results in a general melee—Jones, Mrs. Waters, and Partridge against the landlord, his spouse, and the chambermaid. Unhappily, Tom's diversion with Mrs. Waters is quickly brought to Sophia's knowledge. She has escaped from imprisonment in her father's house in order to avoid a forced marriage with Blifil, and arrives at the inn at Upton at just the moment to discover Jones's perfidy, and to leave immediately on her way to London.

In London, whither both Sophia and Jones have traveled their separate ways, Tom, who believes he has forfeited all claim upon Sophia's respect as well as affection, falls into a dishonorable, because venal, amour with Lady Bellaston, who by an extraordinary coincidence is "a relation" and the protectress of the helpless Sophia. It is to Lady Bellaston's protection that Sophia has fled from her home. But when she finds Sophia the real object of Jones's affection, Lady Bellaston plans to get her out of the way by marrying her to a fashionable acquaintance, Lord Fellamar. Her duplicity is exposed when Tom discovers Sophia is actually a resident in the home of the woman who has been buying his attentions by substantial "loans."

The concluding complications are highly involved, embracing another major digression—the story of Nightingale and Nancy Miller, the memorable little scene of Partridge's visit to the theater, Western's arrival in London to claim his Sophy, Tom's pretended proposal of marriage to Lady Bellaston in order to cure her passion for him, and ensuing further misunderstanding with Sophia, a duel which lands Tom in prison, and finally an approach to reconciliation with both Sophia and Allworthy by Mrs. Miller, at whose house Tom has been a lodger.

If the London incidents are multiplied almost to embarrassment, the denouement is quite as much so. To establish Tom's identity—he is in fact the illegitimate son of Bridget Allworthy by a former resident in Allworthy's hospitable house—the testimony of Mrs. Waters (she is the Jenny Jones of the opening chapter), of Partridge, and of two attorneys is essential. To further vindicate Tom's character, Allworthy has the evidence of Sophia, of Square, of Mrs. Miller, and finally the forced confessions of Blifil himself and of the attorney Dowling, Allworthy's steward. Allworthy and Tom are reconciled, and more surprisingly, Tom and Blifil—a further confirmation of Tom's exemplary good will. As to Sophia and Tom, once Tom is recognized as Allworthy's heir, even Squire Western drops his opposition to Sophia's marrying a "by-blow." And that is the end of the story.

No one who has read *Tom Jones* will grant that I have really told the story here. And I have not. To an unusual degree the story of *Tom Jones* lies in other aspects of interest than plot. And the problem of epitomizing it is not one of scale. We could retell the story in two or three times these dimensions and it would still lack most of the interest which Fielding has given it.

In the first place, mentioning, or even describing, his characters gives no idea of their interest for the reader. The romantic lovers are conventional. Sophia is just a lovely and proper girl, and about all that she looks, thinks, and does is no more nor less than we should expect from a stage ingenue. Tom, too—although it is heresy to say it—might have been drawn from a good theatrical craftsman's stock of youthful and engaging males. But Allworthy, Blifil, Bridget Allworthy, Squire Western, Partridge, Jenny Jones, Lady Bellaston, and Mrs. Miller are portrayed with penetration and vital humor.

In addition there is a small host of personalities glimpsed in single incidents, or employed to give substance to the action rather than as immediate participants in it. These include two members of Allworthy's household, the philosopher Square and the Reverend Mr. Thwackum; Sophia's aunt, Mrs. Western; and such casual acquaintances as the landlord and his wife at the inn at Upton; Sophia's cousin, Mrs. Fitzpatrick, a lady of fragile virtue; and characters in London fashionable life or on the fringe of it, like Lord Fellamar and Mr. Nightingale.

Personal description, either inward or outward, did not appear to advantage in our earlier novels, perhaps because the taste for it had not yet been developed. It tends to be formal and indistinct, as we may see in the first view Fielding gives us of Sophia Western.

> Sophia, then, the only daughter of Mr. Western, was a middle-sized woman, but rather inclining to tall. Her shape was not only exact, but extremely delicate; and the nice proportion of her arms promised the truest symmetry in her limbs. Her hair, which was black, was so luxuriant that it reached her middle, before she cut it to comply with the modern fashion; and it was curled so gracefully in her neck that few could believe it her own. If envy could find any part of the face which demanded less commendation than the rest, it might possibly think her forehead might have been higher without prejudice to her. Her eyebrows were full, even, and arched beyond the power of art to imitate. Her black eyes had a luster in them which all her softness could not extinguish. Her nose was exactly regular, and her

mouth, in which were two rows of ivory, exactly answered Sir John Suckling's description in these lines :—

> Her lips were red, and one was thin,
> Compar'd to that was next her chin.
> Some bee had stung it newly.

Her cheeks were of the oval kind; and in her right she had a dimple, which the least smile discovered. Her chin had certainly its share in forming the beauty of her face; but it was difficult to say it was either large or small, though perhaps it was rather of the former kind. Her complexion had rather more of the lily than of the rose; but when exercise or modesty increased her natural color, no vermilion could equal it. Then one might indeed cry out with the celebrated Dr. Donne :—

> Her pure and eloquent blood
> Spoke in her cheeks, and so distinctly wrought
> That one might almost say her body thought.

Her neck was long and finely turned; and here if I was not afraid of offending her delicacy, I might justly say the highest beauties of the famous *Venus de Medicis* were outdone. Here was whiteness which no lilies, ivory, or alabaster could match. The finest cambric might indeed be supposed from. envy to cover that bosom which was much whiter than itself.

If the object of personal description is to give an inkling of the emotional stir that attends the ocular experience, then this is flat description. Phrases like "middle-sized," "exact but extremely delicate," "nice proportion," "exactly regular," "finely turned," are without emotional suggestion, so induce no appreciative response. Sophia's eyes and hair are black, her teeth white, her cheeks with an agreeable bloom enhanced by blushing, and her features regular. Stylized comparisons are dealt out liberally, and the writer leans heavily upon Suckling's commonplace metaphor (good enough in its original setting) and the superb conceit from Donne. Comparison to the disadvantage of the Venus de' Medici is gratuitous enough to be absurd; and the assurance that Sophia's legs must be shapely and her bosom white—although they are not visible—is the final proof of slavish conventionalism. No doubt it was Sterne's contempt for such bloodless catalogues that prompted him in *Tristram Shandy* to provide his reader with a blank page upon which to write his description of his own mistress.*

---

*But the assumption that tongue-in-cheek was a well established habit with Fielding might justify the view that this is parody of the elegant style. Fielding entitles the chapter "A short hint of what we can do in the sublime, and a description of Miss Sophia Western."

It is rather remarkable that following this exercise in "school" description is a paragraph in which Fielding tells us that the formal approach can accomplish little or nothing in revealing mind and character. These must be developed through thought and action—in other words, in the course of the story.

Yet Fielding is capable of highly effective characterization within small compass. A brief exchange of dialogue will open up the idiosyncrasies of the participants as no substantive account could. Here, for example, Thwackum and Square engage in a debate precipitated by a poaching adventure of Tom's in which he conceals the identity of his fellow in crime upon what he considers a point of "honor." Thwackum makes an issue of the word "honor."

"Honor," cried Thwackum, with some warmth, "mere stubbornness and obstinacy. Can honor teach anyone to tell a lie, or can honor exist independent of religion?"

To this Square answered that it was impossible to discourse philosophically concerning words till their meaning was first established; that there were scarce any two words of a more vague and uncertain signification than the two that he had mentioned, for that there were almost as many different opinions concerning honor as concerning religion. "But," says he, "if by honor you mean the true natural beauty of virtue, I will maintain it may exist independent of any religion whatever. Nay," added he, "you yourself will allow it may exist independent of all but one. So will a Mahometan, a Jew, and all the maintainers of all the different sects in the world."

Thwackum replied this was arguing with the usual malice of all the enemies of the true Church. He said he doubted not but that all the infidels and heretics in the world would, if they could, confine honor to their own absurd errors and damnable deceptions, "But honor," says he, "is not therefore manifold because there are many absurd opinions about it; nor is religion because there are many sects and heresies in the world. When I mention religion, I mean the Christian religion; and not only the Christian religion, but the Protestant religion; and not only the Protestant religion, but the Church of England. And when I mention honor, I mean that mode of Divine grace which is not only consistent with, but dependent upon, this religion; and is consistent with and dependent upon no other. Now to say that the honor I here mean, and which was, I thought, all the honor I could be supposed to mean, will uphold, much less dictate, an untruth, is to assert an absurdity too shocking to be conceived."

"I purposely avoided," says Square, "drawing a conclusion which I thought evident from what I said; but if you perceived it, I am sure you have not attempted to answer it. However, to drop the article of religion, I think it is plain from what you have said that we have different ideas of honor; or why do we not agree in the same terms of its explanation? I have asserted that true honor and true virtue are almost synonymous terms, and they are both founded on the unalterable rule of right and the eternal fitness of things; to which an untruth being absolutely repugnant and contrary, it is certain that true honor cannot support an untruth. In this, therefore, I think we are agreed; but that this honor can be said to be founded on religion, to which it is antecedent, if by religion be meant any positive law—"

"I agree," answered Thwackum, with great warmth, "with a man who asserts honor to be antecedent to religion! Mr Allworthy, did I agree—?"

He was proceeding when Mr. Allworthy interposed, telling them very coldly they had both mistaken his meaning; for that he had said nothing of true honor. It is possible, however, he would not easily have quieted the disputants, who were growing equally warm, had not another matter now fallen out which put a final end to the conversation at present.

We see the same indirect approach in the contrast of Tom and Blifil in their growing years, this time not through dialogue, but through the medium of popular opinion, ironically shaded.

As we determined when we first sat down to write this history, to flatter no man, but to guide our pen throughout by the directions of truth, we are obliged to bring our hero on the stage in a much more disadvantageous manner than we could wish; and to declare honestly, even at his first appearance, that it was the universal opinion of all Mr. Allworthy's family* that he was born to be hanged.

Indeed, I am sorry to say there was too much reason for this conjecture, the lad from his earliest years having discovered a propensity to many vices, and especially to one which hath as direct a tendency as any other to that fate which we have just now observed to have been prophetically denounced against him. He had been already convicted of three robberies, viz.: of robbing an orchard, of stealing a duck out of a farmer's yard, and of picking Master Blifil's pocket of a ball.

The vices of this young man were, moreover, heightened by the disadvantageous light in which they appeared when opposed to the virtues of Master Blifil, his companion, a youth of so different a cast from little Jones, that not only the family, but all the neighborhood, resounded his praises. He was, indeed, a lad of a remarkable disposition; sober, discreet, and pious beyond his age; qualities which gained

---

*"Family" in eighteenth century usage meant all the members and dependents of the household.

him the love of everyone who knew him; while Tom Jones was universally disliked; and many expressed their wonder that Mr. Allworthy
would suffer such a lad to be educated with his nephew, lest the morals
of the latter should be corrupted by his example.

Satire, which pervades all Fielding's fictions, is here a powerful aid to
the illumination of character. Technically, the art of the second paragraph above lies in overstatement; of the third paragraph in ironic—call
it sarcastic if you prefer—misstatement. But the magic of innuendo in
both the first and the third paragraphs gives us the clearest impression not
only of the two boys' characters, but of the sycophancy with which their
neighbors judge them.

Fielding's great art, however, lies not in flashes of suggestive characterization, but in the processes by which we see character ripening under
his hand. We have already noted that his theory of "conservation of character" calls for consistency throughout the story to a clearly defined type.
Modern psychologists tell us that character does not change, and Fielding
had an intelligent adumbration of that view. But character can develop
in the sense that its potentialities emerge as the individual meets with new
experiences. In this sense, the absorbing interest of *Tom Jones,* or at least
its most absorbing *serious* interest, is the maturing of Tom, of Sophia,
and, yes, of Squire Allworthy, who is first presented to us with the appearance of a fully matured personality.

Yet Fielding's depiction of character—and of incident too, for that
matter—is highly colored by his prepossessions. The nineteenth century,
largely through the example of the French realists, come to regard objectivity in character portrayal as an artistic virtue. But objectivity implies an
attitude of mind—impartiality—which is itself a prepossession. There is
little doubt that, as author, Fielding would not have regarded detachment as either an ethical or an aesthetic obligation. For, no less than
Richardson, he considers himself as a moralist, inculcating the principle
of prudent restraint as opposed to pietism, always through character contrasts for the end in view. What he values in character are good will and
honest intentions; what he attacks is self-righteousness.

No character of his illustrates this predilection for humane and open
character better than Allworthy, who combines benevolence and high
moral purpose with shockingly bad judgment, especially of people. One
cannot carry analysis of the plot of *Tom Jones* very far without discovering
that the mainspring of its action is the well-intentioned errors of this
likable blunderer. He fails to penetrate his sister Bridget's guile in foisting
her illegitimate child upon his charity. He fails to fathom the designing
characters of the two elder Blifils, to discern the bread-and-butter ob-

sequiousness of Thwackum and Square, to detect the duplicity of his steward, Dowling, or to see the almost transparent dishonesty of his gamekeeper, Black George. Worst of all, he is putty in the hands of the younger
Blifil, who understands Allworthy's weakness as completely as Allworthy
misunderstands Blifil's hypocrisy. Ultimately, he is deceived by appearances and Blifil's malicious misrepresentations into misjudging and dis-
owning Tom himself. To these cardinal deficiencies in judgment we must
add his injustices to Jenny Jones and Partridge—minor, perhaps, but disastrous to both—due again to his proneness to judge from externals and to
rest upon the rightness of his own moral presumptions.

This is Fielding's portrait of a *good* man, yet an infant in discretion.
Allworthy's is not an amiable or an amusing shortsightedness; for it is only
by the interposition of pure luck that his victims—for they are victims—
are rescued from the embarrassments and sufferings to which his faults
of judgment have consigned them. We have already noted an organic resemblance in *Tom Jones* to *Don Quixote*; but Cervantes' inspired innocent is relatively harmless. Allworthy is not.

It may be objected that *Tom Jones* is comedy, and that balanced judgment of character is out of place in comedy. But Allworthy himself is
neither conceived nor portrayed as a comic character; he is, we repeat, in
Fielding's reiterated view, a good man. Fielding asks us to respect him,
and to like him, as he does himself. All of which is as much as saying that
Fielding is touched with the sentimentality of the period. Allworthy's remark upon Black George, "The dishonesty of this fellow I might perhaps
have pardoned, but never his ingratitude," has the full flavor and bouquet
of sentimentalism. Fielding's partiality for Allworthy is partly his predilection for "class," partly his instinctive admiration for the kind of person
who lives his morality without parading it, and partly his tenderness for
the failings of a character who means to be upright.

We seem to have reached the conclusion that the characters of Fielding's principals are weighted heavily on the romantic-sentimental side.
We are indeed asked to approve Tom as a person, and not wholly on moral
grounds, because, to quote Fielding himself, "in balancing his faults with
his perfections, the latter seemed rather to preponderate." We should admire Sophia because of her fidelity to her romantic prepossessions. We
should accept Allworthy because his mistakes are conscientious ones.

On the other hand, Fielding's drawing of secondary characters tends
to be, if not objective, at least unsentimental. He exploits the simplicity
and awkwardness of even the humble people for whom he feels a patronizing affection—witness Joseph Andrews and Parson Adams. Where his
low characters are without one or another of the primary virtues, Fielding
inclines to make them both blamable and ridiculous—witness Molly Sea-

grim, Partridge, Thwackum, and Square. But good or not so good, these plain people carry, on the whole, more conviction than their sentimentally clothed superiors. This propensity to regard the disadvantaged as natural objects for jocose or satirical treatment is part of the comic tradition, and particularly a convention of theatrical comedy before and down to Fielding's time. It is not surprising, therefore, that Fielding, whose talents had been sharpened in writing for the comic stage, should have accepted this conventional attitude toward the humble and socially untutored.

But the convention carries even deeper implications for Fielding's handling of character. The comedy of the theater had not carried analysis of character very far beneath the surface. A character conceived in the spirit of comic exaggeration did not have to be justified by reason or to have his motives carefully elucidated. *Per contra,* a character less exposed to ridicule, because entitled to the distinction of gentleman or lady, must be handled with fidelity to his breeding and station, and judged also by the morality of his class. These favorable or unfavorable prescriptions, as well as the doctrine of "conservation," put it almost outside the power of a comic writer who observed the conventions to offer profound explanations of character or to inquire seriously into the why of an action which was not necessarily reflective. That is what justified Dr. Johnson's describing Fielding as a man who could tell time from the face of a watch, while Richardson, he declared, could tell how the watch was made.

Profound character analysis, then, is not the object of Fielding's fiction. None of his characters, intelligent or unintelligent, highly placed or humble, virtuous or venial, stands up to an exacting test of lifelikeness. They are interesting because they are pictured with spirit, with comic percipiency, or with sympathy, but they are not deeply explored (at least not in *Joseph Andrews* and *Tom Jones*) and they make analysis superfluous. When Fielding says, as he frequently does, "I shall leave it to the reader to determine," how a character feels or acts, or what his motive may be, we may be sure that it is not only because the answer is likely to be self-evident, but because explanation is beside his purpose.

Plot, on the other hand, was in theatrical comedy a salient, or perhaps *the* salient, interest. Furthermore, a good comic plot must be ingeniously put together—even though the ingenuity might be mechanical rather then imaginative. *Tom Jones* has plot in a sense that *Joseph Andrews* lacked it. At first glance, *Tom Jones* looks episodic; still it takes much more than an initial push to set the story in motion. A rather complicated set of personal relations puts Tom upon the road and underlies the further accumulation of incident. Incident itself is progressively involved, and complication is almost excessive in the final events which bring about Tom's restoration to Allworthy's favor and his reconciliation with Sophia.

In the making of plot, as of character, Fielding tends to work from a fixed pattern with obvious theatrical relationships. So the mechanism of his plots inevitably shows. Once we have been introduced to the central characters—Jones, Sophia, and Blifil—we can guess the channel in which the current of circumstance is bound to run. The only doubt we have of the outcome is as to the means by which Blifil is to be exposed and Sophia and Tom are to be made happy in their mutual love. That is the defect of preconceived character and preconceived design.

But this defect is almost a fixed characteristic of stories and plays with the romantic character-set. Whether or not a plot of this type is interesting in itself depends principally upon what is done with the "middle" of the action. And the question focuses particularly upon such tests of acceptability as specific interest of incident, freedom of the character for voluntary action, and avoidance of forced incident and excessive or irrational coincidence. But most of these tests are tests of the author's command of realistic expedients, and they cannot be applied fairly to fiction before the setting up of a realistic canon.

Even so, they undoubtedly influence our judgment of Fielding's performance. Looking at *Tom Jones* as a novel, and not as programed entertainment, we are aware that time and experience had still much to accomplish before fiction could reach the level of *conviction* that it does in Jane Austen—or even Fanny Burney and Maria Edgeworth. It is interesting, incidentally, that it was principally women writers of fiction who justified the objective of comprehensive truth to life. But we shall come to that later.

The conventional devices of plot, then, are in the main sufficient for Fielding, chiefly because literary tradition had given him little else to work with. Of all the expedients which he accepts without hesitation even though he concedes its weakness, coincidence is, for the modern reader, the most questionable. With all the good will in the world, he must be dissatisfied with Sophia's chance appearance at the very moment of Tom's escapade with Molly Seagrim, her equally fortuitous arrival at the inn at Upton to discover Tom's passing adventure with Mrs. Waters, and the explosive and completely unexpected entrance of her father at the moment that she was about to succumb to the violence of Lord Fellamar—an interposition already worn threadbare in plays and fictions. Or consider the extent to which complication grows out of Tom's loss, while fumbling in his pocket, of the bill for £500 which Allworthy gave him when he was turned out, and later, upon Sophia's loss, in exactly the same fashion, of the bank-bill for £100 her father had given her before she left her home. Such an accident might be accepted once in the course of the story—but twice, and to the two principals?

Then there are the almost numberless instances in which encounters by the purest chance breed critical consequences—Tom's purely fortuitous meeting on the road with Mrs. Waters, his reputed mother; with Partridge, his reputed father; with the attorney Dowling, who is eventually to expose Blifil; with the highwayman who turns out to be Mrs. Miller's cousin; or Sophia's chance meeting with her eloping cousin Mrs. Fitzpatrick; and the constantly repeated overhearing of a random word in an inn-kitchen, with its train of important consequences. Almost the entire machinery of the denouement moves upon the wheels of coincidence, with Mrs. Miller running about as a busy *dea ex machina*. It might seem that Fielding actually prefers an irrational to a rational collocation of events. The fact is, of course, that these were the easy expedients of the theater, in which he was already practiced.

The redeeming feature of plot in *Tom Jones,* perhaps in truth its greatest source of interest, is the accumulation of well handled incident, both dramatic and humorous. But it is adventure—the getting into and out of scrapes—that supplies the steady entertainment. And it is not great adventure, but the stuff, in the main, of well-integrated and almost self-sufficient little episodes, recalling the novelle, but set in the scenes and the culture of eighteenth-century society, and accomplishing a modest something for the progress of the plot and the illumination of character. For "plot is character" in *Tom Jones* only in so far as his sense of honor combines with his unripe judgment to bring about general misunderstanding of his character, and this misunderstanding is dissolved only by the author's final and far-reaching manipulation of good luck.

The remaining artistic ingredient in *Tom Jones* is not typically a characteristic of the novel, and it has at times been subjected to adverse criticism by sticklers for the consistently objective point of viewing fiction. That is, the infusion of the author's own temperament, ideas, and even crotchets—in other words, his personality—into the novel. Fielding may present himself boldly and at length, as in this passage :

> At length we are once more come to our hero; and, to say truth, we have been obliged to part with him for so long that, considering the condition in which we left him, I apprehend many of our readers have concluded we intended to abandon him forever; he being at present in that situation in which prudent people usually desist from inquiring any further after their friends, lest they should be shocked by hearing such friends had hanged themselves.
>
> But, in reality, if we have not all the virtues, I will boldly say, neither have we all the vices of a prudent character; and though it is not easy to conceive circumstances much more miserable than those of poor Jones at present, we shall return to him, and attend upon

him with the same diligence as if he was wantoning in the brightest beams of fortune.

We may also glimpse the author in mere bits of innuendo, or in the unmistakably personal flavor of a word or two.

> It may perhaps be wondered at that the waiting-woman herself was not the messenger employed on this occasion; but we are sorry to say she was not at present qualified for that, or indeed for any other office. The rum (for so the landlord chose to call the distillation from malt) had basely taken the advantage of the fatigue which the poor woman had undergone; and had made terrible depredations on her noble faculties at a time when they were very unable to resist the attack.
>
> We shall not describe this tragical scene too fully; but we thought ourselves obliged, by that historic integrity which we profess, shortly to hint a matter which we would otherwise have been glad to have spared. Many historians, indeed, for want of this integrity, or of diligence, to say no worse, often leave the reader to find out these little circumstances in the dark, and sometimes to his great confusion and perplexity.

Or this :

> Mr. Jones presently opened it, and (guess, reader, what he felt) saw in the first page the name Sophia Western, written by her own fair hand.

We have called this easy intimacy with the reader an "ingredient" of the story. It is, rather, seasoning. For it is after all a matter of style. The sanction for the practice, at least for Fielding, is his reiterated position that he is the inventor of "this new species" of fiction, and can handle it as he likes. At any rate, to an unusual degree the reader feels the presence of the author in the narrative. To some it is offensive; as they think that realistic effect suffers if the manipulator of the marionettes is not kept out of sight. Much, however, must depend upon the author's gift for presenting his personality without intrusiveness. And in this Fielding is usually successful; for the habit appears free from affectation—an altogether natural and mild effervescence of friendliness, something, at its best, approximating the art of conversation.

Much learned discussion of *Tom Jones* has been expended upon Fielding's adoption of classic models (not necessarily *classical*) for his fiction, and in particular upon his defense of the practice in the introductory chapters to the eighteen books into which *Tom Jones* is divided.

Perhaps the problem is no more than academic, though not therefore frivolous. For working upon patterns that have acquired the gloss of authority has never assured a writer's greatness. But Fielding's literary erudition tended to hamper rather than to help him. The debt to Cervantes which he notes in *Joseph Andrews* seems to carry with it too unquestioning a dependence upon the narrative of adventurous episode, and upon the interpolated "little histories." His defense of "epic" method in *Tom Jones* is not only an expression of his erudition in and his profound love of the ancients; it is a belated classicist's illusion that the narrative practice of the ancient epic poets was a sufficient guide for writers of narrative in time to come. Yet he found it difficult to adapt his gay temper, his intellectual independence, and his sharp interest in the normal and the current to the programs and techniques of Virgil—who is, after all, for him the exemplar of epic achievement.* In considering Fielding's apologetic for his use of the epic model, we must remove from the word "epic" a small multitude of scholarly associations that have gathered about it since Fielding's time. Fielding could not have distinguished between the "folk" epic and the "literary" epic. And his predilection for the ancient epic is the product of the academic culture of his time. Ariosto or Tasso—even more notably, Pulci—would seem closer to the temper and method of *Tom Jones* than either Homer or Virgil.

But interspersed classical similes, reminiscences of classical characters (the comparison of Dido in the *Aeneid* with Lady Bellaston in *Tom Jones* or Miss Mathews in *Amelia*), echoes of classical incident (the battle of Upton, and the villagers attack on Molly Seagrim) do not recreate the classical spirit any more than his reiterated protestation of epic purpose. The small debt that *Tom Jones* owes to Fielding's professed models only serves to accentuate his own liberal genius and mental independence. Indeed, when we consider Fielding's fondness for banter, it is possible to interpret the learned disquisitions in the critical passages of *Tom Jones* as mere fun at the reader's expense, or what Sterne would have called "riding a hobby-horse." Fielding's delight in playing with an idea is never more evident than in these passages of sober and learned debate upon aesthetic principles which scholars have been put to it to prove he followed with any more than pretended seriousness. At any rate, this particular ques-

---

*Fielding's plentiful quotations from the ancients make it abundantly clear that Virgil was his favorite poet. He quotes the Latin poets, and very particularly Virgil, almost to the complete exclusion of the Greek dramatists—though in *Joseph Andrews* he tells us that a battered handwritten copy of Aeschylus was the companion of Parson Adams' travels. There is a handful of quotations from Homer in *Amelia,* but almost all are used by Dr. Harrison to confound Mrs. Bennett's pretensions to classical learning.

tion of aesthetic intention and good faith is one of those sleeping dogs that will not bite us if we don't try to pet them. One can read *Tom Jones* without being troubled by the critical interludes.

His last novel, *Amelia,* is in essential respects a departure from all his earlier fictions. In the concluding chapters of *Tom Jones* the distinction between vice and villainy is constantly played up for the greater glory of Tom and the confusion of Blifil, not to speak of the assemblage of deserving or undeserving minor characters. In *Amelia* the failures in prudence are no longer condoned, except in the all-forgiving temper of the heroine herself. If there are real differences between the sins of the head and those of the heart, in *Amelia* they are regarded as only differences in degree. Vice is evil, even petty vice, and Fielding creates a character to prove it, by precept, and by the example of a purely benevolent, moral, and judicious being. That is Dr. Harrison, a Parson Adams without Adams' awkwardness, and a Squire Allworthy without Allworthy's credulity.

If a single word can characterize the distinction between *Amelia* and practically all of Fielding's work that preceded it, it is "responsibility," both moral and artistic. In *Amelia* he no longer plays with moral conceptions; he does not coddle mildly righteous but mildly sinful characters; he does not flirt with his reader; he does not invoke a specious good luck in settling the difficulties of his characters. Perhaps these considerations should not be stated as absolutes; and of course they are all negative.

On the positive side, *Amelia* is a brave arraignment of political and social vices rampant in Fielding's day—more particularly of abuses in the military services, in the judicial system, the prison system, and most of all in political privilege and patronage. But as important as his bold charges were for the overhauling of the political and social sense of his time, they furnished only the setting of the story. The situation of the husband, a faithful servant of his country but shelved by favoritism and corruption in the military administration, and of the wife, equally faithful and devoted to her family but humiliated by her husband's loose habits and bad management of his own interests, brings us very close to the realities of domestic life in the crowded and dissolute London of the midcentury. And the personal relationship of the two, even when strained to tautness by misfortune and misunderstanding, has its own profound and not over-sentimentalized beauty.

Amelia is Fielding's first and only departure from a conventional plot with dangling episodes. Yet even *Amelia* is loose in construction; not because it lacks rational continuity, but because that continuity is again broken up into substantial chunks of intrigue, is interrupted by the favorite little histories, and is brought to a conclusion that is less logical than stagey. However, the principal characters are freer than in *Tom Jones* from the automatism that inheres in Fielding's old attachment to "conservation of character"; and, finally, Fielding has at last reached the point at which a flood of happy coincidences is no longer necessary for the solving of the problems of plot. Even though the threads of destiny are not altogether in the hands of the actors in this comedy of marital adjustments, the characters do show moral energy well applied to the business of living, even in adversity.

To put it all very simply, this is the first of Fielding's novels in which realistic intention is supported by realistic expedients, not unfailingly, but in the main. And to a great extent this rather sudden break into what we might call modernity is due to the nature of the theme—the love of the mature man and woman, responsible, tolerant, and thoughtful, with sufficient romantic affection, but without erotic glamor.

Structurally, at least in the modern view, the novel is out of balance. The opening scene is the arrest and imprisonment of Captain Booth, Amelia's husband, for intervening in a street brawl. The rights of the case are all on Booth's side; the "justice" dealt out to him is the justice of the prejudiced and ignorant Justice Thrasher. The commitment to prison is followed by two extremely long little histories, those of Miss Matthews, a fellow-prisoner, no better than she should be, and Booth himself. Neither is indispensable; Miss Matthews' story, even if we admit her minor part in the plot, is somewhat distracting, like most of these *appliqués* episodes. Booth's has a function, in providing the background for the narrative, and is in itself a well-told story. But the prison episodes and the two lives take up well over a quarter of the narrative before the impending story begins to move.*

The essential story of *Amelia* is the story of a weak man and a strong woman—of a man whose weakness is (after all like Jones's) the want of prudence in the regulation of his day-to-day life. He is a man of courage, a proved soldier, a good man among men, generally right-minded, but, to use a phrase with a clear meaning for every New England housewife, "no manager."

The woman's strength is the strength of affection, for this manly but not-too-clever Captain Booth, and for her children. But it is an affection with little of the knowledgeable and worldly discretion that mark the heroines of the women novelists of the next generations—Miss Burney, Miss Edgeworth, and Miss Austen. Amelia has all the feminine virtues to repletion, but they are the feminine virtues as the mid-eighteenth century construed them, including unquestioning obedience to the will and the

---

*Are such comprehensive flash-backs bad art? They are advantageously used by Meredith, Samuel Butler, Arnold Bennett, and many other later novelists.

whims of her husband and tacit resignation to him of all claims to mental strength and intelligence. Indeed, the presumption of feminine inferiority Fielding fortifies by introducing into his story a female aspirant to masculine learning, Mrs. Bennett, whom Dr. Harrison is put to the pains of humiliating in order to prove man's greater fitness for the heavier struggles of intellect. Fielding would have accepted unblushingly the view that the proper place for a good woman was in a good man's home. And if the man were not so good, that was her proper place anyway.

Captain Booth, then, is beset by debts—the shameful position of many a military servant in times of peace. And his Amelia is beset by attempts upon her virtue; for, as we have already seen, a favorite mark for the seducer's art was the wife of an impoverished gentleman. In fact, before the story ends we are brought face to face with the problem of whether the husband himself might be induced to connive at the demolition of his wife's honor in order to buy the influence which might lead to his restoration to official favor and advancement. This is no rare theme in the fiction of the period, but nowhere treated with more poignant sense of the pity and the shame of the situation.

There is the substance of the story of *Amelia,* which is told with great understanding of the shifts, the humiliations, the temptations, and the abuses that attended the man thrown upon the stony charity of fashionable London. And with equal understanding of the batteries of pretense and cruel subterfuge brought to bear upon a woman with defenses reduced by loneliness and want. The details of intrigue we can leave to the reader interested in a firmly told story. They include the ill designs of men of professed friendship for Captain Booth; and those designs are averted not by Amelia's innocence, which is too perfect for her own protection, but by the grosser understanding of the people about her.

Looking forward and well beyond Fielding's own time, we can put it down for fact that most English novels which rank in the superlative class—*Vanity Fair, The Egoist, The Portrait of a Lady*—are Sophoclean in conception and plot; action depending and building upon some error, some failure of judgment, some *hubris,* the consequences of which dog the principal relentlessly to the end. These, however, are novels of graver import, and Fielding's temperamental bias is comic. The structural unity of all Fielding's "histories" from *Jonathan Wild* to *Amelia* is simply biographic.

And that is Fielding's contribution to the still unknown and unprophesied future of fiction. Plot in Fielding's hands showed an advance over the one-track and far too attenuated plots of Richardson, but it is not a phenomenal advance. In giving us, however, a clear and whole view of a character floundering through the common embarrassments and involvements of the time and the place, he has opened up what we might regard as the normal path of travel of the novel. In this respect *Amelia* seems to have more significance than the much more popular *Tom Jones*. The plot in *Jones* is still the theatrical version of the standard romantic plot, and the characters are still romantic characters, a little too sentimentalized, a little lacking in unliterary humanity. *Amelia* is conceived somewhat romantically, as an eighteenth-century version of the story of Patient Griselda, but with a reprobate husband instead of a jealous one. Yet Amelia herself is no mere piece of literary furniture. She has substance and energy —the tests of reality—and with reason, for Fielding tells us that she is the embodiment of the beauty and virtues of his first wife.

The greater vitality of *Amelia,* the thing that makes it lovable for readers who have seen more of life than their teens, is the simple fact that the character of Amelia has aged, like good wine. She is superior to the minor adolescent disturbances, not because she has become disillusioned, but because she has ripened. Her love for her errant captain is no longer touched by childish sensitiveness; its endurance is the endurance of wisdom, even though it may seem at times patient to the point of folly. *She is the plot,* the enlargement of the theme of feminine staying-power. Captain Booth has a somewhat larger place in the action of the story, but his weakness and his waywardness merely turn the wheels of circumstance, which cannot grind Amelia to tragic dust because she is spiritually superior to the fate of the neglected wife.

If any of Fielding's novels has magnitude, it is *Amelia.* The others are diverting, not sustaining. Yet perhaps Amelia's saintly magnanimity is not quite greatness. When Thackeray created a second Amelia in *Vanity Fair,* he made her a secondary character, and made her complacent constancy to the young jackass George Osborne something less than admirable. Perhaps Thackeray was more nearly right, and perhaps Fielding developed his Amelia too much under the pressure of sentimentalism, the besetting weakness of the art of the period.

It need not be proved that Fielding is not a novelist entirely of the modern stamp. He stands too near the actual emergence of a new literary type, the full potential of which was not to be discovered for at least a century, and was to depend upon the slow accretions of time and experience and the efforts of many minds. Yet his title to pre-eminence in his own century few would dispute. And there is point in the fact that down to Jane Austen's time no real novelist had failed to take a substantial part of his schooling in the art from Fielding's achievement.

If the "moral problem" in Fielding still troubles us, it may be wise to turn back to it, if only to be sure that it is accurately defined. Both Richardson and Fielding had plainly and seriously declared their purpose to be moral. Richardson, however, was temperamentally a preacher. Fielding

was a student of "social behavior," and "social behavior" is the sense of
the Latin *mores,* which it is well to remember gives us our word "moral."
Richardson was also by nurture and long mental habit a puritan, and the
puritan's purity must be snow-white—whether or not he can live up to its
demands. Fielding was by birth and training a gentleman, and in the
gentleman's morality, in the eighteenth century, there was rather more
that a touch of unreflective pragmatism. That tended, as we have seen, to
create different standards for the different social orders, also for men and
for women. Fielding represented his class, as Richardson represented his.

Yet Fielding was not an apologist for careless promiscuity, and certainly not for sexual aggression. Tom Jones, who bears most of the blame
for Fielding's "immorality," is not a rake. There are three sexual adventures recorded for him, with Molly Seagrim, Mrs. Waters, and Lady Bellaston. In each instance the lady was the *provocatrice,* and quite sufficiently
experienced in amatory tactics.

In Tom's expostulation with Nightingale for having seduced the girl
he loved, Tom makes a distinction, clear and even rigid, between predatory love-making and the obligations of "gallantry"; and by implication
between gallantry and real affection. It is, however, a masculine distinction; and when Tom at the moment of his final reconciliation with Sophia
urges it as the excuse for his errant ways, Sophia will not admit it. "The
delicacy of your sex," cries Jones, "cannot conceive of the grossness of ours,
nor how little one sort of amour has to do with the heart." "I will never
marry a man," Sophia answers, "who shall not learn refinement enough
to be as incapable as I am myself of making such a distinction." Her
position is somewhat new and strange, as is evident in Tom's readiness to
offer his line of defense as though it called for forthright acceptance and
forgiveness. Sophia's attitude is in fact a repudiation of the double standard, and Tom's solemn promise to live up to her expectations must be
read as Fielding's sober judgment of the moral issue.

Sophia's word "refinement" in this connection carries a weight of
moral significance. It conveys the sense of Fielding's attitude upon many
moral issues besides that of sex. The distinction that Allworthy draws
between "those faults which candor may construe into imprudence and
those which can be deduced from villainy only" is a refined one—and
quite sanctionable. Tom's forgiveness of the injuries Blifil had done him
is refined. It would be priggish, even Pharisaical, if, his own weakness
having been excused, he failed in sympathy for the weakness of others.

In *Amelia* the purport of the story is plainly, even assertively, moral.
And again it raises honestly, and in the face of commonly accepted social
practice, the question whether a man should expect to live upon a distinct
plane of morality from a woman's. And the answer is unmistakable. The pli-

The only known portrait of Henry Fielding with any claim to actual authenticity, executed after his death from a sketch of Hogarth's believed to have been taken from a silhouette made during Fielding's lifetime. From the first volume of the first collected edition of Fielding's works, edited by Arthur Murphy, 1762. Engraved by James Basire after Hogarth.

able Captain Booth not only is brought to a decenter idea of marital obligation; his entire moral philosophy is broken down and reassembled—in the form of religious conviction. And in Booth's case as in Tom's, the notion that "gallantry" obliges a response to a woman's overtures is overturned. That was a rather courageous stand for a writer to take at that time.

The difficulty of settling these issues is largely the difficulty of defining them. The morality of a book can be judged only by its effect upon the reader—certainly not by its pretensions to morality or its asseverations of moral purpose. Is it honestly to be thought that *Tom Jones* or *Amelia* could make a good man or a good woman evil?

At the same time we must recognize that in the course of his career as a writer of fiction Fielding's own moral stature had grown. It is only in a limited sense that *Shamela* is a moral document. For even though its aim is honest ridicule of moral pretension, it is undeniably ribald. The Lady Booby episodes in *Joseph Andrews* are less objectionable to the "delicate" taste. In *Tom Jones,* however, there is emphasized in Allworthy's little sermon in the last book a defense of sexual purity; and point is made of the fact that although the robust young hero has yielded to temptation, he has not created temptation for any unwary woman.

Finally, in *Amelia,* Booth's early escapade with Miss Matthews is not deprecated with a wink, as the Seagrim and Waters episodes are in *Tom Jones*; it is a matter of prompt and deep penitence for Booth, and he is constantly troubled by the shame of ignoble concealment. Apart from that episode, the purport of the story is uncompromisingly and insistently moral. When Fielding toward the end of the story propounds that curious doubt as to whether Mrs. Atkinson, posing as Amelia, has granted the "last favor" to the libidinous noble lord, in order to secure a commission for her husband, it is with no half-amused glance at feminine duplicity or frailty, and certainly with no purpose of raising a really arguable issue of conscience. It is to contrast a resolute with an irresolute virtue, to the discredit of the latter. The sequence of the four fictions (setting aside *Jonathan Wild* as a moral treatise of another order) is a progress in moral certitude.

Fielding's reputation, no doubt, has suffered, as certainly Voltaire's did, from the compounding of inferences rooted in deep moral or religious prejudices. If a man wrote a questionable book, he must be a bad man, and if he was a bad man, then anything he wrote must be wicked. Wilbur Cross's life of Fielding has done much to clear Fielding on evidential grounds of the personal disrepute for which his first biographer, Arthur Murphy, was originally responsible. The question remains : were his books immoral? The only answer is to be found in the way they affect a normal and normally honest reader.

CHAPTER VIII

Sad Dogs and Saints

Tobias Smollett

ONE THINKS of the formula of a novel by Smollett*—always excepting
Humphry Clinker—as a mixture of wayside encounters, night adventures
at inns, coffee-house quarrels, puerile practical jokes, *chroniques scandaleuses,* politician's levees, gambling, cudgel-fighting, occasional duels,
trivial amours, influence-peddling, fortune-hunting, stories of abandoned
women, debtor's prisons, excursions into criticism, coxcombry, arrogant
egotism, and late repentance, all held together by a frail thread of plot,
and ending in a happy settlement of all the unheroic hero's problems by a
very landslide of wealth, with social resurrrection and marriage to a charming and inflexibly constant young lady who is virginal to the deepest recesses of her thought. They are, in fact, somewhat incongruous blends of
picaresque adventure and romantic sentiment, popular in the most literal
sense—made for the people—but declining in vogue as picaresque and
sentimental motives both fell into desuetude.

Yet these agglomerations of crude story material, undigested and un-
arranged, have, incident by incident, an undeniable vitality, and in the
aggregate an equally undeniable resemblance to the formlessness of life
itself. That, no doubt, is why Fielding, Fanny Burney, and Scott had
good words (though not always unqualified) for Smollett. That is also why
we discern the shadow of Smollett in so much gentler fictions as *Pickwick
Papers* and *Pendennis.*

A purposely picaresque novel was seldom touched with concern for the
primary virtues. Smollett's earliest novels, *Roderick Random* and *Peregrine Pickle* took their pattern from perhaps the best of the rogue romances, Lesage's *Gil Blas.* Lesage's novel, however, was "pure type." Smollett proposed, in his preface to *Roderick Random,* to ask for, and to earn,

---

*Tobias Smollett (1721-1771). *Roderick Random,* 1748; *Peregrine Pickle,* 1751; *Ferdinand,
Count Fathom,* 1753; *Sir Launcelot Greaves,* 1762; *The History and Adventures of an Atom,*
1769; *The Expedition of Humphry Clinker,* 1771.

the reader's compassion, and "that generous indignation which ought to animate the reader against the sordid and vicious disposition of the world."

The words suggest a temperamental bias. Smollett's rogue is to be a rogue, by nature, excess of spirits, and a fondness for rough play—the accepted image of the *picaro*. But Smollett makes him also a victim of society, and his "knavery and foibles" are to voice his resentment for the way the world has treated him. Putting aside for the moment the question whether Smollett succeeds in justifying his unfavorable opinion of society, we can at least note the reasons for his disgruntled feelings.

His own life was filled with adversity and (to his own mind) injustices. He coveted prestige, in literature, in politics, and in medicine—the last career more or less forced upon him. What limited recognition he gained was grudgingly given. He also had the misfortune to be a Scot on the London scene in the years following the union with England, when Englishmen generally looked upon the Scotch as uncouth and unpleasant distant relations. In literature, his early success as a novelist never matched Richardson's, and was promptly eclipsed by Fielding's. So there was on the whole reason enough in his life for feelings of indignity and humiliation. He became unfriendly, jealous, and finally misanthropic—and his writing inevitably reflected these propensities.

Smollett's jaundiced view of human nature and of society found expression in the most cutting form of comedy—satire. And his satire, like Swift's, made pretty liberal use of the physically revolting. Only a generation ago moving picture habitués were frantically amused by the violent contact of custard pies with human faces. Smollett had a penchant for that sort of humor, but instead of pies he favored the contents of chamber pots and closestools—or in one instance, the brains and gore of a sailor whose head had just been carried off by a cannon ball in a naval skirmish. Through his novels we get frequently a pungent sense of the nasty realities of a life into which modern plumbing and personal cleanliness had not yet introduced the physical amenities. His amused description of sewage disposal in the Edinburgh High Street and his grim recital of the all but incredible filthiness of the sick berth on a British man-of-war (both in *Roderick Random*) are rather nauseating to a modern reader. But to Smollett's contemporaries they were simply records of crude fact that could be disregarded if one held his nose, or laughed off if one's senses were not over-delicate. They might, and sometimes did, excite indignation, but they were too familiar to excite disgust.

This was a memorable age in the art of caricature, the graphic method of attacking vices and social inequities by realistic depiction of their physical symbols or by wild exaggeration. Smollett's art is in its own domain exactly of a piece with that of the great caricaturists—Hogarth, and later, Gilray and Rowlandson. The corrective purpose in caricature can, however, be taken too seriously. Behind the caricature, and behind Smollett's writing, there is an appreciable didactic aim, but its impulse is creative expression. Perhaps we might add that the greater the exaggeration, the greater is the artistic gusto, and the feebler the remedial purpose.

Smollett, like Richardson, declares his moral intention in his preface to *Roderick Random* :

> The reader gratifies his curiosity in pursuing the adventures of a person in whose favor he is prepossessed; he espouses his cause; he sympathises with him in distress; his indignation is heated against the author of his calamity; the human passions are inflamed; the contrast between dejected virtue and insulting vice appears with greater aggravation; and every impression having a double force on the imagination, the memory retains the circumstance, and the heart improves by the example.

But does the intention insure the result? Richardson has been repeatedly accused of hypocrisy in declaring his moral intention and then dwelling upon the physical details of a scene of seduction or attempted violation. Unlike Richardson, however, Smollett is not notably concerned with the techniques of sexual aggression. His offense—if it is an offense—is simply nastiness, and it is defended implicitly on the ground that one cannot reach the impressionable senses of the finicky-minded except by direct assault upon the senses.

This argument applies equally to Smollett's handling of human nature. He refuses to fit his characters into preconceived ideas of goodness, of wisdom, even of everyday discretion. The heroes of all his novels of the picaresque type have an aura of greed, parasitism, disloyalty, hypocrisy, rancor, and in general mean and usually ineffectual opportunism. And in this catalogue of inverted virtues, taken over from the older picaresques, their bold and hungry sexuality seems only a minor and venial taint. Are these propensities defects of personality, grafted upon essentially sound character by bad social influences, or are they rooted in the very nature of the young man? The answer must concede something on both sides of the question. Smollett's young men are not nice, either by nature or by social conditioning. But whatever their characteristic defects, Smollett makes the point that they could be nicer than they are, given the right influences; and the best possible influence he conceives as the character and example of a perfect young lady—perfect indeed, even to the most delicate shades of thought and conduct. This profound contrast between the sad dog and the saint is, of course, Smollett's concession to sentiment—

the reprobate's idolatrous fancy of the "pure woman"—yet not so very different from Richardson's, from Fielding's, and from those of a generation of novelists to follow.

Roderick Random is in some part autobiographic, at least in its depiction of Roderick's childhood, education, and early youth. It is also commonly accepted that the character and propensities of its hero are in some degree self-portraiture; but that is a matter of inference.

Its theme and its structure show items of inheritance from many literary sources, principally, as we have noted, from the picaresque. But it shows other family resemblances, to *Don Quixote,* to the sentimental drama and novel of the earlier part of the century, to the *chronique scandaleuse,* to the society novel, so far as that had been developed, to the French romances of the late seventeenth century, and to the novel of manners. So this novel shows, like all of Smollett's fiction, a highly complex inheritance.

The continuity of the story can be briefly summarized. A young man of decent family, but without family backing, comes to London to make his place in the world of wealth and fashion. His character can be simply described as the eighteenth-century version of the swashbuckler—braggart, provocateur, adventurer, fortune-hunter, and ladies' man so far as he can impose upon the credulity and the pliancy of the gentler sex. That he is not thoroughly bad must be taken for granted; for Smollett conceives him as in a definite sense a hero. The people he encounters are as various as his adventures—gamesters, seamen, women of the ancient trade, highwaymen, dealers in influence, sharks both male and female, sexual deviants, politicians lavish with false promises, spongers, and bailiffs. After wasting a substantial inheritance in the most obvious ways, he finally embarks upon a series of desperate ventures to retrieve his fortune, which all end in insolvency both material and moral. Out of this morass of error and waste he is finally dragged by the heroine, whom he has worshipped at a distance for half the length of the story, and who is virtue and sanity personified—except for her unaccountable affection for this half-mature and half-sincere scapegrace.

But there are major episodes which save the story from the curse of aimlessness and triviality. The most memorable is the third of the work which recounts Roderick's service as surgeon's mate on a British man-of-war—an appointment which he had sought fruitlessly through influence and bribery, but which falls to him through a stroke of unrecognized luck when he is shanghaied by a press gang. These chapters have actual historical importance as an exposure of the abuses and cruelties of the enlisted man's life and the all but unbelieveable ignorance and incapacity of the naval command.

Commodore Trunnion and Lieutenant Hatchway; from the fourth edition (the first illustrated edition) of Smollett's *Adventures of Peregrine Pickle*, London, 1769. Engraved by Charles Grignon after Henry Fuseli.

Another significant episode, of a type already familiar in the *chroniques scandaleuses,* and to be matched again in *Peregrine Pickle,* and in Fielding's novels, is the interpolated story of her life told by Roderick's casual acquaintance, Miss Williams. These interpolated biographies, or "little histories," have an almost standard pattern : the descent of a woman of some breeding through seduction and abandonment to prostitution, poverty, and social repudiation. In Miss Williams' case the downward drift is carried still further—to disease, attempted suicide, and imprisonment. If "good taste" is still recognized in our free and easy society, perhaps Smollett can be convicted of an error in taste in employing this Miss Williams as intermediary in Roderick's courtship of the guileless Narcissa. But then Roderick's own gallantry is of the ambiguous order, since he is quite ready to punctuate the rapturous passages in this idealized attachment with passing whoredoms.

What is still enjoyable in *Roderick Random* is its rugged characters and its vigorous action. Two character types which are to become familiar in Smollett's later work—and in Fielding's—are Roderick's rough and ready but kindly patron, his uncle Tom Bowling, and Strap, his valet and companion, and predecessor of the devoted followers who act in every capacity from body servant to money lender and philosopher-counselor for both Smollett's and Fielding's young sparks.

Peregrine Pickle is a better novel, though it is cast in precisely the same mold. The character set shows little change from that of *Roderick Random.* Peregrine is another Roderick; Commodore Trunnion is a more peppery Tom Bowling; Emilia is Narcissa warmed over; Pipes is a less exalted Strap; Lady Vane is a socially superior Miss Williams. The supernumerary characters give us the same noble lords, repainted for a new story, the same ladies of the *ton* and ladies of the town, the same highwaymen, bawds, gamblers, tradesmen's heiresses up for auction in the marriage market, and financially deflated gentlemen competing to annex them, the same greedy politicians, innkeepers, and footmen.

The fabric of the story is also curiously alike in the two novels; but there is more stuff in *Peregrine Pickle.* The superiority of *Peregrine* rests in part also upon a moderate change in tone. Peregrine's character is perhaps no less devious than Roderick's, but his doings are a little less bumptious and futile. Like Roderick, Peregrine has his way to make in the fashionable world, but with a better stock of advantages—if an excess of spending money and a lazy year or so at the University are to be regarded as advantages. So while Roderick has been very much the sport of adversity, Peregrine is permitted to go to the devil with all sails out.

Peregrine is not a gentleman, not even of the homespun variety. He thinks he is, but he is in truth a swaggerer, a pretender, and a good deal of a bully. Let us look at him as he waves his questionable credentials in the faces of society.

It was not long before he made himself remarkable for his spirit and humor, which were so acceptable to the bucks of the university that he was admitted as a member of their corporation, and in a very little time became the most conspicuous personage of the whole fraternity; not that he valued himself upon his ability in smoking the greatest number of pipes, and drinking the largest quantity of ale; these were qualifications of too gross a nature to captivate his refined ambition. He piqued himself upon his talent for raillery, his genius and taste, his personal accomplishments, and his success at intrigue; nor were his excursions confined to the small villages in the neighborhood, which are commonly visited once a week by the students for the sake of carnal recreation; he kept his own horses, traversed the whole country in parties of pleasure, attended all the races within fifty miles of Oxford, and made frequent jaunts to London, where he used to lie incognito during the best part of many a term.

The rules of the university were too severe to be observed by a youth of his vivacity, and therefore he became acquainted with the proctor by times. But all the checks he received were insufficient to moderate his career; he frequented taverns and coffee-houses, committed midnight frolics in the streets, insulted all the sober and pacific class of his fellow-students; the tutors themselves were not sacred from his ridicule; he laughed at the magistrate, and neglected every particular of college discipline.

Smollett sums up his qualifications for a future in society with the observation that he was "in the utmost hazard of turning out a most egregious coxcomb." But his meteoric transit across the Oxford firmament is snuffed out by Trunnion's decision to send him abroad; a decision warmly seconded by his tutors. The change in Trunnion's plan for making him a gentleman has resulted from Peregrine's allowing himself to fall deeply in love—a course which Trunnion can approve only if he is fully informed of the lady's eligibility, both personally and as to her social standing and fortune. Smollett, not satisfied, as Richardson was, with leaving it to the reader to fill out the portrait from his own notions of beauty and charm, presents Emilia as she first appears in Peregrine's eyes.

She seemed to be of his own age, was tall, and though slender, exquisitely shaped; her hair was auburn, and in such plenty that the barbarity of dress had not been able to prevent it from shading both sides of her forehead, which was high and polished. The contour of her face was oval, her nose very little raised into the aquiline form, that contributed to the spirit and dignity of her aspect. Her mouth was small, her lips plump, juicy, and delicious; her teeth regular and white as the driven snow, her complexion delicate and glowing with health, and her full blue eyes beamed forth vivacity and love. Her mien was at the same time commanding and engaging, her address perfectly genteel, and her whole appearance so captivating that our young Adonis looked, and was overcome. . . .

If he was charmed with her appearance, he was quite ravished with her discourse, which was sensible, spirited, and gay. Her frank and sprightly demeanor excited his own confidence and good humor. . . . In short, they seemed to relish each other's conversation, during which our young Damon acquitted himself with great skill in all the duties of gallantry. He laid hold of proper opportunities to express his admiration of her charms, had recourse to the silent rhetoric of tender looks, breathed divers insidious sighs, and attached himself wholly to her during the remaining part of the entertainment.

The interruptions to the course of true love are drawn from the common stock of playwrights and romancists—a misunderstanding caused by the miscarriage of a letter, a cudgel fight with a rival, a duel with no less a person than Emilia's brother Godfrey followed by a warm and lasting friendship, a tiff and reconciliation with his doting uncle, and finally, his departure for the Continent attended by a "governor," Mr. Jolter, and a French valet. Our summary skips quite a collection of japes and escapades.

The Continent—in particular Paris—is the perfect arena for the activities that Peregrine has found most absorbing. In spite of his "fervent vows of eternal constancy" to Emily, he has an observant interest in female faces and forms and a responsive ogle for the roving eye. One sample, perhaps fortunately brief, will serve to illustrate the spirit of Peregrine's most typical encounters :

They were no sooner settled in these lodgings than our hero wrote to his uncle an account of their safe arrival, and sent another letter to his friend Gauntlet [Emilia's brother] with a very tender billet enclosed for his dear Emilia, to whom he repeated all his former vows of constancy and love.

The next care that engrossed him was that of bespeaking several suits of clothes suitable to the French mode, and in the meantime he never appeared abroad, except in the English coffee-house, where he soon became acquainted with some of his own countrymen who were at Paris on the same footing with himself. The third evening after his journey he was engaged in a party of those young sparks at the house of a noted traiteur, whose wife was remarkably handsome, and otherwise extremely well qualified for alluring customers to her house. To this lady our young gentleman was introduced as a stranger fresh from England, and he was charmed with her personal accomplishments, as well as with the freedom and gaiety of her conversation. Her frank deportment persuaded him that she was one of those kind creatures who granted favors to the best bidder; on this supposition, he began to be so importunate in his addresses that the fair bourgeoise was compelled to cry aloud in defense of her own virtue. Her husband ran immediately to her assistance, and finding her in a very alarming situation, flew upon her ravisher with such fury that he was fain to quit his prey and turn against the exasperated traiteur, whom he punished without mercy for his impudent intrusion. The lady, seeing her yoke-fellow treated with so little respect, espoused his cause, and fixing her nails in his antagonist's face, scarified all one side of his nose. The noise of this encounter brought all the servants of the house to the rescue of their master, and Peregrine's company opposing them, a general battle ensued in which the French were totally routed, the wife insulted, and the husband kicked downstairs.

The publican, enraged at the indignity that had been offered to him and his family, went out into the street and implored the protection of the *guet* or city guard, which, having heard his complaint, fixed their bayonets and surrounded the door, to the number of twelve or fourteen. The young gentlemen, flushed with their success, and considering the soldiers as so many London Watchmen, whom they had often put to flight, drew their swords and sallied out, with Peregrine at their head. Whether the guard respected them as foreigners, or inexperienced youths intoxicated with liquor, they opened to right and left and gave them room to pass without opposition. This complaisance, which was the effect of compassion, being misinterpreted by the English leader, he out of mere wantonness attempted to trip up the heels of the soldier who stood next him, but failed in the execution and received a blow on his breast with the butt-end of his fusil that made him stagger several paces backward. Incensed at this audacious application, the whole company charged the detachment sword in hand, and after an obstinate engagement, in which divers wounds were given and received, every soul of them was taken and conveyed to the main-guard. The commanding officer, being made acquainted with the circumstances of the quarrel, in consideration of their youth and natural ferocity, for which the French make large allowances, set them all at liberty, after having gently rebuked them for the irregularity and insolence of their conduct; so that all that our hero acquired by his gallantry and courage was a number of scandalous marks upon his visage that confined him a whole week to his chamber.

The liveliness of Paris, its liberal opportunities for indulging his amours and exploiting his bravado, begin to have their effects upon Peregrine's hitherto healthy conscience. His conceit of himself, which had never been hampered much by native modesty, flourishes in this climate, and at length he even begins to wonder whether he is not throwing away his worldly wisdom and his prospects in continuing to pay court to the gentle Emilia.

We can omit a long digression—over a fifth of the entire work—in which Peregrine parades his self-sufficiency in company with a physician and a painter. Peregrine himself is at times bored by the two; so it is not surprising that their diversions seem to the average reader about as entertaining as the *Congressional Record*. Most of the episodes which make up this digression recall Cervantes, Lesage, Rabelais, and Chaucer at his merriest, but they are dim echoes. They lack the compactness and incisiveness that are the salt of the traditional novella.

One of the trio's more graceless escapades, at the expense of a prince of the blood, results in imprisonment, from which they are released by the intervention of the British ambassador, on the condition that they leave Paris within three days. So they are promptly on the road back to England via the Low Countries, with, of course, opportunities for intrigue and disturbance on the way. After a short stay in London, Peregrine takes the first occasion to visit Commodore Trunnion at his "castle." It is now time for him to renew his addresses to Emilia, but the spirit of his suit is, as we have already hinted, considerably altered, in spite of the fact that Trunnion has by this time withdrawn his opposition to it.

> When he arrived at the door, instead of undergoing that perturbation of spirits which a lover in his interesting situation might be supposed to feel, he suffered no emotion but that of vanity and pride, favored with an opportunity for self-gratification, and entered his Emilia's apartment with the air of a conceited *petit maitre,* rather than of the respectful admirer when he visits the object of his passion after an absence of seventeen months.

There is, happily, enough of the coquette in Emilia to confront Peregrine's assurance with her own proper pride. When at length he is left alone with her,

> instead of that awful veneration which her presence used to inspire, that chastity of sentiment and delicacy of expression, he now gazed upon her with the eyes of a libertine; he glowed with the impatience of desire, talked in a strain which barely kept within the bounds of decency, and attempted to snatch such favors as she, in the tenderness of mutual acknowledgement, had once vouchsafed to bestow.
>
> Grieved and offended as she was at this palpable alteration in his carriage, she disdained to remind him of his former deportment, and

with dissembled good humor rallied him on the progress he had made
in gallantry and address. But far from submitting to the liberties he
would have taken, she kept her person sacred from his touch, and
would not even suffer him to ravish a kiss of her fair hand; so that he
reaped no other advantage from the exercise of his talents during this
interview, which lasted a whole hour, than that of knowing he had
overrated his own importance, and that Emily's heart was not a gar-
rison likely to surrender at discretion.

Disappointed, but still conceitedly confident, Peregrine puts off his
pursuit of Emilia until a more favorable opportunity. With Emilia's brother he sets out for Bath, where the two contrive a scheme, successful in
the outcome, to expose and undo a band of gamesters living upon the
habitués of the spa. This success earns them a moment of social glory and
surrounds them with admiring ladies of all ages and conditions. Peregrine,
however, "exclusive of his attachment to Emily, which was stronger than
he himself imagined, possessed such a share of ambition as could not be
satisfied with the conquest of any female at Bath." In the course of his
sojourn here Peregrine picks up a new acquaintance, Cadwallader Crab-
tree, a misanthrope, pretendedly deaf, who becomes his confidant and
often his companion throughout the remainder of the story. But the stay
at Bath is cut short by the news that Commodore Trunnion is upon his
deathbed. Peregrine arrives at the castle in time to hear his parting words :

"Swab the spray from your bowsprit, my good lad, and coil up your
spirits. You must not let the toplifts of your heart give way because
you see me ready to go down at these years. Many a better man has
foundered before he has made half my way, thof I trust by the mercy
of God I shall be sure in port in a very few glasses, and fast moored
in a most blessed riding; for my good friend Jolter hath overhauled
the journal of my sins, and by the observation he hath taken of the
state of my soul, I hope I shall happily conclude my voyage and be
brought up in the latitude of Heaven. . . . This cursed hiccup makes
such a rippling in the current of my speech that mayhap you don't
understand what I say. Now, while the sucker of my wind-pump
will go, I would willingly mention a few things which I hope you will
set down in the log-book of your remembrance when I am stiff, d'ye
see. There's your aunt, sitting whimpering by the fire : I desire you will
keep her tight, warm, and easy in her old age; she's an honest heart
in her own way; and thof she goes a little crank and humorsome by
being often overstowed with Nantes and religion, she has been a faithful shipmate to me, and I dare say never turned in with another man
since we first embarked in the same bottom. . . .
    "As for that young woman, Ned Gauntlet's daughter, I'm informed

as how she's an excellent wench and has a respect for you; whereby, if you run her on board in an unlawful way, I leave my curse upon you, and trust you will never prosper in the voyage of life. But I believe you are more of an honest man than to behave so much like a pirate. I beg of all love you wool take care of your constitution, and beware of running foul of harlots, who are no better than so many mermaids, who sit upon rocks in the sea and hang out a fair face for the destruction of passengers; thof I must say for my own part, I never met with any of those sweet singers, and yet I have gone to sea for the space of thirty years. But howsomever, steer your course clear of all such brimstone bitches. ... Let me be carried to the grave by my own men, rigged in the black caps and white shirts which my barge's crew were wont to wear; and they must keep a good lookout that none of your pilfering rascallions may come and heave me up again for the lucre of what they can get, until the carcase is belayed by a tombstone. As for the motto, or what you call it, I leave that to you and Mr. Jolter, who are scholars; but I do desire that it may not be engraved in the Greek or Latin lingoes, and much less in the French, which I abominate, but in plain English, that when the angel comes to pipe all hands at the great day, he may know that I am a British man, and speak to me in my mother tongue. And now I have no more to say but God in Heaven have mercy upon my soul, and send you all fair weather, wherever you are bound."

Trunnion's death leaves Peregrine better off to the extent of £30,000, a great fortune for the times. His first impulse is to put a substantial part of the sum into a chariot and six and to set up again in highly fashionable style in London. There he contemplates adding further to his importance by marrying an heiress or a widow of title. But this is only half his planning.

In the midst of these chimerical calculations, his passion for Emilia did not subside, but on the contrary began to rage with such an inflammation of desire that her idea began to interfere with every other reflection, and absolutely disabled him from prosecuting the other lofty schemes which his imagination had projected. He therefore laid down the honest resolution of visiting her in all the splendor of his situation, in order to practice upon her virtue with all his art and address, to the utmost extent of his influence and fortune. Nay, so effectually had his guilty passion absorbed his principles of conscience, honor, and humanity, and regard for the Commodore's last words, that he was base enough to rejoice at the absence of his friend Godfrey, who being then with his regiment in Ireland, could not dive into his purpose or take measures for frustrating his vicious design.

He is on the point of setting out for Emilia's home, "in his chariot and six, attended by his *valet de chambre* and two footmen," when he discovers her one night in a box at the playhouse, dressed plainly, with an unimpressive young woman at her side. Smollett handles their encounter extremely well, although without dialogue, a deficiency in his narrative technique of which modern readers are often uncomfortably sensible.

Emilia, quite aware that his once natural and fresh affection for her has become tainted by affectation and ulterior motive, holds him at a polite distance. The relations of the two lovers drift along for a time, Peregrine studying to overwhelm Emilia by his fashion and consequence; she still all eyes and ears for the object of her heart, but sheltered by her understanding and discretion.

The situation draws rapidly to a climax when she consents to accompany him to a masquerade at the Haymarket. Here he plies her with wine takes advantage of her high spirits, and carries her in a closed carriage, not back to her uncle's house, but to a bagnio. It is all in the mode of Richardson's standard program of seduction. But Emilia wakes to the situation, and rather strikingly takes command of it. She is no mild and tremulous Clarissa. Peregrine falls into the fatal tactical error of trying to further his purpose by argument :

> "Divine creature," cried he, seizing her hand and pressing it to his lips, "it is from you alone I hope for that condescension which would overwhelm me with transports of celestial bliss. The sentiments of parents are sordid, silly, and confined. Seek not, then, to subject my passion to such low restrictions as were calculated for the purposes of common life. My love is too delicate and refined to wear those golden fetters which serve only to destroy the merit of voluntary affection and to upbraid a man incessantly with the articles of compulsion under which he lies. My dear angel, spare me the mortification of being compelled to love you, and reign sole empress of my heart and fortune. I will not affront you so much as to talk of settlements; my all is at your disposal. In this pocketbook are notes to the amount of two thousand pounds; do me the pleasure to accept of them; tomorrow I will lay ten thousand more in your lap. In a word, you shall be mistress of my whole estate, and I shall think myself happy in living dependent on your bounty."

Heavens! What were the emotions of the virtuous, the sensible, the tender Emilia's heart when she heard this insolent declaration from the mouth of a man whom she had honored with her affection and her esteem. It was not simply horror, grief, or indignation that she felt in consequence of this unworthy treatment, but the united pangs of all together, which produced a sort of hysteric laugh while she told him she could not help admiring his generosity.

Deceived by this convulsion, and the ironical compliment that attended it, the lover thought that he had already made great progress in his operations, and that it was now his business to storm the fortress by a vigorous assault, that he might spare her the confusion of yielding without resistance. Possessed by this vain suggestion, he started up, and folding her in his arms began to obey the furious dictate of his ungenerous desire. With an air of cool determination she demanded a parley; and when upon her repeated request he granted it, addressed herself to him in these words, while her eyes gleamed with all the dignity of the most awful resentment. "Sir, I scorn to upbraid you with a repetition of your former vows and protestations, nor will I recapitulate the little arts you have practised to ensnare my heart; because though by dint of the most perfidious dissimulation you have found means to deceive my opinion, your utmost efforts have never been able to lull the vigilance of my conduct, or to engage my affection beyond the power of discarding you without a tear whenever my honor should demand such a sacrifice. Sir, you are unworthy of my concern or my regret, and that sigh that now struggles from my breast is the result of sorrow for my own want of discernment. As for your present attempt upon my chastity, I despise your power as I detest your intention. Though under the mask of the most delicate respect you have decoyed me from the immediate protection of my friends, and contrived other stratagems to ruin my peace and reputation, I confide too much in my own innocence and the authority of the law to admit one thought of fear, much less, to sink under the horror of this shocking situation into which I have been seduced. Sir, your behavior is upon this occasion in all respects low and contemptible; for, ruffian as you are, you durst not harbor the thought of executing your execrable scheme while you knew my brother was near enough to prevent or revenge the insult; so that you must not only be a treacherous villain but also a most despicable coward." Having expressed herself in this manner, with a most majestic severity of aspect she opened the door, and walking downstairs with surprising resolution, committed herself to the care of a watchman, who accommodated her with a hackney chair, in which she was safely conveyed to her uncle's house.

Peregrine, brought at least partially to his senses, tries in every way, but in vain, to re-establish himself in her confidence. He is for a time prostrated by disappointment and chagrin. In time recovered, he resolves to "plunge himself headlong into some intrigue that might engage his passions and amuse his imagination." The depth of his demoralization is sufficiently clear in a comment of his friend Crabtree to one of the ladies to whom he is now paying court:

"Were I an absolute prince, and that fellow one of my subjects, I would order him to be clothed in sack-cloth, and he should drive my asses to water, that his lofty spirit might be lowered to the level of his deserts. The pride of a peacock is downright self-denial when compared with the vanity of that coxcomb."

There follows an intrigue from which evolves "The Memoirs of a Lady of Quality." This is, on good evidence, the story of an actual woman of fashion, written by herself, for which Smollett accepted pay for inserting it in his novel. It is a briefer Roxana story, but in the high-society key of the mid-century. Although it occupies only a single chapter (LXXXI), it comprises a sixth of the entire novel. It is quite as interesting as other typical apologies for a life of dissipation, but no more so.

Then follows a conspiracy of Peregrine and Crabtree to impose on the credulity of society by posing as magicians and fortunetellers. It is downright nonsense, stuffed with childish "business" and leading nowhere. After the fading out of this project, Peregrine falls again upon the amusements of the town, but his appetite for its diversions is already cloying. Out of the general purposelessness of his life there emerges a chance to see Emilia once more, at the approaching marriage of her brother. It takes diplomacy, in fact some steady pressure from Godfrey and his fiancée, to induce Emilia to permit Peregrine to see her again, even on so auspicious an occasion. At the ceremony the two put on a show of indifference, but inevitably overplay their parts. Pretense reaches a climax when Peregrine in the course of a country dance touches Emilia's hand.

> The touch thrilled through all his nerves, and kindled a flame within him which he could not contain. In a word, his endeavors to conceal the situation of his thoughts were so violent that his constitution could not withstand the shock. The sweat ran down his forehead in a stream, the color vanished from his cheeks, his knees began to totter and his eyesight to fail; so that he must have fallen at his full length upon the floor, had not he retired very abruptly into another room, where he threw himself upon a couch and fainted. . . . Emilia . . . was so much alarmed that she could not stand, and was fain to have recourse to a smelling-bottle.

Peregrine is put to bed, and passes a sleepless night, but in the morning he appeals to Emilia's newly made sister-in-law, Sophy, to intercede for him. Sophy takes his letter to Emilia, who at first refuses to look at it, but she is reprimanded by her brother into compliance. She is obdurate, however, as to the point at issue. Her reply :

> She lamented her own fate in being the occasion of so much uneasiness, desired her brother to assure Mr. Pickle that she was not a

voluntary enemy to his peace; on the contrary, she wished him all happiness, though she hoped he would not blame her for consulting her own in avoiding any future explanation or connection with a person whose correspondence she found herself under a necessity to renounce.

Feelings are overheated, and for the time being there is nothing for Peregrine to do but leave the scene of his defeat, which he does with all-round misunderstanding, and ill feeling on the part of Emilia and her brother. When he leaves, it is with the resolve to find consolation as occasion might offer in the bosom of some fair sinner.

The occasion pops up promptly, and the incident which follows (Chapter LXXXVII) has a singular interest in that its theme and even details of incident are so closely parallel to those of Bernard Shaw's *Pygmalion* that it is scarcely possible to escape the thought that Henry Higgins' well-planned effort to achieve the classic experiment with the sow's ear is borrowed from Smollett. The scene in which the residues of vulgarity erupt through unassimilated fine manners is almost as devastatingly funny in Smollett's version as in Shaw's—and considerably more indecorous.

But to return—Peregrine is thrown back once more upon London and its opportunities. And now begins a course of deterioration in fortune, manners, and integrity which is no more nor less than a literary "rake's progress." It is unnecessary to enlarge upon the detail. He runs for Parliament, and is defeated, at great expense to himself; he loans money on false security, and loses it; he buys himself a stable, and throws away a fortune racing; he tries trade, and fails from inexperience and bad judgment; he goes security for a money lender, who absconds. He continues to attend upon the great, in expectation of some profit from their influence, but he is obliged to seek lower companions because he lacks the wherewithal to maintain his place among his fair-weather friends. He joins a club of hack writers, but their interests and conversation are too stale for his tastes. He is offered a bank note "for a considerable sum" by one of his old flames, and has grace enough to refuse it. That is the last step before he is arrested for debt and lodged in the Fleet—the debtors' prison.

After the darkness of these grim days there is a glimmer of dawn with a visit from Godfrey Gauntlet, who has discovered Peregrine's state, and has learned incidentally that the preferment that enabled him to marry his Sophy has come in the greater part through Peregrine's efforts. Understanding is quickly restored between the two friends, and this proves to be a turning point in Peregrine's fortunes. The final shower of blessings is profusion itself. First, a speculation in foreign trade which has been thought to have gone glimmering turns out to be successful. Peregrine has enough to pay his way out of prison, but since ,the debt for which he has suffered has been dishonestly pressed, he refuses to pay it, and continues in the Fleet the while he makes new and more discreet investments. Then— bless her—Emilia inherits £10,000 on the death of her favorite uncle, and an exchange of letters with Peregrine follows. Here is hers.

Sir,
    I have performed a sufficient sacrifice to my reputation, in retaining hitherto the appearance of that resentment which I had long ago dismissed; and as the late favorable change in my situation empowers me to avow my genuine sentiments without fear of censure or suspicion of mercenary design, I take this opportunity to assure you that if I still maintain that place in your heart which I was vain enough to think I once possessed, I am willing to make the first advances to an accommodation, and have actually furnished my brother with full powers to conclude it in the name of your appeased
Emilia.

And here is Peregrine's answer :

Madam,
    That I revere the dignity of your virtue with the utmost veneration, and love you infinitely more than life, I am at all times ready to demonstrate, but the sacrifice to honor it is now my turn to pay; and such is the rigor of my destiny that in order to justify your generosity, I must refuse to profit by your condescension. Madam, I am doomed to be forever wretched, and to sigh without ceasing for the possession of that jewel which, though now in my offer, I dare not enjoy. I shall not pretend to express the anguish that tears my heart whilst I communicate this fatal renunciation, but appeal to the delicacy of your own sentiments, which can judge of my sufferings, and will no doubt do justice to the self-denial of your forlorn
P. Pickle.

The obscurer implications of this solemn renunciation are not beyond Emilia's understanding; and she knows intuitively that a woman's great strength in argument is patience to assert tirelessly an attitude confidently taken. She "gradually decoys him into a literary correspondence," and resolves "to apply herself chiefly to the irresistible prepossessions of his love, which were not at all diminished or impaired by the essays of her pen." Yet even while Peregrine continues obstinately in his decision not to be a wife's dependent, fortune broadens her benign smile upon him. His father, from whom he has been estranged during most of his life, dies intestate, and after due process of law Peregrine will be, as eldest son, heir to an estate which will make the one he has already frittered away look like pocket money.

But no more frittering! Our hero—Smollett himself says he is a hero by this time—presents himself immediately at Emilia's home. There is a sort of *School for Scandal* screen scene from which Peregrine, to Emilia's surprise, emerges after overhearing her exclaim, "If ever I can catch the fugitive again, he shall sing in his cage for life." Peregrine is more than willing to become a singer. Emilia is not saddened by the prospect of Peregrine's hansome inheritance. Perhaps she knows that his ambitious scheme of life will call for it. The obvious remainder of the story is told in a few pages.

We have traversed the greater part of the plot of *Peregrine Pickle*; for what can be dignified with the name of plot is in truth little or nothing more than the love story of Emilia and Peregrine. But *Peregrine Pickle* is a story of action, and what we have had to leave out are the numberless doings, some mischievous, some atrocious, of Peregrine and his cronies. These were, beyond doubt, for most of Smollett's admirers the body and blood of the novel. They must be read just as Smollett presents them to discover their characteristic interest; and there are still many readers of Smollett who find them interesting.

Between the publication of *Peregrine Pickle* (1751) and of *Humphry Clinker* (1771) Smollett spent twenty years in soul-destroying and un-rewarded hack work—compilation and editing, intermitted by the writing of three inferior novels and two unsuccessful attempts at the writing of history.

Humphry Clinker (published under the title *The Expedition of Humphry Clinker*), which was written in the very shadow of death, is a more pleasing narrative than its predecessors. It is in letter form, recounting the travels over much of England and Scotland of a Welsh gentleman, Matthew Bramble, with his immediate family and their entourage of servants. Bramble is an imaginary invalid, and their route of travel is a circuit of some of the health resorts of the period. The character-set in itself implies a departure from the rough and arrogant action of the earlier novels. Here we find, in spite of the ever-present satire of Smollett, kindliness and sympathy, a far more composed view of life, and a quieter humor. There remain vestiges of the extravagance of the earlier novels, but moderated almost to the point of realism. Of all Smollett's novels, the one that shows him at his best as a novelist is *Peregrine Pickle*. But *Humphry Clinker,* if it *is* a novel, is the one that shows Smollett's artistic resources at their best.

The principals of the story, apart from Bramble himself, are his spinster sister Tabitha, middle-aged and a desperate man-hunter; an impressionable niece in her teens, Lydia Melford, gentle and good, but twitching with vaguely conscious romantic urges; her brother, an Oxford undergraduate with quite sufficient undergraduate assurance; and lastly, a natural but unconscious generator of comedy, Humphry Clinker himself, who is introduced in rags and taken into Bramble's service, but will turn out to be the child of a youthful indiscretion of Bramble's. For the moment we can pass over the Scot Lismahago, an original of the first water and one of the most enjoyable serio-comic characters that the eighteenth century produced.

We are going to skip the story sequence of *Humphry Clinker* because the merits of the work rest not on its plot, but upon the amusing breadth and diversity of incident and characters. These include original yet wholly credible human beings, enjoyable scenic background (something almost new in fiction), running commentary upon the society, economy, and politics of the time, recurrent comedy of not too boisterous a sort, and prevailing good nature and good humor.

In Smollett's novels, speaking at large, whatever interest the characters possess for the reader is likely to attach to their limitations, or even to their downright defects. The characters in *Humphry Clinker* are described in large part through their abrasion upon one another, or through contrasted points of view that show through their judgments of the same situations and problems. Smollett does not trouble to tell us that Bramble is a gentleman mellowed by age and experience, that Lismahago is not quite a gentleman, embittered by age and experience, or that both have strong political prepossessions. He simply has them talk to each other. This is Bramble writing to his friend, Dr. Lewis, at home, of a conversation with Lismahago.

His manner is as harsh as his countenance; but his peculiar turn of thinking, and his pack of knowledge, made up of the remnants of rarities, rendered his conversation desirable in spite of his pedantry and ungracious address. I have often met with a crab-apple in a hedge which I have been tempted to eat for its flavor, even when I was disgusted by its austerity. The spirit of contradiction is naturally so strong in Lismahago that I believe in my conscience that he has rummaged and read and studied with indefatigable attention, in order to qualify himself to refute established maxims, and thus raise trophies for the gratification of polemical pride. Such is the asperity of his self-conceit that he will not even acquiesce in a transient compliment made to his own individual in particular, or to his country in general.

When I observed that he must have read a vast number of books to be able to discourse on such a variety of subjects he declared he had read little or nothing, and asked how he should find books among the woods of America, where he had spent the greatest part of his life. My nephew remarking that the Scotch in general were famous for their learning, he denied the imputation, and defied him to prove it from their works. "The Scotch," said he, "have a slight tincture of letters with which they make a parade among people who are more illiterate than themselves; but they may be said to float on the surface of science, and they have made very small advances in the useful arts."—"At least," cried Tabby, "all the world allows that the Scotch behaved gloriously in fighting and conquering the savages of America."—"I assure you, Madam, that you have been misinformed," replied the lieutenant; "in that continent the Scotch did nothing more than their duty; nor was there one corps in his Majesty's service that distinguished itself more than another. Those who affected to extol the Scotch for superior merit were no friends to that nation...."

Though he himself made free with his countrymen, he would not suffer any other person to glance a sarcasm at them with impunity. One of the company chancing to mention Lord B——'s inglorious peace, the Lieutenant immediately took up the cudgels in his lordship's favor, and argued very strenuously to prove that it was the most honorable and advantageous peace that England had ever made since the foundation of the monarchy. Nay, between friends, he offered such reasons on this subject that I was really confounded, if not convinced...

But the most hardy of this original's positions were these : That commerce would sooner or later prove the ruin of every nation where it flourishes to any extent—that the Parliament was the rotten part of the British constitution—that the liberty of the press was a national evil—and that the boasted institution of juries, as managed in England, was productive of shameful perjury and flagrant injustice....

You must not imagine that all these deductions were made on his part without contradiction on mine. No—the truth is, I found myself piqued in point of honor at his pretending to be so much wiser than his neighbors. I questioned all his assertions, started innumerable objections, argued and wrangled with uncommon perseverance, and grew very warm and even violent in the debate. Sometimes he was puzzled, and once or twice, I think, fairly refuted; but from those falls he rose again, like Antaeus, with redoubled vigor, 'til at length I was tired, exhausted, and really did not know how to proceed, when luckily he dropped a hint by which he discovered that he had been bred to the law, a confession which enabled me to retire from the dispute with good grace, as it could not be supposed that a man like me, who had been bred to nothing, should be able to cope with a veteran in his own profession. I believe, however, that I shall for some time continue to chew the cud of reflection upon many observations which this original discharged.

We find a similar mode of characterization in Matthew Bramble's and Lydia Melford's appraisals of the town and society of Bath and of life and activities in London, from which we quote. Are they really describing London or themselves? The first passage is by Bramble :

There are many causes which contribute to the daily increase of this enormous mass, but they may be all resolved into the grand source of luxury and corruption. About five and twenty years ago very few of even the most opulent citizens of London kept any equipage, or even any servants in livery. Their table produced nothing but plain boiled and roasted, with a bottle of port and a tankard of beer. At present, any trader in any degree of credit, every broker and attorney, maintain a couple of footmen, a coachman and postillion. He has his town-house and his country-house, his coach and his post-chaise. His wife and daughters appear in the richest stuffs, bespangled with diamonds. They frequent the court, the opera, the theatre, and the masquerade. They hold assemblies at their own houses; they make sumptuous entertainments, and treat with the richest wines of Bordeaux, Burgundy, and Champagne. The substantial tradesman, who wont to pass his evenings at the ale-house for fourpence halfpenny, now spends three shillings at the tavern, while his wife keeps card-tables at home. She must also have fine clothes, her chaise, or pad, with country lodgings, and go three times a week to public diversions. Every clerk, apprentice, or even waiter of a tavern or coffee-house maintains a gelding by himself or in partnership, and assumes the air and apparel of a petit-maitre. The gayest places of public entertainment are filled with fashionable figures, which upon inquiry will be found to be journeymen tailors, serving-men, and Abigails, disguised like their betters. . . .

The diversions of the times are not ill suited to the genius of this incongruous monster called *the public*; give it noise, confusion, glare and glitter, it has no idea of elegance and propriety. What are the amusements at Ranelagh? One half the company are following one another's tails, in an eternal circle, like so many blind asses in an olive-mill, where they can neither discourse, distinguish, nor be distinguished, while the other half are drinking hot water, under the denomination of tea, until nine or ten o'clock at night, to keep them awake for the rest of the evening. As for the orchestra, the vocal music especially, it is well for the performers that they cannot be heard distinctly. Vauxhall is a composition of baubles, overcharged with paltry ornaments, ill conceived and poorly executed, without any unity of design or propriety of disposition. It is an unnatural assemblage of objects, fantastically illuminated in broken masses, seemingly contrived to dazzle the eyes and divert the imagination of the vulgar. Here a wooden lion; there a stone statue! In one place a range of things like coffee-house boxes covered atop; in another, a parcel of ale-house benches; in a third a puppet representation of a tin cascade; in a fourth a gloomy cave of a circular form like a sepulchral vault half lighted; in a fifth a scanty slip of grass-plot that would not afford pasture sufficient for an ass's colt. The walks, which nature seems to have intended for solitude, shade, and silence, are filled with crowds of noisy people, sucking up the nocturnal rheums of an aguish climate; and through these gay scenes a few lamps glimmer like so many farthing candles. . . .

What temptation can a man of my turn and temperament have to live in a place where every corner teems with fresh objects of detestation and disgust? What kind of taste and organs must those people have who generally prefer the adulterated enjoyments of a town to the genuine pleasures of a country retreat?

Now mark the contrast [with country life] in London. I am pent up in frowzy lodgings, where there is not room enough to swing a cat, and I breathe the steams of endless putrefaction; and these would undoubtedly produce a pestilence if they were not qualified by the gross acid of sea-coal, which is itself a pernicious nuisance to lungs of any delicacy of texture. But even this boasted corrector cannot prevent those languid, sallow looks that distinguish the inhabitants of London from those ruddy swains that lead a country life. I go to bed after midnight, jaded and restless from the dissipations of the day. I start every hour from my sleep at the horrid noise of the watchmen bawling the hour through every street and thundering at every door, a set of useless fellows who serve no other purpose but that of disturbing the repose of the inhabitants; and by five o'clock I start out of bed in consequence of the still more dreadful alarm made by the country carts, and noisy rustics bellowing green peas under my window. If I would drink water, 1 must quaff the mawkish contents of an open aqueduct, exposed to all manner of defilement, or swallow that which comes from the River Thames, impregnated with all the filth of London and Westminster. Human excrement is the least offensive part of the concrete, which is composed of all the drugs, minerals, and poisons used in mechanics and manufactures, enriched with the putrefying carcasses of beasts and men and mixed with the scourings of all the wash-tubs, kennels, and common sewers within the bills of mortality. . . .

A companionable man will undoubtedly put up with many inconveniences for the sake of enjoying agreeable society. A facetious friend of mine used to say the wine could not be bad where the company were agreeable, a maxim, however, which ought to be taken *cum grano salis*. But what is the society of London that I should be tempted for its sake to mortify my senses and compound with such uncleanness as my soul abhors? All the people I see are too much engrossed with schemes of interest or ambition to have any room left for sentiment or friendship. Even in some of my old acquaintance those schemes and pursuits have obliterated all traces of our former connection. Conversation is reduced to party disputes and illiberal altercation, social commerce to formal visits and card-playing. If you pick up a diverting original by accident, it may be dangerous to amuse yourself by his oddities; he is generally a tartar at bottom—a sharper, a spy, or a lunatic. Every person you deal with endeavors to overreach you in the way of business. You are preyed upon by idle mendicants, who beg in the phrase of borrowing and live upon the spoils of the stranger. Your tradesmen are without conscience, your friends without affection, and your dependents without fidelity.

Now Lydia writes, upon the same topic :

The cities of London and Westminster are spread out to an incredible extent. The streets, squares, rows, lanes, and alleys are innumerable. Palaces, public buildings, and churches rise in every quarter, and among these last St. Paul's appears with the most astonishing pre-eminence. They say it is not so large as St. Peter's at Rome, but for my own part, I can have no idea of any earthly temple more grand and magnificent.

But even these superb objects are not so striking as the crowds of people that swarm in the streets. I at first imagined that some great assembly was just dismissed, and wanted to stand aside until the multitude should pass; but this human tide continued to flow without interruption or abatement from morning until night. Then there is such an infinity of gay equipages, coaches, chariots, chaises, and other carriages, continually rolling and shifting before our eyes that one's head grows giddy looking at them, and the imagination is quite confounded with splendor and variety. Nor is the prospect by water less grand and astonishing than that by land. You see three stupendous bridges joining the opposite banks of a broad, deep, and rapid river; so vast, so stately, so elegant, that they seem to be the work of the giants. Betwixt them, the whole surface of the Thames is covered with small vessels, barges, boats, and wherries passing to and fro; and below the three bridges such a prodigious forest of masts, for miles together, that you would think all the ships in the universe were here assembled. All that you read of wealth and grandeur, in The Arabian Nights Entertainments and the Persian Tales concerning Bagdad, Diarbekir, Damascus, Ispahan, and Samarkand, is here realized.

Ranelagh looks like the enchanted palace of a genie, adorned with the most excellent performances of painting, carving, and gilding, enlightened with a thousand golden lamps that emulate the noon-day sun; crowded with the great, the rich, the gay, the happy, and the fair; glittering with cloth of gold and of silver, lace, embroidery, and precious stones. While these exulting sons and daughters of felicity tread this round of pleasure, or engage in different parties in separate lodges, with fine imperial tea and other delicious refreshments, their ears are entertained with the most ravishing delights of music, both instrumental and vocal. There I heard the famous Tenducci, a thing from Italy. It looks for all the world like a man, though they say it is not. The voice, to be sure, is neither man's nor woman's, but it is more melodious than either; and it warbled so divinely that while I listened, I really thought myself in Paradise.

At nine o'clock, in a charming moonlight evening, we embarked at Ranelagh for Vauxhall, in a wherry so light and slender that we looked like so many fairies sailing in a nut-shell. . . . But the confusion of disembarkation was fully recompensed by the pleasures of Vauxhall, which I no sooner entered than I was dazzled and confounded by the variety of beauties that rushed all at once upon my eye. Image to yourself, my dear Letty, a spacious garden, part laid out in delightful walks, bounded with high hedges and trees and paved with gravel; and part exhibiting a wonderful assemblage of the most picturesque and striking objects, pavilions, lodges, groves, grottoes, lawns, temples, and cascades; porticos, collonades, and rotundas, adorned with pillars, statues, and painting, the whole illuminated with an infinite number of lamps, disposed in different figures of suns, stars, and constellations; the place crowded with the gayest company, ranging through those blissful shades or supping in different lodges on cold collations, enlivened with freedom, mirth, and good humor, and animated by an excellent band of music. Among the vocal performers, I had the happiness to hear Mrs.——, whose voice was so loud and so shrill that it made my head ache through excess of pleasure. . . .

Besides Ranelagh and Vauxhall, I have been at Mrs. Cornell's assembly, which, for the rooms, the company, the dresses and decorations, surpasses all description; but as I have no great turn for card-playing, I have not yet entered thoroughly into the spirit of the place. Indeed, I am still such a country hoyden that I could hardly find patience to be put into a condition to appear, yet I was not above six hours in the hands of the hair-dresser, who stuffed my head with as much black wool as would have made a quilted petticoat. And after all, it was the smallest head in the assembly, except my aunt's. She, to be sure, was so particular with her rumpt gown and petticoat, her scanty curls, her lappet head, deep triple ruffles and high stays, that everybody looked at her with surprise. Some whispered, and some tittered; and Lady Griskin, by whom we were introduced, flatly told her she was twenty good years behind the fashion. . . .

I wish my weak head may not grow giddy in the midst of all this gallantry and dissipation, though as yet, I can safely declare, I could gladly give up all these tumultuous pleasures for country solitude and a happy retreat with those we love, among whom my dear Willis will always possess the first place in the breast of her ever affectionate

Lydia Melford.

The two opposed views are a travesty upon two states of mind, the misanthropic (perhaps rather the hypochondriac) and the sentimental. They are also a piquant supplement to the social history of the period, which is one reason why we have quoted so generously. But they are above all effective, though indirect, characterization.

To me, the Scot Lismahago has seemed Smollett's best all-round achievement in character drawing. He has dimensions and depth, his own distinctive humor, and a latent satire that gives his most innocent remarks sometimes the weight of profound judgment. Probably no fictional character between the times of Swift and of Dickens has clothed so penetrating an analysis of the political and social scene in such apparently innocent exchanges of talk. He voices a good deal of the suppressed indignation that any intellectual Scot of that time might have felt toward England and the average Englishman. And Smollett never forgot that, for all his uncomfortable dependency upon English literary taste and fashion, he was after all a Scot.

Lismahago has been kicked around by life, and is not quite sweetly resigned; but in Smollett's way (and it is typical of his perversities) he is finally reconciled to his destiny by marriage to the aging, canting, querulous spinster Tabitha. It does not seem quite right, any more than the faithful Strap's marriage to his master's castoff mistress, Miss Williams. But Smollett is indifferent to aesthetic conformity, and has no respect whatever for poetic justice.

There is a resurgence of Smollett's Scotch memories in the scenic setting of the third quarter of the novel, after Squire Bramble's party has crossed the Tweed. They penetrate into the Highlands and find in the landscape, the life, and the people what they sought in vain in the fashionable British watering places. We are reminded inevitably of the tour that Johnson and Boswell took together into the Highlands and the Hebrides, and of which they both wrote their personal accounts. One has the feeling that Smollett's picture is more generously appreciative. Here are some of Matthew Bramble's impressions, a land-owner's and a gentleman farmer's, yet mellowed by something better than mere economic appraisal.

The Clyde we left a little on our left hand at Dunbritton, where it widens into an estuary or frith, being augmented by the influx of the Leven. On this spot stands the castle formerly called Algluyd, washed by these two rivers on all sides, except a narrow isthmus which at every spring-tide is overflowed. The whole is a great curiosity, from the quality and form of the rock, as well as from the nature of its situation. We now crossed the water of Leven, which, though nothing so considerable as the Clyde, is much more transparent, pastoral and delightful. This charming stream is the outlet of Loch Lomond, and through a tract of four miles pursues its winding course, murmuring over a bed of pebbles till it joins the Frith at Dunbritton. A very little above its source, on the lake stands the house of Cameron, belonging to Mr. Smollett, so embosomed in an oak wood that we did not see it till we were within fifty yards of the door. I have seen the Lago di Gardi, Albano, De Vico, Bolsena, and Geneva, and upon my honor, I prefer Loch Lomond to them all; a preference which is certainly owing to the verdant islands that seem to float upon its surface, affording the most inchanting objects of repose to the excursive view. Nor are the banks destitute of beauties, which even partake of the sublime. On this side they display a sweet supply of woodland, corn field, and pasture, with several agreeable villas emerging as it were out of the lake, till at some distance the prospect terminates in huge mountains covered with heath, which being in bloom, affords a very rich covering of purple. Everything here is romantic beyond imagination. This country is justly styled the Arcadia of Scotland; and I don't doubt but it may vie with Arcadia in everything but climate. I am sure it excels it in verdure, wood, and water. . . .

Notwithstanding the solitude that prevails among these mountains, there is no want of people in the Highlands. I am credibly informed that the Duke of Argyle can assemble five thousand men in arms, of his own clan and surname, which is Campbell. . . . I know of no other people in Europe who, without the use or knowledge of arms, will attack regular forces, sword in hand, if their chief will head them in battle. When disciplined, they cannot fail of being excellent soldiers. They do not walk like the generality of mankind, but trot and bound like deer, as if they moved upon springs. They greatly excel the Lowlanders in all the exercises that require agility. They are incredibly abstemious, and patient of hunger and fatigue; so steeled against the weather that in traveling, even when the ground is covered with snow, they never look for a house, or any other shelter but their plaid, in which they wrap themselves up, and go to sleep under the cope of Heaven. Such people, in quality of soldiers, must be invincible, when the business is to perform quick marches in difficult country, to strike sudden strokes, beat up the enemy's quarters, harass their cavalry, and perform expeditions without the formality of magazines, baggage, forage, and artillery.

The art of bringing scenery and environment within the circumference of the novel has been due in an importamt degree to Smollett's example. In the nature of things, it must always be a subordinate part of the interest; yet there are later novels, most of them romantic, in which this element contributes substantially to the quality of the story. It may be, of course, as it tended to become in Scott, a merely tedious exercise in description. But it takes on importance in the work of the Brontë sisters, Hardy, Butler, and Stevenson.

Perhaps equally important is Smollett's use of "essay passages." It was no innovation, for Defoe had exploited this feature, but generally in the way of flat moralizing. Bramble's letters have a sort of Addisonian roundness and dignity.

> For my part, I am shocked to find a man have sublime ideas in his head, and nothing but illiberal sentiments in his heart. The human soul will be generally found most defective in the article of candor. I am inclined to think no mind was ever wholly exempt from envy, which perhaps may have been implanted as an instinct essential to our nature. I am afraid we sometimes palliate this vice under the specious name of emulation. I have known a person who could not hear even a friend commended, without betraying signs of uneasiness, as if that commendation had implied an odious comparison to his prejudice; and every wreath of praise added to the other's character was a garland plucked from his own temples.

Smollett's humor is never pastel, but cut like a gargoyle out of the granite of human nature, preserving the hardness of its element. It seems in general to have a touch of primal savagery. But in *Humphry Clinker,* in spite of an outrageous jape or two (for which the likable characters are not responsible) the humor is prevailingly temperate and enjoyable. In this novel it is not always easy to distinguish humor from characterization; for it is likely to be implicit in character. In the earlier novels, it is more usually humor of situation—and oftener than not, physical.

In *Clinker* Smollett makes much of malapropisms, both Tabitha's and Winifred's. In this respect too, he is not an innovator, but his have a special interest because they are written, not spoken. Winifred Jenkins, Tabitha's maid, writes, "I have sullenly protested"; "She improves in grease and godliness"; "You have no deception of our doings at Bath"; "Twenty other odorous falsehoods." Some are simply misspellings, as *soot* for *suit, farting* for *farthing, Vails* for Wales (though Winifred is herself Welsh). Smollett's handling of the business is not always consistent, since in spite of these simple illiteracies, Winifred can spell, and use properly, such words as *creditable, lamentations, tabernacle,* and *indifferently,* any of which should prove an obstacle to a real illiterate.

A final word on *Humphry Clinker.* It would be hard to find an epistolary novel which makes better use of the letter medium. There are five correspondents—Bramble, his sister, the two young people, and the servant Winifred. The correspondence is one-sided—in general no answers are returned. The letters are intelligently differentiated as to the points of view of the various writers and the things that would naturally interest them. Although all but Winifred write pure eighteenth century, they have their own recognizable styles. The letters sound like letters, and they do not, as they frequently do in other early novelists, exceed what might be reasonably accomplished within the limits of time, space, and opportunity. Smollett also avails himself fully of the liberties inherent in the letter form. The letters may deviate from the straight path of plot and show an easy discursiveness that introduces diversions, anecdotes, little adventures, sketches of character, and opinions, all interesting in themselves. Could we imagine this, from the pen of the ingenuous Winifred, slipping into the sober lucubrations of one of Richardson's characters?

> As I was troubled with fits, she advised me to bathe in the loffe, which was holy water. And so I went in the morning to a private place, along with the house-maid, and we bathed in our birth-day soot, after the fashion of the country. And behold, whilst we dabbled in the loff, Sir George Coon started up with a gun; but we clapped our hands to our faces and passed by him to the place where we had left our smocks. A civil gentleman would have turned his head another way. My comfit is, he did not know which was which; and as the saying is, all cats in the dark are gray.

Or this, from our young Oxonian, a preview of golf as it is played today.

> Hard by, in the fields called the Links, the citizens of Edinburgh divert themselves at a game called golf, in which they use a curious kind of bats, tipt with horn, and small elastic balls of leather stuffed with feathers, rather less than tennis balls, but of a much harder consistence. This they strike with such force and dexterity from one hole to another, that they will fly to an incredible distance. Of this diversion the Scotch are so fond that when the weather will permit, you will see a multitude of all ranks, from the senator of justice to the lowest tradesman, mingled together in their shirts, and following the ball with the utmost eagerness. Among others, I was shown one particular set of golfers the youngest of whom was turned of four-score. They were all gentlemen of independent fortune who had amused themselves with this pastime for the better part of a century, without having felt the least alarm from sickness; and they never went to bed without having each the best part of a gallon of claret in his belly.

Perhaps we have given more attention to Smollett—viewing him simply as another novelist—than he deserves. Yet there is much to be said for him, and it need not be said with prudish reservations. We have admitted his vulgarity and his robustiousness, but they stand out against the exaggerated propriety and the prissiness of much of the fiction of his time, and of much still to come. If his tone is to be questioned, it is not with wordy confusion over doubtful moral issues. Women have had their word of praise for him, and discriminating women, although he is usually said to be a man's man. If we try to appraise what he did for the novel still to be, it was, principally, to enlarge the area of its resources and to give it variety and bluff humor. For no one of his time viewed his society more comprehensively or presented it more adequately in the peculiar humorous spirit of the period.

CHAPTER IX

Sentimentalism: A Literary Epidemic

OUR INTRODUCTION to Richardson and his followers obliges us to consider more at large the part that sentimentalism played in the literary psychology of the period. We need not go back to its origins, for it is found fully developed in both the French and the English drama of the earlier part of the century. And in attempting to define it, we need not depend altogether upon scientific or dictionary methods of definition; for some of the most enlightening attempts to give meaning to the group of words which cluster about the word "sentiment" (*sentimental, sentimentality*—for which most eighteenth-century usage substitutes *"sensibility"**—*sentimentalist, sentimentalism*) can be regarded as definitions only by suggestion or approximation.

Sentiment itself all of us would recognize as feeling; or perhaps better, *consciousness* of feeling; or in a more specific sense, feeling that has been generally appraised and approved—perhaps elaborately formulated—as creditable or proper, like "patriotic sentiment" and "religious sentiment." But the admirable sentiments were generally identified with the social feelings—those which were felt to draw human beings together, such as affection and sympathy and what is generally implied in our word "benevolence." These sentiments have been ranked probably from the beginning of historic time among the primary virtues—at least when held and practiced with moderation. Our oldest formal treatment of the human virtues, Aristotole's *Ethics,* points out that a virtue in excess may defeat the aim of all virtue, which is to promote satisfaction in life. All ethical systems counsel moderation of the emotions—the balancing of the claims of feeling against those of reason and judgment.

Since sentiment can be communicated, shared, and even grafted into

---

*I am deliberately giving preference to the word *sentimentality*, since the adjective from which it is derived—*sentimental*—can mean only one thing. The adjective *sensible* has at least two completely opposed meanings.

consciousness by the psychology of time and place, it is often difficult to distinguish between genuine feeling and the feeling that we think we owe to ourselves, or to society generally, to profess. Professions of accepted feeling are therefore not necessarily hypocritical, for they may be absorbed from infancy into our stock of inherited and inculcated convictions.

The general ambiguity, even taint, in the word "sentiment" accounts for many efforts to define it by example. Wilson Follett tells us that the cat is the type-sentimentalist, because "it doesn't love you; it loves itself on you." La Rochefoucauld tells us that "if there were no literature, there would be no romance." Stevenson tells us that Burns persistently "battered himself into an affection" for a country wench; for one may not only be infected by sentiment; he may deliberately infect himself.

Tears are the mute language of the sensitive heart. Thackeray confessed that when he wrote highly emotionalized scenes, it was with tears streaming down his own cheeks. Laurence Sterne not only admits the tears; he prides himself on shedding them. Rousseau exclaims, "How sweet are tears of tenderness and joy! How my heart revels in them! Why has it been permitted me to shed so few?" Helen Maria Williams, who wrote as poor poetry as anyone at the end of the century, asks in her ode "To Sensibility" :

> Who, for her apathy, would lose
> The sacred power to weep?

And in her "Sonnet to Twilight," nightfall "Wakes the tear 'tis luxury to shed." In the *Julia de Roubigné* of Henry Mackenzie, the most moist of all the sentimental novelists, Julia, speaking of the carnations sown by her lover's hand in her little garden, tells us that "when they began to droop, I have often watered them with my tears."

Sentimentality, then, is not merely high emotionality; it is a stimulated consciousness of emotion, and even a certain vanity in that consciousness. Needless to say, when self-conscious emotionality becomes a test of fineness of nature, it can, like any other mental trait, become a part of social education. It can likewise become a fad. So when the readers of *Pamela* and *Clarissa* retired to weep over the affecting passages (males in one room, females in another) they were responsive to a more complex psychological pattern than is commonly recognized.

Sentimentalism is the cult or creed of sentimentality. It is the justification of sentimentality as the mark of the finer nature, and it becomes inevitably a sort of literary property for those who care to exploit it.

No doubt eighteenth-century sentimentalism had deeper roots in feminine minds than in masculine, partly because of the general belief that feminine natures were tender and masculine natures rugged. It can be safely said that it was the predominance of women readers of fiction at the mid-century, and of both women readers and women writers of fiction toward the end of the century, that accounted for the extraordinary influence that the cult of sentimentalism exerted upon the novel of the period. Its direct results for fiction were a set of presumptions affecting principally the relations of men with women. Woman was taken to be the "weaker sex"; and the obligation of masculine favor and protection was the corollary of that weakness—an inheritance, of course, from the older notions of chivalry, but to be observed and practiced only where it was justified by social position. There was nothing new in either of these ideas, for they had been a part of all the polities and all the theologies before the eighteenth century. Nor was there novelty in the related feeling that at her best woman showed certain compensating virtues that had the color of moral superiority. Most of them centered in her role as mother or mother-to-be.

There was something new, however, in the common views that woman felt more intensely—and more painfully—than man, that her emotions were on a higher plane, and that emotional stresses, combined with her more delicate physical balance, could result naturally—and not provocatively or disagreeably—in readier tears and in "psychic" or defensive fainting; the latter a boon less readily conceded to man, though not unfamiliar in the literature of the time.

But in the current view, these refinements of personality were to be realized only where birth and breeding could perfect them. For it was felt that upper-class training and class-consciousness were indispensable to produce the perfectly spiritualized woman, or, in default of that training, inherent fineness of character brought by receptive contact with aristocratic people and usages into harmony with the aristocratic ideal—the case, of course, with Pamela. Few women of the time would have quarreled with these presumptions, in part because there were certain advantages for the sex in being regarded as weaklings and (to use Meredith's phrase a century later) "adorable bundles of caprices."

Eighteenth-century England was at least a little muddled as to its socially approved sentiments. It could condemn a man to death for stealing the equivalent of as little as two shillings, but it could also send him to the gallows with an orange in his hand. And while it gave every appearance of gallant protection to the weaker sex, it could be only upon the "respectable" level. A woman of the lower classes was marked as the plaything of the man of wealth, position, and fashion. It is also not surprising that in the individual case "sensibility" was no assurance of an emotionally consistent character. Smollett's Roderick Random, who could weep sentimental tears on parting from a friend, could also plan a heartless and humiliating revenge (his own word) upon a stupid young heiress because she had just enough penetration to see through his plan to marry her fortune.

It seems incongruous that the eighteenth century, which in Europe was called "the age of reason," should be also the age of literary sentiment. Yet the contradiction was not as radical as it appears on the surface; for at any time the intellectuals are certain to be numerically a minority. If the intellectuals of the time were represented by Voltaire, Diderot, Hume, Adam Smith and their like, the true representatives of the mass of readers were the purveyors of romantic imagination and sentiment—the poets, but more particularly the novelists.

The spread of sentimentalism in the mass psychology was furthered by religious enthusiasm among the evangelical sects. Piety, then, had its own, and considerable, share in the building up of the sentimental consensus of the mid-century, and we find sentimentality and conscious piety generally at home in one and the same mind. Despite the cynics of the time, who professed to regard piety and hypocrisy as much the same thing, piety was the sectarian's armor against the temptations of the flesh. For the upper classes, sentimentalism played probably a similar part, since it was supplemented by effective chaperonage and made its contribution to class pride. But among the middle and lower classes it probably tended to weaken resistances, simply by freeing and encouraging the emotions. Indeed, the "men of fashion" of the London coffee houses and pleasure gardens found sentimentalism a favorable terrain for amatory tactics, whether the object went under the name of wench or of lady. The language of sentiment became inevitably the language of aggressive gallantry.

Just how much sentimentality an eighteenth-century reader or theatergoer could, so to speak, soak up, we shall see as we move farther on into the period. But it might be said here and now that even the most fervent apostles of sentimentalism came to recognize decent limits to the sentimental appeal, especially if it played too hard and insistently upon the pathetic fallacy. Clara Reeve, writing in 1782, says that "if there is any defect" in the short novels of Henry Mackenzie (whom we shall meet later), it is that "some of the scenes are shocking representations of human nature and bear too hard upon the reader's humanity and sensibility." Toward the end of the century, the most adored of Mrs. Ann Radcliffe's heroines, Emily St. Aubert, in *The Mysteries of Udolpho*, is cautioned by her father on his deathbed not to indulge herself in "the pride of finer feeling, the romantic error of amiable minds." Frances Burney's *Camilla* (1796) is profuse with the tears of sensibility, yet in the end Camilla's feelings are regarded by her parents as the cause and explanation of her long self-inflicted miseries, which actually bring her to the door of death.

A paradox, clever or entertaining as it may be, must contain more than a modicum of truth if it is to live long. Sentimentalism embodies a paradox —likable, or even admirable, weakness—which common sense could not support beyond the limited period during which any fad may flourish. Yet the sentimental cult had a surprisingly long life in the eighteenth century. Tears of sorrow and of joy become almost as common as punctuation in the works of some of the later and quite ungifted women writers. In novel after novel the heroine "sinks lifeless" not only once but repeatedly in emotional crises.* Lovers may pause in mid-flight to exchange lengthy raptures upon the beauties of the craggy Appenines lying along their course of flight. Invalidism comes to "cast a charm" upon the face of many a delicate woman—or man. Grief at a tragic loss "declines into gentle and not unpleasing melancholy." Before the end of the century consumption has come to make its victim "interestingly pallid"; mental disorder, if not violent, has its precious romantic attraction, and death itself puts a beautiful period to suffering or shock. In Henry Brooke's *Fool of Quality,* a wife, forgiven for "guilt" of which she has been innocent, sinks back upon her pillow, dead. In Henry Mackenzie's *Man of Feeling,* the hero drops dead when the lady of his heart admits she loves him.

As to the impact of sentimentalism upon the love of men and women, evidence is abundant. It induces a retiring and refined affection, surrounded by conventional hesitancies, niceties, rigors, and taboos. The responses of a Pamela or an Ellena (Mrs. Radcliffe's *Italian*) to her accepted lover's gentlemanly advances are so fastidious, so reticent, that one must interpret them as mere maneuvering except for the fact that they are plainly the cachet of her delicacy. If these manifestations were not the expression of conventionalized sentiment, one would be forced to wonder whether the sexual timidity of the eighteenth-century heroine as her wedding day drew near revealed too much curious knowledge of the physiology of love or utter terrifying ignorance. The bridal night precipitates perfect deluges of tremulous apprehension. Pregnancy is announced to a father-to-be, legally and sacramentally qualified as a father, as his shy lady hides her glowing countenance upon his shoulder. These are not natural inhibitions, but deference to fine sentiment.

Between Richardson and Jane Austen sentimentalism gave the prevail-

---

*For the reader who regards arithmetic as good literary evidence, we may cite Mrs. Radcliffe's record in her first romance, *The Castles of Athlyn and Dunbayne,* which is barely a third of the length of *Pride and Prejudice.* Under the stress of emotion, the heroine faints nine times, her mother three, her mother-in-law three, and four assorted gentlemen once each. Within my own reading knowledge, the long-distance record for these alarming physical lapses is Mrs. Mary Robinson's ("Perdita's") *Angelina* (1796). Making up the sum would be arduous and meaningless.

ing tone to fiction; few writers were untouched by its stigma. Miss Austen was the first to reassert with effect the importance of finding and maintaining the balance between judgment and emotion—or, to use her own fine title, between "sense and sensibility." As late as Dickens—even Barrie— sentimentalism could still work black magic upon the susceptible, but by the end of the eighteenth century the average reader had at least the opportunity to learn the difference between "honest" sentiment and counterfeit.

Yet sentimentalism is by no means dead; nor is it likely to die. We still see it in screen versions of human life and behavior, and it accounts in substantial part for the depressing entertainment which interrupts the TV commercials. Thinking people, however, know it today for base coin, and it is safe to guess that most of those who still find it edifying chew gum.

But we must keep clearly before us the distinction between sentimentalism and sentimentality, on the one hand, and what I have called honest sentiment on the other. For sentimentalism is exaltation and exploitation of emotion, an attitude which distorts and even falsifies natural feeling. True sentiment, which is civilized, but not standardized, emotion, gives the humane virtues their proper place in experience. Nineteenth-century reaction against sentimentalism swung far to the opposite extreme. Marx, Ibsen, Nietzsche, and Shaw discounted emotional judgments on moral and social issues so severely that they seem at times to question whether people ought to feel.* But a race without the capacity for feeling, or a society civilized out of its feelings, would give us, presumably, a purely intellectualized life, but a dreary one.

Yet this problem of expounding the feelings is for the writer of fiction a deeply intriguing one. How to present them forcefully—even intensely— without slipping into conventionalized exaggeration? The dilemma is no simple one. It is strange that Samuel Butler, that hard-boiled campaigner against Victorian sentimentalism, who called sentimentality "diarrhea of the sympathetic instincts," should at the very end of the nineteenth century close *Erewhon Revisited* with a parting between father and adult son in these words :

> George burst into tears, and followed him after he had gone two paces; he threw his arms around him, hugged him, kissed him on his lips, cheeks, and forehead, and then turning round, strode full speed toward Sunch'ston. My father never took his eyes off him, but the boy did not look round.

But this is a climactic moment, heavy with drama; and if Butler here al-

---

*However, there seems to be a sanction for regarding "philanthropy," "justice," and "individualism" as socialized sentiments.

lows himself to let his characters go, it is quite a different thing from dragging them through the entire action of the story steadily dripping coagulated feeling.

CHAPTER X

1750:
Retrospect and Prospect

A READER today can walk into even a small-town public library and pick off from the open shelves any of perhaps a thousand novels. There were no public libraries in 1750; and the novels—by any stretch of definition which had been produced down to that time could have been carried off in a handbag.

Yet many readers then could not have afforded to own that little but choice armful of books; for the cost of a novel such as *Clarissa* or *Tom Jones* was the economic equivalent, in relation to the cost of living then and now, of twenty-five or fifty dollars. In addition, an informed guess tells us that no more than a third of the adult population was literate; the illiterate majority could enjoy a novel only if it were read to them. So reading was far from the common resource that it is now. Even in a literate home there might be only half a dozen or a dozen books, ranged on the mantel-shelf or stowed in a closet, to be taken down and read again and again. Probably most of them, in the average family, would have been devotional. In a family of greater pretensions there might be a copy of *Robinson Crusoe* or *The Plague Year;* not *Moll Flanders* or *Roxana,* for they were not "good" books. In a still more impressive household there might be a room for books! There one could find *The Spectator, The Pilgrim's Progress,* volumes of poetry by the admired Mr. Pope, and that fascinating book of travels to remote lands that Dean Swift had written. And there might be some stories by Mrs. Manley or Mrs. Haywood that breathed scandal or told the fancied stories of daring but reprehensible women of the great world.

But most talked about of all in 1750 would have been those new and long, sometimes very long, stories about "people like you and me." Mr. Richardson had written two of them, one about a serving maid who had married her master—think of it! And another about an unfortunate young lady who was . . . but we won't go into that. And Mr. Fielding—the one who wrote those amusing plays before the Haymarket was closed. There was the odd story about Jonathan Wild, who was hanged a score and more of years ago, and Joseph Andrews—tee-hee—Pamela's brother, you know; and Tom Jones—oh, he was the lively one! And Mr. Smollett had written one rather like *Tom Jones,* but not so very like it either—yes, *Roderick Random,* to be sure!

That was really the literary perspective, and it was substantially the whole story of the English novel, down to the middle of the century—all of Defoe and Swift; two novels by Richardson, with *Grandison* still to come; three by Fielding, *Amelia* probably just being thought out; and only the first of Smollett's half dozen or so. Something immensely significant had happened over the previous ten years; but the evidence of its importance was meager and unappreciated. No one called these stories novels, for their authors had not called them novels. *Pamela* was "a series of letters"; *Tom Jones* was a history; *Roderick Random* was just *Roderick Random.* In fact, these three writers, though we think of them as the "greats" of that great decade for the novel, thought they were doing quite distinct things. Richardson said he was writing a treatise on conduct. Fielding said he was writing a comic epic in prose. And Smollett said he was writing a picaresque tale modeled on Le Sage but brought within the compass of common experience.

It requires historical imagination and deliberate isolation from the entire subsequent history of the novel for us to see as their contemporaries saw them the ten or a dozen fictions that we have mentioned. There was not even a vocabulary for discussing them. Opinions could be expressed only as likes or dislikes. And comparisons were limited to that meager array of works that were not even felt to be closely related. The area for our judgment of fiction today is almost infinitely wider, and the grounds of judgment far clearer. But however more comprehensive and intelligent our critical procedures, we have lost something in not being able to judge ingenuously, as their first readers did, these first and quite unconscious trials in the genre. We judge them, as we *must* judge them, from the point of view of an immense accumulated knowledge of what the novel has come to be.

A novel in the emergent and formulative stages is almost inevitably simpler in conception, less effectively designed, and perhaps less competently written. Even so, it is not necessarily less significant or interesting. Novels written two centuries ago are still living, not because scholars keep pumping oxygen into them, but because they have the stuff of life in them. But they are different, over sometimes an immeasurable range of difference, as Rembrandt is different from Paul Klee, and Mozart from

Béla Bartók. Neither age nor novelty is in itself a source of merit. Great works of art defy the calendar. They do not have to be glorified by the patina of age; nor do they have to have glory conferred upon them by swaggering intellectualists.

Not only had the novel as we know it come into existence during the first half of the century; it had also in the varied content and accent of the earlier novelists brought into view conceptions of social range and moral bearing, and, perhaps most importantly, it had found its subject matter in actual life, not in fanciful, idealized, or reminiscent images of life. The word "realism" had not yet come into existence, in a strictly literary sense, but the purpose of realism had underlain the work of all the novelists from Defoe to Smollett. Yet even for us the word embraces a large number of special and not always harmonious conceptions. Defoe's realism was largely circumstantial—what might happen to anyone placed in a situation not too far removed from probability. Richardson's had been psychological, an attempt to examine and interpret the ways of thought. Fielding's had been, in intention, the determination and representation of social truth, and its defense against pietism. Smollett's had been much like Fielding's, but with a confessed predilection for the ways of a man of the world.

After Defoe, whose interest was in the common man, the novel moved to the upper levels of society for subject matter and social point of view. Richardson, Fielding, and Smollett all accepted rank implicitly as the basis of social organization, in Smollett's case not without rumblings of dissatisfaction. Yet all three writers of the great decade entertained no illusions as to how well the upper classes had met their duties to the society which after all maintained them in their privileged position.

From Richardson on, the typical theme of the novel—whatever its range of action—was, and was to be throughout the century, the love of man and woman. There was nothing new in the theme, but it takes on special importance in eighteenth-century fiction because it accompanied, and to some extent accounted for, significant changes in woman's social position and moral influence. The greater part of that transition was accomplished in the latter half of the century, but it was in motion even before Richardson, and it owed a measurable something to his influence. In the novels of both Fielding and Smollett, however, a woman's virtues were still thought to include patient and generous allowances for the recognized masculine frailty. As a corollary, that frailty was given equally generous allowances in the day-to-day lives of most men of the world. Yet both Fielding and Smollett professed to see a difference between a season of wild-oat culture and the practiced vices of the rake. Within another half-century the rake was to have gone out of vogue as an agreeable, or even an amusing, figure, and young men had taken their place in fiction who would not have recognized a wild oat.

Biography had in all these earliest novels, from Defoe on, furnished the typical pattern of fiction. Its characteristic unity had been that of a typical life. That had not necessarily meant, however, that the dominant interest was in character. For the characters of heroes and heroines in both Fielding and Smollett had been generally stereotyped, owing much to the models of the theater. Still, concentration upon the individual encouraged the serious study and appraisal of character. And that interest was to be extended as the century progressed.

The Earl of Chesterfield, who knew literature, writing in 1740 (probably, therefore, before he had seen *Pamela*) says "a novel is a kind of abbreviation of a romance." And a romance, he goes on to say, "is sometimes a story entirely fictitious ... at other times a true story ... but so blended with falsities and silly love adventures that they confuse and corrupt the mind, instead of forming and instructing it." What he had in view, no doubt, was the transcripts of contemporary life of the Behns, Manleys, and Haywoods. Before Fielding the novel had been identified more or less with the "novella," as a short tale of the general design of those in Boccaccio's *Decameron* or Cervantes' *Exemplary Novels*. Fielding hesitated to call his narratives novels not altogether because (as it has been sometimes said) the word "novel" was in disrepute, but because he was quite aware that he was writing something different in aim and design from the novel as it was hitherto understood. By 1750 the word had probably barely begun to take on its new meaning. Yet there is a logical—because historical—relationship between the two apparently distinct genres.

In the earlier phases of long prose narrative the continuity had been less a story for its own sake than a framework or a container for an assemblage of short tales. The *Decameron,* of the mid-fourteenth century, is a case in point. The containing situation is sketchy—the flight of a party of young people from Florence during an epidemic, and their entertainment of one another by telling stories during their short exile. The characters are too indistinct even to be remembered by name, and the brief narrative links between the successive stories are a mere mechanism.

As the longer narrative took more complete form, incidental episodes became less numerous and were related structurally to the major plot by attachment, even though adventitious, to the principal character. In Cervantes' *Don Quixote* (1605–15) we find an example of this type of narrative. It is still a romance, though a romance in burlesque of the older romances of chivalry.

The "little history," an apt term for the interspersed narratives in *Don*

Quixote, continues to be a feature of prose romances right down into the eighteenth century; and when the novel took distinctive form, the little history still found a place in some—not all—of the examples of the newer fiction. Richardson did not use it, but it is introduced unblushingly by both Fielding and Smollett.

The common character of the little histories, at least in English fiction, is briefly this. The narrator is the subject of his own narrative. The story is moral; that is, a commentary upon conduct and its relation to happiness. It usually relates the story of a reckless or vicious life, illustrating the value of virtue by the bad effects of wicked ways. In most cases, therefore, the little histories are stories of libertinism and dissipation, ending in penitence. No single little history need be all of these things; but this is the prevailing pattern.

There are large differences in the extent to which the little history may enter into the real substance of the story. In Fielding, it has been frequently pointed out, these more or less interruptive autobiographic episodes generally attach to characters with importance for the plot. Mr. Wilson's story in *Joseph Andrews,* for instance, brings us in the end to the discovery of Joseph's real identity. The very long little history of Miss Matthews, in *Amelia,* is told by a woman who moves in and out of the action from beginning to end, although she is not a principal. The still longer story of the Man of the Hill, in *Tom Jones,* is pure digression. But even when connection with the main narrative seems slight, these diversions tend to enforce the moral point—in some cases by *contrast* with the moral tone of the central theme. Miss Matthews is an example of feminine libertinism, as Amelia is a model of womanly modesty and loyalty. Mrs. Atkinson, another character with a pathetic story, is scheming and devious, where Amelia is all natural goodness and frankness.

The progress of the novel from 1750 on is in an important degree the history of its slow deliverance from structural looseness. As it grows in distinctive purpose and power, it tends when it introduces such minor episodes to give them essential importance. Ultimately, the increasing respect for the conception of unity will eliminate them altogether. They are, however, so common a feature of mid-century fiction that they must be accepted as an entirely characteristic part of it.

Unity, in all the arts, is a live conception. It is, of course, oneness, sticking to the subject. Unity can be dispensed with in cocktail conversation, but when order and economy give continuous purpose to talk (and literature is, after all, simply glorified talk) it has its virtue. Yet it is not prescriptive. Good works of art have overstepped the principle of unity, though perhaps the best have respected and accepted it. But *criticism* of the arts, or *schooling* in the arts, has always taken unity as a point of departure in aesthetic theory. As the novel of our period developed, it began to subordinate merely incidental material and to eliminate the quite irrelevant. Incidents began to fuse into a rational continuity. Unity was coming in, for the steadily increasing firmness and integrity of the product.

During the next half-century, however, the novel was to show no phenomenal over-all improvement. Laurence Sterne excepted—and his genius defied almost all the "rules" of narrative art—there is no figure before Jane Austen who can rank with the three of the great decade. The romance, which both Fielding and Smollett had repudiated in their introductory discourses, was revived, and existed comfortably side by side with the "new fiction." The sentimental novel was to become more sentimental. The epistolary novel held its place, although it declined in popularity. The masculinity of Fielding and Smollett was displaced by novels of feminine temper and outlook, written by women, and implicitly or explicitly advancing woman's slow social and economic liberation. New names of high secondary importance were to appear—Goldsmith, Fanny Burney, Bage, Maria Edgeworth—and fads of various sorts were to have their day. The six novels produced by the three greats between 1740 and 1750 were within the next generation to be succeeded by dozens appearing in a single year, and literally hundreds toward the end of the century. In number, in variety, in the constant broadening of its social area, in serious social purpose, in precision of form, the novel was over the coming half-century to be "developed." Yet in literary quality and in vitality it was to add little or nothing to the achievement reached just before the mid-century.

There were, however, readable and enjoyable, and even stimulating novels to appear during this slack period, as we shall see.

CHAPTER XI

A Fellow of Infinite Jest

Laurence Sterne

STERNE IS the one professed sentimentalist who is generally ranked among the unarguably great.* Yet there are those who would make argument out of the unarguable, for various and not wholly trivial reasons. The first is that he exceeds (or has been accused of exceeding) the liberal allowances of his own time for sexy suggestiveness. The second is that his use of the written word sometimes narrowly misses obscenity, or perhaps just fails to miss it. The third is that he is demonstrably a borrower from other notable writers. The fourth is that he displays too insistently the defects of his virtues as a purveyor of sentiment. The fifth is that as an author he lacks the grace to keep out of the reader's sight, and insists upon intruding himself into his story. The sixth is that he is frivolous, and that while frivolity may be forgiven a layman, it is unbecoming to the occupant of a pulpit. The seventh is—but why go on? We have already enough for a general indictment.

Not all the articles in the indictment are of equal weight. One or two are all but negligible. The others I am disposed to deal with defensively at the very outset, more or less with the attitude of the lawyer who feels that while his client has a good case, it must be got over to the jury before the prosecution makes too deep an impression upon its receptive consciousness.

As to Sterne's infractions of the sexual taboos, the substance of his offense is that he regards sex as among other things a subject for humor. Sex can be discussed with propriety sociologically, ethically, theologically, psychologically, biologically, pathologically, and no doubt from still other points of view, but good society still seems to balk at discussing it—in public, that is—with amusement. We all know that it furnishes quite an area

---

*Laurence Sterne (1713-1768). *The Life and Opinions of Tristram Shandy, Gent.*, in nine volumes (four instalments), 1760 [1759]-1767; *A Sentimental Journey through France and Italy*, 1768.

of free discourse among males—even to the point of becoming to the fastidious mind tiresome and vulgar. The feminine mind has been said to be less receptive to its humorous implications as matter for unconstrained conversation. Yet I am told that young ladies are beginning to regard it with increasing interest as a supplement to classroom acquaintance with the subject. However, one thing seems fairly certain—that it is not yet accepted as an entirely safe subject for inter-sexual communications except under special conditions, usually justified by legal and/or sacramental sanctions, or with the color of detached inquiry. If, in the progress of sexual enlightenment, detached inquiry should lead in time to greater relaxation in conversation—and in conduct—that may very well be a problem for another generation of moralists.

But let us try to clear our minds as to what we are talking about. Is it morality; is it manners; or is it social expediency? While the three criteria are not completely separable, they furnish an approach to reasonable consideration of what, if anything, is in this respect wrong with Sterne. From the very appearance of *Tristram Shandy* accusations have been leveled at him upon all these heads. Johnson, a captious moralist, thought he was immoral. Goldsmith thought he encouraged the vulgar taste.* Scott thought he was indiscreet. No responsible writer, so far as I know, has thought him innocent.

It would be frivolous to deny that art, and still more, perhaps, pretenses at art, have some tendency to foster curiosity in these matters, and so to stimulate personally or socially unhealthful sexual practices. Yet most discussion of censorship seems to proceed on the supposition that such "evil communications" corrupt minds hitherto and otherwise innocent, generally at the susceptible age—the early teens. Whereas in the experience of most of us sex is quietly (and delightedly) publicized so much earlier than the age of puberty that we are likely to find the beginnings of our curiosity on the subject buried in the obscurity of our very remotest memories. My point is not that that is the best kind of sex education, but that the assumption as to minds still virginal when puberty creeps up on them is in general not an error; it is a falsification.

Sterne *is* sexy at times, cleverly and amusingly so. But I am sidestepping argument as to whether that is wicked, ill-judged, or just vulgar. To a moderate degree it is probably all three.

But the issue of obscenity touches another matter, which is literary taste. In this area it is the word itself that offends, and offends not because

---

*Goldsmith's little essay in reprobation of Sterne can be found in Letter LIII of his *Citizen of the World,* which in Letter XXXII contains a passage of some length rather nastier than anything I know in Sterne, and certainly much less entertaining.

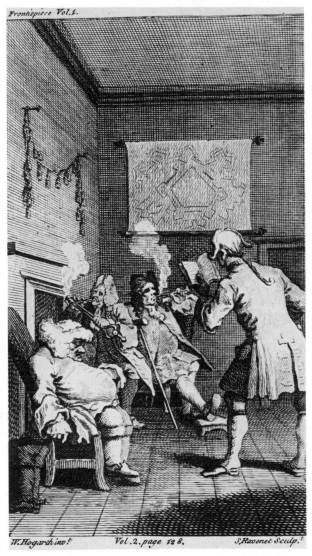

Corporal Trim reading the sermon to Mr. Shandy, Uncle
Toby, and Dr. Slop. This illustration by Hogarth, engraved
by J. Ravenet, appeared in the second edition of *Tristram
Shandy*, 1760; not in the first, and was followed by one of
Tristram's christening in the first edition of the third volume,
1761. The two plates were Hogarth's only illustrations to a
work of English fiction.

of its seductiveness, but because it is foreign to the usage of nice people. Fashion enters here quite as much as propriety; a fact that Sterne himself makes abundantly clear in a passage in his *Sentimental Journey*. I quote the passage in full, vulgar word and all.

> Madame de Rambouliet, after an acquaintance of about six weeks with her, had done me the honor to take me in her coach about two leagues out of town. —Of all women, Madame de Rambouliet is the most correct; and I never wish to see one of more virtues and purity of heart. —In our return back, Madame de Rambouliet desired me to pull the cord. —I asked her if she wanted anything —*Rien que pisser,* said Madame de Rambouliet.
>
> Grieve not, gentle traveler, to let Madame de Rambouliet p–ss on. —And, ye fair mystic nymphs! go each one pluck your rose, and scatter them in your path—for Madame de Rambouliet did no more. —I handed Madame de Rambouliet out of the coach; and had I been the priest of the chaste CASTALIA, I could not have served at her fountain with a more respectful decorum.

Need this shock us? In France this freedom was common in Sterne's time, though strange to an Englishman. It has changed in France—though not unheard of among the peasantry even today. It was perfectly familiar in England in the time of Elizabeth—and did not embarrass the Queen herself. In a word, it is a matter of changing fashion, which Sterne, as a man of the world, accepts and remarks in passing. But the literary turn he gives it—and that closing sentence is admirable if it is not awful—has the mark of both culture and wit. It is not too often that wit excites real, audible, laughter for the well-balanced mind; but it does here; for the incongruity of Sterne's metaphor is absolute, and its audacity compelling. It is only Satanic laughter that is pernicious. This is Adamic, and if it is too ridiculously human for nice minds, let them beware of Sterne.

Is the passage more obscene because it is clever? You, Brother John Bunyan, and you, Messer François Rabelais, will never come together upon that point. So we might as well leave it, with all the allusions to whiskers and bears and noses, and old hats and green gowns. Some of them are pretty recondite anyway, and a *double-entendre* that calls for erudition if it is to be understood is not likely to be very noxious.*

Is an obscenity that is looked at from all sides, turned over, palpated, juggled, and made a sort of intellectual football, more objectionable than

---

*Erudition has in fact so much to do with Sterne's profounder wit that I feel an obligation to suggest that if the reader's edition of *Tristram Shandy* is "one of 800 copies on Japanese vellum of which this is number 654," he give it to the Salvation Army and buy an intelligently annotated edition, such as that edited by James Work.

the single familiar four-letter word? These nice quasi-pornographical and scatalogical questions are as intriguing as the theological—and as unanswerable. It is quite possible that a writer may cheapen his cleverness by spreading it over too broad an area. The long discourse on noses in *Tristram Shandy,* with Slawkenbergius's tale, may be a case in point.* To some readers it is wearisome, once the point of the equivoque is clear. But the problem is not one that seems to call for quantitative analysis.

Sterne has even been called "dirty"—a dirty question-begging word. The only dirty passage in *Tristram Shandy* that sticks in my mind—a play on the phrase "in camera"—has at least three areas of reference, in addition to the scatalogical—optics, art, and domestic architecture. It is a first-rate piece of verbal carpentry, and I refuse to be disturbed by its nastiness, though I would not myself repeat it.

I would cheerfully leave the matter here, on the sound principle that it is vain to carry argument on tastes—or for that matter, on smells—beyond the point at which we can amicably agree to differ.

As to Sterne's plagiaries, the prosecution has a stout case, a very stout one.† It is beyond denial that he has "lifted," quietly and without a word of proper acknowledgment, some of his most notable anecdotes, incidents, and allusions. His principal debts are to Robert Burton's *Anatomy of Melancholy* and to Rabelais, both authors so well known that it is all but impossible to imagine that he really expected to escape discovery. In that fact there is a certain justifiable plea, not of ignorance, but of fair intention. The charge is a moral, not a legal one; for copyright had expired upon every significant work to which he owed a debt. Sterne's undeclared "borrowings" are in a number of instances the very words taken from the figurative mouths of his unwitting creditors. Yet even as a moral charge, it is in some degree defensible, on the ground that works in the public domain become legitimate plunder.

Sterne's offense, then, is not of the first seriousness, because the sum of his illicit debts is a small portion of the actual work; also because the eighteenth century showed in general no marked nicety in these matters. Lastly—and I personally attach some weight to this consideration—the plagiarisms are found not only in *Tristram Shandy,* but in his published

---

*With Sterne, these cases are simply sustained puns, as a rule. And the sustained pun, well carried off, is not contemptible. Witness Thomas Hood's forty-odd plays on the word "double" in as many lines of *Miss Kilmansegg and Her Precious Leg* (probably the punniest poem in the language)—and not a questionable *double entendre* in the lot!

†For the detail of the matter, any of Sterne's major biographers—Wilbur Cross, Walter Sichel, and H. D. Traill—is sufficiently explicit to be convincing. The case against Sterne was originally made by John Ferriar in his *Illustrations of Sterne* (1812), which was, incidentally, not an unfriendly presentment.

sermons; and sermonizing practice, certainly in Sterne's own time, followed the not altogether shameless principle that if someone had already said the thing better than you could say it, the goodness of the cause justified the theft. Sterne may have cultivated in the pulpit that rather careless practice before he adopted it in his fiction. Perhaps we can leave the matter there. It is no longer a problem for Sterne's conscience, and so far as we his readers are concerned, we can deplore or condone the sly business as much as we have a mind to.

On the charge that Sterne overdoes the sentimental, much can be said, but we have already said some part of it in our general talk about sentimentalism. Much of the actual thought of Sterne's day moved in that groove; people did not have to affect it. But to a person like Sterne, sentimental down to the very depths of his real nature, conventionalized sentiment could exert a dangerous charm. And as an accomplished man of letters he would find it a wonderful and always new plaything. No one of his time could act the sentimentalist's role with greater natural aptitude, as well as greater mastery of the techniques of the art.

His real capacity for feeling, then, and his acute consciousness of it, contorted somewhat the mind of a not irrational being. He was fluttery, injudicious, vain, fickle—perhaps in a single word, weak. But he was also genial, amusing, fond of the table, fond of his wine, and fond of his friends, who were never really overnumerous, even when, on the appearance of *Tristram Shandy,* he was much hunted after by London society. Most conspicuously, an incorrigible taste for "philandering" involved him in a number of attachments of varying intensity, permanence, and innocence. For one interested in this more or less extra-literary fact, his published letters carry interesting evidence. But episodes in his *Sentimental Journey* also reflect it with a characteristic blend of parade and truth. While his sentiment is naturally most vigorous and perhaps most interesting in this special phase, it touches a multitude of common experiences, and finds objects of sympathy in the beggar, the beast of burden, the mentally estranged, the aged, the bereaved, most of womankind, and even (a much-quoted instance) the common housefly.

A Victorian biographer of Sterne, H.D. Traill, offers the suggestion that if, or when, Sterne's sentimentalism seems to ring false, it is not because the spirit of the moment is falsified, but because Sterne insists on drawing the reader's attention off the incident and back to himself. The reader becomes aware not only of excess, but of impertinence. There is an idea to ponder. Perhaps what is really wrong with sentimentalism is its raw egotism, and with literary sentiment, its irrepressible intrusiveness. Among other instances Traill quotes the closing sentences from the death of LeFever in *Tristram Shandy* :

—You shall go home directly, *LeFever,* said my Uncle *Toby,* to my house, —and we'll send for a doctor to see what's the matter, —and we'll have an apothecary, —and the corporal shall be your nurse; —and I'll be your servant, *LeFever.*

There was a frankness in my Uncle *Toby,* —not the *effect* of familiarity, —but the *cause* of it, —which let you at once into his soul, and shewed you the goodness of his nature; to this, there was something in his looks, and voice, and manner, superadded, which eternally beckoned to the unfortunate to come and take shelter under him; so that before my Uncle *Toby* had half finished the kind offers he was making to the father, had the son insensibly pressed up close to his knees, and had taken hold of the breast of his coat, and was pulling it towards him. —The blood and spirits of *LeFever,* which were waxing cold and slow within him, and were retreating to their last citadel, the heart, —rallied back, —the film forsook his eyes for a moment, —he looked up wishfully in my Uncle *Toby's* face, —then cast a look upon his boy, —and that *ligament,* fine as it was, —was never broken.—

Nature instantly ebb'd again, —the film returned to its place, —the pulse fluttered—stopp'd—went on—throbb'd—stopp'd again—moved —stopp'd—shall I go on? —No.

It is, Traill, says, a natural and moving scene—down to the last score or more of words, which seem to him superfluous and theatrical. Perhaps the very tokens of death are tampered with for the sake of an effect. And the final words do bring the narrator into the picture, with his forced reminder of his artistic restraint.

Perhaps the critic is right. He cites other instances : the carefully staged gesture of the old peasant in *A Sentimental Journey,* with his crust of bread, as he sits mourning over his dead ass; more particularly, the entire episode of the crazed peasant girl Maria, praised by some as pure feeling, damned by others as pure affectation :

She was dress'd in white, and much as my friend described her, except that her hair hung loose, which before was twisted within a silk net. —She had, superadded likewise to her jacket, a pale green ribband, which fell across her shoulder to the waist; at the end of which hung her pipe. —Her goat had been as faithful as her lover : and she had got a little dog in lieu of him, which she had kept tied by a string to her girdle; as I look'd at her dog, she drew him towards her with the string. —"Thou shalt not leave me Silvio," said she. I look'd in Maria's eyes, and saw she was thinking more of her father than of her lover or her little goat; for as she utter'd them, the tears trickled down her cheeks.

I sat down close by her; and Maria let me wipe them away as they fell, with my handkerchief. —I then steep'd it in my own—and then in hers—and then in mine—and then I wip'd hers again—and as I did it, I felt such undescribable emotions within me, as I am sure could not be accounted for from any combinations of matter and motion.

I am positive I have a soul; nor can all the books with which materialists have pestered the world ever convince me to the contrary. . . .

And the philandering motive creeps almost inevitably into this episode of pure emotion :

Maria, though not tall, was nevertheless of the first order of fine forms—affliction had touch'd her looks with something that was scarce earthly—still she was feminine—and so much was there about her of all that the heart wishes or the eye looks for in woman, that could the traces [of her affliction] be ever worn out of her brain, and those of Eliza out of mine, she should *not only eat of my bread and drink of my cup,* but Maria should lie in my bosom, and be unto me as a daughter.

It is in *A Sentimental Journey* rather than in *Tristram Shandy* that the pursuit of the sentimental experience is seen at its best (if "best" is the right word). In *Tristram Shandy* there are more important things to be looked after. Moreover, *A Sentimental Journey* is not in the strict sense fiction; it merely gives imaginative color to Sterne's actual journey to France and Italy in the winter of 1765–66. Yet it is so very much Sterne and so well supplied with the matter and the method of fiction that we cannot disregard it.

Here again we confront a question almost wholly of literary taste, and there are no acceptable premises on which to decide it. Writers of Sterne's stamp are not merely *in* their books; they *are* their books. And that not in the simple sense that their works bear the impress of an easily recognizable style and explore an equally recognizable world of interests; but that their writing is not tinged with personality, it is flooded with it. It is easy to put the question, what would *A Sentimental Journey,* or even *Tristram Shandy,* be without the constant reminder of Sterne's presence. But the question is unrealistic. Sterne *couldn't* be taken out of either. Perhaps the really important question is what *kind* of personality so persistently begs our attention. We don't, in general, object to personalities in themselves, but to temperaments and habits alien to our sympathies. There is a good deal of the clown in Sterne, and there are readers who can be satisfied with a very moderate amount of clowning.

At this late date probably few of us would protest against Sterne's trivialities on the ground that they are unbecoming a clergyman. Even in his own day only a tender propriety would have taken that offense quite seriously. The clerical calling was a gentlemanly one, like the law and politics, and men entered it not from profound conviction but because with a university degree they were eligible for ecclesiastical preferment, and they could live as gentlemen without conspicuous gentlemanly expenditure. The gamester, the drunkard, and other such uncandid spirits, occupied pulpits, and sacerdotal duties could be taken very lightly—or, what was common, passed on to curates. The churchman who could not laugh at a smutty jest was probably a rare one. And was cracking the jest very much worse than laughing at it?

Most of what has been said and written in adverse criticism of Sterne would convict him on these matters of little more than a mild exhibitionism and an amused indifference to the shrieks of the excessively proper. There remains the question of whether he is vulnerable on the ground of his good faith as an artist.

But first of all, did he think of himself as an artist? Not, I am afraid, with an artist's conscience. He had been an entertainer most of his mature life, and he began to entertain the world at large when his years were nearing the half-century mark. No one could have been more conscious than Sterne that writing was for him literally no more than self-expression—opportunist, void of high aspiration, encouraged and stimulated by a large and more flattering audience than his spiritual charges in and about York. And no one could have worked his own particular field with less compunction, either moral or aesthetic. Discipline was foreign to his temper. His bright particular gift, which was amusement, if smothered by literary discipline, would have vanished in smoke; for his art is little more or less than his exuberance. That places it on a somewhat lower level than disciplined art; but it is *his* art, and it cannot be denied him.

Now what *is* he at his best, viewed as a writer of fiction, rather than a free and easy entertainer with a bag of somewhat unliterary tricks? The purposed jumpiness of his sentences, his disconnection, his dropping of a thread to be picked up later, his promises of chapters that will never be written, his blacked-out, blank, and marbled pages, his profusion of dashes and asterisks, above all, his amused contempt for continuity and for any sort of literary principle—most of them copied from his models, and all of them tending to pall when played upon continuously, these stick to our memories only as idiosyncrasies. In themselves they are quite insufficient to give him literary importance.

What first strikes the reader of *Tristram Shandy* is lack of apparent design, and of homogeneity—things we expect to find in any workmanlike job of fiction. Looking back upon the story with critical purpose, we have to ask ourselves what Sterne was trying to do. What did he conceive as the framework of a narrative undertaken lightly and even irresponsibly? Can we distill consistency out of the mass of deliberate inconsistencies that *Tistram Shandy* seems to be?

First of all, the title has little or no relation to the theme and movement of the story. Yet it must be remembered that *Tristram Shandy* is unfinished, and unfinished because the writer died while it was still under his hands. How long could Sterne have gone on with it? So far as we know, indefinitely. If he had an end in view, he could have delayed it as long as free invention could supply material for the purpose. And no one was more expert at stalling. But as the story stands, we have not a life of Tristram here—although plenty of life in general—and scarcely the shadow of an opinion of Tristram's own.

Then there is no apparent continuity, but this is in the main because interruption and postponement provide the actual technique of this odd narrative. There is a discernable continuity in Tristram's indistinct biographical background, which, we are told, can be untangled by means of dates and allusions by anyone who cares to attempt it.

Yet continuity has minor importance; for the unity of the story consists in the human aggregate that we call a family; and the family is admittedly a queer one. Queer, yet convincing, if we can envisage the closed, almost isolated, social relationships of the country gentleman in Sterne's time. Let us dismiss Tristram, who is not an actor, and scarcely a spectator, in this curious domestic comedy, and look at the real participants in the action. For plot here is not *a* character, but a menagerie of originals occupied in that salient purpose of the eighteenth-century family—keeping the family going. There are only two active figures in *Tristram Shandy* who stand outside the Shandy family itself (in the comprehensive eighteenth-century sense)—Dr. Slop, the accoucheur, and the Widow Wadman, their neighbor. The Russian story men have been equally content with the four walls of a country-house as the entire scene of action, but it is a rare setting for the select-gregarious outlook of the British novelist and reader.

The central figure, as the family head, is Tristram's father, a man, and not an unknown type, whom learning has failed to make rational, and whose pedantry serves only to support an absurd collection of knowledgeable but unbalanced prepossessions. Yet Sterne's picture of him, ridiculously consistent as it makes him, is without savage or even painful satire. Mr. Shandy contrives, elaborates, and preaches a system, his "Tristrapaedia," for the rearing and educating of the perfect gentleman—echoing obviously Xenophon's *Cyropaedia*, similarly conceived for the education of a great ruler. However, character and intelligence, in Mr. Shandy's system, are subordinated to a set of mere notions, chief of which are that the child who is the subject of this program shall have been conceived quietly and earnestly, have an impressive nose, and carry a name of high promise. The crotchety convictions are supported by a fund of false learning, Mr. Shandy being of the not unfamiliar mental temper that collects and cherishes every sententious pronouncement that can provide fuel for his mental flame, and rejects forthwith all the recorded wisdom that fails to lend itself to his eccentric philosophy. He is in a way a travesty upon all systems, in particular, fanciful educational systems. Tristram, the victim of this particular system, is naturally less sure than Mr. Shandy of its efficacy.

Sterne's portrait of Mr. Shandy depends wholly upon mild comic suggestion for its effectiveness. This is partly a matter of temperament, partly of sober conviction; for Sterne's interest is in human frailties, not obliquity. In another social or family setting Mr. Shandy might be more pestiferous than amusing, but he is found in an environment which at once explains and excuses his perversity, and since his notions cannot do much harm in the circumstances, they do not call for indignation. If Tristram is to be in a sense a victim, he will still make a presentable country gentleman. As for the personality of Mr. Shandy, its combination of petulance and benignity, silliness and profundity, makes him humanly understandable, and diverting, in spite of the occasional sharp edge to Sterne's satire.

His brother, Tristram's Uncle Toby, is a still odder creation, yet memorable for many reasons; perhaps, indeed, Sterne's most lasting claim upon a literary place of importance. Sublime innocence and unworldliness lie beyond the mental reach of most of us, and they are subjects for true comedy only when there is true humanity to redeem them from stupidity. In Swift and Anatole France simplicity is amusing but contemptible. In Tolstoy and Chekhov it is affecting but not amusing. In Uncle Toby, Sterne makes the humorous most of an innocence which, to be sure, is pure invention, yet engagingly human. That a man of Uncle Toby's age, both personal and social (and particularly a British army officer of Sterne's time!), should not, as Mr. Shandy puts it, "know the right end of a woman," is not only incongruous but incredible. Yet it is productive of the *purest* humor. One appreciative commentator upon Sterne regards the conclusion of the Widow Wadman episode as "shocking." But for most readers the sustained siege of Uncle Toby's unmasculine ignorance by the knowing widow's quite legitimate and thoroughly womanly curiosity is in every detail of both situation and character a triumph of comic intention. If what is shocking is that Corporal Trim's enlightenment of Uncle Toby ends his interest in the widow, isn't that in perfect accord with Uncle Toby's virginal temper, so completely at odds with all the traditions of the time and the place?

But "my Uncle's" innocence touches other concerns as to which he seems no more informed or experienced. His knowledge of the world in general, outside the army, is almost nothing. In his conversation with his brother as he smokes his pipe, he plays the part of listener, politely attentive, rarely interested, sometimes hopelessly lost in the maze of Mr. Shandy's learned abstractions, but always responsive, if it is only with a frank confession of his puzzlement :

"Do you understand the theory of that affair?" [asked Mr. Shandy].
"Not I," quoth my uncle.
"But you have some ideas," said my father, "of what you talk about."
"No more than my horse," replied my Uncle Toby.

Yet Uncle Toby's own "hobby-horse" is equally alien to Mr. Shandy, though amusing rather than incomprehensible. It takes only a word with a more or less remote military association in it to raise one of Uncle Toby's exasperatingly inconsequential questions or to start a disquisition or a reminiscence upon some phase of the only science with which he is acquainted.

Now it happened then, as indeed it had often done before, that my Uncle *Toby's* fancy, during the time of my father's explanation of *Prignitz* to him, —having nothing to stay it there, had taken a short flight to the bowling-green; —his body might as well have taken a turn there too, —so that with all the semblance of a deep school-man intent upon the *medius terminus,* —my Uncle *Toby* was in fact as ignorant of the whole lecture, and all its pro's and con's, as if my father had been translating *Hafen Slawkenbergius* from the *Latin* tongue into the *Cherokee.* But the word *siege,* like a talismanic power, in my father's metaphor, wafting back my uncle *Toby's* fancy, quick as a note could follow the touch, —he open'd his ears, —and my father observing that he took his pipe out of his mouth, and shuffled his chair nearer the table, as with a desire to profit, —my father with great pleasure began his sentence again, —changing only the plan, and dropping the metaphor of the siege of it, to keep clear of some dangers my father apprehended from it.
'Tis a pity, said my father, that truth can only be on one side, brother *Toby,*—considering what ingenuity these learned men have all shown in their solutions of noses. —Can noses be dissolved? replied my uncle *Toby.*—
—My father thrust back his chair, —rose up, —put on his hat, —took four long strides to the door, —jerked it open, —thrust his head half way out, —shut the door again, —took no notice of the bad hinge, —returned to the table, —pluck'd my mother's thread paper out of *Slawkenbergius's* book, —went hastily to his bureau, —walk'd slowly back, twisting my mother's thread-paper about his thumb, —unbutton'd his waistcoat, —threw my mother's thread-paper into the fire,

Tristram Shandys Implements.

Behold the Learn'd P—d wise & grave,
To bawdy Wit become a selfish slave.

Unsigned engraving, 1761, attacking Sterne, as a prebend of York Cathedral and the author of the "immoral" *Tristram Shandy*. The caricature of Sterne copies Reynolds' portrait; and the nudes chosen to exemplify Sterne's "obscenity" are taken from well-known classic sculptures.

—bit her satin pincushion in two, fill'd his mouth with bran, —confounded it; —but mark! —the oath of confusion was levell'd at my uncle *Toby's* brain, —which was e'en confused enough already, —the curse came charged only with the bran, —the bran, may it please your honours, —was no more than powder to the ball.

'Twas well my father's passions lasted not long; for so long as they did last, they led him a busy life on't, and it is one of the most unaccountable problems that ever I met with in my observations of human nature, that nothing should prove my father's mettle so much, or make his passions go off so like gun-powder, as the unexpected strokes his science met with from the quaint simplicity of my uncle *Toby's* questions. —Had ten dozen of hornets stung him behind in so many different places all at one time, —he could not have exerted more mechanical functions in fewer seconds, —or started half so much, as with one single *quaere* of three words unseasonably popping in full upon him in his hobbyhorsical career.

'Twas all one to my uncle *Toby,* —he smoaked his pipe on, with unvaried composure, —his heart never intended offense to his brother, —and as his head could seldom find out where the sting of it lay, —he always gave my father the credit of cooling by himself. —He was five minutes and thirty-five seconds about it in the present case.

The two brothers provide the meat of *Tristram Shandy.* All the other characters are "feeders" for their humanity and their humors. For both are in the strictest sense "humor" characters, embodiments of the single trait or the single whim that possesses and animates the personality—as purely humor characters as they would have been from the hand of Ben Jonson, but with a gentleness quite foreign to Jonson.

The minor characters have more of the natural in them, perhaps with the exception of Dr. Slop, the only one of the group depicted with a suggestion of satirical malice. Corporal Trim has almost substance enough for a principal, but he is nevertheless a servant, not only in status, to Uncle Toby, but to Sterne, for his comic purposes. The Widow Wadman occupies space as well as position in the concluding chapters, but she, again, is serviceable for Sterne rather than essential.

The workers in the Shandy household seem to furnish more occasion than the principals for a specially graceful aspect of Sterne's art : minute, even exquisite, attention to casual words and gestures, comic but at the same time irrefutably genuine and revealing. Trim has enough gestures, truly in character, to furnish a pantomime. Here is an episode from the kitchen, Corporal Trim holding forth to the servants upon the theme of death.

—To us, *Jonathan,* who know not what want or care is—who live here in the service of two of the best of masters—(bating in my own case of his majesty King *William* the Third, whom I had the honor to serve both in *Ireland* and *Flanders*)—I own it, that from *Whitsuntide* to within three weeks of *Christmas,*—'tis not long—'tis like nothing; —but to those, *Jonathan,* who know what death is, and what havock and destruction he can make, before a man can well wheel about—'tis like a whole age. —O *Jonathan!* 'twould make a good-natured man's heart bleed, to consider, continued the corporal, (standing perpendicularly) how low many a brave and upright fellow has been laid low since that time! —And trust me, *Susy,* added the corporal, turning to *Susannah,* whose eyes were swimming in water, —before that time comes round again, —many a bright eye will be dim. —*Susannah* placed it to the right side of the page—she wept—but she court'sied too. —Are we not, continued Trim, looking still at *Susannah*—are we not like a flower of the field—a tear of pride stole in betwixt every two tears of humiliation—else no tongue could have described *Susannah's* affliction—is not all flesh grass? —'Tis clay, —'tis dirt. —They all looked directly at the scullion, —the scullion had just been scouring a fish-kettle. —It was not fair.—

—What is the finest face that ever man looked at! —I could hear *Trim* talk so forever, cried *Susannah,* —what is it! (*Susannah* laid her hand upon *Trim's* shoulder)—but corruption? —*Susannah* took it off.

Even when the gesture is detached from a significant moment, it may have a commanding pertinence, simply for its homely reality :

Had the same great reasoner looked on, as my father illustrated his systems of noses, and observed my uncle *Toby's* deportment, —what great attention he gave to every word, —and as oft as he took his pipe from his mouth, with what wonderful seriousness he contemplated the length of it, —surveying it transversely as he held it betwixt his finger and his thumb, —then foreright, —then this way, and then that, in all its possible directions and foreshortenings, —he would have concluded my uncle *Toby* had got hold of the *medius terminus*; and was syllogizing and measuring with it the truth of each hypothesis of long noses, in order as my father laid them before him.

Probably the best example of it in the entire story is the scrupulous detail of Mr. Shandy's behavior on the news of the injury to Tristram's nose, a striking mixture of sympathy and absurdities.

The most humbling experience for the critic, historian, or mere writer upon literature is the attempt to explain why the thing that amuses us is amusing. Within the last generation ponderous words upon the forms of literary humor have been written that would do credit to the minuscule mind of Walter Shandy himself. For myself, I can easily forego the labor of typing and labeling Sterne's humor, and content myself with a final word upon what it is not.

All of the inevitable comparisons of Sterne and Rabelais break down upon a critical point—that Rabelais' humor is as coarse and robust as the century that produced it, while Sterne's shows delicacy. And on this point we must make and maintain a distinction between artistic delicacy and what is commonly, and disparagingly, known as indelicacy. On the latter matter we have already said our say.

Again the question of current taste enters. The writers of the eighteenth century were divided in their views of sex as a subject for humor. The Addisons, the Richardsons, the Johnsons, and of course the women novelists, "saw nothing funny" in sex. The Swifts, the Fieldings, the Walpoles, and writers for the theater down to Sterne's time, were generally of a different mind; and they probably represented the prevailing temper. Sterne's humor is not often blatant. Where it is, he seems to be making a deliberate assault upon moral preciousness. There is an animus here, one that many high-minded people have shared. But it is not Sterne at his most admirable.

At its best, his humor would challenge the blandest and purest that our literature has produced. It is particularly attractive when it seasons almost imperceptibly an episode or a passage of some serious import, or when it exudes from a simple and literal mind. The dialogue between Mr. and Mrs. Shandy on putting Tristram into breeches exemplifies it.

> We should begin, said my father, turning himself half round in bed, and shifting his pillow a little towards my mother's, as he opened the debate—We should begin to think, Mrs. *Shandy,* of putting this boy into breeches.—
>
> We should so, —said my mother. —We defer it, my dear, quoth my father, shamefully.—
>
> I think we do, Mr. *Shandy,* —said my mother.
>
> —Not but the child looks extremely well, said my father, in his vests and tunicks.—
>
> He does look very well in them, —replied my mother.—
>
> And for that reason it would be almost a sin, added my father, to take him out of 'em.—
>
> —It would so, —said my mother : —But indeed he is growing a very tall lad, —rejoin'd my father.
>
> —He is very tall for his age, indeed, —said my mother.—
>
> —I can not (making two syllables of it) imagine, quoth my father, who the deuce he takes after.—
>
> I cannot conceive, for my life, —said my mother.—

Humph! —said my father.

(The dialogue ceased for a moment.)

—I am very short myself, —continued my father, gravely.

You are very short, Mr. *Shandy*, —said my mother.

Humph! quoth my father to himself, a second time; in muttering which, he plucked his pillow a little further from my mother's, —and turning about again, there was an end of the debate for three minutes and a half.

—When he gets these breeches made, cried my father in a higher tone, he'll look like a beast in 'em.

He will be very awkward in them at first, replied my mother.

—And 'twill be lucky, it that's the worst on't, added my father.

It will be very lucky, answered my mother.

I suppose, replied my father, —making some pause first, —he'll be exactly like other people's children.—

Exactly, said my mother.—

—Though I should be sorry for that, added my father : and so the debate stopped again.

—They should be of leather, said my father, turning him about again.—

They will last him, said my mother, the longest.

But he can have no linings to 'em, replied my father.—

He cannot, said my mother.

'Twere better to have them of fustian, quoth my father.

Nothing can be better, quoth my mother.—

—Except dimity, —replied my father : —'Tis best of all, —replied my mother.

—One must not give him his death, however, —interrupted my father.

By no means, said my mother : —and so the dialogue stood still again.

I am resolved, however, quoth my father, breaking silence the fourth time, he shall have no pockets in them.—

—There is no occasion for any, said my mother.—

I mean in his coat and waistcoat, —cried my father.

—I mean so too, —replied my mother.

—Though if he gets a gig [whirligig] or a top—Poor souls it is a crown and a scepter to them, —they should have where to secure it.—

Order it as you please, Mr. *Shandy*, replied my mother.—

But don't you think it right? added my father, pressing the point home to her.

Perfectly, said my mother, if it pleases you, Mr. *Shandy*.—

There's for you, cried my father, losing temper—Pleases me! —You never will distinguish, Mrs. *Shandy*, nor shall I ever teach you to do it, betwixt a point of pleasure and a point of convenience.

—This was on a *Sunday* night; —and further this chapter sayeth not.

The humor of the written or spoken word which is wit, Sterne's most memorable gift, calls for no quotation. It permeates almost every scrap of a sentence in *Tristram Shandy*. It is humor for a mature culture and mature minds; not funny, often not risible. It runs with, but is not a part of, his quirks and perversities of style. It is quite separable from his straight-faced nonsense; and probably more than anything else is what is relished by a reader of experience and taste.

A final word seems called for on a matter not always brought to the surface in discussions of Sterne—his distaste for literary pretense.

It is remarkable that Sterne, in both his fictions and his letters, voices no literary judgment upon his great contemporaries. The score of years during which he began to publish *Tristram Shandy* had given the world all of Richardson's novels and all of Fielding's. Smollett was still active, though *Humphry Clinker* was still to appear. Sterne's silence upon what was in an admissible sense the most tremendous twenty years in English fiction was probably not the silence of unfamiliarity. We know he had Fielding's works on his shelves, and that he had a transient and uncomfortable contact with Smollett (the Smellfungus of the *Sentimental Journey*). He was, we know, capable of envy. But more probably he was indifferent or even censorious. If so, for what aspects of their work? And why? Or is nothing to be inferred from the fact that he neglected the courtesy, generous but of course unnecessary, which Miss Burney, Miss Reeve, Bage and Miss Edgeworth, all in one way or another, took pains to express. My own impression is that he was impatient of the literary pose and the residues of conventional romanticism in all three of his great predecessors.

It is simply a fact—and perhaps it is the ultimate word to be said about Sterne—that he was not, in the esoteric sense, literary; but he was obviously and sometimes assertively anti-literary. That he was anti-romantic admits of little or no doubt, in spite of his sentimentalism, which does not have to be romantically dressed up. Indeed, the gravest critics of his temperamental sentimentalism tend to interpret it as disguised sensuality. His correspondence with Miss Fourmentelle and Mrs. Draper (and one particular letter to his friend John Hall Stevenson) give us little reason to dispute the fairness of that judgment, even though it is impossible to adjudge "guilt" in either of these affairs.

The *Sentimental Journey* supports this view that whatever romance he found in his philanderings was self-induced. The romance *in posse* with Madame de L***, picked up, turned to sentimental account, and terminated by La Fleur's diplomatic intervention; the episode of the shopkeeper's wife; the encounter with Madame R****'s *fille de chambre,* fluttering between crass sexuality and elderly good will; even the Maria episode—can anyone imagine the Vicar of Coxwold "taking to his bosom" the unfortunate peasant-girl?—these are not romance, but opportunities for exhibitions of feeling.

Tristram Shandy shows much the same attitude toward women. Mrs. Shandy, unobtrusively amusing, is nevertheless a little contemptible—at least in Mr. Shandy's eyes. The widow Wadham only supports Mr. Shandy's conviction that women account for most of the trouble in the world. Bridget and Susannah live on terms of unblushing freedom with Corporal Trim. These women are all realists, undisturbed, so far, as we can see, by their mild emotions, and unspoiled by romantic prepossessions. Sterne himself, writing to Garrick from Paris, deplores the current French drama, which is "all love, love, love." If his heart can be, as it probably was, intensely moved by Mrs. Draper, it is evidently willing self-deception.* And the cynical burning-out of his young passion for his wife only confirms our conviction of facile and evanescent sentiment. All these things give us apparently his true reaction to the matter of essential romantic interest for every notable writer of fiction from Richardson down to Jane Austen. Both *Tristram Shandy* and the *Sentimental Journey* are totally without literary lovers because Sterne saw in love a situation, not a sustained relation.

But his distaste for literary attitudes touches other matters than romantic love. In spite of Sterne's high spirits, he is scarcely an optimist, as were both Richardson and Fielding. His views of orthodox doctrine are, particularly for a clergyman, extremely noncommittal; that Uncle Toby sees God as the interested director of our personal destinies can be taken as simply another side of the kindly gentleman's simplicity. In all these matters of current conviction, reflected in the literary conventions of the time, Sterne seems not to have been greatly concerned.

But above all, he distrusts literary elegance, in all its manifestations— in its pompous morality, in its servility to the aristocratic tradition, in its manufactured sublimity (remember his parodied apostrophe to sleep in *Tristram Shandy*), and most of all, in its parade of sentience in the dress

---

*There are widely divergent views of the Draper episode. By his biographers generally it has been regarded as on Sterne's part a sincere as well as deep attachment. There are less favorable views of the lady's feelings, which seem to be referred to her restlessness and vanity. Cross, Sichel, and Wright and Sclater (*Sterne's Eliza*) seem to agree that there was a pathological aspect to Sterne's attachment, partly the physical and mental weakness of his final illness, and partly, perhaps, dotage. Cross quotes from one of Eliza's letters her final opinion of her lover; that he was "tainted with the vices of injustice, meanness, and folly."

of magniloquence. Nor is it sufficient to regard the anti-literary attitude as only one aspect of his innate irreverance. The fact that his shelves were filled with the ancient writers, and his aversion to stuffy learning, show that he had literary appreciation—for what he respected and liked.

Nothing is more critical of the grand manner of the eighteenth century than Sterne's relaxed wisdom and unconstrained intimacy with his reader. He was democratic by instinct, not by assertion or contention, but in the obvious range and depth of his sympathies. In spirit, he was the man of his century, in England, most closely akin to Voltaire. *Candide* and the first two volumes of *Tristram Shandy* came out in the same year, 1759—that is no longer a matter of bibliographical dispute—*Candide* early enough, and *Tristram Shandy* late enough, for Sterne to have laughed with the world while busy with his own story. However unlike the two works are, superficially, they were the product of kindred minds, though one was frankly agnostic, the other comfortably and civilly Anglican.

CHAPTER XII

𝕿𝖍𝖊 𝕷𝖆𝖙𝖊𝖗 𝕾𝖊𝖓𝖙𝖎𝖒𝖊𝖓𝖙𝖆𝖑𝖎𝖘𝖙𝖘

Goldsmith and Mackenzie

SENTIMENTALISM IS the dominant note of the great mass of inferior fiction during the latter half of the eighteenth century; so much so that in general usage it is to be taken for granted. In a few cases, however, an individual talent might elevate it to a certain dignity. The two outstanding instances are Sterne, whose importance in other respects has entitled him to a chapter by himself, and Goldsmith, whose once high repute seems to have been undergoing slow but certain eclipse. He shares a berth in this chapter with Henry Mackenzie, a figure of importance in the Edinburgh literary society of his time, but remembered today for only one of his three novels—*The Man of Feeling* (1771). This novel, with no legitimate claim to greatness, has a supportable claim upon our attention. For of all the narratives of the period, it is the most thoroughly saturated with sentimentality; so much, in fact, that it overflows into quite unintended comedy. It takes a peculiar kind of artistic incompetence to make an unimportant writer important. Mackenzie has it.

Goldsmith* calls for our attention first; for *The Vicar of Wakefield* (1766) appeared five years before *The Man of Feeling*.

It is not hard to find reasons for the long popularity of *The Vicar*, but they are not profound reasons. It is short, simple, and good-humored. It has moral weight without somberness, and it leaves no aftertaste of pessimism or cynicism. All these attributes would commend it to the average eighteenth-century reader, and would maintain its popularity throughout the reign of the good Queen Victoria.

Yet *The Vicar* has the defects of its virtues; and the twentieth century likes its realism rational, its characters not altogether transparent, its psychology analytical, and its morality hard-boiled. Only a half-century ago,

---

*Oliver Goldsmith (1728-1774). *The Vicar of Wakefield* (1766) was his only work of pure fiction. *The Citizen of the World* (1762) is an odd sort of social-critical fiction in letters.

The Vicar was still accepted, with *The Scarlet Letter,* as a modest and safe vehicle of instruction in the not wholly communicable arcana of sex— although the moral lesson it actually conveyed, and of which Goldsmith himself was probably quite unconscious, was that sexual ignorance is not always a reliable armor for female virtue.

The plot of *The Vicar* is modeled closely upon the theater, although Goldsmith's own very readable comedies came later. The theme is that of numberless eighteenth-century stories, long or short—the designs of a wealthy man of fashion upon the simplicity of a charming but too trustful virgin. Young Squire Thornhill is no tyro; his villainy is backed by experience and proven tactics, and in the end he is successful in carrying off the fascinated Olivia on a promise of marriage. There follows quickly abandonment of the girl and a proposed marriage with a young lady of fortune, who happens to have been previously affianced to the Vicar's eldest son before the family fell upon evil days.

Thornhill meets the indignant overtures of the Vicar with cruel insolence, and he finally determines to punish his interference by eviction and imprisonment—so powerful then were the advantages of status. But all comes right in the end, with the exposure and humiliation of the villain. The resolving of the plot is brought about through a stretching of coincidence well beyond its permissible limits. The long dispersed family is brought together through a series of purely accidental encounters, and their fortunes are restored by a general reversal of all their supposed misfortunes. Squire Thornhill turns out, quite unintentionally, to be firmly and legally married to Olivia; the second daughter, Sophia, is betrothed not only to a good man, but to an unexpected fortune; the older son marries his former fiancée, who had been all but married to the Squire; and the supposedly wasted means of the Vicar are recovered in full from the absconder who had seemingly ruined him years before. The story is filled out with episodes loosely attached to the plot, the most memorable being the younger son Moses's swapping the family horse to a swindler at a country fair for a gross of all but worthless green spectacles.

This does not seem to be the stuff out of which first-rate fiction is made. If an acceptable plot must be based upon a rational complication, then the plot of *The Vicar of Wakefield* is simply a bad one. But if a human being may be in himself a plot, then we have other grounds on which to consider its merits and its appeal to generations.

For the Vicar himself, though surrounded by a group of theatrically typed characters, is unmistakably a human being. And his humanity consists, as it should, in a likeable blend of force and feebleness, of serene reasonableness and hard-ridden crotchets. And the Vicar's wife is in her own simple way amiable. She is modeled upon the eighteenth century's stock pattern for the rural housewife, as a mixture of practical domestic sense and ambitious aspirations for her young family. But her great importance for the story is to play up the Vicar's exemplary good will, piety, and fortitude. His moral wit is constantly sharpened upon her simplicity. When Moses returns from the fair, her disgust at his costly ignorance is vented in her exclamation, "The blockhead has been imposed upon, and should have known his company better." "There, my Dear," replies the Vicar, "you are wrong; he should not have known them at all." But these well meant exchanges reveal the Vicar's truth to his own nature and his calling, as well as her plain motherly conscience.

There is throughout the story a continuous comedy of character, of which a good sample is Mrs. Primrose's naïve attempt to impress the neighbors, and Squire Thornhill more particularly, with their style, on the Sunday following his introduction to the family as an apparently eligible suitor. The Vicar himself is telling the story.

After tea, when I seemed in spirits, she began thus : "I fancy, Charles my dear, we shall have a great deal of good company at our church tomorrow."

"Perhaps we may, my dear," returned I, "though you need be under no uneasiness about that; you shall have a sermon whether there be or not."

"That is what I expect," returned she; "but I think, my dear, we ought to appear there as decently as possible; for who knows what may happen?"

"Your precautions, my dear, are highly commendable. A decent behavior and appearance in church is what charms me. We should be devout and humble; cheerful and serene."

"Yes," cried she, "I know that; but I mean we should go there in as proper a manner as possible; not altogether like the scrubs about us."

"You are quite right, my dear," returned I, "and I was going to make the very same proposal. The proper manner of going is to go there as early as possible, to have time for meditation before the service begins."

"Phoo, Charles," interrupted she; "all that is very true, but not what I would be at. I mean we should go there genteelly. You know the church is two miles off; and I protest I don't like to see my daughters trudging up to their pew all blowzed and red with walking, and looking for all the world as if they had been winners at a smock-race. Now, my dear, my proposal is this. There are two plough-horses, the colt that has been in our family these nine years, and his companion Blackberry, that has scarce done an earthly thing for this month past. They are both grown fat and lazy. Why should not they do something as well as we? And let me tell you, when Moses has trimmed them a little, they will cut a very tolerable figure."

To this proposal I objected that walking would be twenty times more genteel than such a paltry conveyance, as Blackberry was wall-eyed and the colt wanted a tail; that they had never been broken to the rein, but had an hundred vicious tricks; and that we had but one saddle and pillion in the whole house. All these objections, however, were overruled, so that I was obliged to comply.

The Vicar's principles, we have to admit, must be to the eye of the present-day reader at times quite impervious to reason. Even an exemplar of the every-day uses of religion may rely too unquestioningly upon the letter of the moral law. When Olivia, for instance, tells her father that she has been seduced into a false marriage by a venial priest, whose name she has sworn to conceal,

> "Then we must hang the priest" [the Vicar cries] "and you shall inform against him tomorrow."
>
> "But sir," returned she, "will that be right when I am sworn to secrecy?"
>
> "My dear," I replied, "if you have made such a promise, I cannot, nor will I, tempt you to break it. Even though it may benefit the public, you must not inform against him. In all human institutions a smaller evil is allowed to procure a greater good; as in politics a province may be given away to secure a kingdom; in medicine, a limb may be lopped off to preserve the body. But in religion, the law is written and inflexible, *never* to do evil. And this law, my child, is right; for otherwise, if we commit a smaller evil to procure a greater good, certain guilt would be thus incurred in expectation of contingent advantage.

We need not look too closely at the casuistry of the Vicar's position. Indeed, it is doubtful, as it often is with Goldsmith, whether or not the intent of the passage is humorous.

The Vicar himself is, in an obvious sense, the story. For the action is haphazard and arbitrary, except in so far as it illumines the character of a man whose problems repeatedly involve conflicts between old precept and personal judgment. His rules of conduct are maintained both fervently and rigidly, and are often expressed in passages of worldly wisdom terse enough to be remembered :

> That virtue which requires to be ever guarded is scarce worth the sentinel.
>
> Conscience is a coward, and those faults it has not strength enough to prevent it seldom has justice enough to accuse.

The prolonged popularity of *The Vicar*—right down through the nine-teenth century—is no doubt explained largely by its happy anticipation of the moral temper of the Victorian age. But in our own century its melo-drama, its providential interventions, its sentimentality, and its pietism have been kicked about mercilessly by another order of critics. So among mature readers today an unashamed apologist for *The Vicar* would prob-ably have to be looked for in dark corners with a lantern.

We have placed Goldsmith among the sentimentalists. It is not an ac-cusation. A difference must be recognized between affected or fashionable sentiment and one which expresses a really sensitive nature. Yet how to distinguish with certainty?

In Goldsmith's case there can be little doubt that honest sentiment was well assimilated in a highly sympathetic nature. The rural idyll, the Vicar's simplicity and true goodness, the ingenuous family relations, all confirm Goldsmith's admiration for the simple virtues that we find in the poetry, the plays, and the essays. His humanity, his pathos, his unworldliness, are all manifestations of sentiment, but as free from pretense as a conven-tional feeling can be at its purest.

Henry Mackenzie's claim to literary notice is more frail, resting as it does upon an almost undisciplined sentimentalism. Yet his work shows qualities that might have assured him of some importance as a novelist had he not maimed his talent by forcing it into the sentimental mold.*

The Man of Feeling is scarcely a novel in either scope or form. Its form is quite anomalous, indeed—a "frame" of external incident accounting for the finding of fragments of a manuscript narrating ten or a dozen casual meetings in the brief life of the principal, Harley, called properly enough the man of feeling. His spiritual constitution is almost angelically delicate, and his sensibility to the selfishness and callousness of humanity compels him to shrink from the world, to distrust it, and, in his own word, to "pity" it. It is scarcely necessary to say that with this mental temper Harley is predestined to die young as a spiritual casualty in a heart-lessly competitive society.

The substance of the story is found, as in *The Vicar*, in its principal. Its incident is a series of largely chance meetings with characters who have suffered as he has, but from more immediate and cruel social abuses. He listens to the stories of these unfortunates (a bouquet of little histories, in fact). They embrace the experiences of a young girl crazed by her family's insistence on her marrying a fortune, a crippled and discharged veteran, a ruined tenant-farmer, a victim of seduction now turned prostitute. And

---

*Henry Mackenzie (1745-1831). *The Man of Feeling*, 1771; *The Man of the World*, 1773; *Julia de Roubigné*, 1777.

there are still other and intriguing examples of the human waste of the social system—a beggar cynically resigned to beggary, a misanthropist, a pair of cardsharpers, a penniless and parasitic young man of fashion—all of whom contribute to Harley's conviction that civilization is a *pis aller*. These figures had without exception been previously typed, by Smollett among others, to whom Mackenzie (as a fellow Scot?) seems particularly in debt. Yet Mackenzie depicts them with a freshness that justifies Harley's almost morbidly sympathetic interest in their tales.

The treatment of these episodes follows a formula, the last step in which is almost always a shower of tears in which narrator and listener join, weeping on each other's shoulders. The great scene, however, in *The Man of Feeling* is Harley's death. He has been throughout the action in love with a neighboring landholder's daughter, Miss Walton, but his natural modesty, as well as his sense of the disparity of their fortunes, has kept him silent. When the circuit of his visitations with the wronged and the unhappy has run full course, he returns to his rural home, to fall ill from jail fever contracted during his charitable visits to a local prison. Miss Walton, out of the urgings of her own sympathetic nature, visits him in his illness.

> He was left with Miss Walton alone. She inquired anxiously about his health. "I believe," said he, "from the accounts which my physicians unwillingly give me, that they have no great hopes of my recovery. —She started as he spoke; but recollecting herself immediately, endeavored to flatter him into a belief that his apprehensions were groundless. "I know," said he, "that it is usual with persons at my time of life to have these hopes, which your kindness suggests; but I would not wish to be deceived. To meet death as becomes a man is a privilege bestowed on few. —I would endeavor to make it mine; —nor do I think that I can ever be better prepared for it than now. —It is that chiefly which determines the fitness of its approach." "Those senti-ments," answered Miss Walton, "are just; but your good sense, Mr. Harley, will own, that life has its proper value. —As the province of virtue, life is ennobled; as such, it is to be desired. To virtue has the Supreme Director of all things assigned rewards enough even here to fix its attachment."
>
> The subject began to overpower her. —Harley lifted his eyes from the ground. —"There are," said he, in a very low voice, "there are attachments, Miss Walton" —His glance met hers. —They both betrayed a confusion, and were both instantly withdrawn. —He paused some moments. —"I am in such a state as calls for sincerity; let that excuse it. —It is perhaps the last time we shall ever meet. I feel something particularly solemn in the acknowledgement, yet my heart swells to make it, awed as it is by a sense of my presumption, by a

Harley and the Beggar; from Henry Mackenzie's *Man of Feeling*, London, 1800; engraved by P. Rothwell after Thomas Stothard.

sense of your perfections." —He paused again. —"Let it not offend
you, to know their power over one so unworthy. —It will, I believe,
soon cease to beat, even with that feeling which it shall lose the latest.
—To love Miss Walton could not be a crime; —if to declare it is one,
the expiation will be made." —Her tears were now flowing without
control. —"Let me intreat you," said she, "to have better hopes. —Let
not life be so indifferent to you; if my wishes can put any value on
it. I will not pretend to misunderstand you. —I know your worth.
—I have known it long. —I have esteemed it. —What would you
have me say? —I have loved it as it deserved." He seized her hand—a
languid color reddened his cheek—a smile brightened faintly in his
eye. As he gazed on her, it grew dim, it fixed, it closed. —He sighed
and fell back on his seat. —Miss Walton screamed at the sight. —His
aunt and the servants rushed in the room. —They found them lying
motionless together. —His physician happened to call at that instant.
Every art was tried to recover them. —With Miss Walton they succeeded. —But Harley was gone forever.

Yet we must note a difference, a significant difference, in the quality
and the objects of Mackenzie's sentiment. It is not the vanity of refined
feeling; it is the sentiment of unpretended and comprehensive sympathy,
and its objects are truly unfortunates; for they are the victims of society.
The Man of Feeling is in fact a continuous arraignment of public inequities
and oppressions, and Harley's indignation, though it subsides constantly
into tears, carries with it intelligent judgment of the evils of which he is
a witness. There is topical comment upon political favoritism, the press-
gang, farm tenancy, poaching, land monopoly, military abuses, and—
almost unthinkably, considering the time—British imperialism!* We
quote, in compensatory fairness to Mackenzie, these opening sentences
from his little discourse on British arms in India :

"Edwards," said he, "I have a proper regard for the prosperity of
my country; every native of it appropriates to himself some share of
the power, or the fame, which, as a nation, it acquires; but I cannot
throw off the man so much as to rejoice at our conquests in India. You
tell me of immense territories subject to the English; I cannot think of
their possessions without being led to inquire by what right they possess them. They came there as traders, bartering the commodities they
brought for others which their purchasers could spare; and however
great their profits were, they were then equitable. But what title have
the subjects of another kingdom to establish an empire in India? —to
give laws to a country where the inhabitants received them on the

---

*We must note, too, in *Julia de Roubigné,* a major episode dealing with slavery in the West
Indies.

terms of friendly commerce? You say they are happier under our regulations than the tyranny of their own petty princes. I must doubt it, from the conduct of those by whom these regulations have been made. They have drained the treasuries of Nabobs, who must fill them by oppressing the industry of their subjects. Nor is this to be wondered at, when we consider the motive upon which those gentlemen do not deny their going to India. . . . When shall I see a commander return from India in the pride of honorable poverty? You describe the victories they have gained; they are sullied by the cause in which they fought. You enumerate the spoils of those victories; they are covered with the blood of the vanquished.

Could you tell me of some conqueror giving peace and happiness to the conquered? Did he accept the gifts of their princes to use them for the comfort of those whose fathers, sons, or husbands fell in battle? Did he use his power to gain security and freedom to the regions of oppression and slavery? Did he endear the British name by examples of generosity, which the most barbarous or most depraved are rarely able to resist? Did he return with the consciousness of duty discharged to his country, and humanity to his fellow-creatures? Did he return with no lace on his coat, no slaves in his retinue, no chariot at his door, and no Burgundy at his table? These were laurels which princes might envy—which an honest man would not condemn!

The Man of Feeling, it should be noted in further justice to Mackenzie, has at times a peculiar grace of off-hand style, in passages sensitive to scene and associations, and often touched with the fragrance of reminiscence. This example is from the opening pages.

I looked around with some grave apothegm in my mind when I discovered, for the first time, a venerable pile, to which the enclosure belonged. An air of melancholy hung about it. There was a languid stillness in the day, and a single crow, that perched on an old tree by the side of the gate, seemed to delight in the echo of its own croaking.

I leaned on my gun and looked, but I had not breath enough to ask the curate a question. I observed carving on the bark of some of the trees; 'twas indeed the only mark of human art about the place, except that some branches appeared to have been lopped, to give a view of the cascade which was formed by a little rill at some distance.

Just at this moment I saw pass between the trees a young lady with a book in her hand. I stood upon a stone to observe her; but the curate sat him down on the grass, and leaning his back where I stood, told me. "That was the daughter of a neighboring gentleman of the name of Walton, whom he had seen walking there more than once."

It is a good style for the occasion, but Mackenzie is wise enough not to overuse it. Its complement is a rather rigid and sometimes oracular John-sonese. This, however, is less evident in *The Man of Feeling* than in his two later novels.

There is little need to dwell upon either of these. *The Man of the World* 1773, obviously designed as a counterfoil to *The Man of Feeling,* is a rather shocking tale of planned seduction and desertion, experimentally interesting as the sequent story of two generations, mother and daughter, as in Mrs. Inchbald's *Simple Story* a generation later. The plot is patterned rather closely upon Richardson's *Clarissa,* though the principal's deliberately leading his school companion into crime and eventual transportation, in order to create opportunity for the seduction of the sister, sets a new high in the much-used theme of studied aristocratic villainy.

Julia de Roubigné (1777), Mackenzie's last novel, is the most satisfactory of the three. Its heroine, out of gratitude for a kindness to her father, marries a man of rank, to learn after their marriage that the young man to whom she had once been informally affianced, and whom she had been led to believe already married, had returned, wealthy, from the West Indies, in the hope of making her his wife. The two, sentimentalists of course, arrange an indiscreet because secret meeting before his permanent departure from France. The circumstances of the meeting, although it is quite innocent, are so damning that her husband, "to retrieve his honor," poisons her—to learn of her innocence beside her deathbed. In the agony of regret, he then kills himself.

The plot is well managed—through letters—but by Mackenzie's time it was, of course, quite devoid of originality. The raw sentimentalism of Mackenzie's first novel, brought within control in *The Man of the World,* is in *Julia de Roubigné* neither mawkish, on the whole, nor exaggerative. The high moment of revelation on Julia's deathbed is forcefully handled, although it suffers from the obvious comparison with the poignant passion of the similar scene in *Othello.*

There is in all Mackenzie's novels too much literary artifice, too much sustention of mood, and too inflated a style. His unremitting pressure upon the sympathies is, as Clara Reeve pointed out, painful, but it can also be, when most insistent, ridiculous. Probably no datum in the literature of sentiment can make that clearer than a single sentence from *The Man of the World.*

> Yet those tender regrets which the better part of our nature feels, have something in them to blunt the edge of that pain they inflict, and confer on the votaries of sorrow a sensation that borders on pleasure.

Mackenzie is by no stretch of judgment a great novelist. In the first place, he is notably lacking in originality. For anyone widely read in the fiction of his century, his work betrays him as a sort of literary *chiffonier* —a collector and refurbisher of literary scraps. He apparently worked from wide reading and an appraising memory, but in the fashion of a Hollywood scenarist today, gathering up an idea here, an idea there, and drawing them together into an acceptable but uninspired continuity. There is no character in *The Man of Feeling* whom we have not met before. And in the prostitute's story, the journey in the stage coach, the politician's waiting room, and the ring of dishonest gamblers, we are retreading quite familiar ground.

In style, no one who has written upon Mackenzie has failed to record his indebtedness to Sterne. He employs, to be sure, Sterne's disjunctiveness, his compressed periodicity, his suspended sentences. But I do not feel that the debt goes much beyond the superficialities of Sterne's literary manner and his familiar tricks of asterisks and dashes; and most of these quirks are used sparingly. In fundamental indebtedness, however, in his manifest debts for ideas and situations, he cannot be absolved from borrowing, though borrowing always intelligently adapted.

In the larger estimate of Mackenzie's work one fact stands out that has not been sufficiently recognized by his critics. He is an early, a surprisingly early, humanitarian. It is greatly to his credit that almost a generation before Holcroft and Godwin he was using his novels for honest consideration of the political and social problems of his day. Social intelligence was then in its infancy, and social sympathy, where it existed at all, was likely to be expressed in the pious word and the casual shilling. Mackenzie was aware that the ills of the time called for a positive attitude, and even more, for a program. But in the state then of politics and social sentiment, it could not be expected that Mackenzie himself would be, or could be, a programmist. In England, programs were destined to wait until the French Revolution added the fear of reprisals to the need of understanding. But Mackenzie's role in that slow change from the old order deserves not to be forgotten.

It is unfortunate that Mackenzie's literary reputation has been so persistently judged by his exploitation of the sentimental vogue. For he was a better man, and potentially a better novelist, than his literary penchant could make him. His literary pursuits were dignified and professional, and his miscellaneous and critical writing had merit. But those facts cannot establish him as a novelist; for even at his best in fiction he was out of his element. It takes more than an alert mind and a quantum of literary competency to make a novelist.

CHAPTER XIII

A Young Lady's Entrance into the World

Frances Burney

FRANCES BURNEY'S *Evelina,* probably begun when she was seventeen, and published when she was twenty-six, has been praised as a young woman's view of her contemporary world, and damned (generally, in my experience, by young men) as sentimental, lamely comic, and generally the product of a brash and lamentable amateurism.* It was, however, very popular in its day, and it has been an arresting experience for many discriminating readers in later years.

It has, however, a lasting importance in the history of English fiction as the first novel to examine seriously, through a woman's eyes, the effects of the usages of the time upon the position and the life of a woman. We say the "first" novel to accomplish this, for while Mrs. Behn, Mrs. Manley, and Mrs. Heywood had written fiction more or less in the interest of their sex, no one would think of calling their fictions serious examinations of the social environment. Yet the significance of *Evelina* as a "first" we can note and dismiss. The story impressed the readers of its time as an engaging portrait of an intelligent young lady capable of appraising and recording a new and exacting social experience. It is still a thoroughly readable novel for much the same reasons.

It is not surprising that *Evelina* has seemed to appeal to women rather than men. For a large part of our interest in fiction depends upon our recognition of faithfulness to life in the particular terms on which we know it. There are aspects of the feminine that a gifted woman writer can not only realize but represent with a surer hand than a mere male. In quite different ways Jane Austen, George Eliot, and Virginia Woolf have proved that superiority over, let us say, Dickens, Hardy, and E. M. Forster, all of whom have shown more than ordinary knowledge of women's mental

---

*Frances Burney, *Mme. D'Arblay* (1752-1840). *Evelina, or A Young Lady's Entrance into the World* (1778); *Cecilia, or Memoirs of an Heiress* (1782); *Camilla, or A Picture of Youth* (1796); *The Wanderer, or Female Difficulties* (1814).

viscera. It is no mistake to place Fanny Burney among the able and knowing writers in this respect. In fact, in *Evelina* at least, for her later novels are less rewarding, one may see a sort of island of graceful womanly understanding in a sea of shallow, patronizing, or satirical eighteenth century attitudes upon women and their ways.

The heroine Evelina brings to London two prime assets of personality —innocence and propriety; the second scarcely less important than the first, since London was then a scene of predatory enterprise upon women of all classes. Of her innocence (which is not ignorance) no one is better assured than herself. But country manners were not good currency in the city, and her social embarrassments therefore furnish the sub-stratum of the plot. Like many of the young and inexperienced, she is an adept at getting into false positions, not for want of warnings, cautions, or her own good sense, but simply because she does not know the code of the city. But she learns, and the process of learning is the core of the story.

The bare theme of *Evelina* is simple and romantic—a youngish man, wealthy and well-placed, in love with a charming but at first awkward girl. Awkwardness is, in fact, very much a part of her charm, and it is drawn for us with a delicate humor as well as deep understanding of teenage self-consciousness.

The novel follows the now familiar epistolary form, and the first few of its eighty-five letters give us the setting of the story. Evelina is motherless, and socially fatherless also, since her noble father has refused (for reasons that are to develop later) to recognize her as his child. She has been brought up under the guardianship of a retired clergyman, the Reverend Mr. Villars, and she herself is introduced to us in the eighth letter on the point of being taken to London by Lady Howard, her protectress for the time, "to let her see something of the world." Evelina's personal relation with Mr. Villars is all affectionate duty, thankful and unaffected. She writes here to ask his approval for the visit to London.

> They are to make a very short stay in town. . . . Mrs. Mirvin and her daughter both go—what a happy party! Yet I am not very eager to accompany them. At least I shall be contented to remain where I am, if you desire that I should.
>
> Assured, my dearest Sir, of your goodness, your bounty, and your indulgent kindness, ought I to form a wish that has not your sanction? Decide for me, therefore, without the least apprehension that I shall be uneasy or discontented. While I am yet in suspense perhaps I may *hope,* but I am most certain that when you have once determined, I shall not repine.
>
> They tell me that London is now in full splendor. Two play-houses are open, the opera house, Ranelagh, and the Pantheon—you see I

have learned all their names. However, don't suppose that I make any point of going, for I shall hardly sigh to see them depart without me, though I shall probably never meet with such another opportunity. . . .

I believe I am bewitched! I made a resolution when I began that I would not be urgent; but my pen—or rather my thoughts—will not suffer me to keep it; for I acknowledge—I must acknowledge—I cannot help wishing for your permission.

I almost repent already that I have made this confession; pray forget that you have read it, if this journey is displeasing to you. But I will not write any longer; for the more I think of this affair, the less indifferent to it I find myself. . . .

You will not, I am sure, send a refusal without reasons unanswerable, and therefore I shall cheerfully acquiesce. Yet I hope—I hope you will be able to permit me to go.

I am, with the utmost affection,

gratitude, and duty, your

Evelina.

Shall we set this effusion down as just plain wheedling? Or is it the flutter of a young girl facing a young—and nice—girl's dilemma?

Of course Evelina goes up to London, not without anxious cautions from Mr. Villars. Life opens out invitingly for her, at assemblies, parties, the theater, the opera, the amusement gardens then so popular, and in scenes of quiet and pretty domesticity. Her great moment arrives when for the first time she meets Lord Orville—and dances with him!

Very soon after, another gentleman, who seemed about six and twenty years old, gayly but not foppishly dressed, and indeed extremely handsome, with an air of mixed politeness and gallantry desired to know if I was engaged, or would honor him with my hand. . . .

Well, I bowed, and I am sure I colored; for indeed I was frightened at the thoughts of dancing before so many people, all strangers, and, which was worse, *with* a stranger. However, that was unavoidable, for although I looked around the room several times, I could not see one person that I knew. And so he took my hand, and led me to join in the dance. . . .

He seemed very desirous of entering into conversation with me, but I was seized with such a panic that I could hardly speak a word; and nothing but the shame of so soon changing my mind prevented my returning to my seat, and declining to dance at all.

He appeared to be surprised at my terror, which I believe was but too apparent. However, he asked no questions, though I fear he must think it very strange; for I did not choose to tell him it was owing to my never before dancing but with a school-girl.

His conversation was sensible and spirited, his air and address were open and noble; his manners gentle, attentive, and infinitely engaging; his person is all elegance, and his countenance the most animated and expressive I have ever seen.

In a short time we were joined by Miss Mirvin, who stood next couple to us. But how was I startled when she whispered me that my partner was a nobleman!

The progress of this pretty romance can be taken for granted, its obstacles as well as its fair future. Two rivals appear to challenge Lord Orville's interest in Evelina; object, seduction in both cases. There is at times brisk action in these complications, but Miss Burney is a lady, and she avoids the sensual suggestiveness of Richardson. No duels are fought, though Lord Orville offers to take one on in her behalf; for he has been brought up in the aristocratic punctilio, which still regarded the handling of the gentleman's weapons as part of a gentleman's training.

The chief hindrance to the rapid maturing of the attachment is the opposition, private, friendly, and well-intentioned, of course, of Mr. Villars. He knows the bitter effects of unequal marriages for both Evelina's parents and her grandparents; so he is gravely mistrustful of the suit of the urbane Lord Orville. He fears that Evelina's imagination has been captured by Orville's personal and social glamor, if indeed the nobleman is serious at all.

An unusual, and in the end an unsatisfactorily explained, complication brings Evelina reluctantly around to Mr. Villars' view. This is a letter of audacious gallantry sent to Evelina in Orville's name by one of his rivals. Misled and shocked by this incident, she opens her heart (Letters LX and LXI) fully to Mr. Villars and agrees to refuse further attentions from Orville. It is a finely wrought passage, and incidentally, one that transcends most of the limitations of the epistolary form—a matter in itself of notable art. She resigns herself to her loss, but her spirit is deeply wounded by what she feels is Orville's bad faith, and she falls ill. Her health is, in fact, so endangered that she is sent to Bristol Hot Wells, under proper chaperonage, to recuperate; and there, it may almost be anticipated, she meets Orville again, quite by accident. Mutual interest is re-established, though with a reticence on Evelina's part that reflects her mistrust of both Orville and herself. There is an understandable stiffness on Orville's side too, for he is of course unaware of the cause of Evelina's reserve. The constraints inherent in this ambiguous situation appear in the following dialogue recounted in a letter to Mr. Villars.

When I was seated, I found myself much at a loss what to say; yet, after a short silence, assuming all the courage in my power, "Will you not, my Lord," said I, "think me trifling and capricious should I own I have repented the promise I made,* and should I entreat your Lordship not to insist upon my strict performance of it?" I spoke so hastily that I did not, at the time, consider the impropriety of what I said.

As he was entirely silent, and profoundly attentive, I continued to speak without interruption.

"If your Lordship, by any other means, knew the circumstances attending my acquaintance with Mr. Macartney, I am most sure you would yourself disapprove my relating them. He is a gentleman, and has been very unfortunate, but I am not, I think, at liberty to say more; yet I am sure, if he knew your Lordship wished to hear any particulars of his affairs, he would readily consent to my acknowledging them. Shall I, my Lord, ask his permission?"

"His affairs," repeated Lord Orville; "by no means. I have not the least curiosity about them."

"I beg your Lordship's pardon—but indeed I had understood the contrary."

"Is it possible, Madam, you could suppose the affairs of an utter stranger can excite my curiosity?"

The gravity and coldness with which he asked this question very much abashed me. But Lord Orville is the most delicate of men, and presently recollecting himself, he added, "I mean not to speak with indifference of any friend of yours—far from it. Any such will always command my good wishes. Yet I own I am rather disappointed; and though I doubt not the justice of your reason, to which I implicitly submit, you must not wonder that, upon the point of being honored with your confidence, I should feel the greatest regret at finding it withdrawn."

Do you think, my dear Sir, I did not at that moment require all my resolution to guard me from frankly telling him all that he wished to hear? Yet I rejoice that I did not; for added to the actual wrong I should have done, Lord Orville himself, when he had heard, would have blamed me. Fortunately, this thought occurred to me, and I said, "Your Lordship shall yourself be my judge. The promise I made, though voluntary, was rash and inconsiderate; yet had it concerned myself, I should not have hesitated in fulfilling it; but the gentleman whose affairs I should be obliged to relate—"

"Pardon me," cried he, "for interrupting you; yet allow me to assure you I have not the slightest desire to be acquainted with his affairs, further than what belongs to the motives which induced you yesterday morning—" He stopped but there was no occasion to say more.

---

*Her promise to give Orville her reason for an apparently clandestine meeting with a Mr. Macartney.

"That, my Lord," I cried, "I will tell you honestly. Mr. Macartney had some particular business with me—and I could not take the liberty to ask him hither."

"And why not? Mrs. Beaumont, I am sure—"

"I could not, my Lord, think of intruding upon Mrs. Beaumont's complaisance; and so, with the same hasty folly I promised your Lordship. I much *more* readily promised to meet him."

"And did you?"

"No, my Lord," said I coloring; "I returned before he came."

Again for some time we were both silent; yet unwilling to leave him to reflections which could not but be to my disadvantage, I summoned sufficient courage to say, "There is no young creature, my Lord, who so greatly wants, or so earnestly wishes for, the advice and assistance of her friends as I do. I am new to the world, and unused to acting for myself. My intentions are never wilfully blamable, yet I err perpetually! I have hitherto been blest with the most affectionate of friends, and indeed the ablest of men, to guide and instruct me upon every occasion. But he is too distant now to be applied to at the moment I want his aid. And *here*—there is not a human being whose counsel I can ask."

"Would to Heaven," cried he, with a countenance from which all coldness and gravity were banished, and succeeded by the mildest benevolence, "that I were worthy—and capable—of supplying the place of such a friend to Miss Anville."

"You do me but too much honor," said I; "yet I hope your Lordship's candor—perhaps I ought to say indulgence—will make some allowance on account of my inexperience, for behavior so inconsiderate. May I, my Lord, hope that you will?"

"May I," cried he, "hope that you will pardon the ill grace with which I have submitted to my disappointment, and that you will permit me" (kissing my hand) "thus to seal my peace."

"*Our* peace, my Lord," said I, with revived spirits.

Sophistication is not the state of mind for appraising this sort of dialogue. If it were a scrap from a play of Shaw's, we could properly interpret Evelina's attitude and tone as the well played overture of a minx. But there is here, under the stiff embroidery of eighteenth-century speech, an honest purpose that enables her to surmount her bashfulness and speak with assurance. True, it also adds to Orville's admiration that she shows self-possession and judgment—things which she has learned from contact with the society in which he would have her move.

But better understanding does not lead promptly to denouement; for there is still Mr. Villars' deep prejudice to be dealt with. Evelina, obedient to Villars' will, yields to his summons to leave for her guardian's —and her—home, and to cut herself loose from the man of her heart.

Here is the parting scene, for which we must be prepared with the knowledge that Evelina believes that these words will really be their last.

We all went together to the drawing-room. After a short and unentertaining conversation, Mrs. Selwyn said she must prepare for our journey, and begged me to see for some books she had left in the parlor.

And here, while I was looking for them, I was followed by Lord Orville. He shut the door after he came in, and approaching me with a look of anxiety, said, "Is it true, Miss Anville? Are you going?"

"I believe so, my Lord," said I, still looking for the books.

"So suddenly, so unexpectedly, must I lose you?"

"No great loss, my Lord," said I , endeavoring to speak cheerfully.

"Is it possible," said he gravely, "Miss Anville can doubt my sincerity?"

"I can't imagine," cried I, "what Mrs. Selwyn has done with these books."

"Would to Heaven," continued he, "I might flatter myself you would allow me to prove it."

"I must run upstairs," cried I, greatly confused, "and ask what she has done with them."

"You are going then," cried he, taking my hand, "and you give me not the smallest hope of your return! Will you not then, my too lovely friend—will you not at least teach me, with fortitude like your own, to support your absence?"

"My Lord," cried I, endeavoring to disengage my hand, "pray let me go!"

"I will," cried he, to my inexpressible confusion, dropping on one knee, "if you wish to leave me!"

"Oh, my Lord," exclaimed I; "rise, I beseech you, rise! Such a posture to me! Surely your Lordship is not so cruel as to mock me."

"Mock you," repeated he earnestly; "no; I revere you. I esteem and admire you above all human beings! You are the friend to whom my soul is attached as to its better half! You are the most amiable, the most perfect, of women! And you are dearer to me than language has the power of telling."

I attempt not to describe my sensations at that moment. I scarce breathed; I doubted if I existed; the blood forsook my cheeks, and my feet refused to sustain me. Lord Orville, hastily rising, supported me to a chair, upon which I sunk, almost lifeless.

For a few minutes we neither of us spoke; and then, seeing me recover, Lord Orville, in terms hardly articulate, entreated my pardon for his abruptness. The moment my strength returned, I attempted to rise, but he would not perimt me.

I cannot write the scene that followed, though every word is engraven on my heart; but his protestations, his expressions, were too flattering for repetition; nor would he, in spite of my repeated efforts to leave him, suffer me to escape. In short, my dear Sir, I was not proof against his solicitations—and he drew from me the most sacred secret of my heart.

This is pure eighteenth-century in its elegant clichés, in its sustained politeness, in its reticent confusion on the lady's part, in its attitudinized though real fervor on the gentleman's part, in its prostrating effect upon the happy recipient of the proposal, and most of all, in its rhetorical style—for nicely brought up people in those days *did* speak the language of Dr. Johnson. Yet it is all genuine; for the habits of a generation, mental, social, psychological, determine to a large extent how people act and talk. The proposal, though abrupt, has been anticipated by growing affection and ripening familiarity. All that has prevented it hitherto has been the reserve forced upon Evelina by Mr. Villars' anxieties. With close sympathy once more established, events move steadily to the now inevitable conclusion.

Up to this point we have dealt with the simple merits of Miss Burney's performance. But in some respects her writing is neither consistent nor workmanlike, and we must consider some of her shortcomings.

Many readers have felt that *Evelina* is a concoction, not an artistic composition; that is, that too many incongruous elements have been taken into its plot. But upon this point it is unsafe to try to lay down laws. The central plot is the budding and growth of the affection of Evelina and Orville, which ripens into a somewhat conventional romance. Below the surface of the story is the mystery of Evelina's paternity, relevant because the question of her legitimacy must have a good deal to do with her chances of a brilliant marriage. The denouement is Orville's supplanting of his rivals, acknowledgment of Evelina by her noble father (who *had* married her mother!), and, naturally, the marriage of the lovers. This is a unified and in most respects what might be called a standard plot.

There are two substantial subplots. The first is introduced solely for "comic relief." In it, a Captain Mirvin, a rough naval officer, and son-in-law of the gentlewoman who brings Evelina to London, carries on a running warfare of meaningless quarrels with Madame Duval, Evelina's grandmother, a grossly vulgar one-time English barmaid, long separated from Evelina by her residence in France. It is Madame Duval's intrigues, her impudence, and her utter social impossibility, that account for the fact that after his wife's death Evelina's father has disowned her entire family, and therefore Evelina. Madame Duval's relations on the other side of the family—the Branghtons—are a rather diverting study in social pretensions, and because of their connection with Evelina, although they are not related, they supply a low-comedy accompaniment to Evelina's interest and activity in the life and amusements of the upper classes.

The second subplot introduces halfway through the story an impoverished Scotch poet, Macartney, and toward the very end of the story the girl he is in love with, Miss Belmont. Their link with the action is that Evelina's friendly interest in Macartney's unhappy situation introduces complication into the maturing understanding between Orville and herself. In addition, both Macartney and Miss Belmont are connected incidentally, but not indispensably, with the solving of the problem of Evelina's parentage and position.

If a subplot is to be justified, it should have a recognizable and more or less continuous connection with the central story. The first subplot in *Evelina,* the episodes introducing Madame Duval and Captain Mirvin, is enlivened by the lowest sort of lampooning humor and practical jesting. Without being highbrow, we can safely regard such comic relief as tedious and effete, although many serious novelists and dramatists have condescended to employ it. Comedy, in itself, is another matter, but today most of us would prefer the comedy that gives flavor to a predominantly serious work, to the comedy that takes over intermittently the entire flow of action and introduces a separate set of characters for the purpose. But however it is handled, the important question is whether it is good comedy.

Candor obliges us to say that Fanny Burney's is not.* Her comic interludes are obviously modeled upon Smollett, whose "humor" she thought "exhilarating." But Smollett's comedy is rough and masculine; Miss Burney's is rough and feminine. There is a difference.

Since these comic scenes are not particularly successful, they are superfluous; and since they are pinned carelessly to the central theme through the mere fact that Evelina's grandmother is the victim of them, their usefulness for plot is extremely slight. Captain Mirvin himself, introduced only to make life miserable for Madame Duval, is no more than a parasite upon the action. The goings and comings of the Branghtons, however, are more organic; and although Miss Burney's depiction of their smugness and bad manners is often schoolteacherish rather than amusing, they have a redeeming use. For the Branghtons' affected imitation of the ways of high life presents a strong contrast to Evelina's naturalness and modesty. Furthermore, their ideas of public entertainment, including the theaters, the opera, and the amusement gardens,

---

*There is of course room for difference of opinion here. A recent writer on Jane Austen regards Miss Burney's comic passages as the most memorable part of her work.

T.Lowndes Published Nov.ʳ 24 1779.

Evelina helps Mme. Duval out of the mire. From the fourth edition (first illustrated edition) of Frances Burney's *Evelina*, London, 1779; Anthony Walker after John Mortimer.

give us some of the best close-up knowledge we have as to the way Londoners of the time actually diverted themselves.

The second subplot—the Macartney-Belmont story—is better integrated with the main story than the Duval-Mirvin-Branghton episodes. For Miss Belmont is the innocent subject of an imposture which has foisted her upon Evelina's father as his legitimate daughter, in Evelina's place. That complication is acceptable, since it accounts for her father's rejection of Evelina's proper claims. Macartney, however, Miss Belmont's admirer and suitor, has no useful part in the story beyond furnishing a means of stalling the latter part of the action (call it "creating suspense," if you prefer) in order to roughen the road to the marital bliss of Evelina and Orville. The fact that Macartney turns out to be the natural son of Evelina's father, and therefore her half-brother, is only another instance of the fact that plot can be stretched and padded by the use of easy coincidence. On the whole, all that can be said for this second subplot is that it fattens the story without adding materially to its interest. *Evelina,* then, is not a unified or sharply focused story, not even by the standards prevailing before Miss Burney wrote. And its lack of unity is especially unsatisfactory because the attached episodes are not in themselves very interesting.

Characterization in *Evelina* is sound when it is serious; crudely disappointing when Miss Burney is tempted to copy Smollett (which she does, in spite of her dictum that "imitation cannot be shunned too seduously"). After all, Smollett's vulgar characters have redeeming humanity. Captain Mirvin is only a pestiferous clown. Even the serious characters, however, are conceived with only limited originality, and, except for Evelina herself, who is in temper and training Miss Burney's *alter ego,* they are not profoundly studied. One character, however, is not cut from the familiar eighteenth-century pattern. This is Mrs. Selwyn, a society warhorse, strong-minded and strong-willed, who chaperones Evelina to Bristol, and does her capable best to restore sweet concord to the two lovers. But it is interesting that Evelina—or Miss Burney—accepts her and her helpful activities with reservations :

> Mrs. Selwyn is very kind and attentive to me. She is extremely clever. Her understanding, indeed, may be called *masculine.* But unfortunately her manners deserve the same epithet; for in studying to acquire the knowledge of the other sex, she has lost all the softness of her own. In regard to myself, however, as I have neither courage nor inclination to argue with her, I have never been personally hurt by her want of gentleness, a virtue which nevertheless seems so essential a part of the female character that I find myself more awkward and less at ease with a woman who wants it, than I do with a man. She is not a favorite with Mr. Villars, who has often been disgusted at her propen-

sity to satire; but his anxiety that I should try the effect of the Bristol waters overcame his dislike of committing me to her care.

Strong-minded women were only grudgingly appreciated in Evelina's day; so it is not surprising that she prefers the soft virtues to the rational. But Mrs. Selwyn *is* a creation, tough with dandified males, but aware of character and desert, and amusing in the hearty promulgation of her likes and dislikes. I am not sure that there is a single woman character in the fiction of the period who comes as close as she does to the high bearing and salutary irony of Jane Austen's women.

Fielding, as we have seen, could, in spite of his theatrical experience, suppress theatricality in big scenes. But Miss Burney's handling of highly emotional situations, more like Richardson's and Smollett's, reaches a tension in which the last vestiges of restraint are simply abandoned. The romantic conventions of the time, as a rule, left little for the reader's imagination to fill in; so it would have been unthinkable for Miss Burney to have failed to do full justice to a situation that called for sentimental stress. The recognition scene between Evelina and her father—who at their first meeting had been too overwrought by her resemblance to her dead mother to bear her in his presence—shows Miss Burney's melodramatic energy at its highest, which is not to say its most admirable.

> The moment I reached the landing-place, the drawing-room door was opened, and my father, with a voice of kindness, called out, "My child, is it you?"
> "Yes, Sir," cried I, springing forward and kneeling at his feet; "it is your child, if you will own her."
> He knelt by my side, and folding me in his arms, "Own thee," repeated he; "yes, my poor girl, and Heaven knows with what bitter contrition." Then raising both himself and me, he brought me into the drawing-room, shut the door, and took me to the window, where, looking at me with great earnestness, "Poor unhappy Caroline," cried he; and to my inexpressible concern he burst into tears. Need I tell you, my dear Sir, how mine flowed at the sight?
> I would have again embraced his knees; but hurrying from me, he flung himself upon a sofa, and leaning his face upon his arms, he seemed for some time absorbed in bitterness of grief.
> I ventured not to interrupt a sorrow I so much respected, but waited in silence and at a distance until he recovered from its violence. But then it seemed in a moment to give way to a kind of frantic fury; for starting suddenly with a sternness which at once surprised and frightened me, "Child," cried he, "hast thou yet sufficiently humbled thy father? If thou hast, be contented with this proof of my weakness, and no longer force thyself into my presence."

"Oh, go; go!" cried he passionately, "in pity, in compassion, if though valuest my senses, leave me—and forever!"

"I will; I will," cried I, greatly terrified, and I moved hastily towards the door, yet stopping when I reached it, and almost involuntarily dropping on my knees, "Vouchsafe," cried I; "Oh, Sir, vouchsafe but once to bless your daughter, and her sight shall never more offend you."

"Alas," cried he, in a softened voice, "I am not worthy to bless thee! I am not worthy to call thee daughter! I am not worthy that the fair light of Heaven should visit my eyes! Oh God, that I could call back the time ere thou wast born—or else bury its remembrance in eternal oblivion."

"Would to Heaven," cried I, "that the sight of me were less terrible to you—that instead of irritating, I could soothe your sorrows! Oh Sir, how thankfully then would I prove my duty, even at the hazard of my life."

"Are you so kind?" cried he gently. "Come hither, child; rise, Evelina. Alas, it is for me to kneel; not you—and I would kneel, I would crawl upon the earth, I would kiss the dust—could I by such submission obtain the forgiveness of the representative of the most injured of women."

"Oh, Sir," exclaimed I, "that you could but read my heart!—that you could but see the filial tenderness and concern with which it overflows!—you would not then talk thus; you would not then banish me your presence and exclude me from your affection."

"Good God," cried he, "is it then possible that you do not hate me? Can the child of the wronged Caroline look at—and not execrate me? Wast thou not born to abhor, and bred to curse me? Did not thy mother bequeath thee her blessing on condition that thou shouldst detest and avoid me?"

Evelina's answer is to produce a deathbed letter from her mother. As he reads it, Sir John is overcome with penitence, and Evelina rises from her knees to comfort and reassure him.

I could restrain myself no longer; I rose and went to him. I did not dare to speak, but with pity and concern unutterable I wept and hung over him.

Soon after, starting up, he again seized the letter, exclaiming, "Acknowledge thee, Caroline!—yes, with my heart's best blood would I acknowledge thee. Oh that thou could'st witness the agony of my soul! Ten thousand daggers could not have wounded me like this letter."

He kneels again before Evelina, pleading for her forgiveness.

"Oh then, thou representative of my departed wife, speak to me in her name, and say that the remorse that tears my soul tortures me not in vain."

"Oh rise; rise, my beloved father," cried I, attempting to assist him. "Reverse not the law of nature; rise yourself, and bless your kneeling daughter."

But the scene is too much for the repentant father. Again he begs Evelina to leave him.

"Adieu, my child; be not angry—I cannot stay with thee. Oh, Evelina, thy countenance is a dagger to my heart. Just so thy mother looked,—just so—"

Tears and sighs seemed to choke him, and waving his hand, he would have left me. But clinging to him, "Oh Sir," cried I; "will you so soon abandon me? Am I again an orphan? Oh, my dear, my long lost father, leave me not, I beseech you. Take pity on your child, and rob her not of the parent she so fondly hoped would cherish her."

This is undeniably stagey dialogue, but the situation itself is stagey, recalling the sentimental drama upon which the theater-goers in the earlier part of the century had been nourished.

I have stressed these critical shortcomings in critical fairness. *Evelina* is an altogether readable novel in spite of them. In any summary view of Miss Burney's performance we must balance against the errors and omissions that arise from her inexperience, as well as from the still tentative art of the novel, certain achievements that were important in themselves and that add something to the artistic tradition.

In the first place, as an epistolary novel, *Evelina* is relatively free from much of the awkwardness of narrative through the medium of letters. Writers of fiction in this period gave up slowly a form which seemed to lend itself advantageously to the most mediocre, but the disadvantages of which seemed to overbalance its advantages. Miss Burney, however, used it conscientiously and convincingly. Evelina's letters, contrasted with Pamela's, sound like letters, not dissertations. The correspondence is limited to a well-integrated group of interesting characters; it does not exceed our idea of what letters can actually accomplish; and it conveys happily the spirit of the incidents it depicts, and not merely their details.

For readers of later days, Miss Burney's outlook upon the social spectacle of the time is both intelligent and entertaining, though like all her contemporaries, she tends to think in social absolutes. Bourgeois society she observes only in terms of its aspirations or its shortcomings; people are either polite or common. Evelina herself belongs to the first group; Madame Duval and the Branghtons to the second. On the whole, the novel shows acceptance rather than doubt of the urban caste system. And in the course of the heroine's social education we see not only maturing sagacity and *politesse* but a slow and partly unconscious indoctrination in the snootiness that seemed at that time all but inseparable from aristocratic status. The Branghtons are tried by somewhat different standards from those which Evelina brought with her from the country. She discovers, and reiterates, that nice people do not live up two flights of stairs. She assimilates distinctions; Ranelagh has more tone than Vauxhall (something not quite so clear in other novelists); the really best people go to the opera to listen—not to parade and talk; she learns the right streets, and at length can pick out the right people—there is an amusing early scene in which she comes to the horrified realization that she has been walking the alleys of Marylebone Gardens in company with a pair of strumpets (Letters LIII and LIV), and her innocence in the situation appeals strongly to Lord Orville's protective instinct. But she does learn.

Miss Burney's pictures of good society are informing because she knows good society. There is far more effective instruction in manners in *Evelina* than in Richardson's novels, which were written for the explicit purpose. She can also interpret manners; she knows sincerity from pretense; manners can be really good only when they are an ornament to character.

Undeniably, in *Evelina* Miss Burney's youth and her sex worked powerfully in her favor. Her novel owes its freshness and piquancy to her still romantic and hopeful years, its special percipience to the fact that she was instinctively faithful to her sex, and unwilling to portray it equivocally or cynically. If she deals unkindly with a Madame Duval or a Miss Branghton, it is because she feels that they are not only unladylike but unwomanly.

Whether or not we can find pleasure in *Evelina* will depend upon whether we can override natural prejudices against "dated" situations and dialogue. For Miss Burney's art is conventional and uninventive. Could it have been greatly different, since she was not only the child of her age, but the somewhat pampered pupil of upper middle-class intellectuals when the woman intellectual was occupied largely with herself, while her male contemporaries were busy with intrigue, or perhaps with politics?

Miss Burney's three later novels show a steady progress in complacent failure. She is a literary Bourbon, learning nothing and forgetting nothing. And she is unaware that her audience is moving away from her as surely and rapidly as time itself.

Cecilia (1782) was published when Miss Burney was thirty. *Evelina* had been begun, at least, in her early youth. *Cecilia* is, therefore, not surprisingly, a maturer work in almost every respect; also in all-round merit the best novel of her writing. It embodies a good theme; it is developed rationally upon a substantial plot; its characters are credible. Here, indeed, Miss Burney's understanding of that unpredictable and unaccountable thing we know as character is penetrating and deep. Cecilia herself would be a meritorious creation for a novelist of a much later date. Her view of herself as a woman and her attitude toward marriage are no longer adolescent—although in fact she is just reaching years of discretion.

These are positive merits. The negative merits of *Cecilia* are, first, that it is for its time fairly free from conventional sentiment, and second, that to an important extent the thought and action of its characters are not confined by the environmental determinism of Fielding and Smollett. That is largely because Miss Burney is an intelligent woman choosing to create and develop intelligent women characters. This latter attainment has large importance in the subsequent history of the novel; for it is one of the many respects in which Jane Austen learned from the partial and tentative success of her predecessor. Further, the principal characters in *Cecilia* are clearly conceived and vividly projected. In these determinants of quality, Miss Burney has more than carried on the success of *Evelina*; she has shown added maturity and more skilful command of her medium. What is wrong, then, with *Cecilia?*

It is precisely what is wrong with *Evelina:* a fatuous insistence upon long and tiresome comic interludes. In *Cecilia,* however, the comic characters are not the vulgarians that we met in *Evelina;* they are a sort of chorus of men and women of the *haut monde* who are the purveyors of fashionable chitchat and scandal. As background characters in their proper place, and with no greater part in the story than is called for by their choral function, they are not uninteresting. But as a constant space-consuming interruption to an otherwise well-managed narrative, they are intrusive and at length obnoxious.

There is an error here (as in *Evelina*) not only in taste but in judgment. For these characters are meant to ridicule the vacuous ostentation of people of fashion. Not satirically, however, but with false and condescending humor; false because it lacks the grace of feminine humor, in which Miss Burney had some proficiency, and condescending because it is written down to the level of an audience that she realized and understood only imperfectly. That it is not only an aesthetic error but an error in judgment is clear in the fact that these people and their talk annoy and bore the very likeable Cecilia herself (as Duval *et al* did Evelina). How then could Miss Burney expect them to entertain the reader? Whenever Mr. Meadows, Miss Larolles, Mr. Morrice, and their friends appear, as they do for long intervals throughout the action, we want to escape from them, just as Cecilia did.

Again we confront the fact that Fanny Burney was not a genius; she was a woman of talent, thinking and working not spontaneously but with the brains and habits of a competent artisan. She tells us in the preface to *Cecilia* that she was encouraged to write a second novel through the success of *Evelina*. But she really did not understand what had accounted for that success. *Evelina* is a good novel weakened by humorous irrelevancy. *Cecilia* is a nearly first-rate novel, *spoiled* by the same defect and unredeemed by the entertaining freshness of *Evelina*.

In her third novel, *Camilla* (1796), we find added evidence that maturity seemed to contribute almost nothing to Miss Burney's literary experience. Its principal is a kind of retake of Evelina, but without Evelina's common sense and feminine resourcefulness. She is also, Miss Burney herself tells us in the conclusion, excessively sentimental. The novel as a whole, however, does not seem over-sentimental except in that it is one of the most lachrymose of the period; and by this time tears seem to have become a literary property rather than a touchstone of feeling.

The theme of the story is a common one : an exalted romantic attachment repeatedly interrupted by temporizing and almost deliberate misunderstanding. But there is more interest here than is generally found in the typical situation; for both the young lovers are made to suffer through the solemn cautions and safe advice of, in the girl's case, a devoted mother, and in the young man's case, a generally sensible tutor who has outlived two unfortunate marital ventures. Suspense, however, depends less upon anything integral for plot than upon the fact that at the moment when a word might clarify an ambiguous situation, a door is likely to open and someone appear with a summons to dinner.

The novel is further weakened by the author's ignorance of, or indifference to, some of the most obvious desiderata of realism. The story abounds in coincidence—even to the hero's at last discovering by the sheerest accident the heroine, ill almost to the point of death, in a mean wayside inn. And what is to be thought of a novel that allows significant knowledge to depend, not once but on four separate occasions, upon the accidental reading of a mislaid confidential letter? The plot itself is only moderately satisfactory, hinging as it does upon some improbable financial distresses which accumulate into a deluge before the plot is resolved by marriage to a young man with plenty of what is needed.

But the fatal defect in *Camilla* is neither structural faults nor sentimental prepossessions. Nor—and this must be mentioned too—dialogue carried on in the most stilted Johnsonese. It is the very fault that we have seen in the two earlier novels—interruption of an interesting continuity by disappointing comedy, unattached to anything essential to the plot.

It would be wrong, however, to dismiss *Camilla* as a novel without redeeming merits, even though its merits are those rather of discreet avoidance than of intelligent invention. In the first place, Miss Burney sees that sentimentalism has had its day. *Evelina* is perfumed with sentimentality; the young Cecilia (like Richardson's Signorina Clementina della Porretta) goes temporarily mad through sentimental distress over the seeming loss of her lover; but Camilla, still the victim of her "sensibility," is given us as an example of emotional extravagance, no longer lovely, but shameful and harmful. That is a gain for the novel.

Further, the "machinery" of sentimental fiction has undergone changes for the better in *Camilla*. Fainting, either spontaneous or tactical, is going out of vogue. There are few lapses from the perpendicular in *Camilla,* I should guess no more than a half a dozen, which, considering the literary temper of the times, is a conservative allowance for a novel of almost half a million words. And formal love-making no longer calls for exalted speech-making. Only one of the galaxy of male lovers in *Camilla* goes through the conventional rigmarole of despair and threatened death— and he is a hypocritical fortune-hunter who implements his passionate appeal with a pistol, and whom someone before the end of the story has the good judgment to shoot.

We are scarcely under obligation to deal largely with Fanny Burney's— or at this point we had better say Madame d'Arblay's—last novel, *The Wanderer* (1814). It appeared after Jane Austen's star had risen; and its reminiscent, even antiquated, social perspective places it under great disadvantage in comparison with Miss Austen's bright modernity. *The Wanderer* was written, Miss Burney tells us, over a period of more than ten years, during most of which she had lived with her husband in Paris, through the aftermath of the French Revolution and part of the Napoleonic wars. But the social history of this bitter and sustained international turmoil scarcely enters into the movement of the story, except as a dim background for the heroine, who has escaped from France in disguise as a half-clothed beggar, to undergo in England a life of slow social torture while she waits for restoration of friends and fortune.

It is far from a consistently interesting novel, but it has interesting points. In social environment, *dramatis personae,* complication, and long stretches of group-characterization for comic (and sometimes socialsatiric) effect, it shows family resemblance to its three predecessors. Yet one cannot help feeling that its author has almost pitifully lost touch with living reality. There are the same gallants, the same human cats, the same giddy society girls, the same embarrassments for the heroine, the same noble and incredibly disinterested lover, and the same liberal use of helpful coincidence; but all these are taken over from the stock in trade of fiction at the time *Evelina* was written.

Worst of all, perhaps, is that in persistently playing up the Johnsonian style, Miss Burney had at last developed a sort of literary gobbledegook of her own, so elegant that it becomes all but incomprehensible. Let us sample it.

Wide is the difference between exhibiting that which we have attained only for that purpose, from the power of dispensing knowledge to others. Where only what is chosen is produced; only what is practiced is performed; where one favorite piece, however laboriously acquired, however exclusively finished, gains a character of excellence that, for the current day, and with the current throng, disputes the prize of fame, even with the solid rights of professional candidates; the young and nearly ignorant disciple may seem upon a par with the experienced and learned master. But to disseminate knowledge, by clearing that which is obscure, and explaining that which is difficult; to make what is hard appear easy, by giving facility to the execution of what is abstruse to the conception; to lighten the fatigue of practice by the address of method; to shorten what requires study by anticipating its results; and while demonstrating effects, to expound their cause; by the rules of art to hide the want of science; and to supply the dearth of genius by divulging the secrets of embellishments;—these were labors that demanded not alone brilliant talents, which she amply possessed, but a fund of scientific knowledge, to which she formed no pretensions. Her modesty, however, aided her good sense in confining her attempts at giving improvement within the limits of her ability; and rare indeed must have been her ill fortune, had a pupil fallen to her lot sufficiently advanced to have surpassed her powers of instruction.

Miss Burney means to tell us here that although Juliet was not professionally accomplished as a musician, she knew enough and played well enough to enable her uninspired pupils to put on a good show. The sententiousness of the passage is quite as characteristic as its overloaded diction and its piled-up construction.

Yet *The Wanderer* has moved up somewhat with the spirit of the age. Miss Burney had already touched the humanitarian note in Cecilia's determination to spend her fortune in aid for the oppressed lower classes, and in *Camilla* there is a brief but revealing glance at the miseries of the English prison system. In *The Wanderer* she becomes a participant in the feminist movement, still in its infancy. Two characters in the novel carry the burden of demonstrating the oppressions that attached to woman's position. The first is the heroine, successively known as L.S., Incognita, Miss Ellis, and Juliet, whose sufferings are traceable mainly to the simple fact that she was born a woman, and therefore subject to all the taboos, disqualifications, and special discomforts and inconveniences of the woman's lot. The other "advanced woman" is a prematurely conceived feminist rebel, a tough-minded female who is not willing to accept her soft feminine destiny, but who carries her independence to the extreme of going all but mad because she cannot, in view of his unwillingness, take entire bodily possession of the subject of her desperate passion—who is, it may be guessed, the lover of the heroine. This new motive shows some contact with what was going on in the world, but it is argued (for it *is* argument) confusedly; it is mixed up with vague generalizations about the ill effects of the French Revolution; and its powerful voice is the half-crazed Elinor, whose character is liberated not only from the stultifying conventions, but from common sense.

In her attitude toward the extremes of sensibility Mme. d'Arblay carries on the mission she assumed in *Camilla*—to show the darker side of emotional thinking and acting, although there are still in profusion the tears of sensibility. Here there is again an advance in maturity, but it is merely responsive to the changed attitude of a later generation.

But it is not fair to expect too much of the good Fanny Burney. The best examples before her of unquestionable *excellence* in the English novel were the novels of Fielding, and Fielding's virtues are entirely masculine. Her outlook and her gifts were a woman's, and in opening up a woman's world (no doubt in the main for women readers) she had to find her own way, confining herself to that world as a woman was then permitted to know it—even though it was her own—under the disadvantages of limited contacts and the continuing overweening and unarguable assumptions of male superiority.

We are told by the literary taxonomists that Miss Burney's novels are "novels of manners." That is by way of saying that she is a close and intelligent observer of characters in a specific social setting. There, undoubtedly, lies her proficiency—in the depiction of *both* characters and social environment. Burney's women, however, are always more human than her men. While the world acknowledges a place for a "man's woman," we find less enthusiasm for a "woman's man." And whether or not it is true that Jane Austen and George Eliot shared the same ineptitude in the characterization of their men, it would be hard to deny that Miss Burney's women are drawn with a sure hand; her men are not. But her novels are always *about* women; men are appendages. All her novels but her last take their titles from her heroines' names, and the "Wanderer" is itself an appellation that Miss Burney applies to her principal.

These heroines are, in spite of a discernable variety in their characters, all very young ladies consciously or unconsciously devoted to marriage—

the one way, then, of disposing of person and fortune. None of them is subtle; all have a charming but rather helpless ingenuousness. But Miss Burney *could* create women of greater maturity and complexity, and in all of her novels she gives us at least one woman in whom femininity is a problem rather than a formula. We have already mentioned Mrs. Selwyn in *Evelina*. She is surpassed in *Cecilia* by Lady Honoria Pemberton, a young frivol and a rattle, deriving amusement from embarrassment and mischief. In *Camilla* there is Mrs. Arlbery, so involved in her own criss-crossed motives that we scarcely know whether she ought to be admitted to the lower order of saints or suspended from a gallows. In *The Wanderer*, there is an entire rural society, including a galaxy of some of the grande-damedest grande dames of fiction, engaged in social ritual and indus-triously covering up their natural selves.

These cleverly drawn women are mirrors of sophistication, combina-tions of charm and selfish indifference to everything but their own ideas of amusement. But they are highly interesting studies in the duality of social consciousness. All these portraits owe something to Ben Jonson's "humor" characters—characters that carry the strong impress of a single trait, and that tend, even as in Jonson, to ride the humor to death. In *The Wanderer* they make up Miss Burney's customary chorus, but they are vividly animated, and on the whole probably the best of these activated portraits that she has given us.

Miss Burney's heroes are pure-minded and prematurely wise young men who from their earliest appearance are destined to be not only the husbands, but the mentors and spiritual confidants of her heroines throughout a long and unfailingly happy life together. But on the fringes of her action she almost invariably presents her young men as anything from juvenile comics and mischief-makers to deep and devious villains. It may be suspected that this ambiguous attitude betrays a somewhat imper-fect acquaintance with young men as they are, or with the society of the time in which they moved. More probably, it may reflect shyness and emotional immaturity. It is worth pondering that Miss Burney married at the age of forty-three, although her heroines are always married off, or at least firmly engaged, in their teens.

If we could extract from these novels their labored and sometimes gross humor, their wearisome interations of casual scenes in the social panorama, and the author's unhappy propensity to turn high moments into rhetorical melodrama, we should have left a well-managed narrative with satiric incisiveness that sometimes is comparable to Jane Austen's. But a novel can be, after all, little or nothing but what it was meant to be; and the defect of Miss Burney's work is that after the writing of *Evelina* she was never too sure of her intentions. As an artist, she understood her talents only imperfectly; she took herself too seriously—that is painfully evident in the fatuous introduction to *The Wanderer*; she no doubt over-valued mere labor; and perhaps she over-priced her really substantial prestige as a woman of the upper intellectual and social world.

Yet there is *Evelina*—not pure gold, but certainly not to be forgotten.

CHAPTER XIV

𝔒𝔯𝔦𝔢𝔫𝔱𝔞𝔩 ℜ𝔬𝔪𝔞𝔫𝔠𝔢

Johnson and Beckford

THE PRESENT CHAPTER is anomalous—we seem to be starting right off with one of Johnson's words—for in the first place it hardly fits our scheme of chronology, Johnson's *Rasselas* (1759) coming well before the fictions we have just been discussing, and Beckford's *Vathek* (1786) well after. In the second place "oriental romance" is an accepted but inaccurate phrase for what we are about to consider; since it was oriental only in the imitative sense, and the imitation was, like most of them, generally a rather inferior article. Lastly, there is no sound reason to make the oriental romance a critical category, for it is only one form of "otherwhere" fiction, and the differences among these fictions in treatment, style, authenticity, and objective are much more marked than the similarity in setting that would make them a distinctive class. We might add that it is only by taking a liberty with the customary sense of "oriental" that Johnson's *Rasselas* can be dragged within the definition; for its scene is Abyssinia, and Abyssinia was, we are told, an African kingdom, now dignified with the name of the "empire" of Ethiopia. But we shall abide by the traditional classification, and respect or neglect it as seems convenient!

All the Oriental romances, except for a scattering before the eighteenth century without authentic background, take their origin from Antoine Galland's French translation of the larger part of the *Thousand and One Nights* (1704-1717), retranslated promptly into English. These romances became very numerous, both in France and England,* appearing in a steady stream throughout the entire century and influencing poetry and fiction far into the 1800's. We can consider them only with the highest selectivity, for "the spell of the Orient" seemed to exert little effective magic upon the writers of most of them. In English literature of this period, in spite of experiments in the type from the hands of Addison,

---

*Martha Conant's *The Oriental Tale in England in the 18th Century* numbers over a hundred items in England alone.

Steele, John Hawksworth, Walpole, Goldsmith, Smollett, and Maria Edgeworth, only two stand out as particularly memorable : Johnson's *Rasselas* and William Beckford's *Vathek*.

The forms in which they were best known to English readers were, first, brief moral tales like those from the *Spectator*; second, "letters" from the Orient or from Orientals visiting the European capitals, commenting (usually satirically) upon European institutions and manners, such as Montesquieu's *Lettres Persanes* (1721) and Goldsmith's *Citizen of the World* (1760–1761); and last, romances of substantial length, moral, philosophical, or satirical, such as Voltaire's *Zadig* (1747), his *Princesse de Babylon* (1768), and the two English tales that we have chosen for discussion.

While the vogue of the oriental tale began with the first European translations of the *Arabian Nights,* the most significant of them came to be purposive, which the *Arabian Nights* was not. The reason was fairly obvious—that the deep differences between everything oriental and everything European carried on their surface evaluations of Eastern and Western society that were bound to be critical of one at the expense of the other. At the same time, the dispraise of Western society might, as in Montesquieu's *Lettres Persanes,* carry with it sly implications that the critic himself was not infallible and that affairs at home were not immune from criticism. If satire is not the spirit of an oriental romance, its opposite, the picture of an ideal society looking down, so to speak (as in the *Citizen of the World*), upon effete or corrupt European society, is more than likely to be. Functionally, then, any of the eighteenth-century oriental tales is likely to fall within one or another of the classes of the fiction that compares and discusses two widely different worlds—one of them our own. They may be Utopian; they may be based, like *Gulliver's Travels*, on voyages to strange lands, but without the idealized perspective of the *Utopia*, and they may be the comment of a cultivated foreigner enjoying and judging the queer lives and ways of Parisians or Londoners. *Rasselas** combines in some degree the second and the third of these motives. *Vathek,* however is rather definitely "pure" literature, written for the reader's diversion, the soupçon of morality in it, and the powerful but somewhat inconsistent moral loading of the conclusion, being perhaps afterthoughts or concessions to popular taste.

If the reader approaches Samuel Johnson with an initial prejudice, let him set it aside for the moment. He is the kind of person many of us do not particularly like—too sure of himself to be agreeable, and too dom-

---

*Dr. Samuel Johnson (1709-1784). Johnson's writings are too generally known for notation here. His only substantial work of fiction is *Rasselas* (1759).

ineering to be friendly. And there is his pomposity, and his obstinate moralism. If he were present in the flesh today, perhaps most of us would try to avoid him—though he would inevitably be a friend to many of our friends. In *Rasselas,* however, if you give yourself time to get acclimated to tone and style, you may not be troubled by the buffeting of the literary gale we think of as Johnson. If the story were actually written in the single week it is said to have been, to defray his mother's funeral expenses, there was not time to work it up to the pinnacle of Johnsonian impresssiveness. It is his one fiction of measurable length, and to many of us it will be a surprise because of its relative ease and plainness. *Rasselas* can be read without a dictionary at the elbow.

The key of the romance is given at the very opening in a massive, well-rounded Johnsonian sentence :

> Ye, who listen with credulity, to the whispers of fancy, and pursue, with eagerness, the phantoms of hope; who expect, that age will perform the promises of youth, and that the deficiencies of the present day will be supplied by the morrow; attend to the history of Rasselas, prince of Abissinia.

Decorative rhetoric takes over as the story proceeds.

> The sides of the mountains were covered with trees; the banks of the brooks were diversified with flowers; every blast shook spices from the rocks; and every month dropped fruits upon the ground. All animals that bite the grass, or browse the shrub, whether wild or tame, wandered in this extensive circuit, secured from the beasts of prey, by the mountains which confined them. On one part, were flocks and herds feeding in the pastures; on another, all the beasts of chase frisking on the lawns; the sprightly kid was bounding on the rocks, the subtle monkey frolicking in the trees, and the solemn elephant reposing in the shade. All the diversities of the world were brought together, the blessings of nature were collected, and its evils extracted and excluded.

There is much here that is commonplace and unilluminating. Hillsides with trees and brooksides with flowers are juiceless notations of fact; one primrose by the river's brim would offer something for the imagination. And a phrase here and there seems to be implicitly comical. The "subtle monkey" and the "solemn elephant," tainted with naïve animism, fail to impress us. It is not a promising introduction.

But we find the narrative improves as we go—judging the matter, of course, with the prejudiced modern eye. At any rate, imagery and diction become more flexible as we enter the story.

Rasselas is son of a king, a fact that ought to carry with it some expectation of happiness. But his father's scheme of rule, which, considering the restlessness of aspirants to a throne, may be altogether wise, keeps him confined in a park-like valley surrounded by unscalable mountains until he is old enough to assume some of the cares of state. This is the Happy Valley.

> Here the sons and daughters of Abissinia lived only to know the soft vicissitudes of pleasure and repose, attended by all that were skilful to delight, and gratified with whatever the senses can enjoy. They wandered in gardens of fragrance, and slept in fortresses of security. Every art was practiced to make them pleased with their own condition. . . .
> To heighten their opinion of their own felicity, they were daily entertained with songs, the subject of which was the Happy Valley. Their appetites were excited by frequent enumerations of different enjoyments, and revelry and merriment was the business of every hour, from the dawn of morning to the close of even.

The welfare state! And without taxes! Aldous Huxley had little more to offer in *Brave New World,* though on a considerably higher level of ingenuity. So far as Johnson tells us, they did not have liquor and contraceptives, but they had efficient public relations counsel and policies.

> These methods were, generally, successful; few of the princes had ever wished to change their bounds, but passed their lives in full conviction, that they had all within their reach that art or nature could bestow, and pitied those, whom fate had excluded from this seat of tranquillity, as the sport of chance, and the slaves of misery.
> Thus they rose in the morning and lay down at night, pleased with each other and with themselves, all but Rasselas.

Huxley's Navajo hanged himself in boredom with his crême de menthe existence. Rasselas "sought delight in solitary walks, and silent meditation." His old instructor asks and advises—to no purpose. "I have already enjoyed too much," Rasselas tells him; "give me something to desire." Troubled with his thoughts, he sits down one day to muse, "and remembered that since he first resolved to escape from the confinement the sun had passed twice over him in his annual course."

> "I have lost that which can never be restored : I have seen the sun rise and set for twenty months, an idle gazer on the light of heaven : in this time, the birds have left the nest of their mother, and committed themselves to the woods and to the skies : the kid has forsaken the teat,

and learned, by degrees, to climb the rocks, in quest of independent sustenance. I only have made no advances, but am still helpless and ignorant. The moon, by more than twenty changes, admonished me of the flux of life; the stream, that rolled before my feet, upbraided my inactivity. I sat feasting on intellectual luxury, regardless alike of the examples of the earth, and the instruction of the planets. Twenty months are passed; who shall restore them?"

These sorrowful meditations fastened upon his mind; he passed four months, in resolving to lose no more time in idle resolves, and was awakened to more vigorous exertion, by hearing a maid, who had broken a porcelain cup, remark, that what cannot be repaired is not to be regretted.

This was obvious; and Rasselas reproached himself, that he had not discovered it, having not known, or not considered, how many useful hints are obtained by chance, and how often the mind, hurried by her own ardour to distant views, neglects the truths that lie open before her. He, for a few hours, regretted his regret, and from that time bent his whole mind upon the means of escaping from the valley of happiness.

Rasselas' impatience is relieved by the appearance of a poet and sage, Imlac. The narrative halts for Imlac to tell his personal story. He has traveled much and learned much, and though now poor in pocket, he is rich in the ponderous wisdom that is characteristic of Johnson's own mind. The prince interrupts Imlac's story frequently with inquiries and comments, and in the course of Imlac's replies, we find the kernel of a philosophy, of skepticism as to human happiness, and acceptance of life on the best terms possible. This is the teaching of Voltaire's *Candide*—Johnson himself remarked that if *Rasselas* had not appeared closely upon the heels of *Candide* (both were published in 1759), he would almost inevitably have been charged with borrowing Voltaire's ideas, perhaps more particularly, his portraiture of Candide as an observant and educable traveler and a good man at asking questions.

Imlac joins Rasselas in his plans to escape, not with great hopes, but because he shares Rasselas' distaste for the vacuous life, and "few things are impossible to diligence and skill." At the moment of their fortunate discovery of a means of escape, Nekayah, Rasselas' sister, appears. Nekayah turns out promptly to be one of the great rarities of mid-eighteenth-century fiction—a woman whose mind is not only a storehouse of ideas but a source of power. I am quite willing to set Nekayah down as one of the few mentally living heroines in the fiction of the period. If Rasselas is good at asking questions, she is capable of sharpening them to a point; she speaks and acts throughout with practical and hopeful sense. In the great world, Rasselas and Imlac without her would be philosophical dodderers. Of course Nekayah makes it a party of three, for she too has been thinking and wishing.

Into the world of everyday realities, then, the three emerge. They will, as Rasselas says, "review it at leisure; surely happiness is somewhere to be found."

They begin at Cairo, financing their travels from a stock of jewels which they had taken with them. Nekayah has her maid and confidante, Pekuah, an indispensable for the well-dressed and well-groomed young lady of the time. But they live and travel modestly, once they have passed the mental hazards of sacrificing their royal dignity, learning courtesy, and "being leveled with the vulgar."

The "choice of life," to use Rasselas' phrase, goes forward to new scenes and new encounters. We need only to note that they find dissipation disappointing, the pretensions of an inspired philosopher empty, the pastoral life tasteless and monotonous, wealth and position dangerous. A hermit lets them into his confidence—with illumination :

"I am sometimes shamed to think, that I could not secure myself from vice, but by retiring from the exercise of virtue, and begin to suspect, that I was rather impelled by resentment, than led by devotion, into solitude. My fancy riots in scenes of folly, and I lament, that I have lost so much, and have gained so little. In solitude, if I escape the example of bad men, I want, likewise, the counsel and conversation of the good. I have been long comparing the evils with the advantages of society, and resolve to return into the world tomorrow. The life of a solitary man will be certainly miserable, but not certainly devout."

A philosopher who would "live according to nature" is called upon by Rasselas to tell what "nature" implies :

"When I find young men so humble and so docile," said the philosopher, "I can deny them no information which my studies have enabled me to afford. To live according to nature, is to act always with due regard to the fitness arising from the relations and qualities of causes and effects; to concur with the great and unchangeable scheme of universal felicity; to cooperate with the general disposition and tendency of the present system of things."

Rasselas and Nekayah plan at length to divide the work of investigation; he to "try what is to be found in the pleasure of courts," she to "range the shades of humbler life." He is confused and disgusted by "a continual succession of plots and detections, stratagems and escapes, faction and treachery." She comes to the grave conclusion that "whether perfect happiness would be procured by perfect goodness, the world will never afford an opportunity of deciding. But this, at least, may be maintained, that we do not always find visible happiness in proportion to visible virtue." A Candidean conclusion, but unflavored by humor.

Rasselas and Nekayah discuss institutions—marriage among them; and in this colloquy Nekayah drops little periods of womanly wisdom that would have surprised (if they could have penetrated) the reposeful mind of a Sophia Western or an Evelina. But Imlac recalls them from talk to living (again the reminder of *Candide*), and proposes a visit to the Pyramids. "My curiosity," says Rasselas, "does not very strongly lead me to survey piles of stone or mounds of earth." But after a little argument from Imlac on the value of history as one of the handmaids of culture, Nekayah will "rejoice to learn something of the manners of antiquity." This diversion leads to the only bit of action in the story—the stealing of Pekuah by a troop of marauding Arabs. Nekayah is plunged into depression.

> "The time is at hand," [she tells her companions] "when none shall be disturbed any longer by the sighs of Nekayah; my search after happiness is now at an end. I am resolved to retire from the world, with all its flatteries and deceits, and will hide myself in solitude, without any other care than to compose my thoughts, and regulate my hours by a constant succession of innocent occupations, till, with a mind purified from all earthly desires, I shall enter into that state, to which all are hastening, and in which I hope again to enjoy the friendship of Pekuah."
>
> "Do not entangle your mind," said Imlac, "by irrevocable determinations, nor increase the burden of life by a voluntary accumulation of misery; the weariness of retirement will continue or increase, when the loss of Pekuah is forgotten. That you have been deprived of one pleasure, is no very good reason for rejection of the rest."

But Pekuah reappears, after due payment of the proper ransom for a decidedly marketable young lady, and relates the story of her capture and confinement—the latter an experience productive of some observations upon the Eastern view of woman and woman's society. The Arab chieftan, her captor, had learned, by the bye, in his talks with Pekuah, that feminine conversation, at its best, could add to his only other interest in women— again, perhaps, a matter of reflection for the Sophias and the Evelinas.

The search continues, in conversations with an astronomer whose mind has been turned by his studies, and with an old man who cannot accept age with resignation. We are ready now for the summation of their experiences, given by Imlac in a discourse which shows Johnson at his best. It is not uncommonplace discourse; but it touches the problems of good and evil, of the soul, and of immortality—and brings into line with reasonable hope the now modest aspirations of all three. The incidents of the story have receded in the haze of memory, and closure of the search is given in one brief paragraph :

> Of these wishes that they had formed, they well knew that none could be obtained. They deliberated a while what was to be done, and resolved when the inundation should cease, to return to Abissinia.

As fiction, *Rasselas* cannot be thought to compare favorably with the great formalized novels of the period. But its interest for Johnson's contemporaries did not depend upon its qualities as fiction. That is evident in the cursory view we have given of its content. Yet Johnson's handling of some of the components of fiction has its merits. His characters have substance enough to support the moral purpose, and one, Nekayah, has grace and communicable intelligence, as well as truth to feminine nature when it is not obscured by fashions and conventions. Johnson's dialogue is of course pure Johnson, but intellectualized style is not out of place in intellectual debate; and that is after all just what *Rasselas* is.

The unescapable comparison with *Candide* is not favorable to *Rasselas*. But then Voltaire was writing within his forte; Johnson in an untried medium, carrying the burden of a thesis, and in the shadow of a personal tragedy. In spite of what it is *not, Rasselas* is rewarding reading for one willing to accept narrative as a vehicle for elevated thought.

If Johnson was the most revered man of letters of his time, William Beckford, the author of *Vathek,* was its most lurid figure.* The fact has so definite a bearing on his work that we must pause to look at him before we consider the romance for which he is still remembered.

At the time of Beckford's birth, his father was reputed the possessor of the hugest private fortune in England, amassed principally through West Indian plantations and trade. Beckford, his one son, was largely through the ambition of his mother (a thoroughbred aristocrat) privately educated to add social splendor to that fortune by becoming the most elegant and enviable person in England, in intellect and culture as well as in eligibility for a magnificent marriage.

The intention was partially, indeed in a large measure, fulfilled. He acquired the reputation of a connoisseur in art, beyond the knowledge conceded as a compliment to any buyer with limitless wealth. He had

---

*William Beckford (1759-1844). The one important fiction is *Vathek* (1786), supplemented by the three *Episodes of Vathek* (1912). Other short tales and burlesques of fiction are now all but forgotten.

learning, though rather scattered and precious. He was said to be a pianist of professional finish. Socially he was sought after by the oldest and proudest families—and not merely because his fortune would have reha- bilitated many an old house gone to seed. He had a refined sentimentality that, added to his extremely good looks, made him more than casually interesting to women married or unmarried.

The reverse of the picture may almost be guessed from what has been said. The domestic tyranny of the only son in such a family was more harm- ful to himself than to those about him. He refused or escaped discipline. His isolation, for he had no companions of his own years, and his shelter from competition of every sort, made him monumentally conceited, sharpened his impetuous temper, gave his passions dangerous play, and concentrated all his interests in a conscious and flagrant egotism. What was most dangerous for him—and in the end disastrous—was the combina- tion of aesthetic sensibility and emotional instability which seems some- times to tend to moral astigmatism. At any rate, before he had reached his middle twenties, and before *Vathek* saw the light, he left England because of charges hanging over his head of which homosexuality—then a capital offense in England—was one, and probably the important, item.*

Out of the mixture of impulses in Beckford's nature, two facts emerge with particular bearing upon the writing of *Vathek*. One is his consuming interest during his late teens and early twenties in oriental literature and culture. The other is a state of mind which for the moment we can call diabolism, and which we will return to.

His interest in the Orient was first of all temperamental. Its strangeness fascinated him, and the differences of its moral system from the European intrigued him and encouraged rebelliousness that was partly innate, and partly, no doubt, distaste for his mother's stiff conformity. But most importantly, the vivid animism in which Oriental religions clothed the conceptions of good and evil appealed to his undisciplined and perhaps in some degree superstitious mental habit. He was an avid reader, and over this period he did all he could to exhaust the available sources of literary information upon the East, encouraged and aided by the Rever- end Samuel Henley, an informed Orientalist, of whom more later.

It is hard to say how much of Beckford's diabolism, or Satanism, was due to his immaturity, how much was curiosity, and how much was affectation. With Louisa Beckford, the wife of his cousin Peter, at the same time his mistress during his early twenties, he carried on a sort of

---

*The story may be inferred from any of the earlier biographic studies of Beckford, and is set forth with as much information and intelligent opinion as we are likely to have upon the subject in Guy Chapman's *Beckford,* 1937.

game of being wicked, a significant part of which was the infatuated Louisa's connivance, and even active help, in his other affairs. The sanction of that abnormal relationship she speaks of in their correspondence as "paganism," which we can take to mean considered rejection of the Christian religious-moral code. Beckford's interest in evil, in what might be called affirmative wickedness, is not affected at all by the fact that for a time in his later years, after the tempest of his disgrace and ostracism had blown over, he became ostentatiously devout. That seems to be adequately explained in what we know of human nature, if, indeed, it was not again pretense.

Vathek must be seen, then, as the product of an unquiet mind under strong mental and emotional stimulation. At Henley's suggestion he went to work on the story in a surge of enthusiasm; and Henley was constantly consulted as the story grew under Beckford's hand.

The story was written in French, many English men and women of Beckford's caste at that time being all but bilingual. From that fact developed a complication. Henley had been permitted, perhaps asked, to put it into English, and over a protest from Beckford, published his translation in 1786, surprisingly enough without giving Beckford credit for the original. Accusations of bad faith were exchanged in correspondence, for Beckford was then on the Continent, and because of his involvements unable to return to England. To confirm his authorship, Beckford published at Lausanne in the following year a French version; not, it is said, the original, the manuscript of which was still in Henley's hands, but one retranslated from Henley's published English version. *Vathek* as known today by most readers is Henley's translation.

If it is asked why Beckford did not publish in the first place his French text, the answer is forthcoming. The correspondence of the two shows that he had for some time had under his hand the tales of the four princes whom Vathek and Nouronihar met in the halls of the palace of Eblis, and he wished to complete and add them to his narrative before *Vathek* appeared. In haste to establish his title to the book, Beckford published it without the so-called "Episodes," which were put aside, believed lost, and discovered and published under the title of the *Episodes of Vathek* well over a century later, in 1912, though the number of the princes had shrunk from four to three.

So much, then, for the author of *Vathek* and the curious vicissitudes of its publication. Even with the little we have recorded of Beckford's temperament and personal background, it must be seen that *Vathek* is the invention of a really extravagant and uninhibited mind. This is true not only as to the material of the story, but as to a social and moral skepticism which is disguised by the conventional moral ending. The ending is not surprising for a man who, like Beckford, had all his life spent much ingenuity upon preserving the appearances of conformity while scouting its spirit.

We have taken it as a premise for the discussion of the so-called oriental romance that it is an imitation, and whatever its collateral purpose, an inferior imitation, of the *Thousand and One Nights*. That inferiority is unescapable. The *Arabian Nights* was put together in an age and for a people willing to accept the machinery and embellishments of their own order of superstition. Afrits, Jinn, and their dark magic, mechanical flying horses, wonderful lamps, and magic carpets were, if not matters of absolute belief, acceptable as miracles, therefore real in their own way. A modern reader is not affected by incredulity in these things, any more than in the mythology of Homer and Virgil, because he is not asked to accept them. But when a modern writer uses the same machinery, he confronts incredulity.

Beckford accepted the miraculous, and particularly black magic, as part of the formula of the oriental tale, and he used it (as it is actually used in most religious treatments of the problem of evil in a good world) to amplify and energize the conception of evil. That is not to say that Beckford's miraculous has the vitality that it can have only in a system of true belief. At times, in fact, it is rather puerile invention, as in the case of Vathek's eye that can kill at a glance. But at other times it is really impressive, and cumulatively so as the narrative develops. Again it may be utterly and amusingly fantastic, as it is in the episode of the Indian Giaour, which ends in making the magic-worker a football for the entire population of Samarah.

Vathek's character is not only innately but enterprisingly evil, and being born and bred a king gives him boundless ambition to be the master of the known world not only in power, riches, and luxury, but in knowledge. Knowledge, however, is for him only a form of mental tyranny.

> He was fond of engaging in disputes with the learned, but did not allow them to push their opposition with warmth. He stopped with presents the mouths of those whose mouths could be stopped, whilst others, whom his liberality was unable to subdue, he sent to prison to cool their blood.
>
> Vathek discovered also a predilection for theological controversy, but it was not with the orthodox that he usually held. By this means he induced the zealots to oppose him, and then persecuted them in return; for he resolved, at any rate, to have reason on his side.

A lover of luxury and magnificence, he built his palaces of the five senses; and in pursuit of superior knowledge, his tower of fifteen-hundred steps, from which to "penetrate the secrets of heaven."

His pride arrived at its height when having ascended for the first time the fifteen hundred stairs of his tower, he cast his eyes below, and beheld men not larger than pismires, mountains than shells, and cities than bee-hives. The idea which such an elevation inpsired of his own grandeur completely bewildered him; he was almost ready to adore himself, till, lifting his eyes upward, he saw the stars as high above him as they appeared when he stood on the surface of the earth. He consoled himself, however, for this intruding and unwelcome perception of his littleness with the thought of being great in the eyes of others, and flattered himself that the light of his mind would extend beyond the reach of his sight and extort from the stars the decrees of his destiny.

Mahomet, looking down from his Seventh Heaven, sees Vathek's presumption; "but," he says to his attendants, "leave him to himself; let us see to what lengths his folly and impiety will carry him." The instruments of his destruction appear promptly, in appeals to his avarice, his sensuality, and above all, his desire for esoteric knowledge. The characters sent to encourage his curiosity and ambition are, like those of the genuine oriental tales, both malign and ludicrous.

Not long after . . . arrived in his metropolis a man so abominably hideous that the very guards who arrested him were forced to shut their eyes as they led him along. The caliph himself appeared startled at so horrible a visage, but joy succeeded to his emotion of terror when the stranger displayed to his view such rarities as he had never seen before.

Vathek is so struck with these wonders that "without demanding their price, he ordered all the coined gold to be brought from his treasury, and commanded the merchant to take what he pleased. The stranger obeyed, took little, and remained silent." Vathek asks him in condescension :

. . . who he was, whence he came, and where he obtained such beautiful commodities. The man, or rather monster, instead of making a reply, thrice rubbed his forehead, which, as well as his body, was blacker than ebony; four times clapped his paunch, the projection of which was enormous; opened wide his huge eyes, which glowed like firebrands; began to laugh with a hideous noise, and discovered his long amber-colored teeth, bestreaked with green.

Indignantly Vathek has him thrown into prison under heavy guard, but in the morning the monster has escaped and the guards lie lifeless before the door. "In the paroxysm of his passion he fell furiously upon the poor carcases, and kicked them till evening without intermission." In vain Vathek tries to fathom the hidden meanings of the gifts of the monster, until he falls into a fever followed by an insatiable thirst. He is relieved from this torture by the reappearance of the stranger, who carries with him the inevitable ready remedy. The stranger is lavishly entertained in the palace, where it was found "his loquacity was equal to that of a hundred astrologers; he ate as much as a hundred porters, and caroused in proportion."

In the morning, before the full court, Vathek again plies his guest with questions.

> But the Indian, still keeping his seat, began to renew his loud shouts of laughter, and exhibit the same horrid grimaces he had shown them before, without vouchsafing a word in reply. Vathek, no longer able to brook such insolence, immediately kicked him from the steps; instantly descending, repeated the blow; and persisted with such assiduity as incited all who were present to follow his example. Every foot was up and aimed at the Indian, and no sooner had anyone given him a kick than he felt himself constrained to reiterate the stroke.

Rolling himself into a ball, the stranger is kicked out of the palace, pursued through the streets by the entire populace, and finally disappears in a ravine, above which his pursuers stand looking at one another in astonishment and shame.

The story multiplies extravagant incident as it moves. The final challenge to Vathek's curiosity reaches him in the form of a conditional promise from the stranger.

> "Wouldest thou devote thyself to me, adore the terrestial influences, and abjure Mahomet? On these conditions I will bring thee to the Palace of Subterranean Fire. There shalt thou behold, in immense depositories, the treasures which the stars have promised thee; and which will be conferred by those intelligences whom thou shalt thus render propitious. It was from thence I brought my sabres, and it is there that Soliman Ben Daoud reposes, surrounded by the talismans that control the world."

But the price to be paid is the blood of fifty children, whom Vathek himself selects for the sacrifice. The populace is temporarily appeased, but Vathek, urged on by his mother, Carathis, after an elaborate and nauseating ritual sets forward on his way to Istakar to receive "the diadem of Gian Ben Gian, the talismans of Soliman, and the treasures of the preadamite sultans." The journey is made with an immense retinue and with unparalleled splendor. The numerous and lively incidents of the expedition, we can pass over, to the point of his reaching the house of the Emir

Fakreddin. Here he meets, and falls violently in love with, the Emir's daughter Nouronihar.

Nouronihar has been betrothed to her cousin Gulchenrouz, "the most delicate and lovely creature in the world," a boy of thirteen. Her deep attachment to him, however, fades quickly in the sunlight of the Caliph's presence; and her now vitalized passion is supplemented by a rising ambition when a sort of vision reveals to her that she is destined to be the bride of Vathek. Fakreddin, distressed and frightened by Vathek's impiety, secretes Nouronihar and Gulchenrouz, but their retreat is discovered accidentally by Vathek, and despite the holy làws of hospitality, he escapes with the willing Nouronihar, accompanied by Carathis, who has overtaken him to keep up his faltering purpose. With little interruption they come within sight of the dark summits of the mountains of Istakar, to be confronted by one last plea for repentance and return. Vathek rejects it contemptuously. But the warning has brought consternation to the hearts of his attendants, and most of them vanish during the following night.

Alive with expectation, but also touched by the terror of the surroundings, they approach the entrance of the palace of Eblis.

The gait of these impious personages was haughty and determined. As they descended by the effulgence of the torches, they gazed on each other with mutual admiration, and both appeared so resplendent that they already esteemed themselves spiritual intelligences. The only circumstance that perplexed them was their not arriving at the bottom of the stairs. On hastening their descent with an ardent impetuosity, they felt their steps accelerated to such a degree that they seemed not walking but falling from a precipice. Their progress, however, was at length impeded by a vast portal of ebony, which the caliph without difficulty recognized. Here the Giaour awaited them with the key in his hand. "Ye are welcome," said he to them with a ghastly smile, "in spite of Mahomet and all his dependents. I will now usher you into that palace where you have so highly merited a place." Whilst he was uttering these words, he touched the enamelled lock with his key, and the doors at once flew open with a noise still louder than the thunder of the dog days, and as suddenly recoiled the moment they had entered.

In the midst of this immense hall a vast multitude was incessantly passing, who severally kept their right hands on their hearts, without once regarding anything around them; they had all the livid paleness of death. Their eyes, deep sunk in their sockets, resembled those phosphoric meteors that glimmer by night in places of interment. Some stalked slowly on, absorbed in profound reveries; some, shrieking with agony, ran furiously about like tigers wounded with poison arrows; whilst others, grinding their teeth in rage, foamed along more frantic than the wildest maniac. They all avoided each other; and though surrounded by a multitude that no one could number, each wandered at random unheedful of the rest, as if alone on a desert where no foot had trodden.

Vathek and Nouronihar, frozen with terror at a sight so baleful, demanded of the Giaour what these appearances might mean, and why these ambulating spectres never withdrew their hands from their hearts?

They are greeted by the formidable Eblis himself, "a young man whose noble and regular features seemed to have been tarnished by malignant vapors. In his large eyes appeared both pride and despair." Encouraged by Eblis, they walk about in the amazing chambers. They visit the hall of the tombs of the great infidels, and are accosted by the living-dead Soliman Ben Daoud (the Biblical Solomon). As the ancient king raised his hands toward heaven, "the caliph discerned through his bosom, which was transparent as crystal, his heart enveloped in flames." This is the eternal torment of presumptuous unbelievers. Vathek now calls on Mahomet for mercy, but his Giaour replies :

"Know, miserable prince, thou art now in the abode of vengeance and despair. Thy heart, also, will be kindled like those of the other votaries of Eblis. A few days are allotted thee previous to this fatal period. Employ them as thou wilt; recline on these heaps of gold; command the infernal potentates; range at thy pleasure through these immense subterranean domains; no barrier shall be shut against thee. As for me, I have fulfilled my mission : I now leave thee to thyself."

In the course of their terrified wanderings they come finally to a chamber in which they find "four young men of goodly figure and a lovely female." They ask to be told Vathek's story, and volunteer their own; for this was the point in Beckford's narrative at which he was to introduce the three tales later published as the "Episodes." There is a final momentary diversion with a tang of comedy in the entrance of the self-important Carathis.

She even attempted to dethrone one of the Solimans, for the purpose of usurping his place, when a voice, proceeding from the abyss of death, proclaimed, "All is accomplished!" Instantaneously the haughty forehead of the intrepid princess became corrugated with agony; she uttered a tremendous yell, and fixed, no more to be withdrawn, her right hand upon her heart, which was become a receptacle of eternal fire.

Almost at the same instant, the same voice announced to the caliph,

Nouronihar, the four princes, and the princess, the awful and irrevocable decree. Their hearts immediately took fire, and they at once lost the most precious gift of heaven—HOPE. These unhappy beings recoiled, with looks of the most furious distraction. Vathek beheld in the eyes of Nouronihar nothing but rage and vengeance; nor could she discern aught in his but aversion and despair. The two princes who were friends, and till that moment had preserved their attachment, shrunk back, gnashing their teeth with mutual and unchangeable hatred. Kalilah and his sister made reciprocal gestures of imprecation; all testified their horror for each other by the most ghastly convulsions, and screams that could not be smothered. All severally plunged themselves into the accursed multitude, there to wander in an eternity of unabating anguish.

The three (originally four) "Episodes," since they were designed for insertion in *Vathek* in the very closing period, to give the stories of the three princes condemned like Vathek to atone for their offenses with the eternal fires of hatred and despair consuming their hearts, are of the same temper as the main story and of the same doubtfully moral trend. If there is a distinction between inherent evil and wickedness, then these three princes are like Vathek deliberately wicked. The quasi-religious sanction for their wickedness takes some ritual form of paganism, which apparently in all three, and explicitly in the second, is Zoroastrian. It is opposed to Mahometanism, the "true faith" of the modern East, as pagan cults are similarly opposed to Christianity, the true faith of Western Europe. The parallel is symbolic, for the true faiths are in either case the forms of orthodox righteousness. In an important degree, the action of *Vathek* (as well as of the "Episodes") is a running encomium of pragmatic paganism, whether that paganism is for Beckford self-justification, anti-Christian convictions, or literary pretense. It is probably something of all three. At any rate, the conclusions of *Vathek* and the "Episodes"—that belated and desperate effort to turn to the true belief—are, considering the recusant spirit of the narratives from beginning to end, no more than a compromise with proper opinion. The "Episodes" only intensify the view that the fascination of evil, rather than sensual curiosity, was the important explanation of Beckford's own deviant morality. That is the real theme of all three of the "Episodes," particularly the first two.

The three princes, then, are merely three other Vatheks, different from him in the particular circumstances of their fates, but bent like him upon the pursuit of evil. Prince Alasi is contaminated and finally destroyed by his love for a supremely beautiful princess introduced to him at first as a boy, who is egotistically cruel and madly fanatic. Prince Barkiaroch, teller of the second tale, has his head turned by power and wealth, and like

Alasi is slave to an overwhelming passion. The story of the Princess Zulkaïs and her brother the Prince Kalilah, which is unfinished, is the story of an incestuous attachment, the result ostensibly of a cabalistic baptism of twin brother and sister in their infancy. But the point of all three stories is that the narrator is at peace with life until evil enters it in some pre-emptive form which impels him to destruction.

By general admission, *Vathek* was modeled upon no single and specific antecedent. Yet what might be called its orientality, its assimilation of the authentic tone of Oriental life and culture, brings it closer to the *Arabian Nights* than any other of the eighteenth-century romances of its type. It is not merely tinted with orientalism; it is steeped in it—a fact evident in the copious and sometimes pedantic footnotes upon Eastern languages, mythologies, customs, and government. Even in the psychological set of its principals it is studiously faithful to the Orient.

But it is also to an unusual degree personal, since even before he began *Vathek* Beckford had been deeply influenced by the Near-Eastern social perspective and mental temper. The mind of the Caliph Vathek is in notable respects the mind of Beckford. Its principal characters also show resemblances to members of Beckford's family and to his close intimates. The Nouronihar of the tale is the impulsive and daring Cousin Louisa. Gulchenrouz recalls the handsome and captivating boy who was involved in the scandal that drove Beckford from England. And Carathis, Vathek's mother and the impersonation of arrogant impiety, has been regarded as an inverted caricature of his own obstinately proper mother. These attributions, of course, may be taken or left, but Beckford's correspondence seems to justify them at least in the first two instances.

With the "Episodes," *Vathek* stands as Beckford's one memorable literary work. He outlived the instant fame of his story by more than half a century, wondered at and talked about; for he continued to challenge and puzzle his contemporaries by a strongly assertive but always somewhat unbalanced personality. He bought great paintings, collected an invaluable library, and built an immense modern Gothic abbey at Fonthill which was matter for gossip until its great tower, which had been rushed to completion through Beckford's impatience, collapsed within a few years of its erection. Before he had passed half his life, a great part of his fabulous fortune had been spent, not altogether frivolously, but without judgment. *Vathek* is a strikingly appropriate monument to an extraordinary character and career.

CHAPTER XV

The Gothic Romance

Walpole, Ann Radcliffe, Lewis

LITERATURE, LIKE hats, hairdos, painting, and politics, has its fads. Singular, extravagant, ridiculous, or atrocious, they have flashed in and out of the history of the novel, sometimes without a measurable permanent effect, but sometimes with lasting influence upon writers still to come. The Gothic romance, slow at first to establish its place, but in the last ten years of the century almost incredibly popular, is one of the most conspicuous of these headlong plunges into brief and preposterous importance. Yet the type ranks also among those in which there is some merit to be preserved and worked over by later writers.

This is one case in which full faithfulness to the history of a genre would seem less profitable than closer attention to its highest and most distinctive point of development. So we can skim over the record of its origin and growth, and reach promptly those doubtfully "great" Gothics of the 1790's, and their one and unequaled begetter, Mrs. Ann Radcliffe.

The first of the Gothic romances was Horace Walpole's *Castle of Otranto* (1764), and it was Walpole who first used the word "Gothic" to describe the type.* The so-called Gothic Revival, in which Walpole was one of the conspicuous figures, was a movement to impart to the sophisticated eighteenth century some of the spirit of the late Middle Ages. The movement was more enthusiastic than intelligent, for it originated in the view that the people of the Middle Ages, and particularly the designers and makers of the architectural triumphs called Gothic, led a better life and produced a better art because their spiritual outlook was simpler and clearer. We can pass over the fact that the word "Gothic" was itself a misnomer, at first applied in actual ridicule of the vogue; for the primitive Gothic tribes were extinct long before Gothic cathedrals began to be

---

*Horace Walpole, Fourth Earl of Orford (1717-1797). *The Castle of Otranto* (1764) is his one fiction. His private papers and letters, published many years after his death, are among the most important and often captivating historical and literary remains of his time.

built. We can also take it for granted that the eighteenth century, which
was rather weak on history, and only groping toward understanding of
social evidence and antiquities, interpreted medieval life vaguely and
inaccurately.

At any rate, Walpole (who lacking a Gothic castle of his very own
built, or rather remodeled, one for himself—the much discussed and much
visited Strawberry Hill) decided to render the spirit of this imagined
Gothic culture into English fiction. So he wrote *The Castle of Otranto*.

Except as a sort of literary landmark, it is impossible to take Walpole's
story seriously. In literary charm or grace, it is completing wanting. The
dilettante has rarely either the energy or the sincerity of the artist, and
Walpole's dip into fiction was no more than might be expected from a
literary dandy and a self-appointed arbiter of taste.

In the preface to his first edition, Walpole pretends that his story has
been taken from an ancient manuscript, and he puts on a show of learned
speculation as to its date and its source, defending in particular the liberal
use of the supernatural on the ground that superstition was implicit in
medieval culture. What truly calls for defense, however, are not the supernatural manifestations, but their puerility. A gigantic sword, that requires
a hundred men to lift it, is brought—we don't know how—from the
Holy Land to Italy; a statue bleeds ominously from the nose; the gigantic
figure of a former lord of the castle rises from within to carry it down to
final ruin. Yet these silly prodigies were in all probability devoured as
eagerly as our "space" and "science" fiction today. And they were accompanied by incongruities and improbabilities in the management of incident that reach the depths of the ridiculous.

Here, for example, we find the Princess Isabella fleeing from the mad
pursuit of the lord of the castle. She is only a guest there, and so far as
appearances suggest, knows little or nothing about its remoter recesses.
But finding herself in a subterranean passage, she is frightened on encoun-
tering there an unknown young man, whose protection she begs.

> "Sir, whoever you are, take pity on a wretched princess standing on
> the brink of destruction. Assist me to escape from this fatal castle, or in
> a few minutes I may be made miserable forever."
>
> "Alas," said the stranger, "what can I do to assist you? I will die
> in your defense, but I am unacquainted with the castle, and want—"
>
> "Oh!" said Isabella, hastily interrupting him, "help me but to
> find a trap-door that must be hereabout, and it is the greatest service
> you can do me." Saying these words, she felt about on the pavement,
> and directed the stranger to search likewise, for a smooth piece of brass
> enclosed in one of the stones. "That," said she, "is the lock, which opens

with a spring of which I know the secret. If we can find that, I may escape; if not, alas, courteous stranger, I fear I shall have involved you in my misfortunes. Manfred will suspect you for the accomplice of my flight, and you will fall a victim to his resentment."

"I value not my life," said the stranger, "and it will be some comfort to lose it in trying to deliver you from his tyranny."

"Generous youth," said Isabella, "how shall I ever requite—"

As she uttered these words, a ray of moonshine, streaming through a cranny of the ruin above, shone directly on the lock they sought. "Oh, transport," said Isabella, "here is the trap-door," and taking out the key, she touched the spring, which starting aside, discovered an iron ring. "Lift up the door," said the princess. The stranger obeyed, and beneath appeared some stone steps descending into a vault totally dark. "We must go down here," said Isabella; "follow me; dark and dismal as it is, we cannot miss our way. It leads directly to the Church of St. Nicholas.—But perhaps," added the princess modestly, "you have no reason to leave the castle, nor have I farther occasion for your service; in a few minutes I shall be safe from Manfred's rage—only let me know to whom I am so much obliged."

The absurdities of this sort of thing seem self-evident. The "wretched princess," the opportune "ray of moonshine," the key to the trap-door which the wretched princess (who is only a guest in the castle) seems to have been carrying about with her on the chance that it might "come in handy" some time—all these characteristic details seem to be addressed not to adults, but to children.

The stigmata of sentimentalism are not foreign to the spirit of Walpole's tale. The same young man, Theodore, speaks in this passage to the lady of his heart, Matilda, another princess—Isabella has been, so to speak, only a subterranean acquaintance:

"Give me thy beauteous hand in token that thou dost not deceive me," said Theodore, "and let me bathe it with the warm tears of gratitude."

"Forbear," said the princess; "this must not be."

"Alas," said Theodore, "I have never known but calamity until this hour—perhaps shall never know other fortune again; suffer the chaste raptures of holy gratitude. 'Tis my soul would print its effusions upon thy hand."

But the high note of sentimentalism is reached in the very closing sentences. Matilda has died, stabbed to the heart by her father in a momentary mistake, when he is too angry to look attentively at the lady he is about to assassinate. But there is good reason that the two rival branches of the noble house shall be united by the marriage of Isabella and Theodore (for yes, Theodore is the long lost heir to the title).

> Frederic offered his daughter to the new prince, which Hippolita's tenderness for Isabella concurred to promote. But Theodore's. grief was too fresh to admit the thought of another love; and it was not until after frequent discourses with Isabella of his dear Matilda that he was persuaded that he could know no happiness but in the society of one with whom he could forever indulge the melancholy that had taken possession of his soul.

Happy, happy Isabella! And it might be added in explanation of Theodore's life-long grief for the dead Matilda that he had known her for just two days, and that their conversation might have amounted in all to perhaps twenty sentences, none of which smacked of either love or courtship.

The story itself? It is certainly not worth recounting. But if one is curious, there have been many reprints of *The Castle of Otranto*, many more than it really deserves. The tale can perhaps be fairly dismissed in words taken from the mouth of one of its characters, as a "rhapsody of impertinence."

Yet it was a beginning, and what followed took on greater importance. Walpole had introduced into fiction the furniture and accessories of the Gothic romance—the ancient castle, dismantled and moldering; the ancient noble line, likewise decayed and broken up by family dissensions; the hidden identity of the hero or the heroine, or both; the heroine herself, delicate and fragile, exposed to an unfeeling world, and more particularly to the pursuit of a wicked usurper or a hungry voluptuary; a steady succession of threatened dangers and shattering alarms; and always a placid outcome in which true and loyal love is vindicated, and wealth, position, and title showered upon the deserving. More effects will be added to the Gothic in time, but these Walpole introduced.

The Castle of Otranto had no imitator until twelve years later, when Clara Reeve's *Old English Baron* appeared.* Miss Reeve, who posed as a kind of oracle of taste, believed that prodigies and terrors should not outrage good sense. So she utilized the machinery of marvels that Walpole

---

*Clara Reeve (1729-1807). *The Phoenix* (1772, translated from John Barclay's Latin *Argenis,* 1621); *The Old English Baron* (1777; title of the first edition was *The Champion of Virtue*); *The Two Mentors* (1783); *The School for Widows* (1791). Her *Progress of Romance* (1785) is an early critical discussion of fiction.

had invented, but brought into her story no apparitions, no physical ex-
travagances, that could not be explained, after the fact, in a reasonable
way. She wrote, however, completely without inspiration; so her attempt
to improve Gothic effects for the taste of the more literal-minded resulted
in mere prosiness. Nothing, for example, could be flatter than her painstak-
ing explanation at the end of *The Old English Baron* that the ominous
noises and flickering lights seen at midnight about the old castle were
caused by the presence of a hermit in an abandoned wing of the delapi-
dated structure who, to conceal his presence, adopted nocturnal habits.
Walpole's opinion of it was that "any trial for murder would make a more
interesting story."

Ann Radcliffe appeared upon this corner of the neo-romantic scene
with the publication in 1789 of her brief tale, *The Castle of Athlin and
Dunbayne*.* From the little we know of her life, she seemed to be more
temperamental than her predecessor Miss Reeve; so she went at writing
with more ardor, and consequently better effect. Yet, like Miss Reeve, she
took into her romances only the kind of mystification that could at long
last be rationally accounted for. That concession to probability, however,
did not sterilize her effects, as it had Miss Reeve's. She had enough art to
make them hold their interest until time for the secret to be explained.

In all, Mrs. Radcliffe produced five Gothic romances, the last three of
which show maturity and mastery of her medium—*The Romance of the
Forest, The Mysteries of Udolpho*, and *The Italian*. The three show a
family likeness, for all are built more or less upon the framework of *The
Castle of Otranto*. Her heroines, however, are portrayed more fully and
more spiritedly than Walpole's Isabella and Matilda, though they are
always the children of convention and propriety. Their emotional lives are
troubled, and even melancholy, but their deportment reflects the very best
of breeding. They sketch, paint in water colors, play the lute or the harp,
embroider, sing, read romances, and walk, but not beyond the limitations
of a charmingly delicate constitution; and in their most exalted moments
they write poetry, which Mrs. Radcliffe is always at the pains to quote for
the delectation of the reader. As to their responsiveness to the very best
standards of propriety, we need only note that in *The Italian* Ellena
hesitates to permit her accepted suitor to flee with her from the imminent
danger of death unless she is properly chaperoned.

Mrs. Radcliffe's lovers are equally standard, young men of birth and
breeding, but poorly circumstanced to all appearances, and generally free

---

*Mrs. Ann (Ward) Radcliffe (1764-1823). *The Castles of Athlin and Dunbayne*, 1789; *The
Sicilian Romance*, 1790; *The Romance of the Forest* 1791; *The Mysteries of Udolpho*, 1794; *The
Italian*, 1797; *Gaston de Blondville* (historical romance, published posthumously), 1826.

from the bolder vices of the time. Valancourt, however, in *The Mysteries of Udolpho,* has seen and enjoyed Paris, and that is for a time a serious embarrassment in his suit to the pure-minded Emily St. Aubert.

Mrs. Radcliffe's villains, however, command attention. The usurping villain in *The Castles of Athlin and Dunbayne* is what I believe is known as a "piker." But the Marquis in *The Romance of the Forest* and Montoni in *The Mysteries of Udolpho* have taken on magnitude; and the priest Schedoni, in *The Italian,* has inflexible backbone and sound visceral tone —both of them indispensable for the remorseless part he is to play.

The Romance of the Forest is still readable, and fairly free from manufactured thrills, but none of Mrs. Radcliffe's last three romances is unduly brief. The opening episode shows some mastery of situation. The aristocratic Pierre de la Motte, at the end of his wasted resources, and fallen into evil ways, is trying to escape from Paris in midnight darkness and a pitiless storm. Seeking a direction, he stops at a lonely house on the heath. The door is cautiously opened by a ruffian, who retires momentarily, locking the door after him, and returns, "leading, or rather forcibly dragging along, a beautiful girl, who appeared to be about eighteen."

> Her features were bathed in tears, and she seemed to suffer the utmost distress. The man fastened the lock and put the key in his pocket. He then advanced to La Motte, who had before observed other persons in the passage, and pointing a pistol to his breast, "You are wholly in our power," said he; "no assistance can reach you. If you wish to save your life, swear that you will convey this girl where I may never see her more; or rather, consent to take her with you, for your oath I would not believe, and I can take care you shall not find me again.— Answer quickly; you have no time to lose." . . .
>
> La Motte now turned his eyes upon his unfortunate companion, who, pale and exhausted, leaned for support against the wall. Her features, which were delicately beautiful, had gained from distress a captivating sweetness. She had
>
> > an eye
> > As when the blue sky trembles through a cloud
> > Of purest white.
>
> A habit of grey camlet, with short slashed sleeves, showed, but did not adorn, her figure. It was thrown open at the bosom, upon which part of her hair had fallen in disorder, while the light veil, hastily thrown on, had in her confusion been suffered to fall back. Every moment of farther observation heightened the surprise of La Motte, and interested him more warmly in her favor. Such elegance and apparent refinement, contrasted with the desolation of the house and the savage manners of its inhabitants, seemed to him like a romance of

imagination, rather than an occurrence of real life. He endeavored to comfort her, and his sense of compassion was too sincere to be misunderstood. Her terror gradually subsided into gratitude and grief. "Oh, Sir," said she, "Heaven has sent you to my relief, and will surely reward you for your protection. I have no friend in the world, if I do not find one in you."

La Motte, taking Adeline, joins his wife and servants, and they drive blindly over an unknown road until at the end of the day they approach the dark towers of a deserted abbey.

It stood on a kind of rude lawn, overshadowed by high and spreading trees which seemed coeval with the building and diffused a romantic gloom around. The greater part of the pile appeared to be sinking into ruins, and that which had withstood the ravages of time showed the remaining features of the fabric more awful in decay. The lofty battlements, thickly enwreathed with ivy, were half demolished, and become the residence of birds of prey. Huge fragments of the eastern tower, which was almost demolished, lay scattered amid the high grass, which waved slowly to the breeze. "The thistle shook its lonely head; the moss whistled to the wind." A Gothic gate, richly ornamented with fret-work, which opened into the main body of the edifice, but which was now obstructed with brush-wood, remained entire. Above the vast and magnificent portal of this gate arose a window of the same order whose pointed arches still exhibited fragments of stained glass, once the pride of monkish devotion. La Motte, thinking it possible it might yet shelter some human being, advanced to the gate and lifted a massy knocker. The hollow sounds rang through the emptiness of the place.

The deepening gloom reminded La Motte that he had no time to lose, but curiosity prompted him to explore farther, and he obeyed the impulse. As he walked over the broken pavement, the sound of his steps rang in echoes through the place, and seemed like the mysterious accents of the dead, reproving the sacrilegious mortal who thus dared to disturb their precincts.

From this chapel he passed into the nave of the great church, of which one window, more perfect than the rest, opened upon a long vista of the forest, through which was seen the rich coloring of evening, melting by imperceptible gradations into the solemn grey of upper air. Dark hills, whose outlines appeared distinct upon the vivid glow of the horizon, closed the perspective. Several of the pillars which had once supported the roof remained the proud effigies of sinking greatness, and seemed to nod at every murmur of the blast over the fragments of those which had fallen a little before them.

Even benighted as they are, they decide to move on from this eerie and perhaps dangerous spot. But as they start, their carriage breaks down, and they are obliged to return to the abbey for shelter. With dawn, their spirits rise. Here perhaps is concealment and safety. La Motte examines the ruins more carefully.

[The environs] were sweetly romantic, and the luxuriant woods with which they abounded seemed to sequester this spot from the rest of the world. Frequently a natural vista would yield a view of the country, terminated by hills, which, retiring in distance, faded into the blue horizon. A stream, various and musical in its course, wound at the foot of the lawn on which stood the abbey. Here it silently glided beneath the shades, feeding the flowers which bloomed on its banks, and diffusing dewy freshness around; there it spread in broad expanse to day, reflecting the sylvan scene and the wild deer that tasted its waves. La Motte observed everywhere a profusion of game. The pheasants scarcely flew from his approach, and the deer gazed mildly at him as he passed. They were strangers to man!

This is Mrs. Radcliffe at her romantic best. A poor poet herself—the "interspersed pieces of poetry" in all her romances fully prove it—she nevertheless had poetic sensitivity and perception, and they really add quality to her fiction.

La Motte decides to remain in this secluded refuge until he can learn more of its longer possibilities. Adeline, for she is of course the focus of our interest, finds it sometimes thrilling, sometimes frightening. But peace never provides for long the atmosphere of the Gothic romance; and here the always present threat of danger becomes reality when the Marquis de Montalt, the lord of the demesne, chances to visit it, and finds the La Motte family in residence. Both La Motte and Adeline are endangered by his presence, La Motte because he has incautiously—though we do not yet know how—exposed himself to the Marquis's vengeance, and Adeline because she is fair and lovely and the Marquis is the kind of man we suspected he would be.

Meanwhile, for Adeline a new tension develops. She has found in an ancient chest a fragmentary manuscript in which a former resident of the abbey has recounted his feelings while he is waiting in anticipation of death, as the final act of a conspiracy of which he is to be the victim. Adeline keeps her discovery to herself, and reads the manuscript at night while the rest of the family sleeps. At best, it is rather horrid reading, but it is particularly disturbing at midnight, when the candle gutters in the socket and she hears human sighs and glimpses a shrouded figure and sees the arras disturbed in the chill wind that blows down the corridors and listens to the midnight bell (we wonder who kept the clockwork in order) declaring the hour above the tumult of the outer storm. No, she is not imagining things, for Mrs. Radcliffe conscientiously observes her implied compact with the reader, and all these alarming things can in due time be fully and properly elucidated.

But a livelier, because more imminent, worry for Adeline is the certainty that she has now become the unwilling object of the Marquis's attention. She plans escape, but the plan is discovered, and the attempt ends with her finding herself in the power of the Marquis in his chateau on the edge of the forest. Mrs. Radcliffe sets the stage rather skillfully. Adeline is carried to the chateau in a raging tempest, but within, tranquil luxury and insidious sin are joined in the most approved fashion.

They came to another door; it opened and disclosed a magnificent saloon, splendidly illuminated and fitted up in the most airy and elegant taste.

The walls were painted in fresco, representing scenes from Ovid, and hung above with silk drawn up in festoons and richly fringed. The sofas were of a silk to suit the hangings. From the centre of the ceiling, which exhibited a scene from the *Armida* of Tasso, descended a silver lamp of the Etruscan form. It diffused a blaze of light that, reflected from large pier-glasses, completely illuminated the saloon. Busts of Horace, Ovid, Anacreon, Tibullus, and Petronius Arbiter adorned the recesses, and stands of flowers, placed in Etruscan vases, breathed the most delicious perfume. In the middle of the apartment stood a small table spread with a collection of fruits, ices, and liquors. No person appeared. The whole seemed the works of enchantment, and rather resembled the palace of a fairy than anything of human conformation. . . .

She endeavored with a hope of escaping to open the windows, but they were all fastened; she next attempted several doors, and found them also secured.

Perceiving all chance of escape was removed, she remained for some time given up to sorrow and reflection, but was at length drawn from her reverie by the notes of soft music, breathing such dulcet and entrancing sounds as suspended grief and waked the soul to tenderness and pensive pleasure. Adeline listened in surprise, and insensibly became soothed and interested. A tender melancholy stole upon her heart and subdued every harsher feeling. But the moment the strain ceased, the enchantment dissolved, and she returned to a sense of her situation.

Then the Marquis appears, with a line of select and well tried blandishments.

He now led her, and she suffered him, to a seat near the banquet at which he pressed her to partake of a variety of confectionaries, particularly of some liquors, of which he himself drank freely. Adeline accepted only of a peach. [Was there ever a happier symbol of discreet innocence?]

And now the Marquis, who interpreted her silence into a secret compliance with his proposal, resumed all his gaiety and spirit, while the long and ardent regards he bestowed on Adeline overcame her with confusion and indignation. In the midst of the banquet soft music again sounded the most tender and impassioned airs, but its effect on Adeline was now lost, her mind being too much embarrassed and distressed by the presence of the Marquis to admit even the soothings of harmony. A song was now heard, written with that sort of impotent art by which some voluptuous poets believe they can at once conceal and recommend the principles of vice. Adeline received it with contempt and displeasure, and the Marquis, perceiving its effect, presently made a sign for another composition, which adding the force of poetry to the charms of music, might withdraw her mind from the present scene and enchant it in sweet delirium.

But Adeline's iron virtue triumphs.

. . . He threw his arm around her and would have pressed her toward him, but she liberated herself from his embrace, and with a look on which was impressed the firm dignity of virtue, yet touched with sorrow, she awed him to forbearance.

Adeline is "conducted to her chamber," locks the door carefully behind her, and looks about her upon "airy elegance" and "luxurious accommodations" which "seemed designed to fascinate the imagination and to seduce the heart." But the Marquis, or perhaps his servants, has missed a trick. She discovers an open window, and then in a moment she is in the garden, seeking desperately to find the way out. But waiting there in the garden is Theodore, the young man whom she had already marked with interest in the Marquis's suite; and he has a ladder, an extremely convenient piece of equipment in the circumstances. They go over the wall, down the road, and are on their way to safety, when they are overtaken by the Marquis and his minions. In the scuffle which follows, Theodore seriously wounds the Marquis; and since the Marquis is colonel of his regiment, Theodore is placed under arrest, and is in a promising way to lose his head—this time literally.

And now Adeline is back at the abbey, in La Motte's keeping, and still exposed to the wicked Marquis. But his plans have changed. He no longer wants to seduce her; he wants to kill her. For he has discovered from the seal of an intercepted note from Adeline that she is his brother's daughter, and heir to the estates which he has usurped after murdering her father, and therefore a very undesirable person to have around.

But *noblesse* counts once more. The Marquis has delegated to La Motte the little matter of putting Adeline out of the way; but La Motte, who has not balked at the seduction of Adeline, feels that nice people don't do this other sort of thing. Unexpectedly he liberates the girl, supplies her with a horse and with his servant Peter, and puts her on the road to Savoy and safety.

But La Motte himself is now in the Marquis's vengeful grasp, and, like Theodore, he goes to prison on the Marquis's charge, with every prospect of a sudden and unhappy demise. As for Adeline, we soon find her lodged with the minister, La Luc, in the town of Lelancourt; and La Luc, by one of those pleasant coincidences that simplify problems of plot for Mrs. Radcliffe, has turned out quite unexpectedly to be the father of —can you guess? Yes; Theodore!

The rest of the story is, by comparison with what we have tried to summarize, almost serene. There are idyllic days in Savoy and southern France, although overshadowed by Theodore's imprisonment and jeopardy. But when Theodore and La Motte come up for trial, the Marquis, through one of those sad oversights of even the cleverest minds—he has neglected to pay off one of his sanguinary assistants, who therefore betrays him—is caught up in the trammels of fate. He is put on trial for the death of Adeline's father, and saves his noble head by taking poison before he can be convicted. For the rest, Theodore, the rural minister's son, marries the Marquise de Montalt—Adeline was never her real name anyway—and everything is just the way everybody likes it.

By far the best known of all Mrs. Radcliffe's romances is *The Mysteries of Udolpho,* remembered principally because it is shamelessly lavish of the tricks of Mrs. Radcliffe's trade. It is not an entertaining story; it is atrociously long; and its heroine is a very thin mixture of the human and the angelic. She earns the very highest marks for sensibility. In the meanderings of self-conscious feeling throughout this entire period, there is probably no passage that shows better than the following one the depths of sentimental fatuity into which the resolved sentimentalist can allow himself (or in this case, herself) to sink.

All without was silent and dark, unless that could be called light which was only the faint glimmer of the stars, showing imperfectly the outline of the mountains, the western towers of the castle, and the ramparts below, where a solitary sentinel was pacing. What an image of repose did this scene represent. The fierce and terrible passions too, which so often agitated the inhabitants of this edifice, seemed now hushed in sleep; those mysterious workings which rouse the elements of man's nature into tempest were calm. Emily's heart was not so; but her sufferings, though deep, partook of the gentle character of her mind. Hers was a silent anguish, weeping yet enduring; not the wild energy of passion, inflaming the imagination, bearing down the barriers of reason, and living in a world of its own.

The air refreshed her, and she continued at the casement looking on the shadowy scene, over which the planets burned with a clear light, amid the deep blue ether, as they silently moved in their destined course. She remembered how often she had gazed on them with her dear father, how often he had pointed out their way in the heavens, and explained their laws, and these reflections led to others which in an equal degree awakened her grief and astonishment.

They brought a retrospect of all the strange and mournful events which had occurred since she had lived in peace with her parents. And to Emily, who had been so tenderly educated, so tenderly loved, who once knew only goodness and happiness—to her, the late events and her present situation—in a foreign land in a remote castle—surrounded by vice and violence, seemed more like the visions of a distempered imagination than the circumstances of truth. She wept to think of what her parents would have suffered, could they have seen the events of her future life.

It is all—to borrow a phrase from one of Owen Seaman's parodies—like beginning by being beside oneself, and gradually getting quite a long distance away.

But the precarious reputation of *The Mysteries of Udolpho* rests upon its big moments of superstitious terror excited by some sort of hideous apparition. Most notable are two, and we do not have to recite the substance of a very long story to introduce them. The first is the notorious mystery of the "veiled picture". Emily is exploring deserted corridors in the Castle of Udolpho.

Her imagination was pleased with the view of ancient grandeur, and an emotion of melancholy awe awakened all its powers as she walked through rooms obscure and desolate, where no footsteps had passed probably for many years, and remembered the strange history of the former possessor of the edifice. This brought to her recollection the veiled picture, which had attracted her curiosity on the preceding night; and she resolved to examine it. As she passed through the chambers that led to this, she found herself somewhat agitated, its connection with the late lady of the castle, and the conversation with Annette, together with the circumstance of the veil, throwing a mystery over the object that excited a faint degree of terror. But a terror of this nature, as it occupies and expands the mind and elevates it to high expectation, is purely sublime, and leads us by a kind of fascination

Two woodcuts from John Limbird's first illustrated edition of Mrs. Radcliffe's romances, 1824. Above, scenery in the Pyrenees, from *The Mysteries of Udolpho;* below, the abduction of Ellena, from *The Italian.* Engraved by M. Sears.

to seek even the object from which we appear to shrink.

Emily passed on with faltering steps; and having paused a moment at the door before she attempted to open it, she then hastily entered the chamber, and went toward the picture, which appeared to be enclosed in a frame of uncommon size that hung in a dark part of the room. She paused again, and with a timid hand lifted the veil, but instantly let it fall, perceiving that what it concealed was no picture —and before she could leave the chamber she dropped senseless to the floor.

When she recovered her recollection, the remembrance of what she had seen nearly deprived her of it a second time. She had scarcely strength to remove herself from the room and regain her own; and when arrived there, wanted courage to remain alone. Horror occupied her mind, and excluded for a time all sense of past and dread of misfortune. She seated herself near the casement because from thence she heard voices, though distant, on the terrace, and might see people pass; and these, trifling as they were, were reviving circumstances.

It may be gathered from these brief paragraphs that the experience was, as Mrs. Radcliffe assures us, "a severe shock"; but what Emily St. Aubert saw is hidden from us until almost the end of the romance.

The same reservation holds with regard to the other sensational apparition, in the Chateau le Blanc, in which the later episodes of *The Mysteries of Udolpho* are set. Emily, mystically attracted to the portrait and the mementos of the long-deceased Machioness de Villeroi (who finally turns out to have been her aunt) persuades an old servitor of the Marchioness to accompany her to the death chamber of the lady, which had lain for years as it had been left at the time of her strange last illness and death. The two look with fond recollections and appropriate sentiments upon the relics of the noble lady. But at last Dorothée, the old servant, depressed by this sanctuary of tragic memories, begs Emily to go : "Pray, let us leave the oriel, Ma'amselle; this is a heart-breaking place."

Then, as they sat together upon the bed, she began to relate other particulars concerning it, and this without reflecting that they might increase Emily's emotion, but because they were particularly interesting to herself. "A little before my lady's death," said she, "when the pains were gone off, she called me to her, and stretching out her hand to me, I sat down right there, where the curtain falls upon the bed. How well I remember her look at the time—death was in it. I can almost fancy I see her now. There she lay, Ma'amselle—her face was upon the pillow there. This black counterpane was not upon the bed then; it was laid on after her death, and she was laid out upon it."

Emily turned to look within the dusky curtains, as if she could have

seen the countenance of which Dorothée spoke. The edge of the white
pillow only appeared above the blackness of the pall. But as her eyes
wandered over the pall itself, she fancied she saw it move. Without
speaking, she caught Dorothée's arm, who, surprised by the action,
and by the terror that accompanied it, turned her eyes from Emily to
the bed, where in the next moment she too saw the pall slowly lifted
and fall again.

Emily attempted to go, but Dorothée stood fixed and gazing upon
the bed; and at length said, "It is only the wind that waved it,
Ma'amselle. We have left all the doors open; see how the air waves the
lamp too. It is only the wind."

She had scarcely uttered these words when the pall was more
violently agitated than before; but Emily, somewhat ashamed of her
terrors, stepped back to the bed, willing to be convinced that the wind
only had occasioned her alarm; when, as she gazed within the curtains,
the pall moved again, and in the next moment the apparition of a
human countenance rose above it.

Screaming with terror, they both fled, and got out of the chamber
as fast as their trembling limbs would bear them.

If there is any art in this simple claptrap, it lies in holding back the
solution of the mystery. Once explained, it is deflated. Perhaps for the
reader of today it is not even worth troubling to explain; but perhaps too,
we owe it to Mrs. Radcliffe, or to her one-time admirers.

The veiled picture, which, as Mrs. Radcliffe has forewarned us, is no
picture, was simply a human figure "of ghastly paleness stretched at its
length, . . . partly decayed and disfigured by worms, which were visible
on the features and hands. Had Emily dared to look again, her delusions
and her fears would have vanished altogether, and she would have perceived that the figure before her was not human but was formed of wax."
Why anyone should care to have so unsatisfactory a piece of decor about
the place, Mrs. Radcliffe is also able to explain. A former occupant of the
castle had for some unutterable sin been condemned to a penance of looking daily upon this image of death; and for the spiritual edification of his
heirs and successors he had provided in his will that they also should
observe this penance, on pain of forfeiture of the estate to the Church.

The mystery of the Chateau le Blanc is explained away with more
prosaic circumstantiality. Over the years in which the wing of the chateau
containing the death chamber of the Marchioness had been unvisited, a
band of pirates and smugglers had used the apartments, access to which
was by a subterranean opening upon the seashore, as a rendezvous and
storehouse. On the evening of the visit of Emily and Dorothée, one of the

band had been surprised by the entrance of the two women, and hid himself in the bed. Fearing discovery, he artfully played upon their susceptibilities and scared them off.

More than any other of Mrs. Radcliffe's Gothics, *The Mysteries of Udolpho* is the repository of her once admired scenic descriptions. Although these are too often overstyled, they have merit. They include both formal and incidental descriptions of landscape in the Pyrenees, the Appenines, the plains of Languedoc, and the Mediterranean seacoast, and of the interiors and the environs of the two old castles. The quotation we give is from a journey of Emily and her father in the opening chapters of the story.

> They traveled leisurely, stopping wherever a scene uncommonly grand appeared, frequently alighting to walk to an eminence whither the mules could not go, from which the prospects opened in greater magnificence, and often sauntering over hillocks covered with lavender, wild thyme, juniper, and tamarisk, and under the shades of woods, between whose boles they caught the long mountain vista, sublime beyond anything that Emily had ever imagined.
>
> From Beaujeu the road had constantly ascended, conducting the travelers into the higher regions of the air, where immense glaciers exhibited their frozen horrors and eternal snow whitened the summits of the mountains. They often paused to contemplate these stupendous scenes, and seated on some wild cliff, where only the ilex or the larch could flourish, looked over dark forests of fir, and precipices where human foot had never wandered, into the glen—so deep that the thunder of the torrent which was seen to foam along the bottom was scarcely heard to murmur. Over these crags rose others of stupendous height and fantastic shape, some shooting into cones, others impending far over their base, in huge masses of granite, along whose broken ridges was often lodged a weight of snow that, trembling even to the vibration of a sound, threatened to bear destruction in its course to the vale. . . . The deep silence of these solitudes was broken only at intervals by the scream of the vultures, cowering around some cliff below, or by the cry of the eagle sailing high in the air; except when the travelers listened to the hollow thunder that sometimes muttered at their feet.

This later passage is in a lower key :

> Leaving that town at an early hour, they set off for Padua, where they embarked on the Brenta for Venice. . . . The verdant banks of the Brenta exhibited a continued landscape of beauty, gaiety, and splendor. Emily gazed with admiration on the villas of the Venetian noblesse, with their cool porticos and colonnades, overhung with pop-

lars and cypresses of majestic height and lively verdure, on their rich orangeries where blossoms perfumed the air, and on the luxuriant willows that dipped their light leaves in the wave, and sheltered from the sun the parties whose music came at intervals on the breeze. . . .

Nothing could exceed Emily's admiration on her first view of Venice, with its islets, palaces, and towers rising out of the sea, whose clear surface reflected the picture in all its tremulous colors. The sun, sinking in the west, tinted the waves and the lofty mountains of Friuli, which skirt the northern shores of the Adriatic, with a saffron glow, while on the marble porticos and colonnades of St. Mark were thrown the rich lights and shades of evening. As they glided on, the grander features of this city appeared more distinctly; its terraces, crowned with airy but majestic fabrics, touched, as they now were, with the splendor of the setting sun, appeared as if they had been called up from the ocean by the wand of an enchanter, rather than reared by mortal hands.

The sun, soon after, sinking to the lower world, the shadow of the earth stole gradually over the waves, and then up the towering sides of the mountains of Friuli, till it extinguished even the last upward beam that lingered on their summits, and the melancholy purple of evening drew over them like a thin veil.

Mrs. Radcliffe was, of course, not the inventor of landscape description; nor was she the first to employ it in fiction. Smollett and Mackenzie had anticipated her, and she was familiar with the "nature poets" from Thompson down, often quoting them in her chapter headings. But her scenic effects had not only the sense of beauty, as well as visual clarity and strength; they had finish. Her mastery of descriptive effect is one of her significant contributions to the fictions of another century. It is interesting that although Mrs. Radcliffe enjoyed travel, and took with her husband carriage trips to the picturesque corners of England, she knew little at first hand of the Continent, having visited only northern France and the Low Countries, and crossed the German border. The material for her celebrated landscapes is taken, therefore, from books of travel, some of which seem to have been reliably identified.*

The Italian, her last Gothic romance, perhaps shows Mrs. Radcliffe at her best; that is, if we can regard her as a novelist of sorts, and not merely a specialist in alarms and perturbations. Two of its characters, the villainous monk Schedoni, and his partner in crime, the abbess of the mountain convent in which Schedoni has the heroine confined, may

---

*She is clever enough, however, to handle her material consistently. Her predecessor, Charlotte Smith, in *The Old Manor House,* introduces rhododendrons and cypresses into her St. Lawrence River scenery.

have owed something to characters in Lewis's *Monk,* published in the preceding year. Yet we cannot be too sure. Mrs. Radcliffe's villains were all of a pattern, and it is scarcely surprising that she should have taken one from the religious orders instead of the aristocratic. Schedoni is the motive force of *The Italian,* his saturnine figure dominating the action from beginning to end. Here is our introduction to him.

[His] family was unknown, and from circumstances it appeared that he wished to throw an impenetrable veil over his origin. For whatever reason, he was never heard to mention a relative or the place of his nativity, and he had artfully eluded every inquiry that approached the subject. . . . There were circumstances, however, that appeared to indicate him to be a man of birth and of fallen fortune. His spirit, as it had sometimes looked forth from under the disguise of his manners, seemed lofty; it showed not, however, the aspirings of a generous mind, but rather the gloomy pride of a disappointed one. Some few persons in the convent who had been interested by his appearance believed that the peculiarities of his manners, his severe reserve and unconquerable silence, his solitary habits and frequent penances, were the effect of misfortunes preying upon a haughty and disordered spirit; while others conjectured them the consequence of some hideous crime gnawing upon an awakened conscience.

The elder brothers of the convent said that he had talents, but denied his learning; they applauded him for the profound subtlety which he occasionally discovered in argument, but observed that he seldom perceived truth when it lay on the surface; he could follow it through all the labyrinths of disquisition, but overlooked it when it was undisguised before him. In fact, he cared not for truth, nor sought it by broad and bold argument, but loved to exert the wise cunning of his nature by hunting it through artificial perplexities. At length, from a habit of intricacy and suspicion, his vitiated mind could receive nothing for truth which was simple and easily comprehended.

Among his associates no one loved him, many disliked him, and more feared him. His figure was striking, but not so from grace; it was tall, and though extremely thin, his limbs were large and uncouth, and as he stalked along, wrapped in the black garments of his order, there was something terrible in his air; something almost superhuman. His cowl too, as it threw a shade over the livid paleness of his face, increased the severity of its character, and gave an effect to his melancholy eye which approached to horror. His was not the melancholy of a sensible and wounded heart, but apparently that of a gloomy and ferocious disposition. There was something in his physiognomy exceedingly singular, and that cannot be easily defined. It bore the traces of many passions, which seemed to have fixed the features they no longer animated. An habitual gloom and severity prevailed over the deep lines of his countenance, and his eyes were so piercing that they seemed to penetrate at a single glance into the hearts of men and to read their most secret thoughts. Few persons could support their scrutiny, or even endure to meet them twice. Yet notwithstanding all his gloom and austerity, some rare occasions of interest had called forth a character upon his countenance entirely different; and he could adapt himself to the tempers and passions of persons whom he wished to conciliate, with astonishing facility, and generally with complete triumph.

Though its background and its principal character are drawn from a desecrated monastic life, *The Italian* presents scarcely a variant from the standard Gothic plot. The heroine's detention in a sequestered convent and the hero's false commitment to the dungeons of the Inquisition are little more than scenic changes, although a refreshing departure from the stereotype. The Inquisition scenes are not as galvanic as the similar ones that preceded them in Lewis' *Monk,* which we are on the point of considering, nor are they animated by the strong political intent of the like situations in William Godwin's *St. Leon,* published two years later.*

I have suggested that *The Italian,* while a true Gothic, has closer relations to the accepted novel than its predecessors. Yet it makes a great deal out of very little, and its padding is obvious and inexcusable. The author employs every known device to prolong the action and to sustain its rather transparent suspense. Explanations of motives and emotional states are slow and labored. The scheming Schedoni and his employer, the hero's mother, conduct extremely protracted conspiratorial conversations in which very hush-hush hints of violence are solemnly exchanged. Proceedings at the Inquisitorial trial are spun out by hesitations and minatory silences, and alternate with eventless periods of solitary confinement. But above all, Mrs. Radcliffe revels in slow-motion anecdote—the exasperating roundaboutness, for example, of a servant who can deliver a message only in his own way and at his own time. We sample it here, from *The Italian.* It is not high art, and it had been anticipated in Roman comedy, in Cervantes, and in Walpole, but it shows that when Mrs. Radcliffe is not tempted to be literary, she can produce credible dialogue. The lovely Ellena, tense with anxiety as to whether her lover, Vivaldi, is living or dead, is confronted by her maid with ill news.

"If death be ill news, you have guessed right, Signora; for I do

---

*The Inquisition theme itself is not new. It had entered English fiction in 1737 in [Simon Berington's] *Adventures of Gaudentio di Lucca* as a "frame" for a Utopian story. It appears also in the reading of the sermon in Volume II of Sterne's *Tristram Shandy.*

bring news of that, it is certain.' . . . She stopped on observing the changing countenance of Ellena, who tremulously called upon her to explain what had happened—who was dead, and entreated her to relate the particulars as speedily as possible. . . . "What is the event you would disclose?" said Ellena, almost breathless. "When did it happen? Be brief."

"I cannot tell exactly when it happened, Signora, but it was an own servant of the Marchese's [Vivaldi's father] that I heard it from."

"The Marchese's?" interrupted Ellena, in a faltering voice.

"Aye, Lady, you will say that is pretty good authority."

"Death, and the Marchese's family!" exclaimed Ellena.

"Yes, Signora; I had it from his own servant. He was passing by the garden just as I happened to be speaking to the macaroni man. But you are ill, Lady."

"I am very well if you will but proceed," replied Ellena faintly, while her eyes were fixed upon Beatrice, as if they only had power to enforce their meaning.

" 'Well, Dame,' he says to me, 'I have not seen you for a long time.' 'No,' says I; 'that is a great grievance truly; for old women nowadays are not thought of. Out of sight, out of mind, with them, nowadays.' "

"I beseech you, to the purpose," interrupted Ellena. "Whose death did he announce?" She had not courage to pronounce Vivaldi's name.

"You shall hear, Signora. I saw he looked in a sort of a bustle; so I asked him how all did at the palazzo. So he answers 'Bad enough, Signora Beatrice; have you not heard of what has just happened to our family?' "

"Oh, Heavens," exclaimed Ellena; "he is dead; Vivaldi is dead."

"You shall hear, Signora," continued Beatrice.

"Be brief," said Ellena; "answer me simply yes or no."

"I cannot until I come to the right place, Signora; if you will but have a little patience, you shall hear all. But if you fluster me so, you will put me quite out."

"Grant me patience!" said Ellena, endeavoring to calm her spirits.

"With that, Signora, I asked him to walk in and rest himself, and tell me all about it. He answered he was in a great hurry, and could not stay a moment, and a great deal of that sort; but I, knowing that whatever happened in that family, Signora, was something to you, would not let him go off so easily. And so when I asked him to refresh himself with a glass of lemon-ice, he forgot all his business in a minute, and we had a long chat."

There is still more of it, and the upshot is that it is not Vivaldi who has died, but the Marchesa, his mother, who had been the one insurmountable barrier to their marriage.

In *The Italian* Mrs. Radcliffe's practice of accumulating obscurities

"Tales of Wonder"; cartoon by James Gilray, "an attempt to describe the effects of the sublime and wonderful," dedicated to "Monk" Lewis, 1802.

and mysteries for solution at the end of her story seems to have got the better of her judgment. There are no supernatural hoaxes here, but many concealments of identity and motive; so many, in fact, that when she finally checks them off, one by one, their involutions and interconnections add confusion to tiring detail.

The Italian was the last of Mrs. Radcliffe's truly Gothic romances. A later historical romance, *Gaston de Blondville,* carries no clue as to the date of its composition; and it was not published until 1826, three years after her death, with a biographical introduction. There were no enthusiastic plaudits for this belated work. Mrs. Radcliffe's magic had failed years before she died, and her admirers had long since stopped wondering why she had abandoned writing when at the very pinnacle of her reputation.

What was it that had given this shy little wife of an English businessman so extraordinary a hold upon the readers of her generation? And how much of what she gave her generation has had lasting importance?

The answer to the first question is not that the taste of her day was deplorable. It was, but it can still be debated whether that bad taste explains her romances or the romances explain the bad taste. We are accustomed to call her period the Romantic Revival; and a revival means literally the restoration of life to something either dying or quite dead. She helped in the restoration of life to the romantic tradition. She had her kinship to the romantic poets of the period. Shelley began his literary career with two short Gothic tales in prose. Coleridge reflects the Gothic temper in *Kubla Khan* and *Cristabel.* Byron borrows, or is said to have borrowed, his defiant heroes from her villains. And Scott's poetry and fiction both show her influence. Undeniably she wrote with inventiveness rather than discernment; with energy, not with inspiration; but she was nevertheless responsive to, and to some degree formative of, the spirit of her age.

Her influence, however, survived the rapid decline of her popularity, and even the ridicule that promptly began to displace that popularity. Yet when that ridicule is as cogently expressed as it is in Jane Austen's *Northanger Abbey,* it is not without a sort of affectionate tolerance for the adolescent and unformed taste that could still be impressed by her talents.

When we consider her more lasting influence, we must decide what we mean by "influence." The word has been much abused by scholars; indeed, it is very commonly a lurking place for the *post hoc* fallacy. Influence is not necessarily expressed in appropriation or explicit imitation of prior art, but in an appreciable debt to the spirit or the atmosphere of that art. It is much like rain water, that soaks into the earth to flow in many brooks and to be drawn from many wells.

In this sense, Mrs. Radcliffe's influence is far-reaching, and still very much alive. Perhaps Poe and Emily Brontë never read a word of Mrs. Radcliffe, though it can be suspected that both had done so. Yet she is indubitably present in *The Fall of the House of Ussher* and *Wuthering Heights*. Apart from a broken succession of true Gothics, which include readable works by Robert Maturin, Keith Ritchie, G. P. R. James, Harrison Ainsworth, Sheridan LeFanu, Bram Stoker, and Isak Dinesen, Gothic effects are carried forward into the writings of Mrs. Shelley, Charlotte Brontë as well as Emily, Wilkie Collins, Hawthorne, Poe, Stevenson, writers of our own century like Walter de la Mare and Algernon Blackwood, and the authors of unnumbered dozens of our current mystery stories.

Still the best known, probably, of all the Gothics is Matthew Gregory Lewis's *The Monk* (1796), remembered, unhappily, for the wrong reason —because it has enjoyed the reputation of being the book of the century most exciting in its handling of sexual "business," yet discreet enough to escape the charge of downright pornography.* Be the fact as it may, we can note it and pass on; for so much water has flowed over the dam since Lewis's time that the reader who enjoys vicarious sex sensation will be hopelessly unrewarded if he reads *The Monk* for its "kick."

Argued almost as insistently as the morality of *The Monk* is the question whether it is a true Gothic. Most literary historians have prefered to call it a "tale of terror." The fact that the scene of the tale is a Spanish monastery instead of a crumbling mountain retreat would seem a minor difference. There is also in *The Monk* no carefully nursed mystery to sustain the reader's curiosity down to a lame and impotent conclusion. It does happen that a mystery is born and solved within the last few pages— if we can properly call it a mystery that a rape turns out to have been also incest.

What Lewis attempted to do in *The Monk,* and with no small success, was to raise sexual violence to the level of tragic significance. Yet the story is tainted with juvenility; for Lewis was not yet twenty when he wrote it, although it is supposed to have undergone substantial revision before it was published.

The monk Ambrosio's story is a fall from seeming spiritual strength and grace to Satanic evil and final damnation, and the cause of his fall is his vainglorious confidence in his spiritual invulnerability—a modern case of the Greek tragic *"hubris."* The vehicle of his fall is a sexuality latent under fanatic monasticism, which is brought forward at the very opening of

---

*Matthew Gregory Lewis (1775-1818). *The Monk* (original title, *Ambrosio or the Monk,* 1795) is his one memorable work, though he also translated romances, both prose and poetical, from German, French, and Italian, and wrote a number of contemporaneously successful plays.

the story in his cruel exposure of a girl who has for a moment strayed from virtue with the young man to whom she regards herself as betrothed. She has entered a nunnery as an act of expiation, only to find after she has taken the veil that she is to bear a child. The future of this erring nun and her lover moves along intermittently with the story of the monk himself. These episodes include in turn a digression on her lover's personal history, which in itself contains an all but completely irrelevant piece, the legend of a bleeding nun who haunts a castle far from the essential scene of the story. The romance is therefore involved and interrupted, and scarcely begins to show interest until it is nearly a third completed.

Ambrosio is a preacher of telling power and influence, admired almost to the point of worship for the purity and austerity of his life. One of his most ardent admirers is a young novice, Rosario, who reveals himself at length to Ambrosio as a girl in disguise—Matilda. Their attachment, which has begun on a spiritual plane, becomes earthy, and draws Ambrosio down from his pinnacle of prideful piety. The liaison, carried on in the secrecy of the monk's cell, loses its intensity for him as he becomes satiated, and disgusted with his all too conscious hypocrisy.

Another passion supervenes—a desperate love for the beautiful Antonia. But Antonia lives in the outer world under the protection of a watchful, and ultimately suspicious, mother. Matilda, with a devotion to Ambrosio which will halt at no barrier to his happiness, offers him her help—no empty offer, for she is an adept in the black arts. She proposes to bring the very powers of Hell to Ambrosio's aid in the seduction of Antonia. The monk recoils with horror from her suggestion, but is argued into consent by Matilda's sophistries. She arranges a meeting with the Spirit of Evil himself in the underground sepulchers shared by the monastery and the neighboring convent. With Ambrosio, she descends to these dank resting-places of the religious dead, and performs the ritual which brings Satan into their presence.

"He comes," exclaimed Matilda in a joyful accent.

Ambrosio started, and expected the demon with terror. What was his surprise when, the thunder ceasing to roll, a full strain of melodious music sounded in the air! At the same time, the cloud disappeared, and he beheld a figure more beautiful than fancy's pencil ever drew. It was a youth seemingly scarce eighteen, the perfection of whose form and face was unrivalled. He was perfectly naked; a bright star sparkled upon his forehead, two crimson wings extended themselves from his shoulders, and his silken locks were confined by a band of many-colored fires, which played round his head, formed themselves into a variety of figures, and shone with a brilliance far surpassing that of precious stones. Circlets of diamonds were fastened round his arms and ankles, and in his right hand he bore a silver branch imitating myrtle. His form shone with dazzling glory; he was surrounded by rose-colored light, and at the moment that he appeared, a refreshing air breathed perfumes through the cavern. Enchanted at a vision so contrary to his expectations, Ambrosio gazed upon the spirit with delight and wonder; yet however beautiful the figure, he could not but remark a wildness in the demon's eyes, and a mysterious melancholy impressed upon his features, betraying the fallen angel, and inspiring the spectators with secret awe.

Ambrosio's designs upon Antonia are simplified by her abject devotion to him, and also by her innocence, which implies complete ignorance of the evils to which innocence may be exposed. Yet there is her mother, who knows the world, and does her best to prevent Ambrosio's abuse of his place as Antonia's confessor. When she actually surprises him in a deliberate attempt at seduction, Ambrosio strangles her.

Matilda's powers are brought to his aid again, however. She furnishes him with a potion which will bring about the simulation of death. Antonia is drugged and entombed, and awakes to be made the monk's victim in the very presence of the dead all about her. But chance brings it about that the sepulchers are invaded in the excitement of a riot at the very moment of Ambrosio's triumph; and to prevent Antonia from revealing his guilt there and then, he stabs her to death. He does not escape, however, for the intruding crowd have heard her cries, and track down and arrest both Ambrosio and Matilda.

Up to this moment Ambrosio's relations to Satan might be said to have been only diplomatic; for he has leaned entirely upon Matilda's ingenuity and dark powers. But he has not sold his own soul into perdition. Now, on trial before the Inquisition, he is convicted and sentenced to death at the stake. In this extremity, facing a terrifying end, and dishonor for himself and his order, he decides to buy freedom and life by himself invoking the Father of Evil. Satan, on Ambrosio's performance of the black ritual, appears in the cell.

Scarce had he pronounced the last word, when the effects of the charm were evident. A loud burst of thunder was heard, the prison shook to its very foundations, a blaze of lightning flashed through the cell, and in a moment, borne upon sulphurous whirlwinds, Lucifer stood before him a second time. But he came not as when at Matilda's summons he borrowed the seraph's form to deceive Ambrosio. He appeared in all that ugliness which since his fall from Heaven had been his portion. His blasted limbs still bore marks of the Almighty's thunder. A swarthy darkness spread itself over his gigantic form; his hands and feet were armed with long talons. Fury glared in his eyes, which might have struck the bravest heart with terror. Over his huge shoulders waved two enormous sable wings, and his hair was supplied by living snakes, which twined themselves round his brows with frightful hissings. In one hand he held a roll of parchment, and in the other an iron pen. Still the lightning flashed round him, and the thunder with repeated bursts seemed to announce the dissolution of nature.

A dramatic bargaining scene ensues, Ambrosio striving to secure the boon of freedom with some mitigation of the cost. He begs for a period in Purgatory in which his crimes can be expiated. But Satan answers him :

> "Hope you that your offenses will be bought off by prayers of superstitious dotards and droning monks? Ambrosio, be wise. Mine you must be. You are doomed to flames, but may shun them for the present. Sign this parchment. I will bear you from hence, and you may pass your remaining years in bliss and liberty. Enjoy your existence. Indulge in every pleasure to which appetite may lead you. But from the moment that it quits your body, remember that your soul belongs to me, and that I will not be defrauded of my right."

The warders are at the very door of Ambrosio's cell when in the desperation of what he believes his final moment, he signs the compact, at the price of his soul. Satan catches him up, and the two disappear from the cell.

> [Ambrosio], supported by his infernal guide, traversed the air with the rapidity of an arrow, and a few minutes placed him upon a precipice's brink, the steepest in Sierra Morena. . . . The abbot cast round him a look of terror. His infernal conductor was still by his side, and eyed him with a look of mingled malice, exultation, and contempt.
> "Whither have you brought me?" said the monk at length in a hollow, trembling voice. "Why am I placed in this melancholy scene? Bear me from it quickly ! Carry me to Matilda. . . ."
> "Carry you to Matilda?" [Satan replies], repeating Ambrosio's words.' "Wretch, you shall soon be with her! Hark, Ambrosio, while I unveil your crimes. You have shed the blood of two innocents; Antonia and Elvira perished by your hand. That Antonia whom you violated was your sister; that Elvira whom you murdered gave you birth. Tremble, abandoned hypocrite, inhuman parricide, incestuous ravisher, tremble at the extent of your offenses. And you it was who thought yourself proof against temptation, absolved from human frailities, and free from error and vice. Is pride then a virtue? Is inhumanity no fault? Know, vain man, that I long have marked you for my prey. I watched the movements of your heart; I saw that you were virtuous from vanity, not principle, and I seized the fit moment of seduction. I

London, Published August 25th 1802, by S. Fisher.

W. Tomkins. Del.   E. Hartley. Sculp.

Berthinia rescued from the villainous attempts of Mondford, by the timely assistance of the Marquis.   Page 20.

Frontispiece to one of the early imitations of Mrs. Radcliffe's Gothic romances; *Berthinia, or The Fair Spaniard*, by Isaac Crookenden, London, 1802; engraved by E. Hartley after W. Tomkins. Chap-book, or "blue wrapper" issues of short but sufficiently sensational Gothics were peddled on the streets, this one at sixpence.

observed your blind idolatry of the Madonna's picture. I bade a subordinate but crafty spirit assume a similar form, and you eagerly yielded to the blandishments of Matilda. Your pride was gratified by her flattery; your lust only needed an opportunity to break forth; you ran into the snare blindly, and scrupled not to commit a crime which you blamed on another with unfeeling severity. . . . Hear, hear, Ambrosio! Had you resisted me one minute longer, you had saved your body and soul. The guards whom you heard at the prison door came to signify your pardon. But I had already triumphed; my plots had already succeeded. . . . You trusted that you would still have time for repentance. I saw your artifice, knew its falsity, and rejoiced in deceiving you, the deceiver. You are mine beyond reprieve. I burn to possess my right, and alive you quit not these mountains."

The end comes precipitately. Ambrosio is carried aloft, and "dropped from a dreadful height."

Headlong fell the monk through the airy waste. The sharp point of a rock received him, and he rolled from precipice to precipice till, bruised and mangled, he rested on the river's banks. Life still existed in his miserable frame; he attempted in vain to raise himself; his broken and dislocated limbs refused to perform their office, nor was he able to quit the spot where he had first fallen. The sun now rose above the horizon; its scorching beams darted full upon the head of the expiring sinner. Myriads of insects were called forth by the warmth; they drank the blood which trickled from Ambrosio's wounds; he had no power to drive them from him, and they fastened upon his sores, darted their stings into his body, covered him with their multitudes, and inflicted upon him tortures the most exquisite and insupportable. The eagles of the rock tore his flesh piecemeal, and dug out his eyeballs with their crooked beaks. A burning thirst tormented him; he heard the river's murmur as it rolled beside him, but strove in vain to drag himself towards the sound. Blind, maimed, helpless and despairing, venting his rage in blasphemy and curses, execrating his existence, yet dreading the arrival of death destined to yield him up to greater torments, six miserable days did the villain languish. On the seventh a violent storm arose. The winds in fury rent up rocks and forests; the sky was now black with clouds, now sheeted with fire; the rain fell in torrents; it swelled the stream; the waves overflowed their banks; they reached the spot where Ambrosio lay, and when they abated, carried with them into the river the corpse of the despairing monk.

Lewis, it will be seen, has the power of words. We have quoted only high moments, but they are characteristic; for it is a lurid story, and it is told luridly, as it should be. But *The Monk* is by no stretch of the term great literature. It fell within that period of little more than a decade when many readers could lend a willing ear to poppycock. Lewis's management of his medium was equal to the demands of his situations and his characters; that is all. Apart from his central theme of the apostate monk, which was not unfamiliar, he taps traditional sources for other matters of legend. The wandering Jew, the haunted castle, the demon lover, the wayside inn as a cover for a shambles, all have a part in the continuity of *The Monk*. Yet stale themes are blended into something effective in its own way.

There is no need to deride the extravagance of the story. If one is to introduce the Devil in person, he need not, like Mrs. Radcliffe, set up compromises with reality, or, like Walpole, apologize for the effects he has been at the pains to create. Today the story calls for a well-disposed reader, free from twentieth-century inhibitions, and not worried by blatant irrationality. If there are such readers left, then Lewis's bold tale may appeal to them.

CHAPTER XVI

𝔄n 𝔈ighteenth-ℭentury 𝔖haw

Robert Bage

PERHAPS IT IS impossible to find a novel of the eighteenth century which is not in the broadest view a "novel of purpose." Defoe and Richardson, we have seen, were professed moralists, and even Fielding and gentle Fanny Burney wrote with ameliorative aims. In the last quarter of the century, however, we find a difference. The earlier moral novelists were more interested in personal morality than in public, and they looked trustfully to good breeding, education and religion for the remedies for social ills. By the end of the century, however, it had come to be felt that the roots of social evil were nourished by the aristocratic system, political amateurism and corruption, and judicial ignorance and prejudice.

And with reason; for the times were bad. The American colonies had already been lost, long before a peace treaty had conceded the fact. Britain had been all but strangled by taxes for "defense," much of which was going into private pockets. Political corruption flourished in full daylight, and the King was a principal in it. Abroad, it had been tragically demonstrated that the peers of the realm could not spend time enough from their diversions to play international politics with effect, and that the younger sons and brothers of those peers were more successful as wastrels and casual seducers than as officers in His Majesty's Service.* Good men were rotting in prison for voicing doubts as to the all-round kingliness of the first three Georges, and of the fourth, still in his princely apprenticeship. The drama of the French Revolution was almost equaled in England in 1794 by the notorious "State Trials," in which the government tried unsuccessfully to construe as treason the radical views of Horne Tooke, John Thelwall, Thomas Holcroft, and their friends.

Revolution in the American colonies and in France had given encouragement to the idea that so far as social ills were political ills, they called

---

*It is surprising how often the seducer in novels of the period is an aristocrat, young or old, with a military or naval commission in his tail pocket. The situation appears in Mrs. Haywood, Fielding, Smollett, Bage, Charlotte Smith, Dr. Moore, and many lesser novelists.

for political remedies. But political machinery was distrusted by the group of novelists in the last years of the century who have been called, among other names, "social reformers," "humanitarians," "political novelists," and "revolutionaries."

Three figures stand out in the group : Robert Bage, Thomas Holcroft, and William Godwin, with a possible fourth, Mary Wollstonecraft, who became Godwin's wife, and who was aggressively interested in legal and social justice for women. The last three formed a fairly compact London group. Bage stood somewhat apart, as a North Country businessman. We know that he knew Godwin, through a single recorded visit. On the fringe of the Godwin circle were other literary notables, innocent of disparaging epithets like "revolutionaries." These included some of the best names of the time—Blake, Lamb, Leigh Hunt, Coleridge, Hazlitt, Shelley, later DeQuincey, and more remotely Byron, one of whose uncounted affairs was with a daughter of Godwin's second wife.

"Placing" a writer seems to be the critic's ultimate function. In Bage's case it is not easy.* He was a story-teller without notable technique, a radical without a doctrine, and a moralist without a moral system; a man of unimpeachable integrity in everything he touched, yet the perfect pragmatist. And he had an unusual assortment of distastes, mostly for social shams, sanctified lies, and self-important personages. He is anti-sentimental, anti-aristocratic, anti-sectarian, and anti-Richardsonian in a very explicit sense.†

Bage's first novel, *Mount Henneth* (1781), antedates the earliest fictions of both Holcroft and Godwin. Put baldly, it is the most slapdash performance that could be expected, even as the earliest effort, of a man of really considerable gifts as narrator and student of character. In the first place, it labors under all the worst embarrassments of the letter form; for letters are quite inadequate to reveal the multitude of involved relations of a large group of characters and the intricacies of a constantly shifting action. In addition, the work seriously abuses coincidence. Finally, although we may discount excessive ingenuity of plot, here in *Mount Henneth* we can only deplore Bage's complete indifference to either reason or continuity in the arrangement of his incidents.

Yet the book has unquestioned promise. Its want of artistic discipline is largely atoned for by facile and often charming portraiture, by humor, by

---

*Robert Bage (1728-1801). *Mount Henneth* (1782), *Barham Downs* (1784), *The Fair Syrian* (1787), *James Wallace* (1788), *Man as He Is* (1792), *Man as He Is Not* (popularly known by its subtitle, *Hermsprong*, 1796). The long accepted date of 1781 for *Mount Henneth* is almost certainly in error. See Notes and Queries, N.S. 12 - 27, 1965.

†"Uniformity in goodnesss is uniformity in dullness, and the most uninteresting of all characters that ever were drawn is, I find, the stiff, starched, demure, formal, all-virtuous Sir Charles Grandison."

bland yet penetrating satire, and most of all by an unobscured outlook upon contemporary social and political conventions, illusions, and inequities.

Perhaps Bage's originality is evidenced in *Mount Henneth* most clearly in two women, Julia Foston and Laura Stanley, both of them intelligent and sprightly, but in other ways notably different. The general deficiency of the women in earlier eighteenth-century fiction, even as late as Fielding, is that, like the little girl in Mother Goose, "when they are good they are very, very good, and when they are bad they are horrid." But Bage gives us two women worth studying. Julia is, like so many of her predecessors in the novel, a product of good·breeding and fashion; she is also strong-minded, but her strong-mindedness is not of the sort that subjects those about her to her own whims. It lies principally in an intelligence applied to understanding people, not as mere samplings of the prevalent culture, but as diverse and for that reason interesting individuals. She is proper not by expediency, like Pamela, nor by social station, like Sophia Western, but because she sees a social value in propriety.

Opposed to her is her close friend Laura, who is almost a new creation in either fiction or drama; for without being dirty-minded or technically "impure," she can look upon the raw "mysteries" of sex with both an undisguised interest and a lively intelligence. Her manners and talk upon this point are remarkably frank, particularly so because of their contrast to the ladylike reticences of Julia—who is herself no prude. This peculiar vigor of mind, is, of course, only one aspect of a sound and courageous, though consciously flippant, character, and Bage justifies it with a question—"Why should women be excluded knowledge which so very much concerns them, or denied the communication of it? Will reason forever be at war with our feelings?" What is interesting and significant in these two women is that they have brains, and use them. Brains are not commonly included by the earlier writers of eighteenth-century fiction in their catalogues of the female virtues.

But sexual enlightenment is only one of the objects of Bage's social crusade, which is carried on (much as it is in Goldsmith) by deliberate interruptions of action for passages of what is little more or less than preaching. There are disquisitions upon education, courtroom justice, professed religion, British colonial policy, war, and insular nationalism; and finally, the encouraging picture of an integrated society which is to all intents a social and economic commune in miniature.

In *Mount Henneth* Bage's purpose is accomplished without any broad understanding of the novelist's art. But this is, we repeat, a first novel, and there are five others to come which will show better results, as fiction, than this product of his literary apprenticeship.

Barham Downs shows some maturity. In it Bage again accepts the device of the novel in letters. The narrative is diffuse; the characters embrace not only the conventional pair of lovers, but an entire school of them. Almost everybody, in fact, involved in the action gets married before the end of the story. And even more than in *Mount Henneth,* the interest of the narrative depends upon self-contained episodes and snatches of clever dialogue, dramatic, argumentative, or just smartly amusing. Plot seems so aimless that one almost wonders whether at the outset Bage had any very clear idea of how his story was to end.

It is through dialogue, and not through didactic presentments, that Bage brings into view the serious social philosophy by which he is more generally remembered than by his light touch upon the heart and its concerns. Indeed, his ability to establish and maintain a point of argument through straight talk reflects an intellect that is not to be pushed about by avoidances and evasions. We offer a sample. The situation is recurrent in the fiction of the period—pretty girl, rakish young man of quality, seduction, and abandonment; but followed up in this instance by a second attempt to take advantage of the girl, who has found the protection of friends and has only regrets and tears for her old unwisdom. Since she is no longer pliant to his wishes, the gentlemen takes a more daring course— abduction and violence. But he is prevented, not only by the friends of the girl but by the law. After the abduction, a warrant has been issued for his arrest, and his older brother, the titled head of the family, Lord Cronnot, visits the aged Quaker who has been her chief protection. For Lord Cronnot, to whom these little matters are not unfamiliar, the procedure indicated is simply to quiet all this disagreeable pother by paying the girl a very modest sum from the family wealth.

> Lord Cronnot paid Mr. Arnold a visit the very next day, and the civilities over, he began with saying how extremely sorry he was to wait upon him on such an occasion.
>
> "I dare say thou art," says the Quaker.
>
> "To be sure, my brother is excessively to blame, but the force of love in the minds of impatient young men pleads some exuse."
>
> "As drunkenness excuses murder," replies Mr. Arnold, "or as hunger might have excused Perry Loggan, who robbed thy granary last winter, and yet thou hangedst him."
>
> "Hanged him, Sir! The laws hanged him; not I."
>
> "It is to the care of the laws I design to give up thy brother, Neither thou nor I was ever intended for public executioners."
>
> "Sure, Mr. Arnold, you would not hang him if you could."
>
> "Why not, if his crime deserves it."

"My God, Sir, consider the indelible stain upon an honorable family."

"Did it not cast an indelible stain upon the family of Perry Loggan?"

"Surely, Mr. Arnold, you cannot be serious in the comparison."

"Why not, I pray thee?"

"Who the devil ever thought of uniting the idea of honor with the name of such a family?"

"The idea of honesty they may at least—as useful a quality among plebeians as what thou callest honor amongst the nobility."

"But nobody talks at all of such people."

"Friend Cronnot, this may be the language of pride, but not of discernment. If thou art a lord, the common people are men. Every class of life has *its peerage*. This Nobody of thine is nothing more than the bulk of mankind."

"Consider, Sir, the widespread mischief so cruel a stigma would diffuse over all the correlatives of a noble family."

"Has thy honorable house more uncles, aunts, and cousins, than falls in general to the lot of a plebeian?"

"You are pleasant, Sir. But what has your plebeian to oppose to the deprivation of the honors and offices of the state?"

"The deprivation of bread, a much more terrible calamity."

"Whatever you may think, Sir, I *feel* in a different manner."

"I envy not they feelings."

"Nor do I think the comparison you have all along carried on betwixt the nobility and the refuse of mankind altogether so polite."

"Refuse of mankind! Lay thy hand upon they heart, Neighbor Cronnot, and ask it whether these magnificent ideas have their foundation either in nature or in common sense." My Lord bit his lips, and looked an angry answer.

"Be not in wrath, Friend Cronnot; I design thee no offense, but the point in question, thou knowest, is Truth, not Politeness."

"Well, Sir, if this is your way of thinking, indulge your malice. Let us see how far into the regions of vengeance a Quaker's meekness will carry him. But, Sir, you over-rate your power. You cannot touch my brother's life. In that particular I defy you. You may get a few damages perhaps—a paltry recompense—fully adequate to the offense indeed, and exactly suited to your sordid disposition—your low and groveling ideas—your extraction and education—your—"

"Thy noble blood rises, I perceive, Friend Cronnot; but unless thou canst rail away the laws of thy country, I do not perceive the use of this heat. Doth it make thy intellects clearer?"

"Damn your sarcasm, Sir! Would it not raise the indignation of any man breathing to hear a fellow talk of hanging the son of an earl for a little freedom with an insignificant girl?"

"Would'st thou have talked in this strain if my brother had taken like freedom with thy sister?"

"Curse your comparisons! You are taking every opportunity of putting yourself upon a level with me."

"I am wronging myself then."

But this is after all a problem of personal relationships. There are graver, because more public, issues to be discussed, and Bage is courageous enough to discuss them, even in print. Midway through *Barham Downs* there is a travesty upon Parliamentary debate, in the guise of an act put on at a masquerade. Though we can scarcely quote it profitably, for it is given in terms of the politics of the times, it is brave talk.

His third novel, *The Fair Syrian,* moves upon a higher plane of both characterization and characteristic humor. Structurally, it is the most rambling of them all; the plot, the most improbable. The fair Syrian, who is not a Syrian, and carries the agreeable English name of Honoria Warren, has been taken to the Mediterranean by a captious whim of her father's. Here she suffers humiliating adventures, even to being sold three times as a slave, but surprisingly enough, without losing what would in the Near East, apart from her beauty, constitute her principal salable value. She is brought back to England by her latest purchaser, an Englishwoman, who makes her her principal heiress and shortly afterward dies of poisoning—of which, it may be guessed, Miss Warren is suspected to have been the contriver. Here is the foundation for a story which is developed through incidents sufficiently commonplace to fit the English scene.

In *The Fair Syrian,* as in its predecessors, the story is freshened—or rather in this case *made*—by the presence and talk of a woman whose clear-mindedness is never for a moment obscured by her aggressive wit, a wit which seems at times to be devoted to the service of Satan. A set of rather complicated family relations brings this Lady Bembridge and Honoria together, with resulting debates, renewed from time to time, on the relative satisfactions and rewards of the high life and the quiet life. The issue is scarcely a moral one; rather that of ultimate happiness, Miss Warren speaking as the apostle of enlightened Epicureanism, or, to bring the matter nearer home, of Bage's own moral philosophy. Yet we cannot be too sure—and never can be when Satan is standing by—whether Lady Bembridge herself is not speaking for Bage as much as her fair opponent.

Here, at any rate, is one of these provocative passages. Lady Bembridge's spouse—hers is one of the most loveless of upper-class marriages —has made "indecent advances" to Honoria, which horrify her to the point of determining her to leave her home under Lady Bembridge's roof. Her Ladyship expostulates. These, she says, are trifles. Even her husband's love-making is amusing rather than distressing. Honoria's answer is in character :

"Whatever amusement it might be to My Lord to sport with moral sanctions, to me—"

But Lady Bembridge interrupts her with a response equally expressive of her convictions as a woman of the world :

"Moral sanctions! Oh, my Dear!"

Honoria persists however. The dialogue continues in a letter to her friend Aurelia :

"Will Your Ladyship have the goodness to permit my immediate departure?"

"Will your gravityship please to behold itself in that mirror? See now—this moral gloom—what an awful solemnity it gives to these sweet features!"

"I wish the same mirror had the power of reflecting the true image of wit."

"Good—what then?"

"Your Ladyship would see how little genuine it is when—"

"It sports with moral sanctions—true. It is a sad affair when wicked wit sports with things serious, as it will do sometimes, even in our august senate. And you are a thing serious just now, my Dear; so pray, pray, forgive me, and I never will be witty again."

It was impossible to resist a smile.

"That is the smile of peace and mercy—is it?"

I shook my head.

"One has much ado to get a substantial Christian forgiveness here, I see. If saints above are as unrelenting as angels below, it will go hard with some of us."

"Neither saints nor angels, Lady Bembridge, are exorable but to repentance; and what kind of repentance is that which sins even while it deprecates?"

"Well, like Shakespeare's clown, I shall never be aware of my own wit till I break my shins against it. But, my Dear, I suspect your judgment is none of the best."

A footman here announced Lady Mary Hapsenberg; for it was rout night, Aurelia, and Lady Bembridge had taken the trouble to come into my dressing room to repeat her persuasions that I would make one.—"Well, my Dear," says she, "I must go; but first I will tell you a secret. Your wisdom is too evangelical—fit only for celestials. It wants a sprinkling of folly to humanize it. Come amongst us. Condescend to be a Venus at night, and I will allow you to be a Minerva in the morning. Remember your father's maxim, Child, *not anything too much.* Always wisdom, wisdom—I tell you, my Dear, we were not designed for it. Nature created us imperfect beings, and you want to counteract the operations of nature. Think of the impiety of it!"

As to the letter of womanly virtue, Honoria, who is unalterably pure not only by precept but by temperament, is disturbed by her own obstinate maidenliness. Bage gives us a scene in which her lover, and savior, Sir John Amington, makes overtures to gain her as his mistress— averse as he is, in the old tradition, to lower his status by marrying a woman without visible prospects, family, or fortune. Her refusal mixes withering resentment with genuine sorrow over this alteration in their friendly relations. But in the long watches of the night, she reflects upon her rigor and his disappointment. And when she finds that he has fallen seriously ill as a result of his penitence, she actually offers her purity upon the altar of gratitude. Why, she asks herself, should she place that purity above her profound debt to him for saving her, as he has done, from ignominious death and ruined reputation?

This is not a sacrifice of principle. It is weighing a moral constraint against a moral gratification; so it is not irrational and it is certainly not ridiculous. But the strength of her emotional preference is clarified for both her own mind and his when he refuses her surrender, and she falls upon her knees in tears crying "Great God, I thank thee."

But in the background of Honoria's story is another excursion into the casuistry of love which constrasts Eastern and Western viewpoints, and which sounds a curious echo of Voltaire's *Candide.* It is a lengthy exchange of views between Honoria, at the time a slave destined for a Turkish harem, and Amina, a young but amply experienced Near Eastern girl in the same situation. Honoria begs pity for her unhappy lot, but is answered by the young Georgian with a quick summary of her own history, the end of which is reconcilement with her fate and a truly dispassionate unconcern for the vicissitudes of sex under the Oriental system.

"Let me tell you," [she advises Honoria] "when you yield to the oppression of an aching heart, you afflict yourself more cruelly than fortune can. I advise you to be merry. Every situation has its pleasures if the mind is disposed to pleasure, and they are fools that do not make the most of it. . . .

"After nine years experience, I have found that when bad luck comes, to double it by sadness is the silliest thing we can do. See now— if you are the most unfortunate of womankind, half your woes at least are of your own creating."

Honoria expostulates. "I know not," she says, "whether I should choose to change the sensibility that pains me for the unfeeling merriment that constitutes your pleasure." She reproaches Amina for her want of Christian conscience in surrendering herself willingly to a succession of owners. "This we call impurity and wickedness,—unsanctified by marriage rites." Amina's answer is a burst of laughter.

It is not necessary to regard this exchange of arguments as an attempt on Bage's part to repudiate European sexual morality; it is, however, certainly a trial balloon for the consideration of sex upon more objective grounds than the puritan. And it is typical of Bage to use argument of this sort not to affront conventional susceptibilities, but to encourage better understanding of the obscurer grounds for the moral sanctions.

Upon its specific merits as a novel, we can afford to deal briefly with Bage's next novel, *James Wallace*. It is scarcely more interesting than *The Fair Syrian*, and there are two to come which will be more worth our attention.

There are two things, however, which make *James Wallace* memorable. One is that it is the first novel of any importance to accept business as a career for a gentleman. Out of Wallace's impressive mental and moral endowments there emerges a gift for management which changes him from an unhappy dependent to a man of acknowledged capacities, and ultimately of means. That leads to the discovery that he is not an abandoned foundling, but the son of upper-class parents, properly married, and heir to a modest title and an estate. The conclusion, then, is gratuitous and conventional. What is important in this aspect of the story is that Bage has accepted commerce as a decent alternative to the highly financed *mariage de convenance* as a means of maintaining a costly estate or re-establishing an impoverished one. For he still thinks of the aristocrat as the axis of an acceptable social system; but not the aristocrat of decayed estate and social worthlessness. The aristocrat, he is heretic enough to believe can be made as well as born. Bage has not achieved complete democracy—nor is it clear in any of his novels that he was a democrat in sympathies.

Another notable thing in this novel is a daring but cautiously expressed doubt that ritual marriage is under all conditions benign or desirable. He does not, like Mary Wollstonecraft, think it demeaning, but he questions it seriously enough to have disturbed many traditionalists of his time. Scott, who included three of Bage's novels—*Wallace* among them—in Ballantyne's *Novelists' Library*, thinks his influence in this respect regrettable.

But Bage's attitude is neither dogmatic not contentious. If we trace it through the entire course of his fiction, we find a striking parallel to the development of Bernard Shaw's views from his early novel, *The Irrational Knot,* to his play *Getting Married.* But there are behind Shaw three or four generations of added social experience and speculation. He has also a more positive view of remedial expedients—in particular, easy and uncontestable divorce. Bage does not press expedients; indeed, he does little more than pose the problem; though in *James Wallace* and the novel to follow he considers fairly the conditions underlying the problem.

Bage is not an analyst of sexual experience, although he accepts its unpredictable effects as the reason for examining the complex questions surrounding marriage. When he faces the problem directly, he allows one character—always a male—to voice his doubts as to whether masculine nature and propensities are not promiscuous and therefore undomestic. If so, he appears to say, it can be only under favoring conditions and with intelligence, good will and forbearance, that the disparate interests of husband and wife can be fused into common purpose and produce contentment.*

In making his case, Bage dares to view the libertine not as a moral monstrosity, but as a distinct kind of human being. He questions the common representation of the rake in fiction as the vicious or spoiled child of a debased aristocratic culture. He is a man of different urges, Bage suggests, whether brutal or merely indelicate, and therefore to be judged thoughtfully. But the problem, as he presents it, is of pre-emptive importance for woman, and the more so as her liberty of choice increases. In so far as his fictions are vehicles of good counsel, it seems to be directed to women, as they assume the greater risk in marriage.

For all this show of liberalism, Bage's novels end invariably in affectionate and contented marriages—at least so far as expectation can carry us—on a basis of understanding thoroughly clear before the decisive step is taken. Understanding, however, does not imply for him insurance, for he accepts the fact that marital experience exerts its pressures differently upon different people. In *James Wallace* he makes his point rather surprisingly through clearing up his plot by two presumably happy marriages, but dissolving a third attachment through the unwillingness of a girl, deeply in love but also aware of her own sensitiveness, to marry a libertine and the equal unwillingness of the libertine to surrender the kind of liberty he enjoys. There is no theater in it, no manufactured sentimental stress. Two sensible people do a sensible thing, in full knowledge of themselves, though not without pain for the young lady and a sense of tragic consequence on the part of the young man. The last word of the story,

---

*He seems to present the problem without personal prejudice. One of his letters quoted by Scott would make it apparent that his own marriage was a satisfying one.

curiously enough, is a letter from the gay blade in question felicitating himself upon preserving not only his liberty but his personality. There is profound point beneath the mannered frivolity of the letter.

The point is not made, however, at the expense of woman's position, feelings, or intelligence. For Bage recognizes sanctions for purity that are fundamental in the feminine nature, and not merely conventional social and economic responses. The diagnostic of feminine affection, he believes, is at its best intelligent loyalty; as that of the masculine nature is, and not necessarily at its best, the interest of the chase.* The problem of civilized marriage is the reconcilement of the two opposites.

Man as He Is has been called by a discriminating critic† the best of Bage's novels. It is a judgment I feel no inclination to question, though the novel betrays most of Bage's shortcomings. It is beyond doubt the subtlest of his novels, focusing upon a question already lurking in the background of *The Fair Syrian* and *James Wallace*. That question is, how far the observance of moral conventions should be permitted, in personal opinions and conduct, to impair the freedom or cloud the happiness of others. Honoria Warren, we may remember, posed this question to herself, but the inhibitions of her sex and her moral nurture made it an act of pure courage to face it honestly, and an indescribable relief not to have to answer it. In *Man as He Is* Miss Colerain lives wholly in the comfortable assurance that feminine purity can mate and subsist side by side only with masculine purity. It is not a doctrine, not a religious conviction, but a spiritual conviction maintained with almost fantastic intensity, and exercised against the man, admittedly, of her affections.

The central situation follows rather curiously that of *Amelia* or of one of Smollett's earlier novels : young man, full of the stir of youth, balancing continuously a heartfelt devotion to an idealized though flesh-and-blood mistress against the recurrent temptations of the moment—which are frequent and lively enough in all conscience. But there is a difference : Miss Colerain has the iron in her constitution which Amelia and Smollett's heroines have not.

"Happiness," [she says to her lover's, Sir George Paradyne's, tutor] "is too important to be made the subject of experiment. I will be candid with you, Mr. Lyndsay; and to prove to you that I am not without my sex's weakness, I own that I love Sir George, fondly love him; so much the more necessary is it to guard against the errors of my heart. That heart shall break, as perhaps it will, before I marry a man

---

*Morton, in *James Wallace*, declares, "I look upon women as the true *ferae naturæ* [wild animals], and by God, I will hunt them down."
†Miss J. M. S. Tompkins, *The Popular Novel in England*, 1770-1800.

cried Sir George.   You dare not then
truſt your happineſs in my hand.
You dare not confide in my promiſe
to be all you deſire."

"Indeed, Sir George," Miſs Colerain replied, "I am too young for a
preceptreſs; and you are young. It is
from experience in the great ſchool of
the world you muſt learn what is wanting—if any thing is wanting—to com-
pleat the charaćter of a gentleman.
You are going abroad."

"From whence have you this intelligence?" Sir George aſked.

"Once," replied Miſs Colerain,
"I had it from yourſelf. Miſs Carlill alſo has lately mentioned it."

"I fear," ſaid Sir George, "I
am not obliged to Miſs Carlill. It is
ſhe who learns and communicates my
little errors, I ſuppoſe, in form of
anecdote."

"You would not wiſh to do good
and great things unnoticed," ſaid Miſs

Cole-

Typical printed page of a late eighteenth-century novel. Note the long s's and the
catchword at the bottom of the page. From the first edition of Robert Bage's *Man
as He Is,* 1792. The page contained less than half the text of the average modern
page of fiction, and a volume usually contained from 200 to 250 pages; so it is not
surprising that even moderately long novels ran to six or eight volumes.

to whom I cannot give my entire esteem. But this esteem must not be upon credit. I cannot admit as a plea the possibility that he may one day deserve it."

The issue of Sir George's actively masculine habits is raised time and again throughout the story. He is, in truth, the over-age bad boy. Unfortunately, Bage is not resourceful enough to prevent coincidence from playing far too important a part in the piling up of evidence against the unfortunate culprit. When Miss Colerain should be peacefully at home in her quiet rural English town, she is certain to appear suddenly in London or Paris and quite by chance to run across Sir George in his unlucky moments of amorous relaxation, or, in one case, to hear a groundless rumor of his engagement. So when Sir George's honest but over-confident proposal is finally made in form, he is confronted by indignant virginity, bristling with sarcasm. And the comedy—likewise the tragedy—of it all is that Sir George has been driven into his course of petty debauchery by the humiliation he has suffered at the stoic virgin's hands. In the end, of course, all comes right—for Bage is not by temperament a maker of tragedy—but only after Miss Colerain discovers that in his disappointment Sir George has become as much of a penitent recluse as his gentlemanly status will permit. It should be added that Bage in the end justifies his thesis by awakening Miss Colerain's consciousness to the fact that rampant virginity may be a serious disturbance to the flow of life in a world of human beings and of unstable moral fashions.

That is the story, and it is far from a bad one. But this central theme is overlaid by digressions, good in themselves, but intrusive in a modern novel. There are little histories of Lyndsay (Sir George's sensible tutor); of Mowbray, victim of a worthless wife and now an apostle of rational divorce laws; of a mysterious and fascinating Balkan countess; and of the Jamaican slave Fidel. Bage shows a special talent for such short narratives —even at times a genius—as in the story of the schoolmaster of Nibbiano in *Barham Downs*. But the digressions do open up cracks in the continuity.

Then too, *Man as He Is* is overpopulated. A host of characters not at all necessary to the action move on and off the scene; yet they can not infrequently force their individual interest upon the reader. Inevitably they tend to be one-sided, since they are so casually introduced and abandoned, but they are often purely enjoyable. There is Miss Carlil, a charming straight-laced Quakeress and an adept at moral dialectic; Bardoe, a consistent exponent of the view that nothing matters; Lyndsay, the apostle of restraining prudence—even in the practice of the primary virtues; and Mrs. Almon, an adventuress, who is either benign or wicked, it is hard to say which. No reader need lament having encountered these people, though they are all brought in to exemplify the fact that human nature defies definition and social philosophy is not a science.

One last act of justice with respect to *Man as He Is* must be to note Bage's gift for coining aphorisms pregnant with hard Northern humor. Nothing in Bage's performance, incidentally, is more Shavian.

> Those who have property are the only people who have a chance of losing it.
> That is the most desirable prudence which is the most dearly bought.
> If rank could save people from the gout, it would be worth something.

At times they strike the very note of Carlylean wisdom :

> One sees a greater value in health for having been sick.

Or this, anticipating probably the most quoted scrap of Carlyle's caustic sense :

> "I wish," said Lord Auschamp, rather peevishly, "I wish, Sir George, you would be content to take the world as it is."
> "I must, My Lord," Sir George answered.

Into his final novel, *Hermsprong*—we may call it by its popular title —Bage poured all his reforming energy. What in the early novels had been accomplished generally by amused satire becomes central, insistent, and even severe. The aim of the novel is to dissolve the illusions of caste, state religion, social salvation through politics, and feminine inferiority, by aggressive debate in which cool reason confronts prejudice and privilege. Yet this novel of reason is built upon the most fanciful of assumptions— the fallacy of the "noble savage," current and recurrent in fiction from Mrs. Behn's *Oroonoko* on.

The "noble savage" conception is, of course, that primitive man is naturally kindly, sincere, and just. The conventional vehicle for the idea is to introduce the ingenuous savage into European society, and allow him by his principles, his conduct, and his intellectual curiosity, to expose its hollowness and falsity. In *Hermsprong* the alien is a young man of European parentage whom circumstances have placed during his youth among a tribe of American Indians. He is not really a primitive; for his parents have by their presence and instruction also given him all the advantages of European culture, and in the end great wealth. As an unusual (and unthinkable?) social hybrid, he should therefore represent the best of two deeply opposed civilizations. Yet in spite of the influences of a very complete, though informal, education, he has favored the life and the outlook of the savage up to the point at which he is introduced to the society and traditions of the British aristocracy.

The key to Hermsprong's social character is an uncompromising frankness, so uncompromising that it often becomes effrontery. And the special object of his contempt is the upstart peer and possessor of a vast Cornish estate, with whose daughter he has fallen in love. At least we have here a situation productive of embarrassments and conflicts of interest and feeling.

The girl, Miss Campinet, suffers from a disease of civilization which she calls "duty," and with it, in the good old fashion, she does her best to unite a daughter's affection. But how can one love a father who is self-seeking, morally decrepit, and tyrannical? Hermsprong would liberate not only herself but her mind. Her love for him is manifest and demurely acknowledged, but the mournful text of her personal creed is that the claims of filial duty come before love. When the truth finally emerges from a complicated situation, Hermsprong, it turns out, is the true heir to Lord Grondale's title and property. This he has known all along, but it is no solution to Miss Campinet's problems of the heart. Hermsprong's reason, however, is kept at work, with the result that she at last consents to marry him if he will allow her father during his lifetime the full use and enjoyment of social place and estate. The claims of aristocratic privilege seem to have cheated those of reason and everyday justice, but Hermsprong's surrender is not as ignoble as it sounds, for it is attended by a correspondence between the two lovers in which the most refined of aristocratic preciosity is made to harmonize with the most noble of savage simplicity and candor.

It scarcely needs to be pointed out that this outline suggests a plot neither new nor clever. But the effectiveness of the story depends not upon mechanical contrivance nor upon situation, but upon first rate characterization, at times sympathetic, at times satiric, and upon the same kind of ethically directed dialogue we have already illustrated from Bage's earlier novels. No novel of Bage's is stronger in dialectic than *Hermsprong*. The interested can find the best examples of it in debate upon the illusions of "progress" in Chapter XXVII and in a random though sharply pointed discussion of woman's education in Chapter XLIII.

Hermsprong, as the repository of Bage's maturest convictions, is also the vehicle of his most telling irony. We may sample it in a passage from a sermon of Dr. Blick's in praise of the Tory-Anglican securities of property, rank, and creed—no unworthy companion-piece to Sinclair Lewis's speech of Babbitt before the Zenith Rotary Club.

"If ever the Church can be in danger, it is so now," said the good doctor. "Now, when the atheistical lawgivers of a neighboring country have laid their sacrilegious hands upon the sacred property of the Church; now, when the whole body of dissenters here have dared to imagine the same thing. These people, to manifest their gratitude for the indulgent, too indulgent, toleration shown them, have been filling the nation with inflammatory complaints against a constitution, the best the world ever saw, or will ever see, against a government, the wisest, mildest, freest from corruption that the purest page of history has ever yet exhibited. Besides this political daring, one of their divines, if anything divine could be predicated of so abhorred a sect, has absolutely denied the most important tenet of holy religion, the Trinity in Unity; has endeavored to take from us the comfortable doctrines of atonement and grace—and indirectly, the immortality of our precious souls; —for, unless they are immaterial, how can they be immortal? But," said the doctor, rising in energy, "what can be expected from men who countenance the abominable doctrines of the Rights of Man? Rights contradicted by nature, which has given us an ascending series of inequality, corporeal and mental, and plainly pointed out the way to those wise political distinctions created by birth and rank. To this failure of respect to the dignitaries of the nation, and, let me add, to the dignitaries of the Church, is to be ascribed the alarming evils which threaten the overthrow of all religion, all government, all that is just and equitable upon earth."

Since argument is in *Hermsprong* so cardinal a matter, it is necessary that Bage's raisonneurs be manipulators rather than mere participants in the lengthy exchanges of talk. Hermsprong himself is of course the author's mouthpiece, but he is powerfully seconded by one of Bage's most winning characters, the artful and vivacious young Miss Fluart, who has an aptitude for transfixing her opponents on cleverly contrived ethical dilemmas. Her fencing with Lord Grondale in defense of his daughter's almost nonexistent liberties has something of the rapidity and thrust of one of Wilde's comedies. Equally, the losing cause must have its champions, upholders of the good old traditions, armed with the fondest and stupidest clichés of class. The eminent one, we have already noted, is Lord Grondale. His less intelligent and less practiced second is his chaplain, whom we have just quoted—pluralist and toady, fatuous, vindictive, and short-tempered, one of the stiffest ecclesiastical grandees of fiction, and almost good enough for Trollope.

Bage's final position as a politico-social thinker involves no large program for social betterment. Politics, he constantly makes clear, he distrusts, for the reason he puts in the mouth of Hermsprong :

"I call you [the English] no names; I lay no crimes to your charge; I impute to you nothing more than the having followed the usual course of things. You are rich, and addicted to pleasure, to luxury. It is a consequence that has always followed wealth; and a consequence of this addiction is political carelessness, the immediate precursor of political corruption."

Hermsprong enlarges this indictment in a general conversation toward the end of the novel.

"I cannot, I fear, submit to be fettered and cramped throughout the whole circle of thought and action. You Europeans submit to authority with regard to the first, and to fashion with regard to the last. I cannot get rid of the stubborn notion that to do what we think it right to do is the only good principle of action. You seem to think that the only good principle of action is to do as others do. You allow fashion to be often folly, and believe it right to be fools when you have so great a sanction; and by some ingenious use or abuse of words you are always and eternally right. It is my misfortune that I cannot be right upon such easy terms. Servile compliance is crime when it violates rectitude, and imbecility at least when it is prostituted to folly. When it has become habitual, what a thing it has made of man."

"My friend," said Miss Fluart, "you have indulged yourself in a pretty satirical vein; but will you not have the goodness to allow us some good qualities?"

"Many, Madam. I am not now drawing your whole picture as a people; I am only placing before you some things I dislike. . . . [My complaint] is your politics, Madam, a subject on which the English delight to dwell, on which no two people ever thought wholly alike, and on which you have brought yourselves to so charming a degree of rancor that you can bear no deviations from your own opinions. Before you can set up an undisputed title to be an amiable people, you must first learn to agree to differ. Your religion has been teaching you love and good will to men ever since you were born, and you have not yet got beyond the primer of the science. This it is that deforms your societies, or, to preserve your tempers and politeness, drives you to insipidity and cards."

But if we repudiate the political framework for a society which must, by its mere size, be organized, then what recourse have we for administrative and judicial control? A Kropotkin would object that the word "must" begs the question. But Bage himself is after all a dissident rather than a political philosopher. His answer is—so far as he ventures upon an answer—the escapist's. Having by force of circumstances to accept the political framework, the dissatisfied can find a plan of living in the small nonpolitical commune, so small that it is little more than a neighborly aggregation of families of similar culture and tastes.

> "I have sixty thousand acres of uncleared land upon the Potowmac" [says Hermsprong]. "It cost me little. I have imagined a society of friends within a two-mile ring; and I have imagined a mode of making it happy. In this, it is possible, I may not reach the point I desire; but with common prudence we cannot fail of plenty, and, in time, of affluence."

The proposal, vague enough, to be sure, echoes the conclusions of both *Mount Henneth* and *Barham Downs,* in which contented subsistence is to be gained through just such voluntary social unities. The principle of the plan underlies, after all, the workers' communities of Owen and of Noyes a half century later, but with the notable difference that Bage's unifying idea is cultural rather than industrial. Whatever we may think of the communal theory, in the tentative and temporary viability it has shown when uncontaminated by political absolutism, the desideratum of limited size seems to have been critical, as Bage thought it would be.

This last of Bage's novels is the most forceful of them all; perhaps not the most convincing. For Hermsprong's effective trait is not common sense but rampant intellectual vigor. In addition, he is almost untouched by saving humor. To overlook the latter consideration would be to disregard the fact that Bage's social satire at its best shows the bland spirit of Chaucer, not the flame of Swift.

Perhaps one way to appraise Bage's merits, strictly as a novelist, and not as a social interpreter, is to compare his artistic endowments with those of Fielding, by common consent the first English novelist of his century. The comparison will not be altogether to Bage's advantage; but it may highlight his individuality and his literary independence.

Fielding's novels have design. They are the work of an already experienced writer, not only well-read, but unusually attentive to literary form. Bage's are natural and unschooled. Whatever his wide reading taught him, it gave him no formal (and perhaps constrained) ideas of artistic dignity. He has respect enough for the inherent dignity of the well-chosen word, but little or none for literary elegance. Compared with Fielding's, his writing flows easily from the pen, and shows little evidence of studied or self-conscious style.

Fielding's humor is also the product of literary learning and awareness, not infrequently labored, particularly when he pursues the mock-heroic fashion. Bage's humor is to all appearances effortless, the issue of an amusing mind. It seems also to inhere in his characters, to season their contacts and their conversation. We never feel with Bage, as we may with Fielding, that he calls upon us to admire his cleverness, rather than his characters and the "inevitable" ways and talk that should express them, not him. Fielding tends to show his wit with an air of consequence, sometimes with almost disturbing assurance; Bage intimately and winningly. It is possible for one to be bored with the unremitting flow of Fielding's cleverness; not by Bage's more modest humor.

Fielding's morality, which seems to be still a live issue, shows a somewhat precarious balance between gentlemanly respect for feminine purity and amused tolerance for raffish male morality. His tongue-in-cheek attitude toward the roving male affections is usually set down by Fielding-ites as the mark of his freedom from Richardsonian hypocrisy. But is it specially creditable, particularly at a time when male depravity—there is no gentler name for it—stood in no need of a devil's advocate? Bage's attitude is steadily sensible of the social recoil of the double standard, and evokes no specious amusement over the abuse of masculine liberty and opportunity. My inclination is to call Bage's position the more honest as well as the more socially intelligent. At the same time, it must be admitted that Bage lived in a period of more mature social conscience.

We have already noted that Bage's characters tend to present a single surface to the reader, yet that is a deficiency by no means uncommon in the period, quite understandable before the novel had taken on psychological subtlety or had developed a psychological technique. Yet as simply conceived as they are, these characters have the air and speech of human beings, largely because they are without literary stuffing. And partly because of their one-sidedness, they are clearly differentiated. We may feel that Fielding in *Tom Jones* and *Amelia* presents the same pair of purely fictional lovers, depicted in the earlier novel in the urgency of adolescent passion, in the latter with the maturer affection of approaching middle-age. No one of Bage's highly individualized women characters could be thought a mere reprocessing of an earlier one.

We have commented in passing upon the peculiar quality of Bage's dialogue. It is probably too incisive, too *staccato,* even in its best passages, to be quite realistically convincing. Yet as a departure from the sustained oratorical dialogue of his predecessors, it approaches conversation as we hear it in our everyday contacts. It is surprising that Fielding, experienced in writing for the theater, which does not tolerate speech-making, should in his fiction allow a single character uninterrupted discourse which can run to a page or more. And Fielding's followers—Smollett and Burney, for example—can outdo Fielding in these liberal allowances for full and gracefully rounded but unreal conversation.

Many readers find one type of character in Fielding even more engaging than his youthful lovers—the friendly purveyors of adult wisdom who play a balancing or even a corrective part in the destinies of his romantic principals. In *Joseph Andrews* it is Parson Adams; in *Tom Jones,* Squire Alworthy; and in *Amelia,* Dr. Harrison. Fielding's interest in these characters seems primarily pictorial. They are personalities in their own right, teachers and counselors only as they are good men speaking (but not always acting) from a fund of experience and natural prudence. In Bage we find a different and newer sort of guiding intelligence—*young* men and women, but matured in imagination as well as reason. They are the forerunners of the raisonneurs of Meredith and Henry James, representatives if not actual voices of the author.

In Bage they play a curious and distinctive part, men like Holman in *James Wallace* and Lyndsay in *Man as He Is* speaking for the male interest (creative intellect, as Shaw, following Bergson, later conceives it), and women such as Lady Bembridge in *The Fair Syrian,* Miss Lamounde in *James Wallace,* and Miss Carlil in *Man as He Is,* representing woman's interest—the unprofaned personality, the home, and the race of the future. None of these characters except Miss Lamounde is a principal. In *James Wallace* Bage gives some particularly sharp collisions of masculine and feminine "reason" in conversations between raisonneurs; and in *The Fair Syrian* and *Man as He Is* they have an important share in breaking down barriers of prejudice in the principals.

These distinctions seem to emphasize, in the main, Fielding's cultivated gifts and Bage's natural gifts. And properly so; for Bage is not a cultivated writer. Well read as he was, and thoroughly conversant with the thinking of his day, he had not had the discipline, as Fielding had, of a great English public school and a Continental university. The meaning of that discipline is evident in Fielding's greater circumference and depth and his greater control of his purpose. The instinct for narrative is not enough; after all, genious does imply among other things a capacity for taking pains. And Bage did not take pains. He wrote because he found it fun, and, we are told, to take his mind off the cares of business. These are not great motives, but they have given us a star of one of the lesser magnitudes.

To me personally, Bage is a fond disappointment; fond because he is full of endearing traits and uncodified wisdom; a disappointment because he seemed satisfied with "the little less." Yet if I were asked which of the obscurer novelists of the century could provide a tolerant reader with a new and rewarding experience, I should say unhesitatingly Bage.

CHAPTER XVII

Social Justice

Holcroft, Godwin, Mary Wollstonecraft

THE MORE SERIOUS, but certainly less entertaining, apostles of social reform in fiction were, most importantly, William Godwin, and in a lesser way, his friend Thomas Holcroft, and Godwin's wife, better known by her maiden name of Mary Wollstonecraft.

Self-educated, and working successively as hostler, shoemaker, and strolling actor, Holcroft had no exalted view of social and political make-believe.* He became both a playwright of some note, and a novelist because he saw fiction as an available platform for his aggressively radical views. As a radical, he had the brave distinction of having voluntarily surrendered himself for trial in the notorious state trials of 1794 on a charge of treason, but his case was dismissed when the government was defeated in successive prosecutions of three of his associates.

I have found it easy to be effusive over Bage, but I know of no reader who has admitted enthusiasm over the novels of Thomas Holcroft. Two of his novels are readable, even by the standards of our discriminating day, but unsparing of the reader's time and patience. Those are *Anna St. Ives* and *Hugh Trevor*.

Probably no epistolary novel proves the inadequacies of the form more completely than *Anna St. Ives*. Three characters occupy the center of action. There are Anna herself, a high-minded aristocratic girl with enormous confidence in her moral energy, and her two lovers. The first, Frank Henley, is plebeian, but the perfect example of the perfect man whom the perfectibilians delighted to honor. The other, Coke Clifton, is shrewd, scintillating, and as dissolute as the reckless young heir to a peerage was customarily pictured. The correspondence follows a curious pattern, which Bage, however, had already used with effect. Each of the three has a confidant from whom no experience, and even no thought, is concealed,

---

*Thomas Holcroft (1745-1809). *Alwyn*, 1780; *Anna St. Ives*, 1792; *The Adventures of Hugh Trevor*, 1794-7; *The Memoirs of Bryan Perdue*, 1805.

but they are merely receivers of what is to be conveyed to the reader in this essentially unrealistic fashion. The insufficiency of the letter medium is perhaps particularly evident because the story presents meticulously some powerful though perhaps theatrical dialogue which is quite good enough to stand on its own merits but seems too precisely reported for the limitations of a letter.

Henley we have already described as perfection. More specifically, he combines kindliness and generosity, physical fitness and courage, with complete clear-mindedness as to the rights, and more particularly the wrongs, of the social structure. Anna is fully aware of this, and she loves him more than wholeheartedly—with a kind of adoration for his spiritual greatness as well as for his personal charm. But like Miss Campinet in *Hermsprong,* she opposes love to her sense of social duty, and duty embraces for her the necessity of marrying within her class. Not that she has any illusions as to the caste system, but because an unsuitable marriage will make her father and her remoter relations unhappy. She writes her dear friend Louisa (who is, incidentally, Coke Clifton's sister) :

> I have been making some efforts to decide the question, not of love, but of duty. Love must not be permitted till duty shall be known. I have not satisfied myself so well as I should wish, yet my former reasons seem invincible. Ought my father and my family to be offended? Ought I to set an example that might be pernicious? Is it most probable that by opposing I shall correct or increase the world's mistakes? The path before me is direct and plain; ought I to deviate?

This is obviously reason reduced to the narrow compass of mere family interests and affections, with the interests of society reflected rather dimly in the concerns of the family. And it is interesting that her friend Louisa sees from the first—despite the fact that it is her own brother who will profit from Anna's choice—that Anna's "duty" is a dubious sanction for dealing so imperiously with her own heart.

Anna's convictions, once she has reached her decision to place her duty before her love, demand that she deal honestly with Frank Henley. He naturally expostulates, for she had declared her love for him; but she answers :

> You confound, or rather you do not separate, two things which are very distinct : that which I think of you, and that which the world would think of me, were I to encourage hopes which you would have me indulge. . . . It is not my heart that refuses you; it is my understanding; it is principle; it is a determination not to do that which my reason cannot justify.

Finally, she not only persuades Frank to accept her decision—and what else can he do?—but even enlists his support in attempting to alienate Clifton from his wicked ways and to retrieve his character so that he will make a desirable husband for her.

The comedy takes a new turn. For it is comedy, and Holcroft is fully aware that devious notions can masquerade in the dress of reason. Anna begins to work upon Clifton. She discounts the violence of his passion—he is genuinely in love with her—and tries to discipline him for her purposes. At first he seems gratefully compliant, but his letters to his confidant shows that it is only politic compliance. As time goes on, he grows restless, then indignant, and finally rebellious. The end of the noble experiment is Clifton's astute argument upon the very premises that Anna has laid down—that the individual's right to freedom of action justifies their sexual relations before their marriage, which circumstances must delay for a time. She explodes with disdainful anger, but there can be little doubt that her indignation results as much from the deflation of her system as from her personal discomfiture.

The plot now borrows a motive from Richardson's *Clarissa*. Clifton, still the spoiled and arrogant child of the aristocracy, resolves on a pitiless revenge for his humiliation. He enlists a lawless band to abduct and confine both Anna and Henley; Anna in a remote and deserted dwelling and Henley in a madhouse. Of course he plans to ravish Anna, but compunctions and vacillations delay the act. When he finally commands his courage to the point of performance, she adopts the beseiged girl's most reliable defense. When he tries to break into her bedchamber, her foot against the door proves more effective than his shoulder.

The conclusion of the plot is melodramatic. Anna escapes, but unhappily to seek refuge in the nearby madhouse where Frank is confined. The final scene is an attempt at rescue and a general melée, with blood and broken bones, the escape of the two lovers, and, naturally, their union according to the laws of the heart. In a rather useless coda, except for its pertinence to the lesson of general benevolence, Frank and Anna join in a somewhat patronizing effort to make a man of Clifton.

The absurdity of the story is what, as satire, justifies it. Holcroft, with his broad dislike of conventions, attacks expediency in the guise of "reason" when brought to the defense of an almost indestructible convention of the time and the class—the *mariage de convenance*. For the purpose, he uses an intelligent but self-assured woman as its champion, not to depreciate woman's power to think independently, nor to argue unnecessarily the principle of free choice, but to expose one of the fallacies of caste through a mind which feels itself superior to the system yet assumes the need of remaining a part of it. That personal vice enters into the problem in this particular case is almost beside the point of Holcroft's presentment; for vice itself he treats as an altogether characteristic weakness of the upper classes, wasteful and degraded and imbued with the feeling that their privileges include exemption from responsibility to society for their actions. Anna herself, threatened and calmly anticipating attack from her rejected and resentful lover, with a certain moral exaltation transfers that responsibility from the man to the society which produced him :

> Is there enmity in my words? Surely I do not feel it. The spirit of benevolence and truth allows, nay, commands me to hate the vice, but not its poor misgoverned agents. They are wandering in the maze of mistake. Ignorance and passion are their guides, and doubt and desperation their tormentors. . . . Be kindness and charity mine.

This is Christian sentiment in a rational key; but it is typically Holcroft, and it is voiced again in his next novel.

The Adventures of Hugh Trevor is generally regarded as Holcroft's best novel. My own vote would be cast for *Anna St. Ives. Hugh Trevor* is in the first place a novel of purpose undisguised. It anticipates rather amusingly an Educationalist program highly favored today—vocational guidance. But Holcroft's counsel is addressed to youth at large, and his advice with regard to four polite professional callings—the university, theology, the law, and politics—is "Don't"! The four professions are, or were at the time, obviously those devoted in an important degree to the control of public opinion and the discouragement of individual thinking. The action of the story is concerned with repeated instances of the classic collision of respectable rascals with the trusting and the helpless. Its nominal hero is a young man undergoing his schooling in life and learning everything the hard way, repeatedly skinning his nose by running in the dark into stiff-necked university officials, unprincipled churchmen, designing pettifoggers, and over-reaching politicians. The story itself has little importance, but the characters are vigorously depicted; two in particular : Turl, regarded by the master of his college as "a very dangerous fellow," but a young man of all-round wisdom, undaunted by public incompetence and corruption; and Belmont, who appears rather late in the story, a latter-day pragmatist and stoic, with an irreducible minimum of personal responsibility. Turl is, like all of Holcroft's principals, a revolutionist, but one surprisingly endowed with prudence. His system?

> To speak so as to produce good, not bad, consequences. He that would sweep the streets of pea-shells lest old women might break their necks, would doubtless have good intentions, yet his office would be only that of a scavenger. Speak, but speak to the world at large, not to insignificant individuals. Speak in the tone of a benevolent and

disinterested heart, and not of an inflamed and resentful imagination. Otherwise you endanger yourself and injure society.

There is no real intimacy between Trevor and Turl, who is just barely the older of the two; for Turl is not only thoroughly serious, but somewhat distant, by temper a counselor rather than an intimate; but he checks Hugh's vanity, questions his unripe convictions, dissuades him from the practice of law—"in its origins and essence absolutely unjust"—and acts generally as the restraining hand upon the impetuous shoulder.

It is much to Hugh's advantage that he has Turl's composed mind to watch his mental growth; for he is all fire and indignation. Yet his mental liberation is unfortunately void of significant result, since the story is brought to a conventional end by Hugh's inheritance of a fortune. The story is too multiplex, too unassembled, to attempt to summarize. Too many events just happen; too much is said about too many things. If this novel is Holcroft's best, then it is not surprising that the world seems contented to have consigned his fiction to oblivion.

Far more important in the eyes of his contemporaries, and of posterity, is William Godwin.*

I have felt over many years that no writer of fiction before Henry James is so much like James himself as Godwin. It was Stuart Sherman who suggested that James's unfaltering interest in a self-chosen and self-satisfied high society was after all a deliberate revelation of its underlying ugliness. That is even more emphatically true of Godwin's fiction. His recurrent theme is the lush growth of the worst human traits in the hotbed of high breeding and privilege. Godwin, however, writes with more conscious animus than James, and it must be admitted that all his novels are disappointingly pedestrian and sober. The important resemblance between Godwin and James lies in the fact that Godwin, particularly in the novels written after 1800, is not only a perceptive but a systematic psychologist—a distinction that could not be conceded to any novelist before his time.

Godwin's fictions must be approached with some idea of one of the great documents in political and social liberation—his *Enquiry Concerning Political Justice,* published in 1793. For while none of his novels can with strict accuracy be called doctrinaire, all of them are infiltrated with his social philosophy. The sources of that philosophy we can scarcely go into. He was extremely well-read, and no thinker, particularly from Locke

---

*William Godwin (1756-1836). *Enquiry Concerning Political Justice* (1793); *Things as They Are, or the Adventures of Caleb Williams* (1794); *St. Leon* (1799); *Fleetwood, or the New Man of Feeling* (1805); *Mandeville* (1817); *Cloudesley* (1830); *Deloraine* (1833).

Crayon drawing by Sir Thomas Lawrence of Thomas Holcroft (LEFT) and William Godwin at the State Trials, 1794.

on, could have failed to influence him. We can, however, note the cardinal points of *Political Justice*.*

First, character is, from the point of view of social values, the product of circumstances (which we can interpret as environment) rather than of inborn propensities. But perfection is not to be found or attained within the limitations of human nature—a fact which vitiates neither aspiration nor effort. Social aggregates can be improved since individuals can be improved.

Second, the rule of reason must prevail over the feelings, in both public and private concerns. Reason rejects efforts at quick and violent social changes. Social betterment is a long road to be traveled.

Third, the first assumption argues the possibility of an approach to social perfection—the "perfectibilian" view. It also argues equalitarianism, since inherent endowments are less determinative than environmental factors, and the accident of birth should give no undue advantage to the individual.

Fourth, government, statutory laws, the courts, the churches, and all similar institutions which are presumed to regulate society and protect it against itself, are in reality the instruments of privilege, working for the advantage of those who have and for the oppression of those who have not.

Upon these premises the structure of Godwin's philosophy was built. It need not be said that none of them was new. But they had not been publicized in England as they had been upon the Continent; and to that extent their assembling and their enlargement was an influential contribution to English social thought and a stimulus to reform.

Caleb Williams (the subtitle has replaced the original title), published in 1794, is a purposeful novel embodying and illustrating those views.†
The original three volumes divide the novel into three distinct "movements." In the first third we are introduced to Ferdinando Falkland, "a

---

*Our notation assumes Godwin's revisions in the later editions of *Political Justice*. A summary of the work may be found in Chapters VI and VII of Ford K. Brown's *Life of William Godwin*. A lengthier critical analysis is contained in the "Introduction" to Volume III of F. E. L. Priestley's edition, University of Toronto, 1946. Godwin's philosophy and intellectual relations are treated in Rosalie G. Gryll's *William Godwin and His World* and in Burton R. Pollin's *Education and Enlightenment in the Works of William Godwin;* at less length in Chapter XI of Basil Willey's *Eighteenth Century Background*.

†Godwin's first ventures in fiction were three "novels" written and published in 1783-1784, two of which have been recovered from oblivion. *Imogen*, a rather conventional pastoral romance, was republished in 1963 in the *Bulletin* of the New York Public Library. The second, *Italian Letters, or the History of the Count de St. Julien,* is announced for publication by the University of Nebraska.

country squire of considerable opulence," a man of every gentlemanly excellence—education, taste, charm, and a high sense of both his prerogatives and his obligations as a member of the upper classes. To him is contrasted Barnabas Tyrrel, his opposite in everything but wealth and social position. Tyrrel is vulgar, vain, aggressive, and intolerant; and as a landlord, he is unscrupulous and brutal. As the two conspicuous figures in their community, these two are brought into constant and often painful collisions, each playing his part in conformity with his background and character. Falkland attempts to reconcile their growing differences by a courageous and candid talk with Tyrrel. But his magnanimity is wasted. Tyrrel continues to travel his own road in his own way, until in the end a policy of peculiar brutality to a dependent relative ends in her death, and in consequent condemnation of him by his neighbors. Stung by his ostracism, he blames his misfortune upon Falkland and provokes a quarrel in which he publicly trounces Falkland in the parlor of an inn.

Tyrrel does not live to triumph in this cheap glory. He is found the same night murdered within a few yards of the inn. Falkland is brought before a magistrate's court, conducts his own defense, and is acquitted "with every circumstance of credit," to the applause of the entire countryside. The search for the murderer ends in the conviction and execution of two of Tyrrel's former tenants named Hawkins, father and son, whom he had persued relentlessly and ruined.

But Falkland's complete exculpation apparently cannot console him for the injury that Tyrrel's attack and triumph have done his pride. He lives in poignant regret that Tyrrel's untimely death has robbed him of the opportunity to vindicate his name.

> From thenceforward his habits became totally different. He had before been fond of public scenes, and acting a part in the midst of the people among whom he immediately resided. He now made himself a rigid recluse. He had no associates, no friends. Inconsolable himself, he yet wished to treat others with kindness. There was a solemn sadness in his manner, attended with the most perfect gentleness and humanity. Everybody respects him, for his benevolence is unalterable; but there is a stately coldness and reserve in his behavior, which makes it difficult for those about him to regard him with the familiarity of affection.

In the second third of the story, the relator, Caleb Williams, is seen as the secretary and librarian of Falkland. Williams himself (the "I" of the story) is a self-educated but intelligent young man whose spirit of inquiry, unhappily, is not exercised wholly within the field of intellect, but deteriorates at times into plain inquisitiveness. This prompts him into an intru-

sive interest in the secrets of Falkland's household and personal effects.
And the upshot of his investigations is the slow growth of a doubt that
Falkland was innocent of Tyrrel's murder. Lacking the judgment to rest
satisfied with a single warning from Falkland, Williams persists in spying
upon his employer. His suspicions grow, and are finally verified, not by anything he has actually discovered, but by Falkland's voluntary confession.

We must pause a moment to note that *Caleb Williams* is frequently
dignified with the title of "the first detective story." This, however, is not
an accurate pronouncement. The mystery of the murder, and all its attendant suspense, dissolves, we have seen, when the story is scarcely more than
a third completed. The process of detection is not ratiocinative—to use
Poe's word—but is forwarded by mere blundering curiosity. There is not a
single shred of *evidence* of guilt presented to the reader at any point in the
story, although Williams appears to be on the verge of discovering it in
a locked chest when his employer, in a sort of panic fear that Williams
may verify his suspicions, confesses the murder to him, and so binds him to
secrecy. Finally, the true interest of the story, because it is the *purposed*
interest, begins with this confession. There is in reality no single respect in
which the story conforms to the technique of the modern detective story.
The point is rather immaterial, but it has to be made. The process of
revelation, incidentally, is much the same as that followed by Dostoevski
seventy years later in *Crime and Punishment* : the breakdown of the
criminal's morale, resulting finally in voluntary confession.

Cornered, Falkland tells Williams in detail the circumstances of the
murder :

> "Look at me. Observe me. Is it not strange that such a one as I
> should retain lineaments of a human creature? I am the blackest of
> villains. I am the murderer of Tyrrel. I am the assassin of the Hawkin-
> ses."
> I started with terror and was silent.
> "What a story is mine! Insulted, disgraced, polluted in the face
> of hundreds, I was capable of any act of desperation. I watched my
> opportunity, followed Mr. Tyrrel from the rooms, seized a sharp-
> pointed knife that fell in my way, came behind him, and stabbed him to
> the heart. My gigantic oppressor rolled at my feet.
> "All are but links of one chain. A blow! A murder! My next
> business was to defend myself, to tell so well-digested a lie as that all
> mankind should believe it true. Never was a task so harrowing and so
> intolerable!
> "Well, thus far fortune favored me; she favored me beyond my
> desire. The guilt was removed from me, and cast upon another; but this
> I was to endure. Whence came the circumstantial evidence against

him, the broken knife and the blood, I am unable to tell. I suppose by some miraculous accident Hawkins was passing by, and endeavored to assist his oppressor in the agonies of death. You have heard his story; you have read one of his letters. But you do not know the thousandth part of the proof of his simple and unalterable rectitude that I have known. His son suffered with him; that son for the sake of whose happiness and virtue be ruined himself and would have died a hundred times.—I have had feelings, but I cannot describe them.

"This it is to be a gentleman, a man of honor! I was the fool of fame. My virtue, my honesty, my everlasting peace of mind, were cheap sacrifices to be made at the shrine of this divinity. But, what is worse, there is nothing that has happened that has in any degree contributed to my cure. I am as much the fool of fame as ever. I cling to it with my last breath. Though I be the blackest of villains, I shall leave behind me a spotless and illustrious name. There is no crime so malignant, no scene of blood so horrible, in which that object cannot engage me. It is no matter that I regard these things at a distance with aversion;—I am sure of it; bring me to the test, and I shall yield. I despise myself, but thus I am. Things are gone too far to be recalled."

But Falkland has learned to know his confidant. He has risked nothing in making his confession; the pursued has turned on the pursuer.

"I had no alternative but to make you my confidant or my victim. It was better to trust you with the whole truth under every seal of secrecy than to live in perpetual fear of your penetration or your rashness.

"Do you know what it is you have done? To gratify a foolish, inquisitive humor, you have sold yourself. You shall continue in my service, but can never share my affection. I will benefit you in respect to fortune, but I shall always hate you. If ever an unguarded word escape from your lips, if ever you excite my jealousy or suspicion, expect to pay for it by your death or worse. It is a dear bargain you have made, but it is too late to look back. I charge and adjure you by ·everything that is sacred and that is tremendous, preserve your faith."

Williams' first view of the new situation is sympathetic and foolishly confident :

I will never become an informer. I will never injure my patron; and therefore he will not by my enemy. With all his misfortunes and all his errors, I feel that my soul yearns for his welfare. If he has been criminal, that is owing to circumstances. The same qualities under other circumstances would have been, or rather were, sublimely beneficent.

But he soon appreciates the reality; he is condemned not only to secrecy but to oppressive servitude. "He watched me, and his vigilance was a sickness to my heart. For me there was no more freedom, no more hilarity, of thoughtlessness, or of youth." The servant resolves to seek "an amicable adjustment of interests," but the employer will have no intimacy, no forced friendliness. "I will not always be," he says, "the butt of your simplicity and inexperience, nor suffer your weakness to triumph over my strength." In the young man indignation is succeeded by terror, and he resolves at any risk to break for liberty. But it is all useless. Falkland anticipates his escape and prevents it. Williams' feelings and fears rise to a passion of resistance, in spite of Falkland's dire threats. He escapes at night; but he is followed, apprehended, put on trial for a theft of plate, which, needless to say, is a trumped-up charge, and thrown into prison. More than that, the temper of the courtroom proceedings and the hostility of the spectators have convinced him that even the revelation of Falkland's guilt can result only in disbelief and even greater punishment.

Here is the nub of Godwin's purpose. He has carried his somewhat unadmirable hero through a course of action that, effectually or ineffectually, demonstrates the superiority of position and influence to all the claims of common justice.

> For myself, [the prisoner reflects] I looked round upon my walls, and forward upon the premature death I had too much reason to expect. I consulted my own heart, that whispered nothing but innocence; and I said, "This is society. This is the object, the distribution of justice, which is the end of human reason. For this sages have toiled, and midnight oil has been wasted."

The terror of the situation would be scarcely possible for Godwin to exaggerate. The threat of death for minor offenses was real; hanging was then prescribed punishment for well over a hundred crimes. The prison system itself was inconceivably brutal and indescribably filthy. The remainder of this second part of the novel is devoted to graphic argument in favor of the prison reform movement which in England had been set in motion in 1777 by John Howard's *State of Prisons in England and Wales,* to which Godwin refers in a footnote. From the misery and danger of his situation the prisoner at length escapes on his second attempt.

The final portion of the book should, by all the weight of fictional usage, vindicate the victim and bring the privileged criminal to well merited justice. It does not. The tragic end of this bitter conflict of personalities, and of impotent justice with rank and pertinacious injustice, is a stalemate. For years after the prisoner's escape he flees from place to place with a price on his head. For a time he is harbored by a band of highway-men led by a Robin Hood in an eighteenth-century dress. Attempting to escape to Ireland, he is mistakenly apprehended as a robber of the mails, but he buys his release by a ruinous bribe. He hides himself in the Jewish quarter of London and earns a pittance as a hack writer. Then he hires himself to a watchmaker to learn his trade, but is betrayed by his employer for the reward on his head. Always he is overtaken and obliged to move on, but in this last episode he is arrested on the old charge of theft, and exasperated beyond endurance, he defends himself by at last declaring Falkland's guilt in open court. The magistrate will not even lend an ear to the accusation :

> "First, I have to tell you, as a magistrate, that I can have nothing to do with your declaration. If you had been concerned in the murder you talk of, that would alter the case. But it is out of all reasonable rule for a magistrate to take an information from a felon, except against his accomplices. Next, I think it right to observe to you, in my own proper person, that you appear to me to be the most impudent rascal that I ever saw. Why, are you such an ass as to suppose that the sort of story you have been telling can be of any service to you, either here, or at the assizes, or anywhere else? A fine time of it, indeed, it would be if, when gentlemen of six thousand a year take up their ser-vants for robbing them, those servants could trump up such accusations as these, and could get any magistrate or court of justice to listen to them. Whether or no the felony with which you stand charged would have brought you to the gallows, I will not pretend to say; but I am sure this story will. There would be a speedy end to all order and good government if fellows that trample on ranks and distinctions in this atrocious sort were upon any consideration suffered to get off."

Williams is remanded for trial, and to his amazement, when his case is called, there is no one to press the charge against him. He is again free.

But free only for further pursuit. Wherever he decides to settle, Falk-land's agents discredit him. He can retain no friends, keep no employment. For a brief period he leads a quiet life as artisan and teacher in a little Welsh town, but this modest career too collapses before Falkland's plot-ting. A plan to escape to the Continent is blocked by Falkland's emissary. Williams finally decides to write down his story, to be published after his death, when the event should justify him and expose Falkland. To the astonishment of his tormentors, he then turns back to Falkland's own village, the scene of his first misfortunes and his imprisonment. He goes to the magistrate who had first sentenced him, to lodge a formal charge of murder against Falkland. The magistrate declines to hear the charge, and tries to expostulate with him; but the accuser is adamant; he will risk everything—even the chance of his own death—upon this throw of the die, and the magistrate is obliged to issue a summons for Falkland's appearance.

The final scene is all but incredible. When Williams confronts his old accuser in court, his courage and his desire for vindication melt within him.

> I can conceive of no shock greater than that I received from the sight of Mr. Falkland. His appearance on the last occasion on which we met had been haggard, ghost-like, and wild, energy in his gestures, and frenzy in his aspect. It was now the appearance of a corpse. He was brought in a chair, unable to stand, fatigued and almost destroyed by the journey he had just taken. His visage was colourless; his limbs destitute of motion, almost of life. His head reclined upon his bosom, except that now and then he lifted it up, and opened his eyes with a languid glance; immediately after which he sunk back into his former apparent insensibility. He seemed not to have three hours to live. He had kept his chamber for several weeks; but the summons of the magistrate had been delivered to him at his bed-side, his orders respecting letters and written papers being so peremptory that no one dared to disobey them.

Falkland, Williams sees, has been brought to this state by his own inward torture. But Williams is called upon to press his accusation. Against his sympathies, even against his will, Williams reviews Falkland's conduct. But he concludes his statement with :

> "I have told a plain and unadulterated tale. I came hither to curse, but I remain to bless. I came to accuse, but am compelled to applaud. I proclaim to all the world, that Mr. Falkland is a man worthy of affection and kindness, and that I am myself the basest and most odious of mankind! Never will I forgive myself the iniquity of this day. The memory will always haunt me, and embitter every hour of my existence. In thus acting, I have been a murderer—a cool, deliberate, unfeeling murderer.—I have said what my accursed precipitation has obliged me to say. Do with me as you please! I ask no favour. Death would be a kindness, compared to what I feel!"

The effect upon Falkland is equally unexpected, and even equally bizarre.

> When I expressed the anguish of my mind, he seemed at first startled and alarmed, lest this should be a new expedient to gain credit to my tale. His indignation against me was great for having

retained all my resentment towards him, thus, as it might be, to the last hour of his existence. It was increased when he discovered me, as he supposed, using a pretence of liberality and sentiment to give new edge to my hostility. But as I went on, he could no longer resist. He saw my sincerity; he was penetrated with my grief and compunction. He rose from his seat, supported by the attendants, and—to my infinite astonishment—threw himself into my arms.

"Williams," said he, "you have conquered! I see too late the greatness and elevation of your mind. I confess that it is to my fault, and not yours, that it is to the excess of jealousy, that was ever burning in my bosom, that I owe my ruin. I could have resisted any plan of malicious accusation you might have brought against me. But I see that the artless and manly story you have told has carried conviction to every hearer. All my prospects are concluded. All that I most ardently desired is forever frustrated. I have spent a life of the basest cruelty to cover one act of momentary vice and to protect myself against the prejudices of my species. I stand now completely detected. My name will be consecrated to infamy, while your heroism, your patience, and your virtues will be forever admired. You have inflicted on me the most fatal of all mischiefs, but I bless the hand that wounds me. And now"—turning to the magistrate—"and now, do with me as you please. I am prepared to suffer all the vengeance of the law. You cannot inflict on me more than I deserve."

Falkland dies, worn out by his self-torment, shortly after the conclusion of the trial.

Why this tame and sentimental ending to a story weighted down with passion? The answer is found in Godwin's equitable nature and his strong convictions. Both Falkland and Williams, he proposes, are victims of the legal system; Falkland also the victim of false standards of aristocratic honor. In *Political Justice* Godwin had already taken the position that law is itself a fetter upon liberty, since it cannot be administered in the spirit of humanity, but only through the weaknesses and class interests of time-servers and corrupt instruments of privilege. In this sense, *Caleb Williams* is obviously a sort of appendix to the doctrine of *Political Justice*.

St. Leon, Godwin's next novel, is developed upon two long familiar themes—the elixir of life and the philospher's stone. The mere statement of that fact implies the point of view of the story—that immortality is no blessing, and that great wealth is not an unmixed blessing. St. Leon himself, like Caleb Williams a hero without much heroism, has wasted a patrimony and learned that bad luck can intensify the effects of bad management. When, in his despair for his dependent family, he is persuaded to accept the doubtful gifts of immortality and immeasurable wealth, his use of the gifts, in spite of his benevolent intentions, leads to lasting disaster, alienating him at last from all human associations and sympathy—even to the contempt of the most cherished members of his family.

One major episode, however, puts power into an otherwise rambling and repetitious tale. That is, St. Leon's imprisonment and trial by the Spanish Inquisition. It is a moving passage, the more striking because it is in fact a travesty upon English law, the English courts of justice, and the English prison system; in particular, the notorious abuses of police power and judicial inquiry in the proceedings of 1794 against Holcroft and his friends.

Fleetwood, or The New Man of Feeling (1805) appeared in the interval between Jane Austen's (or rather, her father's) first efforts to find a publisher and the appearance of *Sense and Sensibility* years later. So it barely falls within our area of discussion. Like its two predecessors, it is put together haphazardly. There is, we have already seen, no canon of unity or coherency in the novel; yet we recognize readily enough one which suffers from diffuseness or inconsecutiveness. *Fleetwood* presents three loosely articulated episodes, the first and third depicting two quite distinct passages in the life of the principal, and the second a prolonged excursion into the life of his benefactor.

The hero is introduced to us as a young child, a fascinated pupil of nature. The mood of the opening pages recalls nothing so much as Wordsworth's *Tintern Abbey*. The emotional strength, even beauty, of these pages far surpasses the formalized description of scenery and its effects that we find in even the best of the earlier romantic fictions. When in the course of time the young man is sent to Oxford, all this is changed.* Fleetwood falls into evil ways, not because he has a relish for dissipation, but because his vanity impels him to adopt the life of the place and the manners of his companions. This episode is followed by his father's death, a transient stage of remorse, and his departure for the Continent, where he sinks again into an aimless and dissolute life.

The end of Fleetwood's *Lehrjahre* is a meeting in Switzerland with an old friend of his father's, Mons. Ruffigny. His story fills the entire second quarter of the novel. It is poignant narrative, like all of Godwin's themes philosophically, or rather sociologically, loaded. Ruffigny recounts his experience among the children working twelve hours a day in the silk mills of Lyons. He escapes from this cruel apprenticeship, is tossed about in

---

*Godwin, like his friend Holcroft, speaks of the traditional universities with evident antipathy. His own education terminated with five years in a dissenting academy at Hoxton; but they made him a serious and accomplished scholar.

beggary in the streets of Paris before the Revolution, and is rescued and put on the road to wealth by Fleetwood's father.

With the grateful and kindly Ruffigny, Fleetwood returns to England, but they separate when Ruffigny discovers that Fleetwood has embarked upon a new liaison in London. The breakup of this arrangement is followed by Ruffigny's death, Fleetwood's repentance (a rather repetitious business), his entry into Parliament, his disgust with practical politics—which echoes Holcroft's presentment in *Hugh Trevor*—and final return to the Continent, in search of someone deserving to be made a friend, rather than a parasite upon his wealth and a companion in dissipation.

The concluding half of *Fleetwood* makes him acquainted with a Scotchman, Macneil, once a friend of Rousseau's, now married to a woman who has lived down a seduction and become a devoted and intelligent mother. Macneil turns out to be the proper physician for Fleetwood's ailment, which is no more nor less than the inevitable boredom of a prodigal and irresponsible life. After delays and heartsearchings, Fleetwood, now a man of forty, marries Macneil's youngest daughter, still in her teens. Disparity of years soon exposes disparity of interests, and these are accentuated by his wife's melancholy over the loss of her family at sea. Complication is clinched when Fleetwood generously adopts into his family two young half brothers. The first is a model of the gentle virtues; the other proceeds to reward Fleetwood by alienating his wife, cheating him out of his fortune, and finally attempting to murder him. Under this young Gifford's influence, Fleetwood is driven into a frantic and wholly unwarranted jealousy, and abandons and divorces an innocent wife. The details of discovery and reconciliation need not be gone into. Suffice it to say they are sufficiently faithful to the still popular romantic tradition.

We could afford to pass over this Othello-like narrative, with its happy ending, if it were not for one fact. Godwin's title for the book is, we remember, *Fleetwood, or the New Man of Feeling.* The echo of Mackenzie's title has its point. The *new* man of feeling is not to have his susceptibilities shared and his tears multiplied by an oversensitized reader. Fleetwood has lived on his emotions until they have exhausted his taste for life and destroyed his happiness. We have not only a new theme there, but a well conceived and well developed method. Mackenzie's naïve repetition of incident is displaced by a minute and penetrating study of the anatomy of obsessive feeling; in other words, an approach to the psychological fiction of Meredith and James two full generations later. Godwin had already attempted the study of the effect of a distorted passion upon morale, so also upon personality, in *Caleb Williams,* but with dramatic purpose rather than analytical. That achievement in *Fleetwood* was recognized and appreciated by a few of his friends, and by still fewer critics and reviewers. Shelley, always an admirer of Godwin's work, even when their personal relations were at their most tenuous, regarded *Fleetwood* as one of the great achievements in fiction. *Fleetwood* shared for some years with *Caleb Williams* and *St. Leon* a moderate popularity; but it was in fact the last of his novels to contribute importantly to his reputation, which was already on the decline when *Fleetwood* appeared.*

Godwin's analytical method was carried on later at long intervals in *Mandeville* (1817), *Cloudesley* (1830), and *Deloraine* (1833), but Jane Austen and Scott had by that time established their place, and the later novels could only be called failures. Yet not utter failures. Even admitting his penchant for melodrama, there is the stuff of a really first-rate story at least in *Fleetwood* and *Deloraine,* but spoiled by the effort to wring the last drop of emotion out of a situation by restatement, enlargement, sentimental emphasis, and tedious moralizing. We need do no more than note the later novels as possibilities for a reader disciplined in "skipping"; for they lie beyond the terminus of our study.

All of Godwin's major novels are written in the first person, perhaps a reflection of his own strong egotism. All of them, also, deal with negative morality, psychotic disturbance, or crime—a fact of interest in view of his perfectibilian, or even partially perfectibilian, views. But these morbid themes are not pursued merely for their drama, nor do they raise discord with his theories. For they all illustrate his conviction that man's character is determined by his circumstances. His principals are all, however good their natures, victims of some form of social constraint, perversion, or vice, which is in turn the product of institutionalism.

There have been preachers who were also novelists, preachers by profession such as Kingsley and Newman, and preachers by temperament such as Richardson and Holcroft. But it seems particularly unfortunate for Godwin—as a novelist—that his early career was in the pulpit. It developed a wordy propensity—for after all a sermon aims to enlarge the sense of a text of ten or a dozen words into a half-hour's discourse. To the novel, then, which he conceived first as a vehicle for political and social discussion, and only secondarily as a means of entertainment,† he brought a cultivated expansiveness which adds nothing to its missionary purpose and detracts seriously from its interest as a story. That was the judgment of the critics of his time, and the years have only emphasized it. Godwin's novels, even when they contain an acceptable story, portray

---

*Yet Burton Pollin, *op. cit.*, notes that *Caleb Williams* has been reprinted in over fifty new issues and translations.

†This statement conforms with his own statement of his aim in the cancelled preface to the first issue of *Caleb Williams*.

characters of some interest, and show high dramatic moments, are tedious. And unhappily his lavishness of mere words and often inflated rhetoric did not disappear as experience and the success of other writers accumulated. In fact, they became more wearisome as he persisted, although his audience was falling away before his eyes.

Godwin's closing days were, in the general view, a long story of deterioration in literary power, in reputation, and in character. Shelley, now Godwin's son-in-law, for he had married the one child, Mary, of Godwin's marriage with Mary Wollstonecraft, continued to worship Godwin for *Political Justice* and the earlier novels. But he also furnished the wherewithal for Godwin's actual subsistence; for Godwin had gone through bankruptcy, become a borrower, and fallen so hopelessly in debt to his friends that most of his old intimates dropped him. The three novels of his later years appeared at long intervals in the writing of children's books, compendiums, and other hack work. But his general decline never diminished his vanity nor his conviction that the world—which meant his family and friends—owed him a living for what he had long before accomplished.* These closing years were largely fruitless and pathetic. What he had achieved was finished before Jane Austen's star had risen; so we dismiss them with propriety as well as relief.

We have now to consider a woman whose conspicuous indiscretions and almost comic emotional defeats have all but buried the memory of thoughtful positions bravely taken and books—not always well written—with only somewhat less influence upon contemporary thought than, let us say, Tom Paine's and Godwin's.

Mary Wollstonecraft's "love-life" we can note and pass—her unhappy and quite unreciprocated adoration of the painter Henry Fuseli, followed by her desperate and finally betrayed attachment to an American adventurer, Gilbert Imlay, and her "irregular" connection and subsequent marriage to Godwin. It can simply be said that she was not, as her detractors represented her, a woman of reckless passions. She condemned marriage on rational grounds, and because she had seen in her mother's and her sister's marriages the devastating results of improvidence and abuse. That she was indifferent to notoriety simply ranks her with her companions in the cause of social, including sexual, emancipation. Her widely known *Vindication of the Rights of Woman,* a plea for educational opportunities for women, had appeared in 1792, before *Political Justice,* but it had not particularly interested Godwin. Indeed, his first impres-

---

*Basil Willey, *op. cit.,* makes the point that his dependence upon his friends was justified in his view on the ground that since one should share his surplus with those in need, not as an act of charity, but as a social debt, it was equally implied that the needy were justified in expecting that aid upon just that understanding.

sion of her was not favorable. She appropriated too much of a dinner-table conversation; and Godwin himself, like Johnson and Coleridge, enjoyed not only talking but being listened to. Godwin and Mary were married in 1797, after they had been living together for some time and Mary had become pregnant. They married without false understandings or illusions. They were both mature—he past forty, she in her late thirties; they reconciled their connection with their social philosophy; he loved her deeply, and he complied with her wish that they maintain, even after marriage, separate homes in order to lead their busy lives without intrusion upon each other. The marriage was short-lived, ending in Mary's death after the birth of a daughter within the year. It was a union of two forceful and assertive egos, but Godwin's record of it reveals a profound though not always unshadowed affection.

If Godwin was not by his natural gifts a great novelist, his wife was still less so. She was a publicist and a controversialist rather than a teller of stories.* A brief narrative, *Mary, a Fiction,* published in 1788, is a somber story of coercive marriage, unsanctioned love, exile, morbid illness (with more than a touch of the eighteenth century's sentimental interest in invalidism), the death of the lover by consumption, then the death of his uncontaminated mistress by sheer physical inanition, with a final note of hope that the two will be joined "where there is neither marriage nor giving in marriage." It is a story of youthfully idealized passion, but naïve and feeble in the extreme. Her *Original Stories from Real Life* (1788) were written for children, with the hard and distressingly adult didacticism that marked the children's stories of her time. An extrinsic interest attaches to them in the fact that the edition of 1791 contained the only published illustrations by William Blake to a work of fiction; and that implies at least their acquaintance, and in all probability some exchange of ideas between two apostles of social revolt.

The more mature *The Wrongs of Women, or Maria,* was left unfinished at her death, and published in 1798 by Godwin in his collection of her *Posthumous Works.* Even the first third of the novel, which was all she had finished, was unrevised. The remainder exists only in scraps, and finally mere notes, from which a reader may form a vague idea of her intention. As a social document in the dress of fiction, it has the single merit of taking up the woman's cause where Bage and Holcroft had left off.

---

*Mary Wollstonecraft Godwin (1759-1797). *Mary, a Fiction* (1788); *Original Stories from Real Life* (juvenile, 1788); *The Wrongs of Women, or Maria* (posthumously, 1798). Her influence as thinker and agitator has also its importance for the fiction of the period: *Thoughts on the Education of Daughters* (1787); *Vindication of the Rights of Men* (1790); a reply to Burke's *Reflections on the Revolution in France,* 1790, which also called forth Tom Paine's more notable *Rights of Man,* (1791-2); *Vindication of the Rights of Woman* (1792).

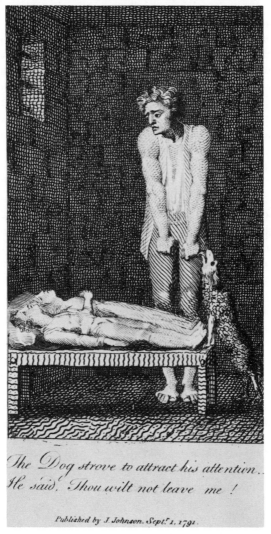

The Dog strove to attract his attention...
He said, Thou wilt not leave me!

Published by J. Johnson. Sept.ʳ 1, 1791.

Illustration designed and engraved by William Blake for the second edition of Mary Wollstonecraft's *Original Stories from Real Life,* 1791; Blake's only published design for a work of fiction.

The scene of the novel is a madhouse; the characters four—Maria, confined by her husband's knavery in order to secure her fortune; her husband, a conventional sampling of eighteenth-century male peccancy, to which is added the demoralizing effects of trade upon an avaricious character; Jemima, Maria's keeper and attendant; and Darnford, confined like Maria and for much the same atrocious reason. Environment is sketched in only faintly; the action is meager—for what can one do in a madhouse?—and three quarters of the narrative as it remains comprises the "little histories" of Maria, Jemima, and Darnford. Seduction has its day, or rather, its days, in the stories of the two women. Jemima's mother was seduced, Jemima has been seduced, and finally Maria is seduced by Darnford. The number of illegitimate children tallies with the number of seductions, and in each case with the final desertion of the trusting mother.

But the focus of the story is the married life of Maria, as written by herself and given to Darnford. Perhaps it adds little to the theme of woman's ignoble dependency, which had been explicit or implicit in earlier fictions. But it does state the situation in its worst possible aspects, with a husband who is purely a rascal. His final abomination is to offer his wife as a mistress to a friend from whom he wishes to borrow money. Maria's real case, however, is against society, which binds her irrevocably to a man who is sunk in depravity, egotism, and abuse of herself and her fortune, and who sharpens the pain of every new injustice by ridiculing her woman's nature and the helplessness to which laws and institutions have condemned her.

In its fragmentary state, how the novel ends would seem almost immaterial; and it is, as a matter of fact, quite undetermined. Godwin prints two contemplated endings. One was Maria's suicide when she finds herself pregnant and abandoned by Darnford. The other was purposed suicide averted by the discovery that the one child of her marriage, whom she had thought dead, still lives and can have a mother's care. "I will live for my child," Maria declares, a sound sentiment, though smacking of the cliché.

The urgency of the theme is indisputable; but the language of fiction, regrettably, was not Mary Wollstonecraft's language. The story had been under her hand for some time before Godwin published its fragments, and it may be doubted whether any possible ending for it would have added to the force of Maria's own little history. The author herself suggested that the part she had finished called for "rearrangement"; and it did. But its real defect is plodding prosiness. That, however, does not destroy Miss Wollstonecraft's importance as a pioneer in the fiction of purpose. As a promulgator of social enlightenment, more particularly as an early feminist, she occupies a more significant position, and in that connection we shall have occasion to return to her briefly when we come to the discussion of Jane Austen.

Though the four writers we have considered in the last two chapters were in fact revolutionaries, their views showed ponderable differences. All agreed that the underlying principle of a good social life should be reason, but their definitions and applications of reason were colored, as they are always bound to be, by their own circumstances and prepossessions. Bage was probably the one person in the group whose "reason" was untouched by personal bias and free from special pleading. Godwin's began in revolt from the revealed religion of which he had been a preacher, and throughout the course of his life underwent some surprising and contradictory changes—perhaps proof that his reason did him some real intellectual service. Mary Wollstonecraft's was infiltrated by strong emotions and was expressed as aggressive feminism. Holcroft's anticipated the general position of nineteenth-century philosophical anarchism—that society should be permitted to flourish upon the least possible amount of statutory law and officialdom.

But all agreed that man's natural propensities were good, and that he was spoiled by social institutions—a doctrine straight out of Rousseau. All deplored great accumulations of wealth and of political power. All favored a revision (not necessarily the destruction) of sexual sanctions and taboos.* Only Bage was in any accurate sense a Utopian, and his little Utopias would not have been recognized by Sir Thomas More.

Their power over their hour rested upon their hopeful interpretation of the spirit of the times. When Burke, Hannah More and Southey were imploring their countrymen to accept and respect things in England as they were, this stalwart four maintained that reckless bloodshed in France had not vitiated the idea of liberty. But they were a minority trying to outface the prejudices of a disillusioned and frightened England, and they wrote under the heavy disadvantage of continuous hostility from the conservative organs of opinion.

None of the four—Bage is the only possible exception—was born to the career of literature. Temperamentally they were preachers and teachers. Only Bage had a touch of literary charm in his fiction, and only Godwin contributed much of value for the matter and fashioning of fiction still to be. Neither Miss Wollstonecraft nor Holcroft ever gained the appreciation of readers of fiction. Bage and Goodwin continued to be read throughout the first third of the new century. But none of them survived the wave of

---

*Godwin in *Political Justice* declared marriage one of the most useless and tyrannical of social institutions, but later, in *St. Leon, Fleetwood, Mandeville,* and *Deloraine,* he accepted it as a benign and refining influence.

fiction from Miss Austen, Scott, Dickens, Thackeray, the Brontës, and many others. In the long view, their inexperience, their ineptitude, above all, their lack of the authentic gift, were enough to account for an always moderate and a swiftly declining repute.

CHAPTER XVIII

End of a Century

Principally Maria Edgeworth

AGNES REPPLIER once wrote an engaging little book, *A Happy Half-Century,* to the effect that the years from 1775 to 1825 were the most fortunate in our literary history for the moderately gifted writer. For there was never a period in which mediocrity had so splendid a chance of wearing the dress and colors of genius. She is speaking not only of literature in general, but of the fringes of literature—literary correspondence, gift books, children's reading, and other matters of social context. Her assertion is in no sense a general condemnation of the literature of the period; she tells us only that low-grade authorship was very low-grade, and that fiction shared in that ignoble distinction.

There was no dearth of fiction between the last of Smollett's novels and the first of Jane Austen's; for the spread of literacy had increased the demand for books, but upon a regrettably lower level of taste. Culture expands more slowly than literacy. Subscriptions to the private circulating libraries in the stationers' and book-sellers' shops in cities and fashionable towns kept the supply of new novels flowing; but these libraries were regarded, even by the writers of the time, as the repositories of silly and insignificant stories, if not actually dangerous to young and impressionable minds. "Good" novelists of the period disparaged what Maria Edgeworth called "common novels"; and while the sense of her phrase is vague, it probably applied less to the Gothics than to inept imitations of the "greats" of the mid-century.

Prose fiction was produced in such quantity in the latter half of the century that following its history would involve a meaningless pursuit of names, some of them conspicuous in fashionable life, the Church, the theater, politics, and public scandal; others properly forgotten except by the antiquarian bookseller or the curious reader. But a name was not necessary to establish a writer of fiction. Hacks wrote under an assortment of pseudonyms for printer-publishers, who in turn lived upon the demand from circulating libraries. Novels fell from the press in such rapid succession that they might appear and be forgotten in a fortnight or two. When an issue of only five hundred copies was supposed to show a profit, almost anybody could get almost anything published.*

In spite of the low quality of the product, fiction in the latter half of the century showed both technical development and diversification; and that was not wholly due to the example of the more accomplished writers of the period. Before the word "novel" had come into general use in the modern sense, there had been no serious effort to determine what the novel was. But novelists themselves were thinking of a common denominator for their diverse output; in other words, thinking of "form." Ideas of form had by the end of the century actually settled down into vague conceptions of length, method, and serious purpose. We are little nearer a definition of the novel today. In fact, we see wider diversification today than in Miss Burney's time; for we have novels of thirty thousand words, and of a million; novels with two characters and with two hundred; novels with or without specific setting, philosophy, psychological or social bearing, internal consistency, time sequence, stylistic embellishment, syntax, or everyday grammar.

If by evolution we mean progressive experiment tending toward a normal and more or less permanent form, then there has been no true evolution in the history of the novel. In that sense, the novel, unlike the sonnet or the ode, is not susceptible to exact definition; and unlike a play or an essay, there are no governing conditions of presentation or publication that suggest length or definiteness of form.

At the end of the eighteenth century, however, we do find a more or less settled conception of the social area of the novel, of length, of breadth of treatment, and of vaguely observed unity. But it touched only one type of novel—the novel of manners—and it furnished no formula. But it determined roughly, and for a century to come, what readers might expect to find in a novel. As a matter of fact, the novelists of this period would probably have been more sensible of the limiting conditions of their performance than at any other time either earlier or later.

There were many writers over this half-century who either for their command of the form of the novel, or for what they contributed to the flow of ideas in their time, must interest the serious student. But it is beside our purpose to accumulate names of the third, fourth, and fifth orders.

---

*On this question of the causes and history of the deterioration of popular taste, Mrs. Q. D. Leavis's *Fiction and the Reading Public* is the best source of information and opinion. More compactly, Chapter II of Ian Watt's *The Rise of the Novel* covers the matter for the first half of the century, and the opening chapters of Miss J. M. S. Tompkins's *Popular Novel in England, 1770-1800* for the later years.

There is, as an instance, the busy Charlotte Smith, who, after her separation from her husband—and she was married at fifteen, largely to retrieve her father's wasted fortune—made her living during the last twenty years of the century from still readable novels that were specially sensitive to the changes in contemporary thought. She was not without invention, but in every aspect of her performance there was a novelist or two who could do better. Her *Old Manor House* (1793) anticipates mildly some of Mrs. Radcliffe's effects, notably landscape, and is probably her most rewarding work. In *Emmeline* (1788) and *Desmond* (1792) she moves with the liberative feminism of her time. *The Wanderings of Warwick* (1794), a sequel to the *Old Manor House,* contains a poignant episode on slavery in the British West Indies. In *Marchmont* (1796) she supports Godwin's attack upon legal abuses and the brutalities of the prison system. *The Young Philosopher* (1798) borrows Bage's theme of the European youth who learns humanitarian principles among the American Indians (for whom she had already spoken a kind word in the *Old Manor House*). These interests reflect an alert as well as a humane mind; but no one who has read Mrs. Smith's novels is likely to think of her as more than a respectable bread-and-butter novelist with an appraising eye for literary vogue.*

These closing years of our century brought to something like maturity the historical novel. Historical setting was far from new in fiction, going back indeed, though quite unreliably, to the medieval romances. I confess an aversion to (or "from" if you prefer) the historical novel. My distaste is in the first place that I prefer my history and my fiction in separate compartments. Further, I respect the academic objection to it—that so far as it is inventive, it is not history; and so far as it is history, it is not fiction. There are, it must be conceded, wide differences in the liberties taken with the historical component.

In so-called historical fiction before 1800 there is no problem at all of faithfulness to the record. It is fiction; and it is not history. The first reputed historical novel of the period, Thomas Leland's *Longsword* (1762), a tale of the time of Henry III, is confusion itself so far as its historical characters are concerned; and as fiction, it is insufferably dull. Furthermore, its priority is asserted only because it shows something of the developed form of the novel; for historical characters had been brought

---

*On the other side of the question of Mrs. Smith's interest as well as importance, Miss Tompkins (*op. cit., passim*) deals explicitly with her formative influence in almost every phase of then current fiction. The topical plan of Miss Tomkpins' work precludes her treating Mrs. Smith at length as a subject, but her comments add up, I think, to a better opinion of her novels than I have ventured. Florence M. A. Hilbish's *Charlotte Smith, Poet and Novelist* (1941) discusses her place and achievement fairly and interestingly.

into less completely formulated fiction by Nashe and Deloney in the Elizabethan period.

What is generally accepted as the first historical novel in the modern temper is Sophia Lee's *The Recess* (1785), which was highly thought of in its day. Its historicity is, however, far from unimpeachable. For Miss Lee is really not interested in history; she is romantically interested in Mary Stuart. To the ill-fated queen she generously presents two girl children through a secret marriage with the Duke of Norfolk, who of all the great Elizabethans is probably the most difficult to inflate to the dimensions of a hero. There is naturally, a handful of historic figures; Drake, Sidney, Leicester, and even Elizabeth herself, for whom Miss Lee, as a good Mariolater, has, and glories in having, a lively aversion.

In the management of her story, Miss Lee leans hard upon physical detail straight out of *The Castle of Otranto*—the discovery of an ancient manuscript purporting to give the source of her story, the trap door with its secret lock, the subterranean passage leading to the convent a half-mile distant (for the problem of earth disposal never bothered the romantics), and the moldering ruins, "the Recess," in which the two sisters not only find refuge but grow to maturity. But Miss Lee does better with scenery and atmospheric effects :

> A peal of thunder, which shook the ruins to their foundations, seemed to reprove his boldness. The livid lightning pervaded our dungeon through many a time-worn aperture. During every tremendous illumination I gazed awe-struck on the pallid face of my love; till, suddenly glancing around, I gave a cry which startled even myself— glowing, gasping, transported, yet still unable to speak, I sunk before my lord, and clasping both his hands, prest them to my heart, and lifted them with mine towards Heaven. . . . [She has discovered a sealed secret door in the recess]. In the corner, on the right hand, covered with lumber, placed long since on purpose, you will find a trap-door.

This shows improvement upon Walpole; and its effectiveness is tacitly acknowledged in the later Gothics and in the historical novels of Jane Porter and her sister Anna.

What is really wrong with Miss Lee's historical romance is that it is without historical perspective. Of the tensions of politics behind Elizabethan court life we get only a distorted echo, and almost nothing of its social setting. The interrelationships of her characters, whether historical or imaginary, involve the favor or the animosities of small people doing small things—not the quiet but deadly competition of ambitious people caught in the swirl of partly constructive and partly stupid statecraft. In particular, her two heroines, one of whom loses her mind through disappointed love for the canny Leicester, are just two eighteenth-century women, with eighteenth-century tempers and sensibilities, dropped into an environment that is Elizabethan only in name.

Jane Porter in her turn gave added respectability to the type by tempering imagination to the demands of the subject. *Thaddeus of Warsaw* (1803), and still more, *Scottish Chiefs* (1810), retained a certain popularity almost through the nineteenth century. Both preceded Scott's *Waverley* (1814). While Miss Porter is more respectful of the written record than Miss Lee, yet she deals in *Scottish Chiefs* with a subject—Sir William Wallace—sufficiently wrapped in legend to encourage freedom in her interpretation of events and characters. Her Wallace is something too high-minded, and she is lavish of fine speeches with no warrant whatever in her sources, which are in themselves apocryphal. Most notably, Miss Porter sheds the fragrance of sentiment upon the masters of Scottish destiny who were allied with Wallace, and the odor of criminal enormity upon the adherents of Edward I—a not altogether accurate appraisal of clan politics of the time. Her women, who are far more conspicuous in Wallace's entourage than history presents them, are patterns of selfless female virtue—except for the Countess of Mar, stricken with unreturned love for Wallace and dedicated to a rejected woman's vengeance.

Yet *Scottish Chiefs*, in spite of length, strained rhetoric, and homemade history, can still be read—particularly, perhaps, because Miss Porter surpassed most of her contemporaries in the creation of atmosphere, both in the violently disturbed society she revivifies for us and in the wild outdoor life of the Highlands.

It would be an unkindness to the reader to pass in review writers once accepted, even esteemed, but now consigned to the lover levels of inexcellence.* We must go on to consider one more writer who had a peculiar power to convey in a few of her novels a sense of the life of the time, and whose sympathetic eye saw straight to the center of an isolated corner of contemporary life, peopled it with bewildering but altogether human

---

*For one who has the courage to pursue the novel of the latter half of the century into its darker corners Miss Tompkins' *Popular Novel in England, 1770-1800* is the indispensable lead. The difficulty is to find the novels themselves in any but the best-stocked institutional libraries. It might be added that most of the novels of the period worth reading were reprinted (unless they were still inaccessible because of copyright) in one or more of three comprehensive collections of late eighteenth-century fiction: *The Novelist's Magazine*, 20 volumes, 1780-1788; Anna Laetitia Barbauld's *British Novelists*, 50 volumes, 1810; and Ballantyne's *Novelist's Library* (with introductions by Sir Walter Scott), 10 volumes, 1821-1824. But these collections are themselves hard to locate, and the copyright difficulty explains inadequate representation of authors as deserving as Mrs. Smith and Miss Lee.

beings, picked up and fused its scraps of country lore, extracted its curious social ethos, and naturally, and so all but unconsciously, produced one of the greatest—perhaps the greatest—piece of descriptive realism of her century. The young lady was Maria Edgeworth, her book *Castle Rackrent,* a story of Irish landlordism in the grim closing years of the century. She was not without literary experience; for she had already written children's stories under the domineering eye of a self-important father.* Happily, he was not about the house when Maria was accumulating the material for *Castle Rackrent* and writing it. So it is her single work of fiction written before her father's death that is known to be free from his pedantic corrections. She was to live many years more, to write a handful of presentable but oppressively didactic novels and tales, but never again to deal so exquisitely with the lives of insignificant but exhilarating people.

The effects of this father-daughter relation have been variously gauged by her biographers and critics. Too little is known of it beyond the fact that her opinion of her father was almost idolatrous, and that she cheerfully, and probably thankfully, accepted all he had to offer. Byron records in his diary a meeting with the two at dinner in 1813 :

> Everyone cared more about *her.* She was a nice, unassuming Jeanie-Deans-looking body—and if not handsome, certainly not ill-looking. Her conversation was as quiet as herself; no one would have guessed she could write her name. Whereas her father talked, not as if he could write nothing else, but as if nothing else were worth writing.

Probably her father's influence as editor with full powers was less hurtful than the stamp upon her mind of his authority as what we should call today an "Educationist"—that is, a promotor of pedagogical notions for which he demanded the solemn respect due to demonstrable truth. His personal hobby as an Educationist was utilitarian : nothing addressed to the mind should be without its firmly impressed and fully elucidated moral lesson. Except in *Castle Rackrent,* didactic purpose oozed from all Miss Edgeworth's fiction. Latterly, her medium was fashionable life. In that glittering setting she places hardy apostles of "integrity" and "prudence" —two favored, perhaps abused, words in her ethical vocabulary. But firm as her characters are in their convictions, and impeccable in their social demeanor, they are relentless promulgators of their own virtues, tyrannically because unvaryingly right, and offensively modest.

Of all her fiction, *Castle Rackrent* alone is a work of the free spirit,

---

*Maria Edgeworth (1767-1849). *Castle Rackrent,* (1800), *Belinda* (1801). *A Modern Griselda* (1804). *Leonora* (1806). *Tales of Fashionable Life* (including *The Absentee* and *Ennui,* 1812), *Patronage* (1814) and other novels down to 1834.

undampened by sententiousness and unspoiled by her father's officiousness. It is so very good that there is the best of reason to lament that she was never again tempted (or perhaps allowed) to write herself out. The charm of the work depends upon its temper—benevolent without sentimentalism, satiric without contempt. And its fidelity is the product of her intimacy with every phase of Irish country life; for from her fifteenth year she had lived in the midst of it with her family on the family estate at Edgeworthtown. Its order is inherent in the unreflective memories of the old servant who has his tale to tell. There is no "preparation." The opening breaks on the reader like a sunrise, and its movement is simply the high flood of talk.

Having, out of friendship for the family, upon whose estate, praised be Heaven! I and mine have lived rent-free time out of mind, voluntarily undertaken to publish the *Memoirs of the Rackrent Family*, I think it my duty to say a few words, in the first place, concerning myself. My real name is Thady Quirk, though in the family I have always been known by no other than "Honest Thady"; afterward, in the time of Sir Murtagh, deceased, I remember to hear them calling me "Old Thady," and now I've come to "Poor Thady"; for I wear a long great-coat winter and summer, which is very handy, as I never put my arms into the sleeves; they are as good as new, though come Hollandtide next I've had it these seven years; it holds on by a single button round my neck, cloak fashion. . . .

Now it was that the world was to see what was in Sir Patrick. On coming into the estate, he gave the finest entertainment ever was heard of in the country; not a man could stand after supper but Sir Patrick himself, who could sit out the best man in Ireland, let alone the three kingdoms itself. He had his house, from one year's end to another, as full of company as ever it could hold, and fuller; for rather than be left out of the parties at Castle Rackrent, many gentlemen, and those men of the first consequence and landed estates in the country—such as the O'Neills of Ballynagrotty, and the Moneygawls of Mount Juliet's Town, and O'Shannons of New Town Tullyhog—made it their choice, often and often, when there was no room to be had for love nor money, in long winter nights, to sleep in the chicken-house, which Sir Patrick had fitted up for the purpose of accommodating his friends and the public in general, who honored him with their company unexpectedly at Castle Rackrent; and this went on I can't tell you how long. The whole country rang with his praises. . . .

However, my lady was very charitable in her own way. She had a charity school for poor children, where they were taught to read and write gratis, and where they were kept well to spinning gratis for my lady in return; for she had always heaps of duty yarn from the tenants, and got all her household linen out of the estate from first to last; for after the spinning, the weavers on the estate took it in hand for nothing, because of the looms my lady's interest could get from the Linen Board to distribute gratis. Then there was a bleach-yard near us, and the tenant dare refuse my lady nothing, for fear of a law-suit Sir Murtagh kept hanging over him about the water-course. With these ways of managing, 'tis surprising how cheap my lady got things done, and how proud she was of it. . . .

Another time, in the winter, and on a desperate cold day, there was no turf in the parlor and above stairs, and scarce enough for the cook in the kitchen. The little gossoon was sent off to the neighbors to see and beg and borrow some, but none could he bring back with him for love or money, so, as needs must, we were forced to trouble Sir Condy—"Well, and if there's no turf to be had in the town or country, why, what signifies talking any more about it; can't you go and cut down a tree?

"Which tree, please your honor?" I made bold to say.

"Any tree at all that's good to burn," said Sir Condy; "send off smart and get one down and the fires lighted before my lady gets up to breakfast, or the house will be too hot to hold us." . . .

And the next morning it came into my head to go, unknown to anybody, with my master's compliments, round to many of the gentlemen's houses where he and my lady used to visit, and people that I knew were his great friends, and would go to Cork to serve him any day in the year, and I made bold to try to borrow a trifle of cash from them. They all treated me very civil for the most part, and asked a great many questions very kind about my lady and Sir Condy and all the family, and were greatly surprised to learn from me Castle Rackrent was sold, and my master at the lodge for health; and they all pitied him greatly, and he got their good wishes, if that would do; but money was a thing they unfortunately had not any of them at this time to spare. I had my journey for my pains, and I, not used to walking, nor supple, as formerly, was greatly tired, but had the satisfaction of telling my master when I got to the Lodge all the civil things said by high and low.

Few stories are so crowded with telling incident, often extravagant beyond words, but marked with truth, and often footnoted as to their actuality within the author's own experience or knowledge. The theme is the unheeded tragedy of a family's decay and ruin. Almost every sentence is pregnant with the irony of improvidence and irresponsibility. The buoyant loyalty of the teller of the tale is the loyalty of ignorance and sentimentality; and his hearty praise of his masters and their prodigal ways is implicit condemnation of an entire system.

Few writers have surpassed Miss Edgeworth, at least in this one particular story, in conveying the wholeness of a situation not by large and elaborate design, but by light brush-touches upon characters, customs, manners, thoughts and feelings, color, even landscape; nothing accented, yet all unfailingly clear and integral. Here it is in a passage in which Old Thady recounts Sir Kit's home-coming with the wife he had married to bolster the decrepit estate.

The very morning after they came home, however, I saw plain enough how things were between Sir Kit and my lady, though they were walking together arm in arm after breakfast, looking at the new building and the improvements.

"Old Thady," said my master, just as he used to do, "how do you do?"

"Very well, I thank your honor's honor," said I; but I saw he was not well pleased, and my heart was in my mouth as I walked along after him.

"Is the large room damp, Thady?" said his honor.

"Oh, damp, your honor, how should it be but as dry as a bone?" says I, "after all the fires we have kept in it day and night? It's the barrack-room your honor's talking on."

"And what is a barrack-room, pray, my dear?" were the first words I ever heard out of my lady's lips.

"No matter, my dear," said he, and went on talking to me, ashamed-like I should witness her ignorance. To be sure, to hear her talk, one might have taken her for an innocent, for it was "What's this, Sir Kit?" and "What's that, Sir Kit?" all the way we went. To be sure, Sir Kit had enough to do to answer her.

"And what do you call that, Sir Kit?" said she; "that—that looks like a pile of black bricks, pray, Sir Kit?"

"My turf-stack, my dear," said my master, and bit his lip.

Where have you lived, my lady, all of your life, not to know a turf-stack when you see it? thought I; but I said nothing. Then, by-and-by, she takes out her glass, and begins spying over the country.

"And what's all that black swamp out yonder, Sir Kit?" says she.

"My bog, my dear," says he, and went on whistling.

"It's a very ugly prospect, my dear," says she.

"You don't see it, my dear," says he; "for we've planted it out; when the trees grow up in the summer-time—"says he.

"Where are the trees," said she, "my dear?" still looking through her glass.

"You are blind, my dear," says he; "what are these under your eyes"?

"These shrubs," said she.

"Trees," said he.

"Maybe they are what you call trees in Ireland, my dear," said she; "but they are not a yard high, are they?"

"They were planted out but last year, my lady," says I, to soften matters between them, for I saw she was going the way to make his honor mad with her; "they are very well grown for their age, and you'll not see the bog of Allyballycarricko'shaughlin at-all-at-all through the screen, when once the leaves come out. But, my lady, you must not quarrel with any part or parcel of Allyballycarricko'-shaughlin, for you don't know how many hundred years that same bit of bog has been in the family; we would not part with the bog of Allyballycarricko'shaughlin upon no account at all; it cost the late Sir Murtagh two hundred good pounds to defend his title to it and boundaries against the O'Learys, who cut a road through it."

Now one would have thought this would have been hint enough for my lady, but she fell to laughing like one out of their right mind, and made me say the name of the bog over, for her to get it by heart, a dozen times; then she must ask me how to spell it, and what was the meaning of it in English—Sir Kit standing by whistling all the while. I verily believe she laid the cornerstone of all her future misfortunes at that very instant; but I said no more, only looked at Sir Kit.

There were no balls, no dinners, no doings; the country was all disappointed—Sir Kit's gentleman said in a whisper to me, it was all my lady's own fault, because she was so obstinate about the cross.

"What cross?" says I; "is it about her being a heretic?"

"Oh, no such matter," says he; "my master does not mind her heresies, but her diamond cross—it's worth I can't tell you how much, and she has thousands of English pounds concealed in diamonds about her, which she as good as promised to give up to my master before he married; but now she won't part with any of them, and she must take the consequences."

The tiff turns out to be the opening scene of an act of almost incredible cruelty—the imprisonment of a wife in her own chamber for almost seven years, by a husband who cannot coerce her into surrendering her possessions to supply his prodigality.

Belinda, published in 1801, on the tide of popularity of *Castle Rackrent,* is today no more than a readable novel. Its social milieu, its characters, and its literary manner owe something to Fanny Burney. But as a novelist of manners Miss Edgeworth is something less than a Burney.

The heroine is sent up to London by an aunt notorious as a matchmaker, to be placed under the chaperonage of Lady Delacour, a brilliant woman of the world whose badinage turns out shortly to be a screen for her suffering from a malignant illness. Belinda, more or less forced into the position of a matrimonial adventuress, is in fact a girl of rigid principles. Two eligibles present themselves, both seemingly meritorious, and possessed of handsome fortunes. The story is concerned with their chances and mischances as suitors; for Belinda, almost from the beginning, is plainly in a position to make her own choice. Both Lady Delacour and Lady Anne Percival, Lady Delacour's opposite in every way, try to influence that choice, but Belinda's unfailing good judgment guides her heart to the right decision despite the worldly wisdom of her counselors. A complication with some importance for the suspense of the story is that the successful lover, Clarence Hervey, has involved himself in a visionary plan to rear and educate a young girl in order to marry her when she reaches marriageable age. The situation is said to have been actually paralleled in the experience of one of father Edgeworth's intimates. (Was this one of the bright ideas of the old Educationist himself?) What saves Hervey is that the young lady falls in love with the picture of a youthful naval officer, whose appearance in full life before the end of the story resolves the difficulty.

The salient defect of *Belinda*, however, is the complete lack of elasticity in the heroine's character. Described as everything sweet and lovable, she is really a good deal of a prude, a somewhat passionless calculator, and the complacent admirer of her own perfections. Worst of all, she has the insufferable habit of squeezing the last drop of moral juice out of situations which seem to reveal quite clearly their moral import. In this disagreeable habit she is solemnly abetted by the little group of consciously right-thinking young men who attend her. We give an instance. Sir Charles Percival, one of Miss Edgeworth's model husbands, is telling the story of the frivolous Miss Moreton, concluding with these sentences :

"I am inclined, in spite of scandal, to think the poor girl was only imprudent. At all events, she repents her folly too late. She has now no friend on earth but Mrs. Freke, who is, in fact, her worst enemy, and who tyrannizes over her without mercy. Imagine what it is to be the butt of a buffoon!"

"What a lesson to young ladies in the choice of female friends!" said Belinda. "But had Miss Moreton no relations who could interfere to get her out of Mrs. Freke's hands?"

Mr. Percival goes on to explain that a brother had attempted to intervene, but Mrs. Freke had been so indignant at his "insolence" that she took effective steps—he was a clergyman—to deprive him of a living he had been led to expect.

"That was the story," said Mr. Vincent, "that effectually changed my opinion of [Mrs. Freke]. Till I heard it, I always looked upon her as one of those thoughtless, good-natured people who as the common saying is, do nobody any harm but themselves."

"It is difficult in society," said Mr. Percival, "especially for women, to do harm to themselves without doing harm to others. They may begin in frolic, but they must end in malice. They defy the world—the world in turn excommunicates them—The female outlaws become desparate, and make it the business and pride of their lives to disturb the peace of their sober neighbors. Women who have lowered themselves in the public opinion cannot rest without attempting to bring others to their own level."

"Mrs. Freke, notwithstanding the blustering merriment she affects, is obviously unhappy," said Belinda; "and since we cannot do her any good, either by our blame or our pity, we had better think of something else."

Two of Miss Edgeworth's shorter novels, both included in the *Tales of Fashionable Life,* reintroduce the Irish scenes of *Castle Rackrent.* They have a common theme—the impoverishment of a great Irish estate to meet the extravagant cost of breaking into London society; this followed by a return to the patriarchal estate, and the setting up of competent management to restore its resources.

Ennui, the first of the *Tales of Fashionable Life,* pictures a young man bred in the lap of luxury who becomes bored to despair by dissipation. Under a promise to see some day the Irish estate which has supported his prodigality, he goes to Ireland, learns slowly the business of estate management, despite the suspicions and ill will of neighbors and tenants, only to discover that he is a changeling, without the shadow of legitimate title to the properties. He is above concealing his false position, which in the circumstances would be easy. What follows (apart from the inevitable love story) is the resolution to find happiness and independence in a life of well-directed labor as a barrister. The story might carry political and social significance, were it not for its manifest inferiority to both *Castle Rackrent* and *The Absentee,* the latter the best remembered of Miss Edgeworth's fictions after *Castle Rackrent.*

Even *The Absentee,* however, lacks the sparkle of its predecessor. But it has, what *Rackrent* has not, the dimensions and program of a novel, and it is on the whole the most enduringly satisfactory novel that Miss Edgeworth has left us. It really belongs to her earlier period, for it was finished in play form in 1804, but its appearance was delayed until it was used to fill out the last volume of the *Tales of Fashionable Life.*

The complication is the belief that the heroine is illegitimate—as we have seen in *Evelina,* a matter sufficiently grave to bar her marriage to a discriminating man of rank. The essential story, however, is that of Lord Clonbrony, and even more particularly his wife, who are rapidly wasting a patrimony upon the entertainment of London society, which laughs at them behind their backs and even openly flouts them. Lord Colambre, their son—the lover of the heroine, Grace Nugent—fresh from the university, deeply attached to his parents, and indignant at their humiliation by fashionable society, decides to look into the situation at the home estate, travels incognito to Ireland, finds that his family is being grossly cheated by the agent for the estate, and the tenants heartlessly exploited, and returns to London in time to avert his father's bankruptcy and to end the attempt to break into society.

On familiar ground, Miss Edgeworth does full justice to the Irish scene and the deplorable economic situation. *The Absentee* is a serious indictment, pressed with all her moral earnestness. Again the heroine is too fine, too perfectly poised in both affection and prudence, to be enjoyable. But this fault we must expect to find in Miss Edgeworth's later works. Her perfectibilian convictions (the elder Edgeworth was a sworn Rousseauian) draw her constantly into the creation of exemplary characters in whose veins runs the ichor of exalted and conscious virtue—but like the ichor of the ancient gods, deficient in red corpuscles.

In spite of the stiffness of her moral attitudes, realistic processes matured under Miss Edgeworth's hands. Her description of character is clear and explicit, even when not deeply touched by imagination. Development of her characters in personality and social intelligence is equally clear, though as a rule annoyingly didactic. Yet there are moments in which we hear an anticipation of the voice of Miss Austen. Here is a nicely balanced bit of sympathetic-satiric characterization, with something of the verve that animates the familiar openings of *Northanger Abbey* and *Emma*. It is from *Belinda*.

Clarence Hervey might have been more than a pleasant young man if he had not been smitten with the desire of being the most admired person in all companies. He had been early flattered with the idea that he was a man of genius; and he imagined that as such he was entitled to be imprudent, wild, and eccentric. He affected singularity in order to establish his claims to genius. He had considerable literary talents, by which he was distinguished at Oxford; but he was so dreadfully afraid of passing for a pedant that when he came into the company of the idle and the ignorant he pretended to disdain every species of knowledge. His chameleon character seemed to vary in different lights, and according to the different situations in which he happened to be placed. He could be all things to all men—and to all women.—He was supposed to be a favorite with the fair sex, and of all his various excellences and defects, there was none on which he valued himself so much as on his gallantry. He was not profligate; he had a strong sense of humor and quick feelings of humanity; but he was so easily led, or rather, so easily excited by his companions, and his companions were now of such a sort, that it was probable he would soon become vicious.

Yes, it lacks the magic of Miss Austen's humor, her felicitous understatement, her feeling for style, and most of all, perhaps, her flexible sentences. Yet it has analytical ease and precision. There is something added here to the resources of the writer of fiction.

And we add an agreeable foretaste of those great moments in which a character of Jane Austen's is arrested in her satisfied view of herself, to look inward and reappraise. The source is again *Belinda*.

The reflections, however, which Miss Portman made upon the miserable life this ill-matched couple led together did not incline her in favor of marriage in general; great talents on one side and good nature on the other had in this instance tended to make each party unhappy. Matches of interest, convenience, and vanity, she was convinced, diminished instead of increasing happiness. Of domestic felicity she had never, except during her childhood, seen examples. She had, indeed, heard from Dr. X— descriptions of the happy family of Lady Anne Percival, but she feared to indulge the romantic hope of ever being loved by a man of superior genius and virtue, with a temper and manners suited to her taste. The only person she had seen who at all answered this description was Mr. Hervey, and it was firmly fixed in her mind that he was not a marrying man, and consequently, not a man of whom any prudent woman would suffer herself to think with partiality. She could not doubt that he liked her society and conversation; his manner had sometimes expressed more than cold esteem. Lady Delacour had assured her that it expressed love; but Lady Delacour was an imprudent woman in her own conduct, and not scrupulous as to that of others. Belinda was not guided by *her* opinions of propriety, and now that her ladyship was confined to her bed, and not in a condition to give her either advice or protection, she felt that it was peculiarly incumbent on her to guard not only her conduct from reproach, but her heart from the hopeless misery of an ill-placed attachment. She examined herself with firm impartiality; she recollected the excessive pain she had endured when she first heard Clarence Hervey say that Belinda Portman was a compound of art and affectation; but this, she thought, was only the pain of offended pride—of proper pride. She recollected the extreme anxiety she had felt, even within the last four and twenty hours, concerning the opinion which he might form of the transaction about the key of the boudoir—but this anxiety she justified to herself. It was due, she thought, to her reputation; it would have been inconsistent with female delicacy to have been indifferent about the suspicions that necessarily arose from the circumstances in which she was placed.

The paragraph conveys no more psychological truth than we might expect upon the lower levels of ethical consciousness. But there is both psychological approach and method, certainly beyond anything we find in Miss Edgeworth's contemporaries, with the exceptions due Miss Burney and Godwin.

Perhaps the thing most to be regretted in Miss Edgeworth's career is her failure to make the most of an undeniable gift of irony, particularly in her pictures of married life. It is not especially evident in her better known novels—not even in the Delacour episodes in *Belinda,* where it could have been used advantageously. It is highly effective, however, in some of her slighter stories. *The Modern Griselda* is an ironic title for probably the best of them; for this Griselda is simply a thoroughly spoiled child who must have her whims and her "sensibility" indulged by an affectionate husband, himself a model of patience. Temperamentally, Griselda might have been modeled after Lady Teazle, though it goes without saying that Miss Edgeworth has not the fine hand of Sheridan. The story ends in separation, a conclusion almost unheard of in the fiction of the time. In the short series of *Letters of Julia and Caroline,* a brisk satiric opening moves into more sober, and really more characteristic, treatment. Misunderstanding here, which ends in the wife's foolhardy elopement, is simply the result of a fashionable marriage embarked upon without either affection or shared interests. In both these stories there is facile handling of a theme that might have been treated with greatness by a greater mind. Still, there is importance in the fact that they were attuned to a changing sense of woman's social place and of husband-wife relationships, even though Miss Edgeworth's attitude is unmistakably the good old-fashioned one. One wonders where the middle-aged spinster picked up her experience of marital failures—certainly not within her own family—and also whether it was by the advice of her much married father that she was dissuaded from going on with these piquant little glimpses of marriage at its worst.

In spite of the closeness of the moral atmosphere in her fictions, Miss Edgeworth was widely read, and became in a small way a literary lioness. Her popularity can be seen in the returns from her works. In 1800 she was paid £100 for *Castle Rackrent,* rather better than the going price for short fictions from unproved writers. A year later she received £300 for *Belinda.* But *Patronage* brought her £2100 in 1815, at the very moment that Jane Austen was offered £450 for copyright to *three* novels—*Sense and Sensibility* and *Mansfield Park,* both previously published at her own expense, and *Emma,* as yet unpublished.

Probably what more than anything else accounted for Miss Edgeworth's popularity was the fact that she was a resolute uplifter. But it was not an altogether vain role. Her depiction of upper middle class and aristocratic society for lower middle class readers was in the best sense "improving"; for she nursed few illusions, yet could appraise fairly the upper-class virtues. She knew her times and she knew her people. And although her rather spinsterish prepossessions may amuse us today, we can scarcely ridicule her mild but convincing sincerity.

Maria Edgeworth survived Jane Austen by thirty-two years, and she managed to hold her audience almost down to the time of Dickens. Miss Austen names her with Fanny Burney as a writer of the first excellence. No doubt modern readers will smile at Miss Austen's superlatives. But the point here is not whether she overpraised her lesser contemporaries; it is that she recognized kindred spirits with something of her own grasp of life, and so absorbed, consciously or not, literary virtue from them.

It will not have gone unnoticed that in this conspectus of late eighteenth-century fiction women have taken an important, even a pre-eminent position. Miss Burney and Miss Edgeworth still hold a respected place, and writers like Charlotte Smith and Sophia Lee may be assigned by scholars a comfortable but transient place beside them. But many names are all but forgotten which in the opinion of the time had acknowledged status. Elizabeth Inchbald, Mary Robinson, Susanna Gunning, Regina Roche, Charlotte Lennox, Amelia Opie (all married at some time in their generally eventful lives), had for a time almost Miss Burney's importance; but the years have been unkind to them. There were men novelists too, as we have seen, but in the last quarter of the century the women novelists held the more conspicuous place.

A fact worth remarking is generally worth trying to explain. In this case, a substantial part of the explanation seems to be that women were rapidly becoming important; so it should not be surprising that their increasing participation and influence in the extra-domestic life of their time should be watched, justified, and pleaded by women rather than men. We can concede Bage's, Holcroft's, and Godwin's place in the "emancipation" of women without questioning the greater importance of women, because they *were* women, in forcing issues and promulgating influence.*

But even more important, for the novelist, than a change in political and legal status was its interaction with a change in woman's intellectual and social maturity. One cannot fail to recognize the transformation in the personal stature of women in the years between *Tom Jones* and *Pride and Prejudice*. It is not explained by woman's being able to demand greater recognition, but by her awareness of what she wanted recognized. In Sophia Western's time the great purpose of marriage was succinctly stated in the Book of Common Prayer. But Elizabeth Bennett could see,

---

*The matter is interestingly discussed at length in B. G. MacCarthy's *Women Writers; their contribution to the English novel, 1744-1818,* Dublin, 1947.

because she was qualified to see, a considerably broader purpose for her married life than the duly sanctioned right to bear some man's children and to approve his view, however benign, of her serviceable unimportance. Furthermore, Elizabeth's awareness of what she could expect to receive without having to claim it was not the product of the agitation of the Charlotte Smiths and the Mary Wollstonecrafts, but of the clearer covenant with society that may be read in the transition from Fanny Burney's *Evelina,* of 1778, to her *Wanderer,* a third of a century later. And the new understanding was not to be measured by the extension of Miss Burney's mental horizon (for her capacity for mental growth was not phenomenal), but by her rather puzzled awareness of change. For both Burney and Edgeworth the guarantee of woman's autonomy lay in her wise use of her personal attraction and influence as a woman. And while that realistic attitude might have been honored at almost any time in history as well as in the reign of George III, it could be argued in these later years upon broader grounds of privilege, as well as of education, social nurture, and public policy. In a word, women had become in later eighteenth-century fiction not objects but subjects of interest, for themselves and also for men. Fiction had had much to do not only with recording that change, but with furthering it.

CHAPTER XIX

And
Jane Austen

1   The Name and the Novels

IF WE turn back to our comparison of Miss Edgeworth's returns from her fiction with Miss Austen's,* we may draw two inferences. First, that in her own lifetime—she died in 1817—her popularity was not at all comparable to Miss Edgeworth's. There are other items of evidence of similar import. Sales of the original issues of her novels, which meant all the copies printed down to Bentley's collected edition of 1832, were evidently about four thousand for *Pride and Prejudice,* always the most popular, and only about two thousand for *Emma.*† This compares with ten thousand for Scott's *Waverley* in 1814, "within a few months of publication." Miss

---

*Jane Austen, 1775-1817. *Probable* dates of composition are given in order, with dates of publication in parentheses. "Elinor and Marianne," 1795, was the first draft of *Sense and Sensibility*, 1797 (1811); *Pride and Prejudice* (original title, "First Impressions"), 1796-7 (1813); *Northanger Abbey*, 1798, revised for publication, 1803 (1818); *Mansfield Park*, 1811-3 (1814); *Emma*, 1814-5 (1815); *Persuasion*, 1815-6 (posthumously, 1818, with *Northanger Abbey*). All the novels published during her lifetime were issued anonymously, and any or all of the earlier novels may have had extensive revision before publication. In addition, Miss Austen left three small manuscript volumes of "Juvenilia"; ten chapters of an unfinished novel, *The Watsons*, probably written about 1803 (1871); a short satirical sketch in letters, *Lady Susan*, of about the same period (1871); and a small portion of an unfinished last novel, *Sanditon*, written in 1817 (1925). It will be seen from the dates of publication given above that the "Juvenilia" and unfinished novels were withịeld from publication for many years after her death.

The concise and authoritative discussion of her life and writings is R. W. Chapman's *Jane Austen, Facts and Problems*. Two recent anthologies of criticism relating to her contain pertinent essays and extracts: *Jane Austen, a Collection of Critical Essays*, edited by Ian Watt, and *Discussions of Jane Austen*, edited by William Heath.

†R. W. Chapman, *Jane Austen, Facts and Problems*, 156-157.

Burney's *Wanderer,* published in the same year, for which she was to receive contingent royalties of £3,000, sold 3,600 copies within the first half-year, although it had been unfavorably reviewed. So Miss Austen's sales, and her profits, were almost pathetically modest, even for her time.

But our interest in her sales is not sentimental. They are significant because they tell us whether she was read; and obviously she was not. Our second conclusion from "the figures" is that her reputation grew gradually and slowly; for today she is with little doubt the most widely read of the pre-Victorian novelists, not even excepting Fielding—or Scott, whose reputation has declined as hers has risen.

Her early obscurity may be explained in part by her insistence upon her anonymity, even down to her death. Few outside of her family knew her as an author; and although there were recorded slips from that tight secrecy, it remained a fact that, unlike Scott, who peeked out from behind his anonymity, Miss Austen threw out no hints of her authorship and encouraged no guesses. Even Miss Edgeworth, her sister in art and something of a trader in literary gossip, who was sent copies of *Mansfield Park* and *Emma* as they came out, was apparently ignorant of the identity of the sender. She notes in a letter that *Emma* was sent her by "the authoress of *Pride and Prejudice.*" Reasons for that concealment have been mooted— personal shyness, perhaps the feeling not uncommon in her time, that novels were somewhat disreputable, and most probably, if we can judge from hints in her letters and the reminiscences of her family, her aversion from the public life that would have been forced upon her had she admitted her authorship. Perhaps all these reasons had weight.

But anonymity is not in itself enough to explain lack of recognition. Nor is the fact that there was not time enough in the six years from the publication of *Sense and Sensibility* to her death for her reputation to take root and grow. The cool reception of the four of her novels which came out before her death must be accounted for upon the probability that many of her contemporaries simply did not care for her. Many readers today do not. And disparagement, when it appears, cannot be brushed aside as unintelligent or tasteless; for it has been voiced by critics of discrimination.

Some of this criticism has been more devastating than scrupulous—for example, the remark attributed to Mark Twain that a library without a volume of Jane Austen must be a good library, even if it contained no other books. Some of it has been (to my own thinking) finicky or esoteric. Much of it has been marked by the ineliminable prejudices of sex. Women like Miss Austen because she is womanly. Males have been known to frown upon her because she is womanish—and that apart from the specific issues of sex, which she usually takes for granted or manages to side-step.

But the indifference of her contemporaries, at any rate, seems to show that after the simplicity and comfortable optimism of Miss Burney and Miss Edgeworth, Miss Austen's intellectual firmness and dry humor were strange and perhaps formidable. It may be thought even more confidently that her scorn of sentimentalism and headlong romance estranged readers who had reveled in the sentimental and the bizarre. But explained or unexplained, her failure to impress her own generation deeply must be accepted as a fact.

The dates of composition of Miss Austen's novels were given from memory in a note by her sister Cassandra, which gives the impression, rightly or wrongly, that the three earlier novels were finished before 1799, *Pride and Prejudice,* however, undergoing later "alterations and contractions"; and that the three later novels were written from 1811 to 1816 and published as they were completed. The almost inevitable impression from the bare facts as Cassandra presented them would be that Miss Austen had two brief periods of activity, from roughly 1795 to 1798, and from 1811 to 1816, with a long and completely unproductive interval between. Evidence that might affect that conclusion was given to the public belatedly and at long intervals, in her nephew J.E. Austen-Leigh's *Memoir* of his aunt (1870), in such of her letters as Cassandra herself had not destroyed, a substantial mass of "juvenilia," and three unfinished or unsatisfactory novels—in addition, of course, to items of external evidence.

There is substantial agreement today that Miss Austen's career cannot be summarized as a burst of youthful energy which produced three novels (*Sense and Sensibility, Pride and Prejudice,* and *Northanger Abbey*), then a lapse of a dozen years or so followed by three rapidly composed and mature novels (*Mansfield Park, Emma,* and *Persuasion*). The present critical consensus would have us believe, rather, that no novel of hers, with one exception to be noted, failed to be carefully studied and revised almost down to the final date of publication. The one novel that may not have been retouched in later years was *Northanger Abbey,* the manuscript of which was sold to a publisher in 1803, shelved by him until it was repurchased by her brother Henry, and finally published with *Persuasion* after her death. The facts seem to justify the presumption that she may have done no further work on *Northanger Abbey,* and even, perhaps, that she may not have wished to see it published.

We can proceed to look, then, at her career, not necessarily as two brief and intermitted flashes of activity, but as a continuity, beginning, in fact, far back in her early teens, without discernible literary aspirations, and proceeding, perhaps with some major interruptions, down to the time of her death.

Jane Austen's juvenilia have considerably more interest than is com-

monly to be found in precocious authorship. They were written principally to amuse her brothers and her sister. But unlike the Brontë children's
adolescent writings, they were not her part of a game in which all could
play. She was the entertainer; the others were the audience. Furthermore,
if they provided fun for her family, they provided still more for herself.
They were written in the pure spirit of fun; for they are, all except
Catherine, the longest, parodies upon the things they were all familiar
with. She had read, and had liked, not only the Burneys and the Edge-
worths but the Radcliffes. But her young mind had seen through and
beyond them. She knew even then things that they did not know, and she
found amusement, at once intelligent and tolerant, in their conventional-
ity, their commonplaceness, and their artificialities.

Probably these early writings were finished before the appearance of
Mrs. Radcliffe's *Udolpho* and *The Italian,* but she could have read her
three earlier romances; and we know that she had read in her green years
Charlotte Smith's *Orphan of the Castle,* a more or less Gothic extravagance, and others of Mrs. Smith's fictions. We also have it on the evidence
of the letters that "tales of terror," even quite inferior ones, were not unknown or unesteemed in the household of the Reverend George Austen,
her father.

Yet the strong features of Gothic romance (which she pokes fun at
later in *Northanger Abbey*) are less the object of ridicule in these earliest
pieces than the apparatus of romantic sentiment in the novels of manners.
There were dozens of this type to her purpose; but we find, particularly in
Love and Freindship (sic) passages in unmistakable parody of Fanny
Burney, good-natured but in their way critical—and she admired Miss
Burney. In the "letters" found in the copybooks there are amusing echoes
of Richardson, her opinion of whom seemed to be nicely balanced between
praise of his knowledge of the heart and distrust of his moral influence.

The score or more of these short pieces cannot be dated closely, but
from the few that she did date it is known that they went back at least as
far as June, 1790, when Jane was fourteen and a half. This is the date of
Love and Freindship. Some of the shorter pieces appear on the evidence
of temper and style to have been written even earlier.* *Love and Freindship* is probably the most familiar of the juvenilia. Its humor is girlish,
perhaps forced, as girlish humor can be forgiven for being. Yet although
young Miss Austen is taking off literary attitudinizing, she gives us also
surprising glimpses of the adult mind and emotions.

The "collection of letters" in the second volume of the manuscript
share the naiveté of *Love and Freindship,* and also its critical awareness :

---

*My own pronouncement, which I am willing to risk.

Lady Bridget came this morning, and with her, her sweet sister Miss Jane—. Although I have been acquainted with this charming Woman about fifteen Years, yet I never before observed how lovely she is. She is now about 35, in spite of sickness, sorrow, and Time is more blooming than I ever saw a Girl of 17. I was delighted with her, the moment she entered the house, she appeared equally pleased with me, attaching herself to me during the remainder of the day. There is something so sweet, so mild in her Countenance, that she seems more than Mortal. Her Conversation is as bewitching as her appearance; I could not help telling her how much she engaged my Admiration—"Oh! Miss Jane (said I)—and stopped from inability at the moment of expressing myself as I could wish—"Oh! Miss Jane— (I repeated)—I could not think of words to suit my feelings—She seemed to be waiting for my Speech—I was confused—distressed—my thoughts were bewildered—and I could only add "How do you do?" She saw and felt for my embarrassment and with admirable presence of mind relieved me from it by saying—"My dear Sophia be not uneasy at having exposed yourself—I will turn the conversation without appearing to notice it." Oh! how I loved her for her kindness! "Do your ride as much as you used to do?" said she—"I am advised to ride by my Physician. We have delightful Rides around us. I have a charming horse, am uncommonly fond of the Amusement, replied I quite recovered from my Confusion, in short I ride a great deal." "You are in the right, my Love," said she. Then repeating the following line which was an extempore equally adapted to recommend both Riding and Candour—

"Ride where you may, Be Candid where You can,"* she added, "I rode once, but it is many years ago"—She spoke this in so low and tremulous a Voice, that I was silent—Struck with her Manner of speaking I could make no reply. "I have not ridden," continued she fixing her Eyes upon my face, "since I was married." I was never so surprised—"Married, Ma'am!" I repeated. "You may well wear that look of astonishment, said she, since what I have said must appear improbable to you—Yet nothing is more true than that I once was married."

"Then why are you called Miss Jane?"

"I married, my Sophia without the consent or knowledge of my father the late Admiral Annesley. It was therefore necessary to keep the secret from him and from everyone, till some fortunate opportunity might offer of revealing it—Such an oportunity alas! was but too soon given in the death of my dear Capt. Dashwood—Pardon these tears, continued Miss Jane wiping her Eyes, I owe them to my Husband's Memory. He fell my Sophia, while fighting for his country in America after a most happy Union of seven years—. My Children

---

*Parodies Pope's "Laugh where we must; be candid where we can" (*The Essay on Man*).

two sweet Boys and a Girl, who had constantly resided with my Father and me, passing with him and with every one as the Children of a Brother (tho' I had ever been an only child) had as yet been the comforts of my Life. But no sooner had I lossed my Henry, than these sweet Creatures fell sick and died—. Conceive dear Sophia what my feelings must have been when as an Aunt I attended my Children to their early Grave—. My Father did not survive them many weeks— He died, poor Good old Man, happily ignorant to his last hour of my Marriage."*

There is a sharp eye here for literary make-believe—for the sentimental convention, for assumed modesty, for instantaneous affection and effusive confidences, for the pleasure of melancholy memories, and for the piling up of tragic incident. But even more, there is parody of self-conscious and ill-managed style, and of the lapses and inconsistencies that betray careless workmanship.

Some of the juvenilia are extremely sketchy—even less than a page. Others, perhaps the latest, though we cannot be sure, show capacity to stay with and work over an idea. *Catherine,* which takes up most of the third volume of the manuscript, and exhibits the first signs of perhaps purposeful authorship, is a story of promise, touched with irony, but in the main soberly and even laboriously intent upon straightforward characterization. It stops abruptly in the midst of things, the characters undisposed of, the bearing of incident undetermined.

These narratives, however, though diverting, have a sameness of tone resulting naturally from their single sprightly intention and from the conventions of the sentimental fiction they burlesque. But they do give us a glimpse of intelligent apprenticeship; and they are also the expression of a spirited girl's exuberant and unaffected humor, contrasting with the sobering views of youthful character and conduct which were then being inculcated in the *Moral Tales* of Maria Edgeworth and the *Sandford and Merton* of Thomas Day.

The oldest form of any of Miss Austen's completed novels, the "Elinor and Marianne" which her sister Cassandra believed Jane wrote in or about 1795, followed closely upon these amusing exercises of fledgeling talent. This was rewritten as *Sense and Sensibility,* but not until after she had begun and finished a novel called "First Impressions," later to be thoroughly revised as *Pride and Prejudice. Sense and Sensibility,* therefor, was in its genesis at any rate the first step out of her adolescent fictions

---

*From *Jane Austen's Volume the Second,* edited by B. C. Southam, 1963, by permission of the Clarendon Press, Oxford University.

and into her maturer work. It is, indeed, in every way, with the possible exception of *Northanger Abbey,* the most youthful in spirit of any of her completed novels.

To one who has first become acquainted with Miss Austen's maturer novels, *Sense and Sensibility* is lacking in subtlety and quiet irony. The human relations are seriously and directly dealt with; the characters rigidly defined, neither endearing nor intriguing; the dialogue is scarcely touched by innuendo, though incisive enough in the strong scenes. Most of all, from the point of view of the characteristic in Miss Austen, the two great identities which she developed in her later works—the woman of sense and the civilized moral man (in this case Elinor Dashwood and Edward Ferrars)—are only imperfectly realized. Their passion is so austerely in control that it reaches one only through the author's assurances. *Sense and Sensibility* is, in a word, a first and not too effectual attempt to handle a situation in which the pressures of feeling and of reason are to be brought into balance. And its ineffectuality lies at least partly in the fact that for some, particularly of her early readers, Marianne's romantic intensity challenged the sympathies, while Elinor's reserve tended to strike them as cold and unwomanly.

Of Marianne's emotionality, and of Miss Austen's ability to bring it to the surface, both in the dialogue and in discursive comment, there can be no doubt :

> Marianne would have thought herself very inexcusable had she been willing to sleep at all the first night after parting from Willoughby. She would have been ashamed to look her family in the face the next morning had she not risen from her bed in more need of repose than when she lay down on it. But the feelings which made such composure a disgrace left her in no danger of incurring it. She was awake the whole night, and she wept the greatest part of it. She got up with an headache, was unable to talk, and unwilling to take any nourishment; giving pain every moment to her mother and sisters, and forbidding all attempt at consolation from either. Her sensibility was potent enough.
>
> When breakfast was over, she walked out by herself, and wandered about the village of Allenham, indulging the recollection of past enjoyment and crying over the present reverse for the chief of the morning.
>
> The evening passed off in the equal indulgence of feeling. She played over every favorite song that she had been used to play to Willoughby, every air in which their voices had been oftenest joined, and sat at the instrument gazing on every line of music that he had written out for her, until her heart was so heavy that no further sadness could be gained; and this nourishment of grief was every day applied. She spent whole hours at the pianoforte alternately singing

and crying, her voice often totally suspended by her tears. In books too, as well as in music, she courted the misery which a contrast between the past and the present was certain of giving. She read nothing but what they had been used to read together.

The hardness of outline in these early characters is specially apparent in the "big scene," in which for the obvious purpose of the novel the stronger character should be fully justified by its strength. Here Elinor is obliged by circumstances to reveal to Marianne that while she was endeavoring to ease her sister's grief, she herself was suffering under the same distress of disappointed love.

Elinor's office was a painful one. She was going to remove what she really believed to be her sister's chief consolation, to give such particulars of Edward as she feared would ruin him forever in her good opinion, and to make Marianne, by a resemblance in their situations, which to *her* fancy would seem strong, feel all her own disappointment over again. But unwelcome as such a task must be, it was necessary to be done, and Elinor therefore hastened to perform it.

She was very far from wishing to dwell upon her own feelings, or to represent herself as suffering much, any otherwise than as the self-command she had practiced since her first knowledge of Edward's engagement might suggest a hint of what was practicable to Marianne. Her narration was clear and simple; and though it could not be given without emotion, it was not accompanied by violent agitation nor impetuous grief. *That* belonged rather to the hearer, for Marianne listened with horror, and cried excessively. . . .

Her first communication had reached no farther than to state the fact of the engagement, and the length of time it had existed. Marianne's feelings had then broken in, and put an end to all regularity of detail; and for some time all that could be done was to soothe her distress, lessen her alarms, and combat her resentment. The first question on her side, which led to further particulars, was :

"How long has this been known to you, Elinor? Has he written to you?"

"I have known it these four months. When Lucy first came to Barton Park last November, she told me in confidence of her engagement."

At these words, Marianne's eyes expressed the astonishment which her lips could not utter. After a pause of wonder, she exclaimed :

"Four months! Have you known of this four months?"

Elinor confirmed it.

"What! while attending me in all my misery, has this been on your heart? And I have reproached you for being happy!"

"It was not fit that you should then know how much I was the reverse."

"Four months," cried Marianne again. "So calm! so cheerful! How have you been supported?"

"By feeling that I was doing my duty. My promise to Lucy obliged me to be secret. I owed it to her, therefore, to avoid giving any hint of the truth; and I owed it to my family and friends not to create in them a solicitude about me, which it could not be in my power to satisfy."

Marianne seemed much struck.

"I have very often wished to undeceive yourself and my mother," added Elinor; "and once or twice I have attempted it; but without betraying my trust, I never could have convinced you."

"Four months! and yet you loved him!"

"Yes. But I did not love only him; and while the comfort of others was dear to me, I was glad to spare them from knowing how much I felt. Now, I can think and speak of it with little emotion. I would not have you suffer on my account; for I assure you I no longer suffer materially myself. I have many things to support me. I am not conscious of having provoked the disappointment by imprudence of my own; and I have borne it as much as possible without spreading it farther. I acquit Edward of all essential misconduct. I wish him very happy; and I am so sure of his always doing his duty, that though now he may harbor some regret, in the end he must become so. Lucy does not want sense, and that is the foundation on which everything good may be built. And after all, Marianne, after all that is bewitching in the idea of a single and constant attachment, and all that can be said of one's happiness depending entirely on any particular person, it is not meant—it is not fit—it is not possible that it should be so. Edward will marry Lucy; he will marry a woman superior in person and understanding to half her sex; and time and habit will teach him to forget that he ever thought another superior to *her*."

"If such is your way of thinking," said Marianne, "if the loss of what is so much valued is so easily to be made up by something else, your resolution, your self-command, are perhaps a little less to be wondered at. They are brought more within my comprehension."

"I understand you. You do not suppose that I have ever felt much. For four months, Marianne, I have had all this hanging on my mind, without being at liberty to speak of it to a single creature; knowing that it would make you and my mother most unhappy whenever it were explained to you, yet unable to prepare you for it in the least. It was told me—it was in a manner forced on me by the very person herself whose prior engagement ruined all my prospects; and told me, as I thought, with triumph. This person's suspicions, therefore, I have had to oppose by endeavoring to appear indifferent where I have been most deeply interested. And it has not been only once; I have had her hopes and exultation to listen to again and again. I have known myself to be divided from Edward forever, without hearing one circumstance

that could make me less desire the connection. Nothing has proved
him unworthy; nor has anything declared him indifferent to me. I have
had to contend against the unkindness of his sister, and the insolence
of his mother, and have suffered the punishment of an attachment
without enjoying its advantages. And all this has been going on at
a time when, as you too well know, it has not been my only unhappi-
ness. If you can think me capable of ever feeling—surely, you may
suppose that I have suffered *now*. The composure of mind with which
I have brought myself at present to consider the matter, the consolation
that I have been willing to admit, have been the effect of constant and
painful exertion; they did not spring up of themselves; they did not
occur to relieve my spirits at first; no, Marianne. *Then,* if I had not
been bound to silence, perhaps nothing could have kept me entirely—
not even what I owed to my dearest friends—from openly showing
that I was *very* unhappy."

Marianne was quite subdued.

"Oh! Elinor," she cried, "you have made me hate myself forever.
How barbarous have I been to you! you who have been my only
comfort, who have borne with me in all my misery, who have seemed
to be only suffering for me! Is this my gratitude? Is this the only
return I can make you? Because your merit cries out upon myself, I
have been trying to do it away!"

It is rather a fine lesson in civilized affection as Miss Austen conceived
it. But it has a didactic clang. Elinor's sermonizing speeches are too long,
too rhetorically precise. Furthermore, both Elinor and Marianne seem to
be acting up to the demands of their constructs or images of idealized
personalities. We feel a subdued and ambiguous sympathy for Marianne,
and however we may respect Elinor's strength of character, we incline to
grudge her some of the glory of her self-discipline.

Miss Austen has created Marianne as the expiring echo of eighteenth-
century sentimentality—of rapturous surrender to emotion and vanity in
feeling and feeding it. And it is sensibility in the full eighteenth-century
dress, not merely in susceptibility to impetuous love, but in adoration of
intense people, effusive love of nature, ecstatic responsiveness to romantic
poetry (though her favorite poet was Cowper, apparently; not Burns or
Blake), contentious faith in her own criteria of behavior, "the irritable refinement of her own mind," and of course, tears in profusion.

The novel is comedy only in the limited sense that it offers an agreeable
ending. There are comic passages in it, but they take the form of well-meant
intrusions of amusing but conventionally typed minor characters upon
Marianne's acute misery. Here again we seem to hear an echo of Miss
Burney's comic interludes, though without her annoying irrelevancy.
There is satire, too, of a mature order in the smug selfishness of the Dash-

woods' elder brother and his wife, and in the single-minded worldliness of Edward's mother, Mrs. Ferrars. But the temper of the novel appears on the whole to confirm Bergson's dictum that when sympathy or censure enter, comedy tends to disappear.

There is a challenging interest in the fact that in 1796, while *Sense and Sensibility* was still under Miss Austen's hand, Fanny Burney had published her *Camilla,* the first novel of quality to take critical issue with the ideal of sentimental love, and, as in *Sense and Sensibility,* through the portrait of a girl suffering from that emotional ailment. That Miss Austen had read *Camilla,* and immediately upon its appearance, is certain, for her name appears on the list of subscribers. In addition, she has recorded her admiration of it, and defended it against the fatuous John Thorpe's belittling of it in *Northanger Abbey.* It is worth a thought, then, that her interest in this theme may perhaps have been started by Miss Burney's less explicit and certainly less captivating approach.

Sense and Sensibility is Miss Austen's link with the eighteenth century; it is also her adieu to it. In this first novel she has liquidated the greater part of her debt to her immediate predecessors. In the next one, *Pride and Prejudice,* she discovers and exploits a new independence. The adolescent energy and earnestness of *Sense and Sensibility* give place to a flow of detached ironic humor, not a new medium for Miss Austen, but hitherto handled bluntly and somewhat unskillfully.

In *Pride and Prejudice* the counsel of prudence is urged not against an unhealthy sentimental impulse, but against the deceptiveness of hasty impressions.* It is again a study in the attainment of experience; therefore a repudiation of unreflective feeling. First love, first impressions, both are held up, not to ridicule, because they may not be far wrong, but to judgment, for if they are wrong, they may be perilously misleading.

Pride and Prejudice is not unworthily the general favorite of Miss Austen's readers, although cultivated opinion seems to prefer one of the three novels of the later period. Probably the chief reason for its greater popularity is its livelier comedy. But it is not Fielding's comedy; still less Smollett's or Sterne's. Its nearer relations are Miss Burney's comedy of

---

*The original title, "First Impressions," was replaced by the more apt *Pride and Prejudice,* which is generally thought to have been taken from the last chapter of Miss Burney's *Cecilia:* "The whole of this business," said Dr. Lyster, "has been the result of PRIDE AND PREJUDICE. . . . Yet this, however, remember: if to PRIDE AND PREJUDICE you owe your miseries, so wonderfully is (sic) good and evil balanced, that to PRIDE AND PREJUDICE you will also owe their termination." Miss Burney's capitals are certainly forceful enough to leave an impression; yet the phrase appears also in the concluding pages of Sophia Lee's *The Recess* (1785), twice in Charlotte Smith's *Old Manor House* (1793), and twice again in Bage's *Hermsprong* (1796). Perhaps it was a current byword.

manners (without the "made" comic scenes) and Miss Edgeworth's comedy of character when she is at her too rare best. Miss Austen's own contribution, however, is pre-eminently important. Neither Burney nor Edgeworth could have conceived a character as beautifully poised yet animatedly charming as Elizabeth Bennett. And if Miss Austen's men are, as they have been said to be, drawn unmistakably by a woman's hand, Darcy has at any rate not been drawn from the fish-pond of eighteenth-century aristocratic males.

What is new in the comedy of *Pride and Prejudice* is that it is not pictorial nor (in the most literal sense) diverting; it is essential. It is the fabric of the story. And since the story has moral direction, comedy is therefore largely the medium of moral judgment. It permeates the entire work, from the moment we are introduced in the opening chapter to the Bennett family. But its high points are little duets of caustic wit. We see one in a triangular conversation involving Darcy, Elizabeth, and the crafty Miss Bingley, who serves merely as "feeder" for the other two.

Miss Bingley . . . soon afterwards got up and walked about the room. Her figure was elegant, and she walked well; but Darcy, at whom it was all aimed, was still inflexibly studious. In the desperation of her feelings, she resolved on one effort more, and, turning to Elizabeth, said :

"Miss Eliza Bennett, let me persuade you to follow my example, and take a turn about the room. I assure you it is very refreshing after sitting so long in one attitude."

Elizabeth was surprised, but agreed to it immediately. Miss Bingley succeeded no less in the real object of her civility; Mr. Darcy looked up. He was as much awake to the novelty of attention in that quarter as Elizabeth herself could be, and unconsciously closed his book. He was directly invited to join their party, but he declined it, observing that he could imagine but two motives for their choosing to walk up and down the room together, with either of which motives his joining them would interfere. "What could he mean? She was dying to know what could be his meaning"—and asked Elizabeth whether she could at all understand him.

"Not at all," was her answer; "but depend upon it, he means to be severe on us, and our surest way of disappointing him will be to ask nothing about it."

Miss Bingley, however, was incapable of disappointing Mr. Darcy in anything, and persevered therefore in requiring an explanation of his two motives.

"I have not the smallest objection to explaining them," said he, as soon as she allowed him to speak. "You either choose this method of passing the evening because you are in each other's confidence, and have secret affairs to discuss, or because you are conscious that your figures appear to the greatest advantage in walking; if the first, I should be completely in your way; and if the second, I can admire you much better as I sit by the fire."

"Oh! shocking!" cried Miss Bingley. "I never heard anything so abominable. How shall we punish him for such a speech?"

"Nothing so easy, if you have but the inclination," said Elizabeth; "we can all plague and punish one another. Tease him—laugh at him. Intimate as you are, you must know how it is to be done."

"But upon my honor I do *not*. I do assure you that my intimacy has not yet taught me *that*. Tease calmness of temper and presence of mind! No, no—I feel he may defy us there. And as to laughter, we will not expose ourselves, if you please, by attempting to laugh without a subject. Mr. Darcy may hug himself."

"Mr. Darcy is not to be laughed at!" cried Elizabeth. "That is an uncommon advantage, and uncommon I hope it will continue, for it would be a great loss to *me* to have many such acquaintances. I dearly love a laugh."

"Miss Bingley," said he, "has given me credit for more than can be. The wisest and the best of men—nay, the wisest and best of their actions—may be rendered ridiculous by a person whose first object in life is a joke."

"Certainly," replied Elizabeth—"there are such people, but I hope I am not one of *them*. I hope I never ridicule what is wise or good. Follies and nonsense, whims and inconsistencies, do divert me, I own, and I laugh at them whenever I can. But these, I suppose, are precisely what you are without."

"Perhaps that is not possible for anyone. But it has been the study of my life to avoid those weaknesses which often expose a strong understanding to ridicule."

"Such as vanity and pride."

"Yes, vanity is a weakness indeed. But pride—where there is a real superiority of mind, pride will be always under good regulation."

Elizabeth turned away to hide a smile.

"Your examination of Mr. Darcy is over, I presume," said Miss Bingley; "and pray what is the result?"

"I am perfectly convinced by it that Mr. Darcy has no defect. He owns it himself without disguise."

"No," said Darcy, "I have made no such pretension. I have faults enough, but they are not, I hope, of understanding. My temper I dare not vouch for. It is, I believe, too little yielding—certainly too little for the convenience of the world. I cannot forget the follies and vices of others so soon as I ought, nor their offenses against myself. My feelings are not puffed about with every attempt to move them. My temper would perhaps be called resentful. My good opinion once lost, is lost forever."

"*That* is a failing indeed!" cried Elizabeth. "Implacable resentment *is* a shade in a character. But you have chosen your fault well. I really cannot laugh at it. You are safe from me."

"There is, I believe, in every disposition a tendency to some particular evil—a natural defect, which not even the best education can overcome."

"And *your* defect is a propensity to hate everybody."

"And yours," he replied with a smile, "is wilfully to misunderstand them."

Pride and Prejudice opens up here a new comic intention, in which responsive laughter, even Meredith's "thoughtful laughter," may have little or no place. Character, not action, is its source; its object the "follies and nonsense, whims and inconsistencies," which divert Elizabeth Bennett; and its final aim to project a more socially enlightened conception of personality and conduct. The progress of enlightenment is the substance of the story. If there is much to be gained by classification, then we may set it down as a datum in the history of fiction that *Pride and Prejudice* has moved out of the area of Miss Burney's "novel of manners," since its concern is with personal rather than fashionable conduct, and provided a reason for a new descriptive term—the "novel of social satire."

The material for corrective comedy can be set down as any and all of the traits involved in the putting on of a personality—the wearing of a "front." This is quite as likely to be a matter of self-deception as of insincerity or hypocrisy. It may, indeed, be the result of misdirected training, and it is not uncharacteristically the accompaniment of social position. It may be accentuated by luxury, by refinement, by gallantry, by flattery; so high society is a specially favorable environment for it, and is likely to furnish for the comic artist the most desirable models for his purpose.

Darcy is such a model : a man of high character, finished behavior, but insulting vanity—which is not altogether of his own making. He is presented to us exactly as he presents himself to Longbourn society—as a social object; not as a case-history. Why he is what he is, we are to learn in time. But he enters our vision as he does Elizabeth's, provoking manners passing as good, conceit as pride, egotism as superiority. His fatuity breaks through its concealments in phrase after phrase from the passage we have just quoted : "the wisest and the best of men may be rendered ridiculous;" "the study of my life to avoid those weaknesses which often expose a strong understanding to ridicule;" "I have faults enough, but they are not, I hope, of understanding."

But the comic instrument, Elizabeth herself, is not unambiguous. Her faults are summarized in the word "prejudice"; and for those she herself, unlike Darcy, is in the main to blame. But correction also is within her own power, though it waits upon self-discovery. That comes to her following Darcy's rejection, in a moment of painful revelation—an experience shared by all of Jane Austen's heroines except the two "solitaries," Fanny Price and Anne Elliot.

> She grew absolutely ashamed of herself. Of neither Darcy nor Wickham could she think without feeling that she had been blind, partial, prejudiced, absurd.
>
> "How despicably have I acted!" she cried; "I, who have prided myself on my discernment! I, who have valued myself on my abilities! who have often disdained the generous candor of my sister, and gratified my vanity in useless or blameable distrust. How humiliating is this discovery! yet, how just a humiliation! Had I been in love, I could not have been more wretchedly blind. But vanity, not love, has been my folly. Pleased with the preference of one, and offended by the neglect of the other, on the very beginning of our acquaintance, I have courted prepossession and ignorance, and driven reason away, where either were concerned. Till this moment I never knew myself."

The change in Darcy himself—it is not a change of character, but of essential humor—is fairly rapid and complete. At the opening of the novel his conversation is almost wholly self-centered. At the close, it verges on humility. The change has come about almost entirely through the abrasion of character upon character. But once Elizabeth's tart rejection has opened Darcy's eyes, she no longer works upon him through direct contact. Much has happened between Darcy's departure from Rosings and Elizabeth's visit to Pemberley, but it has happened in the unquiet reflections of Darcy and herself.

The perfection of that program of comic regeneration is what chiefly differentiates Jane Austen's work from Burney's and Edgeworth's. It had been somewhat dimly anticipated by Bage, but we have no certainty that Miss Austen had read Bage. If she had, she would probably have regarded his skeptical humor as unrefined and overly masculine. She does share with Bage, however, a sometimes amused, sometimes troubled, interest in the ambivalence of the lessons of experience. And that idea never disturbed the minds of her two popular spinster predecessors, who were quite sure of the eternal verities.

Pride and Prejudice shows no sharp cleavage from the structure of the later and more finished examples of the eighteenth-century novel. Yet it shows some of the less desirable features of type. The "little history" had already disappeared from the novels of Fanny Burney and Maria Edgeworth; and while there are still vestiges of it in Colonel Brandon's story in *Sense and Sensibility*, and even as late as Mrs. Smith's story in *Persuasion*, in *Pride and Prejudice* the substantial chunk of Darcy's personal background is organic and is given us in passages of dialogue with Darcy's housekeeper. But subordinate incident is still introduced in substantial mass and without close adhesion to plot. The visit to Charlotte Collins is such an incident—opportune, diverting, but useful only as it creates the occasion for Darcy's first proposal, although there has been at Rosings no contact with Darcy that would suggest that his affection for Elizabeth had reached the boiling point. The Lydia-Wickham episode is even more extraneous. Why should the seduction of Elizabeth's sister, with its long train of concealment and negotiation, be necessary to forge the last link in her affection for Darcy? These incidents are, to be sure, integrated with plot by skillfull contrivance, but that does not make them integral. There is, then, in this well-conceived novel a carry-over of loose and lumpy plot construction. Even Miss Edgeworth in *Belinda* had written a more coherent novel than Miss Austen had so far achieved.

In the character-set also Miss Austen shows her literary tutelage. The theme of the pair of lovers struggling toward the solution of a problem of compatibility is anything but original. The problem, however, is cast in a new mold. For this is the first time in a major fiction that a conflict of emotional interests involves criticism of the aristocrat not on the familiar ground of the traditional vices of his class, but for the injury that birth and breeding have done to his personality. The theme is adumbrated in Burney's *Cecilia* and Edgeworth's *Ennui,* but not developed with Miss Austen's flair for clear issues and sharp characterization to give them significance.

In her comic characters, however, she shows her debt to the conventions; yet a debt that no one would hold against her unless he were impervious to high humor. She has no comic principals like Parson Adams or Humphry Clinker; and she dispenses with purely comic menials like Partridge and Strap and Winifred Jenkins. But her most amusing comics, perhaps best of all her clerics like Mr. Collins and Mr. Elton, contribute not only to the entertainment of the novel but to its movement and its intellectual interest. The clerics support her insistence upon the dignity of their office by showing its peculiar indignity when filled by servile or conceited fools. That is organic comedy, in the larger view, even though her stupid curates are never brought into direct apposition with the three clergymen who play for her the parts of modest heroes.

Miss Austen has cut herself completely free, however, from Miss Burney's comic chorus and elaborate comic business. At the same time she has blest us with some memorable individual satiric-comic creations : Mr. Collins and Lady De Bourgh, notably, in *Pride and Prejudice,* and later Miss Bates in *Emma*; in all of them the balance between pure amusement and ironic censure depending upon the quantum of simplicity or pretension in the particular character. In the wisdom and tolerance underlying her comedy Miss Austen is more closely related to Fielding than to her immediate predecessors, although her ethic is as different from Fielding's as a good nineteenth-century woman's can be from a good eighteenth-century man's.

Probably it is clear from what has been said that the perfectly integrated realistic novel has not come into being in *Pride and Prejudice.* Yet realistic intention is apparent in all of Miss Austen's fiction. It is not implemented, however, by the relentless objectivity and the proletarian sympathies of later realists. Realism for her—and she would not have recognized the word, at least in its literary relations—was felt and expressed negatively, in her rejection of the sentimental optimism of earlier women writers. But realism is imperfectly achieved when reservations are made with regard to any social level or interest. The simple fact is that not only Miss Austen but English society could not at that time have understood, much less have accepted, the implications of a comprehensive and impartial social-critical method. Furthermore, Miss Austen was not by temperament a realist. It is difficult to think of a modern realist untainted by fervor or amused in any degree by the thing he deprecates. And a realist without an animus, indignant, sympathetic, nevertheless not impartial, would be a stranger among us. Amusement, unhappily, tended to be refined out of Miss Austen's later work—even including *Emma*—yet it was never completely lost, let us be thankful, in the greater seriousness of her maturer work.

The next novel, *Northanger Abbey,* is not one to compel enthusiasm, unless one can see its purpose—to deflate literary exaggeration and affectation. It would have been much more to the purpose if it had appeared in 1803, when she sold it for publication, hard upon the heels of Mrs. Radcliffe's and Monk Lewis's successes. She herself realized when it was returned to her hands years later that the time for it had passed. Perhaps, too, she felt that its effervescence marked it as youthful, too youthful to be ranked with the novels that had made her reputation.

Possibly Miss Austen would have been unhappy if she had felt that her story would be taken to be downright condemnation of Gothic and sentimental fiction. Her ridicule was tempered, no doubt, by agreeable recollections and critical fairness. The fun she makes of *Udolpho* in Chapter VI of *Northanger Abbey* is honest fun; not contemptuous. She simply finds rational amusement in the effects of high-flown romanticism upon sentimental minds; in this case adolescent, and therefore doubly susceptible. The one articulate opinion Miss Austen voices—that of Henry Tilney, the hero—is not only tolerant, but appreciative.

"The person, be it gentleman or lady, who has not pleasure in a good novel, must be intolerably stupid. I have read all Mrs. Radcliffe's works, and most of them with great pleasure. *The Mysteries of Udolpho,* when I had once begun it, I could not lay down again; I remember finishing it in two days, my hair standing on end the whole time."

This is not exalted criticism, but it is not heavy-footed. It is critical testimony, sententious as youthful criticism is likely to be; but it places Mrs. Radcliffe without needlessly shaming her.*

As to fiction generally, even in its then indeterminate state, Miss Austen steps into *Northanger Abbey* in person to defend it. She has her sensible say as to pretended taste, and offers tribute, somewhat casual, perhaps, to the fictions of which she herself thought well.

I will not adopt that ungenerous and impolitic custom, so common with novel writers, of degrading, by their contemptuous censure, the very performances to the number of which they are themselves adding; joining with their greatest enemies in bestowing the harshest epithets upon such works, and scarcely ever permitting them to be read by their own heroine, who, if she accidentally take up a novel, is sure to turn over its insipid pages with disgust. Alas! If the heroine of one novel be not patronized by the heroine of another, from whom can she expect protection and regard? I cannot approve it. Let us leave it to the Reviewers to abuse such effusions of fancy at their leisure, and over every new novel to talk in threadbare strains of the trash with which the press now groans. Let us not desert one another; we are an injured body. Although our productions have afforded more extensive and unaffected pleasure than those of any other literary corporation in the world, no species of composition has been so much decried. From pride, ignorance, or fashion, our foes are almost as many as our readers; and while the abilities of the nine-hundredth abridger of the History of England, or of the man who collects and publishes in a volume some dozen lines of Milton, Pope, and Prior, with a paper from the *Spectator,* and a chapter from Sterne, are eulogized by a thousand pens, there seems almost a general wish of decrying the capacity and undervaluing the labor of the novelist, and of slighting the performances which have only genius, wit, and taste to recommend them. "I am no novel reader; I seldom look into novels; do not imagine that I often read novels; it is really well for a novel." Such is the common cant. "And what are you reading, Miss—?" "Oh! it is only a novel!" replies the young lady; while she lays down her book with affected indifference or momentary shame. "It is only *Cecilia,* or

---

*This conversation on romantic fiction is anticipated in the *Catherine* of the juvenilia, with Charlotte Smith, not Mrs. Radcliffe, as the subject.

Camilla, or *Belinda*"; or, in short, only some work in which the greatest powers of the mind are displayed, in which the most thorough knowledge of human nature, the happiest delineation of its varieties, the liveliest effusions of wit and humor, are conveyed to the world in the best chosen language. Now, had the same young lady been engaged with a volume of the *Spectator,* instead of such a work, how proudly would she have produced the book, and told its name.

The story of *Northanger Abbey* develops from Catherine Morland's readiness to carry the exciting stuff of romance into the realities of her own life. With a mind filled with the "horrid" effects of *Udolpho,* she surrenders herself to silly imaginings of mysteries lurking in the old abbey which houses the Tilney family. But she is brought to her senses by Henry Tilney at a moment of willfully extravagant curiosity. What might be called normal romance takes up from that point, and the remainder of the story is no remarkable departure from the familiar novel of sentiment. There are well drawn characters, some personable, some vain and pretentious, some industriously idle with their little affairs, and one, General Tilney, father of the hero, a rather frightening domestic martinet. Plot is designed, in the necessities of the case, partly upon the Gothic pattern; the final complication is artificial. But the story ends with the expected improvement in Catherine, notably in common sense, under the hopeful and not disinterested encouragement of Henry. Good opinion would consign *Northanger Abbey* to the lowliest place among Miss Austen's novels.

Here we come to an unavoidable stopping-place. In the once accepted but now somewhat questionable view of Miss Austen's literary growth, *Northanger Abbey* was regarded as the last of the "early" novels, all practically completed before 1800, to be shelved for more than a decade, and to be rescued for publication—at her own risk and expense—from 1811 on. Two earlier tries for publication are recorded. Her father made a cautious approach to a publisher in 1797 with "First Impressions," the early form of *Pride and Prejudice.* It was flatly refused, without a reading. In 1803, after revision for the purpose, she herself sold *Northanger Abbey* to a printer—for ten pounds! The going price to an unknown for a first novel was commonly regarded as fifty. He lacked even the courage of his convictions; the manuscript was put aside, until it was repurchased by her brother, held until after her death, and, as we have seen, published with her last novel, *Persuasion,* in 1818.

The corollary to the accepted chronology of the novels was that the three later novels were written in a splendid burst of activity from 1811 to 1816, the year Cassandra gives for the completion of *Persuasion.* That leaves a gap of about a dozen years in which, it was assumed, she produced nothing of consequence and published nothing at all. Various attempts

were made to account for the long pause. One explanation was the un-
settlement of the Austen family after the removal from Steventon, Jane's
birthplace, to Bath in 1801, again to Southampton after her father's death
in 1805, and finally to Chawton in 1809. The explanation covers only parts
of the period in question, and it seems in itself insufficient. Another supposition, not unsupported, was that these years were marked by at least
one affair of the heart that ended in disappointment.* But the dates
proposed for any circumstantially confirmed attachment take us barely
into the first years of the long silence. In addition, what little we know of
these obscure episodes would seem to make it doubtful that any of them
resulted in a long paralysis of her energy. Finally, from what we know of
her personality, it would seem improbable that she was the kind of woman
to hide herself in moody retirement, even after a serious emotional defeat.
There is also the further suggestion that her failure, and her family's, to
put her into print when the worst of fictional claptrap could find a market
was disheartening. That would be completely understandable. Yet *if* the
long pause reflected a real failure of energy and interest, when vitality and
ambition should have been at their best, then it might be a mistake to
accept any one of these explanations to the exclusion of one or all of the
others.

Two short fictions, however, break the hiatus, neither of them largely
significant, and both of them withheld from publication for more than a
half-century after her death. These were the unfinished *The Watsons*,
probably planned for the dimensions of a novel, and the other a novelette
(deplorable term!), *Lady Susan*, which is finished only in the sense that it
is brought to a conclusion so abrupt that we are almost obliged to think
that Miss Austen herself had tired of it. There is uncertainty as to when
either was composed, though there is ground for a presumption of 1803 or
thereabouts for *The Watsons* and 1804-5 for *Lady Susan*. Yet there are
also reasons for thinking that *Lady Susan* preceded *The Watsons*, though
the fair copy may have been made later. In point of comparison with Miss
Austen's other works, *The Watsons* is not specially remarkable. *Lady Susan*
is definitely so.

Even what we have of *The Watsons* cannot be judged as finished writing. The opening pages recall the manner of *Sense and Sensibility* and
Pride and Prejudice, but not the verve. Yet there are points at which
proved skill takes possession.

The background of the principal anticipates in some measure that of
Fanny Price in *Mansfield Park*. Emma, daughter of a lower middle class
family, has been brought up in the luxury and calm of a well-to-do house-

* For light on her possible attachments, see R. W. Chapman, *op. cit.,* Chapter V.

hold by an aunt whose late marriage throws her back upon her own boorish and quarrelsome family. A favorite brother, however, seems (as in *Mansfield Park*) to be able to offer her the comfort of friendly understanding. The characters are not strongly marked as types, yet they show relations to similar characters in her better known novels, both earlier and later. There is the heavy and consequential elder brother, like John Dashwood in *Sense and Sensibility*; the thoroughly practical-minded young woman (a reminder of Charlotte Lucas in *Pride and Prejudice*) who "could like any good-humored man with a comfortable income"; the inevitably spoiled young man of fashion who recurs in most of her novels; and the valetudinarian father, as in *Emma*. These can be identified in the little we have of the story, and their "lines" perhaps predicated from their personalities. But the detail of the story can only be guessed at.*

Lady Susan is Miss Austen's only attempt to depict fashionable urban society, matter of prime interest for both Miss Burney and Miss Edgeworth. It is also her one mature work in letter form. As an epistolary novel, it is among the few in which letters seem to serve their purpose completely and neatly; for much of the interest of the story, which *is* interesting, derives from the raciness of these letters from women of fashion, with their undertones of cynicism, deceit, and self-deception.

Lady Susan herself is utterly different from the women of Miss Austen's more familiar fictions. She is an accomplished liar, ingrate, and mistress of palaver, improvising her morality as she goes, wickedly humiliating her daughter by denying her an education and nagging her because she is uneducated, finding most of her enjoyment in intrigue and delighting in the jealous rancors of the women she has wronged. A single word to do her justice must be both profane and obscene.

But she is portrayed with satiric polish scarcely surpassed in any other of Miss Austen's works, without reprehension, question, or directive comment. She is brought to no untimely end, suffers no poetic justice, is unchanged in character from first to last, and is left comfortably wedded to a man who can indulge her extravagance, stomach her duplicity, and not wince at her contempt. The ironic doubt expressed in the "Conclusion" (which abandons suddenly and unaccountably the letter form) as to whether she will be happy is supplemented by doubts as to whether any of the characters are to be blest with that vital satisfaction, since their futures have been poisoned by Lady Susan's abominations. *Lady Susan* has the

---

*Cassandra told her nieces the intended development, but in only the sketchiest terms. Elizabeth Jenkins, in her largely personal study, *Jane Austen*, sees even in the unfinished state of *The Watsons* a novel of nascent promise. Edward Austen-Leigh's *Memoir* of his aunt suggests that she may have abandoned it because she found herself writing a story of more commonplace people than could really interest her. See also the footnote to page 353.

cruelty of *Pere Goriot*—though a woman's picture of a heartless woman can be more merciless than a man's. It is Miss Austen's only work that is seemingly indifferent to personality except as a moral enigma. There seems, incidentally, support for the belief that an acquaintance of the Austen family sat unawares for the portrait.

But *Lady Susan* should be read, if for nothing more than its surprising contrast to the more familiar novels.

It is generally admitted that there is a profound difference between the earlier novels and the later. A growth in maturity must, of course, be taken for granted between the art of a girl not long out of her teens and that of a woman nearing forty. But *Mansfield Park, Emma, Persuasion* (and *Pride and Prejudice* also, assuming that late and thoroughgoing revision places it in the maturer class) belong to a quite different intellectual order from *Sense and Sensibility* and *Northanger Abbey*. That marked difference can scarcely be dissociated from the sustained silence for which, as we have seen, speculation has been busy with possible explanations, most of them assuming more or less tacitly some defeat or emotional disturbance followed by exhaustion of interest or energy.

Yet a massive increase in creative power, maturity, and artistic command would seem an improbable sequel to a long period of intellectual enervation. Another explanation has been offered—that these years were not sterile years at all, but were spent in careful and unremitting working over of material already at hand. Mrs. Q. D. Leavis has propounded a theory which sustains this view : that these years were spent in the reconstruction of a number of earlier works, developing gradually out of sketches and briefer tales the fully formed and well polished novels of the later period.* The detail of the theory we can pass over, as well as inevitable doubts that arise from so radical a reconstruction of the Austen canon. External evidence, including the letters, makes it pretty clear that from 1811 to 1816 she was occupied with the writing of *Mansfield Park, Emma,* and *Persuasion.* No matter how far back their supposed sources may lie, we are still confronted with the fact that that surge of power contrasts

---

*Q.D. Leavis: *A Critical Theory of Jane Austen's Writings, Scrutiny,* vols. X, XI, XII, 1941-44. This comprehensive revision, Mrs. Leavis believes, included items from the "Juvenilia." As part of the process of rebuilding earlier work, completed or uncompleted, *The Watsons* furnished the germ of *Emma*—a suggestion already put forward in R. Brimley Johnson's *Jane Austen. Lady Susan* is similarly taken to have supplied the material for *Mansfield Park. Pride and Prejudice* is assumed to have been completely revised, and *Persuasion* to have drawn upon the store-house of early materials. The articles show great ingenuity in the gathering and interpretation of evidence. While I feel a certain doubt of a method which involves building inference on inference, the argument does offer in general a ponderable explanation of why Miss Austens' energy seems to have been dormant over so long a time.

strongly with the dozen years or so which brought into daylight no novel which she herself was willing to publish. Doesn't the gap still confront us, even if it is a term of depressed and intermittent activity rather than of idleness?

No critical argument, at any rate, has erased the record that the early novels were completed *in some more or less final form before* 1800, and that the three "later" novels, whatever their genesis and development, belong to another period and to a different class—always with the qualification that *Pride and Prejudice* as we know it was not the *Pride and Prejudice* of 1797 or thereabouts. The pendant question would seem to be whether *Emma,* to take a random instance, was under Miss Austen's hand for ten years after the writing of *The Watsons,* or for only two or three years. How significant is the question?

For us, who have been considering what the fictional art of the eighteenth century had put into Miss Austen's clever hands, the question has a good deal of significance. For the gap marked the end of her apprenticeship, and during her apprenticeship she had used the models of the eighteenth-century ateliers. That is true even though her original genius had shown clearly in her early work, and her later work still gives us echoes of the eighteenth century. For our limited and practical purposes, we might close at this point our consideration of Miss Austen's artistic and intellectual debts to her predecessors except in so far as the literary *manners* of the eighteenth century continued to affect her work, and its social usages to determine the channel of her interest in the society about her.

None of the novels has stirred more deep-seated conflict of opinion than *Mansfield Park.* On the surface, the theme of the novel is the unresolvable antithesis of the social temper and the religious. That seems to approximate Miss Austen's meaning when she wrote her sister that the novel was to be "about ordination."

There are two distinct character-groups here; how distinct is somewhat obscured by the fact that their members are a part of the same social community and mesh and intermesh with one another. One group represents good society, with its security and charm, also, at its less admirable, its flippancy and its irresponsibility. The other represents the inwardly religious life, without disturbing dogmatic insistencies or sectarian primness, but with its conscious rectitude and its own security. The first group makes the proximate purpose in life amusement; the second goodness.

The differences are matters of social disposition, not of argument, except that for two of the principals, Edmund Bertram and Mary Crawford, unvoiced argument permeates their whole vivid relation. Miss Crawford would like to marry Edmund, but she has an aversion to clerical status and style. Edmund would like to marry Mary, but he would make her a clergyman's wife. This situation provides what might be called the active romance of the story, though the opposition of ideals makes it arm's-length romance.

The love of "little Fanny Price" for her Cousin Edmund, accumulated through years of sympathy and kindness while she has been growing up in the Bertram household, is, however, the pervasive theme of *Mansfield Park*. Their affection is mutual, but felt on Edmund's part unsuspectingly and passionlessly. For Fanny it is slow martyrdom, the more acute because she cannot bear to see her idol appropriated by a coquette; and Mary Crawford is that, even expertly.

Fanny is the heroine of the story, if Miss Austen's insistence can prevail to make her so. But probably there are few readers who wholeheartedly like her or approve of her. The unfavorable attitude is explained in large part by the fact that *Mansfield Park* embodies views of conduct that to the modern reader are likely to seem overrefined, or even effete. What at first glance seem to be social issues become moral issues, for Fanny inseparably so; and it is not always easy to see why, for the cases of conduct usually seem to involve discretion rather than conscience.

For example, the core of the middle action, the amateur theatricals, is determined by the attitude that "Father would not like it." Yet that deference to Father's judgment has to do in an important degree with the possible effects of amateur acting upon untried susceptibilities and urges. That *is* an issue of the moral order, as both Edmund and Fanny are wisely aware. Even less disputably, Miss Austen conceives—and she may be right or wrong—that acting may give artful insincerity a permanent hold upon character; again a moral issue. But these questions are not superficially clear, and moral judgment, so far as the reader can see, is made to rest upon differences of opinion as to whether the play in question is an immoral play. As these questions are developed in talk between Edmund and Fanny, they seem, unfortunately, to be approached illiberally and primly.*

The unfavorable response to *Mansfield Park* seems actually to be heightened by the artistic justice of Miss Austen's picture of Mary Crawford and her friends. They are likable because they have been educated in likableness. They wear "the graces" as their birthright and their aristocratic vesture. And perhaps what is wrong with Fanny, viewed as a

---

*A sharp and highly interesting interpretive conflict as to the attitudes and sympathies in *Mansfield Park* can be found in Chapter VI of Marvin Mudrick's *Jane Austen: Irony as Defense and Discovery,* and Lionel Trilling's defense of *Mansfield Park,* reprinted in the Austen anthologies of both Ian Watt and William Heath.

heroine, is that in spite of her well advertised virtues, and despite Miss Austen's insistence, she does not possess the graces—not, at least, in Chesterfield's authentic sense.

We have spoken of ambiguous moral issues. The transcendant moral issue in *Mansfield Park,* which is concerned with the making and breaking of a liaison, is quite unambiguous. It is the one instance in which Miss Austen has given, if only within a single sector of the action, full topical importance to a sexual sin. And she regards it as a sin, not merely as a shocking indiscretion, destructive to both the participants. Like the Lydia-Wickham story in *Pride and Prejudice,* the escapade serves as a catalyst for the conclusion of the main plot. But here in *Mansfield Park* it has its own structural integrity, and its relevance to the theme of the deterioration of character through the indulgences and the fatuities of the idle and the bored.

But *Mansfield Park* has its defenders, with reasons both aesthetic and ethical. However one may think of little Fanny, and however one may dissent from rigid pronouncements upon some perhaps indistinct moral issues, this novel stands as the most uncompromising expression of Miss Austen's disrelish for façade. Conversely, it voices her conviction that the ultimate social grace is unadvertised and unoffending sincerity.

It is not wise to condemn a book because we do not like a character in it, even a principal. We don't like Macbeth. We don't like Becky Sharp (unless we are not afraid of too clever women). But we don't interpret tragic faults as faults of the book. In these instances, however, we are not called upon to admire or to love. But in *Mansfield Park* a character is held up before us as a pattern of natural and modest virtue. If we don't like Fanny Price, we fail to meet Miss Austen upon her own ground. Is the failure ours or hers?

The sharpness and intimacy of the portrait of Emma Woodhouse in Miss Austen's all but last novel has lent encouragement to the idea that it was drawn from the life—her own. Yet there is little to support that guess beyond her admission that she liked her Emma, and a certain affectionate condonement of Emma's repeatedly humiliated but always resurgent self-confidence and of her propensity to take charge of other people's lives.

There are readers of *Emma* who believe it is the faultless novel. There are others who maintain that, assuming woman's inevitable and insuperable incapacity as novelist, *Emma* is at least as good as a woman could be expected to write. Still others, not so very numerous, take *Emma* as final proof that Miss Austen knew and depicted only the sides of woman's nature most to be feared and avoided. Such diversity of judgment suggests a character of baffling complexity—unless one holds that the simple diagnostic of feminine nature *is* baffling complexity. Emma, the young lady herself, is a great stimulus to argument, for both sexes, for all ages, and from every angle of prejudice or partisanship. But argument usually resolves itself into the simple question of whether, apart from its strictly biogenetic bearing, the creation of "fair Eve, our general mother," was really carefully thought out. At all events, Emma seems to be a woman to be praised or dispraised by men, but to be properly known and valued only by women.

Although five marriages are achieved or to be achieved in the course of *Emma* (one of them an accomplished fact just before the opening of the narrative), this is Miss Austen's one novel in which the central theme is not the politics and strategy of the heroine's search for a husband. It would be unsafe to say that Emma is not engaged in such a search; for the apostles of the subconscious would be instantly upon us. But if we credit Emma's own words, and accept her surprise when she discovers she is in love with Knightley as something more than an author's artifice, we must acknowledge that Emma's interest in marriage, vicarious as it is, is an artist's rather than a postulant's. For the first time, Miss Austen here studies her heroine not principally in relation to her marital problem, but in relation to herself.

At the same time, it must be realized that the matchmaker's function was not then, as it might be now, dishonored or superfluous. In a marrying and getting married world it was important, sometimes indispensable. Mothers, aunts, and chaperones might even attain the expertness of what are known in our dog shows as "professional handlers." Miss Edgeworth depicts that accomplished showmanship particularly well—though quite without humor. But Emma is new, a marriageable young lady herself conducting the business of getting a young woman married with the energy and assurance, if with something less than the infallibility, of the old and knowing. Emma's promotional activities should not be regarded altogether as meddling, nor as compensation for a sexual apathy of her own. I am inclined to leave Freud out of the question and to take her at her creator's valuation.

Something has been made critically of the distinction between the literary character we identify with ourselves, and the character whose person and actions we can watch only as spectators. Problematical characters belong, of course, in the second category; and Emma is one of them. If she were quite transparent, like Sophia Western, for example, or Evelina, we should readily like or dislike her, and know why. But since Emma is a problem, judging her is a matter of the intellect as well as of the responsive feelings. Not only is Emma de-sentimentalized; she must be judged without sentimentality. She is not a sweet child, like Fanny Price, nor an ardent one, like Marianne Dashwood. She has much practical sense, though her own criteria of practical sense may mislead her, since she is still a girl in experience as well as in years. Her affections—and therefore her appeal—are on the extra-dry side, as Jane Fairfax, with sympathy, and Mrs. Elton, without sympathy, both clearly see. Her errors in judgment usually entail some blindness or indifference to other people's susceptibilities. That is principally what is wrong with her nagging encouragement of Harriet Smith's fluid affections, although, to be sure, she misjudges Harriet's worth in almost every possible way. It is that also that in an instant converts our amusement at Miss Bates into indignation when Emma insultingly snubs her, and that still more arouses our irritation over her busybodyish concoction of romantic tales to account for Miss Fairfax's reticences.

It is difficult for many readers to clarify their own response to Emma. She scarcely demands sympathy, because she has so firm a grasp upon her own personality. She scarcely needs to be censured, for her mistakes are in the upshot not serious. She does not, I believe, usually command affection, as Elizabeth Bennett commonly does, and Anne Elliot certainly and always. As to her growth in understanding, both of herself and of the world, we accept it as the theme of the story, but our interest in it depends in large part upon how deeply her personality has affected us. *Emma* is, after all, pure comedy, in the sense of Meredith, on the one hand, looking forward; but also, looking backward, in the more obvious but indiscriminate sense of Fanny Burney. It is Miss Burney's "comic relief" that Miss Austen employs in the loosely attached Miss Bates passages, but with better, because more natural, power to amuse, and with much closer relation to plot.

If we can assimilate the paradox of "profound comedy," that is just what Miss Austen gives us here. The more delicate the balance between possible tragedy and possible comedy, the more absolute the effect of comedy—if things turn out that way. Emma's exclamation, at the end of her attempts to make a lady of Harriet Smith—"O God, that I had never seen her!"—is comic only after the atmosphere has cleared. Emma speaks the words in an agony of fear and jealousy—all the result of her tinkering with the clockwork of an insipid young woman's heart.

In characterization, *Emma* cuts the last cord of dependence upon the theater for the characters of fiction. Complication, however, as in all of Miss Austen's novels, smacks of the theater. Emma blindly mistakes the object of Mr. Elton's charades, and finds encouragement for Harriet in her error. She mistakes Harriet's gratitude to Knightley, and consequent adoration, for thankfulness to Frank Churchill for rescuing her from the band of gypsies. In both cases everything depends upon whom the "he" and the "she" refer to, and Emma's mind is never stirred to recognition of the ambiguity. These contrivances are clever but unconvincing.

Yet by the test of either entertainment or social enlightenment *Emma* remains a great novel, not without faults inherent in a still immature fictional economy, but glorified by its humanity and its lively charm.

My feeling for *Persuasion,* the last completed novel, approaches reverence. There is an exquisite closeness to the reader, a contact assured, ripened in sympathy, and perhaps retrospective of things deeply marked in Jane Austen's own life. Perhaps, too, she worked with the solemn consciousness that this was to be her final effort.

It is an unusual story of mature love, sustained over years of disappointment and carried into the years in which the gloss of passion has become the patina of confident and secure attachment. The outlook for a life together is of an order quite different from the lyric hope of beginners in the arts of affection.

On the surface, *Persuasion* seems to call into question the doctrine of the prudent marriage, the familiar theme of all the earlier novels. Yet Anne Elliot's regrets, she tells us explicitly in the concluding chapter, raise no doubts as to the rightness of the principle, or of her own wisdom in acting upon it :

> "I have been thinking over the past and trying impartially to judge of the right and wrong; I mean with regard to myself; and I must believe that I was right in being guided by the friend whom you will love better than you do now. To me she was in the place of a parent. Do not mistake me, however. I am not saying that she did not err in her advice. It was, perhaps, one of those cases in which advice is good or bad only as the event decides; and for myself, I certainly never should, in any circumstance of tolerable similarity, give such advice. But I mean that I was right in submitting to her, and that if I had done otherwise, I should have suffered more in continuing the engagement than I did in giving it up, because I should have suffered in my conscience. I have now, as far as such a sentiment is allowable in human nature, nothing to reproach myself with; and if I mistake not, a strong sense of duty is no bad part of a woman's portion."

If there is a touch of sophistry in this, it is the comforting sophistry of all of us who make our convictions part of our stock of self-respect.

Narrative art in *Persuasion* reaches a high point scarcely touched in the novels before it. Plot is tighter, action less diffuse; interest focused steadily upon the principals; emotions are handled with depth, but without glitter or sentimental stress. It opens, like *Pride and Prejudice* and *Mansfield Park,* with a satirical view of the home background, presenting the heroine only after the immediate environment has been carefully sketched in. Anne's family, "the Elliots of Kellynch Hall, in Somersetshire," is one of Miss Austen's great satirical group-portraits. Anne is the unexpectedly sensible scion of this stuffy family. She scarcely enters the story before the fourth chapter, where the making and breaking of a former engagement with Frederick Wentworth is given us in what is to all intents a perfectly designed and self-contained short story which bears comparison with a tragic episode of Turgenev or Chekhov.

Other marriages, little or big, hopeful or doubtful, are being arranged upon the horizon of the central action, and contrast manners and motives with those of the generally higher and healthier marital activities of the principals. But these other marriages are well wrought into the action, not appendages, however diverting, to the main story. Complication is neat, though not unconventional. It is almost necessary to introduce apparently rival claims upon both Anne's and Wentworth's affections in order to re-activate a devotion which had been allowed to decline into injured pride on his part and moody regret on hers. So mirages of affection enter the story which must be dissolved before truth can emerge. Yet it is as clear in the opening chapters as in the conclusion that these two are destined lovers, and no contrivance of the author's will thwart their wholly shared purpose.

Persuasion shows, if not a greater sensitiveness, a freer interest in scene and atmosphere. Any reader who remembers the stiff constraint in the description of Pemberley in *Pride and Prejudice*—the hill that, "crowned with wood, was a beautiful object," "the stream of some natural importance," the "rooms lofty and handsome, and their furniture suitable to the fortune of their proprietor"—will feel an unaccustomed responsiveness to the enjoyment Anne draws from the soft touch of external beauty upon the senses—the breath of wind and the breathlessness of calm, the spacious presence of the sea, "the influence so sweet and so sad of the autumnal months in the country," "the last smiles of the year upon the tawny leaves and withered hedges," the consoling voice of music, and the stir of the heart in the presence and movement of people. We need not invent romance for Miss Austen to account for this added grace; at the same time, it is hard to escape the feeling that reminiscence has its part in the symphonic fulness of this last novel. Her brilliant mind is less taken up with the fascinating goings-on of Mister and Miss; the reflective mind is more deeply sensible of the ambience of life. In addition to the delight we feel in the culmination of a love story of unusually pure and flowing color, there is in the prevailingly tranquil atmosphere of *Persuasion* amenity and charm less familiar in the earlier novels.

The twelve chapters left us of the unfinished and untitled novel now known as *Sanditon* show marked departures in both intention and design from any of Miss Austen's previous works. The earlier novels used a formal and somewhat stereotyped introduction—rapid but careful outlining of the domestic setting : the heroine's family background and interests, with scattered hints as to the light in which the principal characters were to be viewed and judged. *Sanditon,* however, opens with a lively bit of action, the overturning of a carriage; and with that as a fulcrum, proceeds to elaborate a theme of broader social bearing than any Miss Austen had hitherto attempted—the promotion of an ambitious building development in a quiet and pretty sea-front village.

The approach differs again in the rapid, perhaps too rapid, accumulation of characters—twenty-five, to be precise—in the dozen chapters outlined before the work was laid aside. And while some of these must be secondary, or even supernumerary, a more varied action seems to be in the making, with a plot possibly greater in both mass and complexity than we have found customary with Miss Austen. One character, familiar in eighteenth-century fiction, she had so far refused to use with the rest of the properties of the novel of manners—the young fop in the role of seducer. She introduces him with a new approach, affected literary chit-chat, and a technique for which he owns himself indebted to Richardson's Lovelace. Perhaps intrigue was to play a greater part in the action, though we seem to be put on notice that the two candidates for the place of heroine are sensibly aware of the young man's designs.

Little can be guessed as to the probable course of the story, not merely because it stops short before complication is set in motion, but because an unconventional character-set seems to promise more than a conventional plot. The one fact that is both clear and important is that *Sanditon* was to deal with the allurements and dangers of speculation, and that "Mr. Parker of Sanditon" was to embody the vulgar optimism of the single-minded money-maker, to anticipate the Christopher Newman, the Silas Lapham, and the Teddy Ponderevo of fictions still many years in the future. And while the aspect of the theme that would have attracted Miss Austen's interest must have been the comedy of personality rather than the pitfalls of economic delusion, it is still true that what we know of *Sanditon* intimates a notable enlargement of her horizon. A devoted "Janeite" may be forgiven for lamenting that it was this particular novel that failed of completion; for in it Miss Austen seems to have been moving into a world of larger dimensions and more critical issues.

2   *The Mind of the Novelist*

OUR FINAL look at Jane Austen is to summarize her debt to tradition both literary and intellectual and to measure the significance of her own contribution to tradition.

Accepting Jane Austen as Virginia Woolf's "common reader" must accept her, I have tried to present her as a sympathetic and articulate judge of her own society; simple in the most acceptable sense, but not naïve, profound but not sententious (for she was wise enough to distrust the wisdom of the adage), satirical but not above sincerity and good humor. In the three prayers still preserved which she wrote for the family devotions, she asks in effect in all three to be enabled "to consider our fellow creatures with kindness, and to judge of all they say and do with charity." She seems to intimate here a misgiving that her incomparable gift of irony might slip into sarcasm (as it rarely does) or even cynicism. What is most distinctive and most memorable in her work is that unmuddied flow of ironic genius, implicit in and inseparable from her personality. For as Kierkegaard suggests, irony is not a trick of the artist, but a trait, ingrained in character and judgment and liberated in the work of art.

Fair appraisal of Miss Austen's art must entail first of all recognition of the still unproved art with which she was familiar and from which her earliest novels took their pattern; also of the fluid state of social criticism, particularly as it touched woman's place and outlook. She dates, indisputably, as in the eyes of the future we all will; but dating is for the fully civilized reader a significant part of the literary personality.

It should be clear from what has been said that her early years were a conscious but not a passive literary pupilage, not the less serviceable because she was amused as well as instructed by her preceptresses. And it was not a matter of choice that her intructors were schoolmarms rather than schoolmasters, for we have seen that over the previous quarter of a century, and apart from the fictions of the revolutionaries, the better novels of the period came from the hands of women.

Reading was, indeed, the liberating part of Miss Austen's education, more important than the home schoolroom, whatever it may have offered. Her formal schooling stopped at nine. Her reading was probably not severely directed, if we can judge from the startling titles of the minor Gothics mentioned in *Northanger Abbey*. Yet except where she offers in her novels an occasional but meagerly favorable opinion, we are without a clue as to where a more than common familiarity with fiction left her. Her own reminder in a letter to Cassandra that the Austen family were "great readers of novels" stands plain but unglossed. Even in the letters there is no word of serious discussion of the novels the family read.

We have suggestions, for the most part only memoranda or allusions, as to the range of her reading.* Allusions cannot always be safe evidence of

---

*The literary allusions in novels, letters, and *fragmenta* are indexed in an appendix to Volume V of R. W. Chapman's (Oxford) edition of the novels.

reading, but in Miss Austen's case there seems to be no reason to question their pertinence. Of course she had read all Fanny Burney's novels, and Miss Edgeworth's *Belinda*; but her silence upon the *Tales of Fashionable Life* and even *Castle Rackrent* is misleading; for she makes it clear in one of her letters that she read Miss Edgeworth faithfully. Casual references tell us that she was acquainted with *Robinson Crusoe, Tom Jones, Tristram Shandy, The Sentimental Journey, Clarissa,* and *Grandison,* but she mentions neither *Pamela* nor *Amelia.* Her brother Henry's "biographical notice" to the posthumous *Northanger Abbey* and *Persuasion* tells us that "she did not rank any work of Fielding quite so high" as *Grandison,* "which gratified the natural discrimination of her mind, whilst her taste secured her from the errors of his prolix style and tedious narrative." An undeveloped episode in *Sanditon,* however, shows misgivings as to the moral effect of *Clarissa.*

Probably she knew all of Ann Radcliffe, though she does not refer to her first two very minor tales. She had read many other Gothics and the near-Gothics of Charlotte Smith; and in one of her letters she indulges herself in a mild "rave" over Eaton Stannard Barrett's spoof of the Gothics, *The Heroine* (1813).

Her single reference to Godwin, in the letters, is a slap at his seedy appearance, but that was common talk. If she had ever read a novel of his, it would be particularly interesting to know what she thought of it. Of course she knew *Rasselas,* for Johnson was her favorite prose writer. *The Vicar of Wakefield,* alluded to in *Emma,* she apparently thought of as a story for a commonplace mind. She preferred Scott's poetry to his fiction. She is silent, surprisingly, on Smollett, for whom Fanny Burney had good words, likewise on Beckford, Bage, Holcroft, Mary Wollstonecraft, and, less surprisingly, on most of the minor women novelists—even though when her preferences are strongly expressed, they are for the superior writers of her own sex.

As to her reactions to poetry, again we learn little that is explicit; but she knew her Shakespeare and all the better eighteenth-century poets. In *Persuasion,* however, there is talk about poetry. Anne Elliot discusses Scott and Byron—vaguely again, so far as Miss Austen records the conversation—with the bereaved Captain Benwick. The talk is a sort of sentimental holiday for Benwick, but it opens up no hint of whether at this late day Scott and Byron had displaced Crabbe and Cowper in Miss Austen's own preferences. One thing, however, is clear. Anne, in the conclusion, "thought it was the misfortune of poetry to be seldom safely enjoyed by those who enjoyed it completely; and that the strong feelings which alone could estimate it truly were the very feelings which ought to taste it but sparingly." That mistrust of emotional responsiveness to poetry is echoed in the unfinished *Sanditon*. But it should be added that it is romantic excess, not the romantic impulse, that bothers Anne. Miss Austen has, in fact, voiced much the same feeling here as in *Northanger Abbey* when she deplores "the luxury of a raised, restless, and frightened imagination" in Catherine Morland's absorption in *Udolpho*.

Evidently Miss Austen had done a great deal of reading in the British theater. Her opportunities of seeing plays were probably limited. The whole record, however, of fiction, poetry, drama, with Boswell, books of travel, sermons, and miscellaneous reading, is not unimpressive.

Miss Austen adds to the remark that her family are great novel-readers, that they are "not ashamed" of it. The defensive note is significant. Yet defense does not entail argument; and where much professional criticism was conservative, and as yet not too articulate, perhaps we should not expect to find literary small talk expressing much more than simple likes or dislikes. Miss Austen herself, even when most consciously appreciative, only notes her feelings; she does not explore them or bring them into discussable order. So it is difficult to judge what she thought of her contemporaries or of the novelist's art.

There can be little doubt, however, that the weightiest direct influence in her reading, and ultimately upon her writing, was Fanny Burney. Indeed, one of her fonder critics traces that influence into examples of what might appear to be servile copying.* But the residues of reading that stick to the unconscious memory have often accounted for what might seem to be imitation. On the other hand, particularly admirable (and therefore memorable) "bits" are what competent and self-respecting writers would be careful to avoid repeating. Where Jane Austen looks most like Frances Burney is where Miss Burney herself is patently the child of her time; and if we detect echoes of Miss Burney in Miss Austen's earliest work, they vanish in the later—a fact that needs no argument if·we compare *Mansfield Park* with *The Wanderer,* published in the same year.

The most obvious resemblance between Miss Burney and Miss Austen is in style. The simple fact is that both labor with the burden of late Johnsonese. But with what a difference! Miss Burney's idolatry of her great preceptor was never relaxed; indeed, it became more constrained, more binding, as her years accumulated, until her prose became hopelessly stilted, involved, and obscure.† Miss Austen's Johnsonese never exceeds the standards of "elegance" still current in her time. Yet even in her dialogue

---

*R. Brimley Johnson, *The Women Novelists,* 1919, pp. 117-130. There are interesting items of evidence, but I feel sure that in two instances of phrasal parallelism Miss Austen quotes in the confidence that the phrase *will* be recognized. The argument on the whole seems to prove too much.

†See page 222.

she shows Johnson's circuitousness and turgidity. It was a confined and confining tradition upon which she had to build; so her writing lacks some of the ease and grace of plain English that remained to be rediscovered by later novelists.

These insufficiencies in Miss Austen's prose are probably mental hazards for the reader of today; these, and her overloading of dialogue. For it must be admitted that she stretches the conversational tolerances beyond their limits of elasticity. The point may be illustrated by this substantial quotation from *Persuasion*. Wentworth and Anne Elliot are discussing Benwick's engagement, a development not particularly wise in itself, yet a deliverance from misunderstanding on the parts of both speakers. Wentworth opens the conversation.

"With all my soul I wish them happy, and rejoice over every circumstance in favor of it. They have no difficulties to contend with at home, no opposition, no caprice, no delays. The Musgroves are behaving like themselves, most honorably and kindly, only anxious with true parental hearts to promote their daughter's comfort. All this is much, very much in favor of their happiness; more than perhaps—"

He stopped. A sudden recollection seemed to occur, and to give him some taste of that emotion which was reddening Anne's cheeks and fixing her eyes on the ground. After clearing his throat, however, he proceeded thus :

"I confess that I do think there is a disparity, too great a disparity, and in a point no less essential than mind. I regard Louisa Musgrove as a very amiable, sweet-tempered girl, and not deficient in understanding, but Benwick is something more. He is a clever man, a reading man; and I confess that I do consider his attaching himself to her with some surprise. Had it been the effect of gratitude, had he learnt to love her because he believed her to be preferring him, it would have been another thing. But I have no reason to suppose it so. It seems, on the contrary, to have been a perfectly spontaneous, untaught feeling on his side, and this surprises me. A man like him, in his situation! with a heart pierced, wounded, almost broken! Fanny Harville was a very superior creature, and his attachment to her was indeed attachment. A man does not recover from such a devotion of the heart to such a woman! He ought not; he does not!"

Either from the consciousness, however, that his friend had recovered, or from some other consciousness, he went no further; and Anne, who, in spite of the agitated voice in which the latter part had been uttered, and in spite of all the various noises of the room, the almost ceaseless slam of the door, and ceaseless buzz of persons walking through, had distinguished every word, was struck, gratified, confused, and beginning to breathe very quick, and feel a hundred things in a moment. It was impossible for her to enter on such a subject; and yet, after a pause, feeling the necessity of speaking, and having not the smallest wish for a total change, she only deviated so far as to say :

"You were a good while at Lyme, I think?"

"About a fortnight. I could not leave it until Louisa's doing well was quite ascertained. I had been too deeply concerned in the mischief to be soon at peace. It had been my doing, solely mine. She would not have been obstinate if I had not been weak. The country round Lyme is very fine. I walked and rode a great deal, and the more I saw, the more I found to admire."

"I should very much like to see Lyme again," said Anne.

"Indeed! I should not have supposed that you could have found anything in Lyme to inspire such a feeling. The horror and distress you were involved in, the stretch of mind, the wear of spirits! I should have thought your last impressions of Lyme must have been strong disgust."

"The last few hours were certainly very painful," replied Anne. "but when pain is over, the remembrance of it often becomes a pleasure. One does not love a place the less for having suffered in it, unless it has been all suffering, which was by no means the case at Lyme. We were only in anxiety and distress during the last two hours, and previously there had been a great deal of enjoyment. So much novelty and beauty! I have traveled so little that every fresh place would be interesting to me, but there is real beauty at Lyme, and in short," with a faint blush at some recollections, "altogether my impressions of the place are very agreeable."

As she ceased, the entrance door opened again, and the very party appeared for whom they were waiting.

No one who knows the authentic note of Miss Austen's dialogue would think this passage an exceptional one. Admitting all extenuations, and conceding the stiff ritualism of conversation, as of every aspect of manners at the time, the fact remains that both Wentworth and Anne are making speeches. We miss the short periods of the spoken word, whatever their insufficiency for instant and clear understanding. To make dialogue sound like talk, yet to give it the circumference and depth that talk rarely achieves—that is the novelist's problem. Miss Austen has not solved it, though in her hands the instrument is used more deftly than in Miss Burney's.

These relics of eighteenth-century prose mechanics simply show the evanescence of literary fashion. Yet Miss Austen gives us compensating passages, regrettably rare, of sparkling and beautifully balanced prose :

The remembrance of a person and face of strong, natural, sterling insignificance.

Prettier musings of high-wrought love and eternal constancy would never have passed along the streets of Bath than Anne was sporting with from Camden Place to Westgate Buildings. It was almost enough to spread purification and perfume all the way.

It seemed as if there were an instantaneous impression in her favor, as if his eyes received the truth from hers, and all that had passed of good in her feelings were at once caught and honored.

But prose of this transparency is memorable just because it is exceptional. Her aptitude for plain but penetrating phrase she usually sacrifices upon the altar of elegance.

Yet her style is never highly orchestrated. The problem of the word, and of the setting for the word, is for her an intellectual one, her aim precision and refinement. If by style we mean conscious beautification, then it must be said that the early novels are extremely sparing of it. Even at her best—say, in *Emma* and *Persuasion*—her style is disciplined rather than ingratiating.

To the mind of the conscientious eighteenth-century writer, no art could be practised without deference to the appropriate principle of form. But Miss Austen seems to have been little concerned with critical premises. She accepted form as it came to her hands, and problems of structure seem to have been settled upon lines of convenience. Her assiduous revision proves her capacity for self-criticism, but her happy freedom from twaddle about "my art," even in her family letters, would imply that her critical views were largely empirical. In the mere handful of references to her literary labor we find scarcely a word of the theoretical approach. Her most sustained critical pronouncements are found in a series of letters to her niece, Anna Austen (Lefroy), written in 1814 when Anna was trying her hand at a novel of her own. Even here, her suggestions seem less technical than tutorial—matters of probability, consistency, diction, even topography. When she drops her brief comments upon the novels of her lesser contemporaries, they seem as a rule deliberately trivial.

Her easy attitude toward problems of construction is confirmed in her indifference to a consistent narrative point of view. Though she adopts in general the omniscient perspective, at times she steps boldly into her narrative to drop a suggestion of motive, to record a personal judgment, or even to indulge a whim. And her omniscience, it must be added, penetrates only the minds of her women characters. She never displays the mental workings of her males except through speech and act.

Doubt as to whether she stands among the greatest of novelists seems to rest in large part upon the feeling that her novels lack hard impact. It is at any rate certain that the qualities she admired in Burney and Edgeworth, and that furnished the staging for her own work, could be (to borrow an analogy) compared with those of Vermeer or LeBrun; not of El Greco or Rembrandt. Indeed, she would perhaps have been a more broadly accomplished artist if she had cared more about the arts in general. But there is reason to think that she was not at home in other areas of art.

Although pianos and harps are familiar in her novels, and young ladies, including her heroines, play them, there is, I believe, in the whole breadth of her work only one allusion to a composer—Frank Churchill's off-hand reference in *Emma* to "Cramer", a momentarily popular pianist-composer then in London. A determining incident in *Persuasion* is the concert at the Rooms in Bath at which Anne Elliot's cultivation is called upon to supply a translation for the words of an Italian song; but it is just a song, written apparently by nobody and set to music by nobody. Would it have spoiled the situation to have supplied a title for it? There are possibly a score of references to music in the novels and letters, most of them intimating that she knew what she liked and refused to be interested in what she did not like.

> . . . . A concert with Illuminations and fireworks; to the latter Eliz. & I look forward with pleasure, and even the concert will have more than it's usual charm for me, as the gardens are large enough for me to get pretty well beyond the reach of its sound.

This is all very honest, but perhaps it reveals a somewhat obstinate aesthetic insensibility.

As to painting—just as she went to the concerts in Bath, she visited the galleries in London during the months she lived there with her brother Henry. But a remark in one of the letters suggests that she went to look at people rather than paintings. That was good for her own art, no doubt, but disappointing if we would think of her as a woman of informed and expressive tastes. And in *Pride and Prejudice* she takes pains to tell us, as a sort of tribute to Elizabeth Bennett's candor, not only that she knew little about painting, but that she could really prefer a commonplace decorative home product to a presumably first rate work of art:

> The picture gallery, and two or three of the principal bedrooms, were all that remained to be shown. In the former were many good paintings, but Elizabeth knew nothing of the art; and from such as had been visible below, she had willingly turned to look at some drawings of Miss Darcy's, in crayons, whose subjects were usually more interesting, and also more intelligible.

It does not excuse Elizabeth's ignorance that it marks her as still provincial. But it is unfortunate that Jane Austen should appear to think her frankness in the matter commendable; for it seems to reflect her indifference to "effects" in her own art; and that is, with equal frankness, something at times to be regretted.

In setting, the novels again give us occasional reminders of Miss Burney or Miss Edgeworth, but in the main only when her characters are away from the home base. In *Northanger Abbey* and *Persuasion* much of the action takes place in Bath, with which Miss Austen was familiar. It was the one haunt of urban society that she depicts for us with any show of pleasure in the scene or the people. London in *Sense and Sensibility* is a dreary place because of the very circumstances which brought the Dashwood girls there. In *Pride and Prejudice* and *Mansfield Park* the minor London action is off-stage.

But Miss Austen's brief excursions into fashionable life are very different from those of her predecessors. *Evelina* and *Northanger Abbey* both deal with the education of an ingenue; but the reader is left in *Evelina* with a doubt as to whether the girl has become educated in anything but society manners. Catherine Morland, on the other hand, has acquired social dimensions, and a trifling theme has taken on significance. Pride of family and position, which Miss Burney makes the focus of complication in *Evelina* and *Cecilia*, she liquidates by conventional compromises—in *Evelina* by the timeworn theatrical expedient of making a supposedly illegitimate daughter legitimate, in *Cecilia* by the heroine's surrendering a claim upon a fortune which has been largely dissipated and for which there is another conveniently at hand to replace it. When Miss Austen adopts the same theme in *Northanger Abbey, Pride and Prejudice,* and *Mansfield Park,* she reduces it to ridicule in *Northanger Abbey,* solves it by comic regeneration in *Pride and Prejudice,* and settles it in *Mansfield Park* by a common-sense recognition of the realities.

The rural social setting is with Miss Burney little more than a point of departure in her first two novels. Miss Edgeworth in her Irish novels makes it a point of safe return. For Miss Austen it is the circumference of her interest. She chooses, and almost confines herself to, the county estates and villages, with their cultivated upper middle-class society, landed or comfortably wealthy, worldly-wise but orthodox, caste-conscious, familiar with marital arrangements and settlements, and making rare but brilliant incursions into the closed aristocracy of the neighborhood when beauty, charm, intelligence, and social endowments combine for the greater glory of one of their women. Miss Burney, and for that matter Bage and Miss Edgeworth, have a weakness for the crossing of the social orbits of the country-bred young lady and an unimpeachably aristocratic hero. Miss Austen, however, likes her self-contained society, and it is only in *Pride and Prejudice* that her heroine marries both fortune and social eminence, and then only in the landed gentry. She has, indeed, a weakness for saving her heroine from a "brilliant" marriage by placing her in the chaste arms of a clerical younger son. Yet she really pictures her chosen society with distinction, and with cheerful confidence in its rightness as well as its comfort and security.

It is easy, with a well-ripened social prejudice, to interpret that satisfaction with her own society as snobbish. That is not just to Miss Austen, whose outlook upon the world outside her own social periphery is incurious rather than superior. If she accepts her environment with complacency, it is the complacency of modesty, not of smugness. It is difficult to find an English word that takes in the whole of her social consciousness. It embodies both personal and class pride, but free from arrogance or parade; it embraces dignity, but not affected dignity; it respects propriety, but not modish manners or taboos; it interprets the full life as one of material well-being, as well as of leisure, mental and spiritual resources, and opportunity for enjoyment.

Beyond these criteria of a satisfying social balance, she seems to cherish certain, perhaps unescapable, idols of the cave. These are hers by inherence and habit, rather than by choice and approval.

For example, her father was a clergyman; two of her brothers became clergymen; and she accepts the spiritual calling as a polite and respected way of life, but without an active show of interest in the meaning of the spiritual life for the man who chooses it. Three of her heroines marry clergymen (four, if one counts the proposed ending for *The Watsons*), all of them with moderate but independent fortunes to prevent the holy life from becoming exigent. They are nice young men, but apparently quite free from spiritual ferment.

Two of her brothers were naval officers—both in time admirals. Naval rank, like the Church, was a desirable social placement. Yet in *Persuasion,* the story of a naval officer's romance, only sentimental words are said of the life of the captain of a frigate in the great Nelson's day. For Miss Austen, the navy was status rather than life, and Captain Wentworth, so far as his social perspective and habits are revealed to us, might about as well have been a landsman.

These would seem to be for Miss Austen the two noble professions. In the army, always less glittering to a maritime nation, she was less interested, and apparently less confident of its requirements of character and its effects upon character. But it furnishes her with a gentlemanly retired colonel in *Sense and Sensibility,* a sparkish captain in *Northanger Abbey,* and a rascal in *Pride and Prejudice.*

The Church, in general, and the services, sheltered the younger sons

of the landed families, but the éclat of the system was kept up by the
eldest sons, inheritors of rank and estates. The life Miss Austen shows us is
their life of gentlemanly pursuits, of carefully managed income and outgo,
its background well designed but not very ancient houses, landscaped
shrubberies, gardens and espaliers, carriages and footmen, sprigged mus-
lins and embroidered waistcoats, and furniture declared by Miss Austen to
be "in the best taste."

But what taste means for the decorative setting of that life we are
never told. Pemberley, she assures us, is a revelation of aristocratic taste in
landscaping, furniture, and objects of art. It is, of course, a carefully contrived setting, to play a part in Elizabeth's changing estimate of Darcy.
Her instant impressions are favorable, but her phrases of commendation
are without substance. Apparently her eye is not drawn to what is blest by
years and tradition, but to what exhibits the seal of Darcy's choice. That
she has any sense of values is shown only in the conventional distinction
she makes between "splendor" and "real elegance," and that seems simply
to echo drawing-room conversation.*

I have noted the dimness of association in Miss Austen's word "taste,"
not because it could be easily bettered by any considered mode of satisfying
either the eye or the mind, but because she presumes upon its vagueness.
We can imagine her saying, "if you could understand what I mean, you
would not have to ask." That *argumentum ad ignorantiam* would strike
many of us as not only unreasonable but arrogant.

But if Jane has little to tell us as to taste in things material, that may
not be greatly important; for that aspect of taste is part of the flow of time.
In deportment and manners, however, it is not merely a matter of fashion
or ephemeral. There are durable values here, though changeable; and
her criteria of taste in this area are intelligibly developed, not by precepts,
but as they should be, in the actions and attitudes of her men and women.
In spite of her reliance upon taste as the cachet of quality, however, she
does not accept it as the matter of determining interest in the life she
depicts. She never confuses it with understanding, as the society novel
before her time tended to do.

It has been held against Miss Austen that her society is not only a
confined society but a woman's society, seen through a woman's eyes.
The objection itself is one-sided, for it is pressed, naturally enough, by

---

*Elizabeth Bowen (*Notes on Writing a Novel*) regards Jane Austen's indifference to the detail
of scene and setting as "proof of her mastery of the novel." I agree that "effects" that have
no significant connection with action, character, or mood can be very questionable contributions to interest, But I maintain my point that when Miss Austen insists on taste as an
attribute of gentility, the reader can be forgiven for wondering whether it means anything
more to her than fashion, if, indeed, it means anything at all definite.

men rather than women. Granted that a woman is bound as a woman to depict life as a woman sees it, is it to be thought that she judges it with less intelligence? Some critics have said yes, that women writers and women readers of fiction (who no doubt outnumber men readers) have deprived the novel of muscle and blood. But have muscle and blood more to do with the wholeness of life than what women have brought into the novel?* There is an even deeper implication in this impatient attitude toward the woman as novelist—that men know more about women than women know about men—a matter not to be argued temperately.

The defense of the woman novelist, if it needs to be urged, is after all the nature of her social intelligence, which has been adequately set forth in George Meredith's essay on comedy.† He credits the woman of intelligence with a special aptitude for discovering and judging the self-deceptions of the superior male. This is the area in which Miss Austen's comic perception appears at its best. The voices of her admirable women are the voice of Jane Austen, whether in the high moral mood of Elinor Dashwood and Fanny Price, or in the ironic humor of Elizabeth Bennett and Emma Woodhouse. And it is to her credit that in giving her women that commentative function, she has made them neither priggish nor shrewish.

The fact remains that Jane Austen's one plot (with a single exception) —the capturing of a well-placed and well-to-do husband—approaches its problem, and solves it, from the point of view of a woman's thoughts, feelings, and interests. However the husband-to-be may look like the active mind in the transaction, as Knightley does in *Emma* and Wentworth in *Persuasion,* it is the woman's experience that Miss Austen submits to analysis, because she understands it and can voice it.

The eighteenth-century novelists were generous to their heroines with both love and fortune, and youth with which to make the most of both. Fortune was, in fiction and theater, a postulate of the theme of love, whether it smiled beside the cradle of the heroine or proved her skill at angling. If it was conceived as a reward for anything, it was for looking pretty and behaving nicely. Miss Austen, still favoring the happy conjunction of love and fortune, took a different view of their relationship. Fortune, at least a comfortable freedom from want, she did regard as a reward —for prudence. Love was, as Miss Austen depicted him, no reckless child of a more reckless goddess-mother, but an Eros sitting in the broad warm lap of a matronly Athena and bending his bow as she wisely approved. But she distinguishes between the judicious marriage and the mercenary, a distinction necessary for her purpose when she defines it, in *Pride*

---

*I dismiss the challenge to declare plainly what it *is* that women have brought into the novel, because that is in large part what I have been writing this book about.
† *On the Idea of Comedy and the Uses of the Comic Spirit,* 1877.

and Prejudice,* but one that can never be free from a suggestion of casuistry. For however comprehensive the accepted idea of prudence may be, Miss Austen herself makes the case for it to an important degree in terms of income. And since she had only begun to assimilate the conception of trade as a not dishonorable source of wealth, her "prudence" is usually referable to an assured and handsome inherited affluence. Even her clergymen who turn out to be successful suitors are younger sons who have quite enough of what it takes.

In Miss Austen's view, the instinct for security, no doubt a part of woman's physical and social nature, was particularly important for a woman whose acceptance of life was determined by other pressures than the struggle against poverty and squalor. In taking that position, she follows the lead of the women novelists of another generation. But her insistence upon the disciplining of the heart almost inevitably raises uncertainty as to the value she places upon what is commonly called "true" affection. There are readers who complain that her ear is deaf to the coloratura passages of lyric love. The matter has been put even more strongly; her women, it has been said, cannot interest the he-man because they exhibit only moral passion, not physical.

One must distinguish here. Any appreciative reader will admit her cleverness and delicacy in the treatment of the social aspects of sex—the fluttering interest of her women in the apparition of a new eligible, the amusing rituals of flirtation, and the pressure of expertly schooled charm. But these are merely the furniture of traditional romance. She still seems to distrust and avoid the impulsions of highly emotionalized and undisguised passion. Her lovers are never seen or heard to breathe a word to each other of demonstrative affection. In the whole range of her fiction she records just one embrace—in *Mansfield Park*—but it is a brotherly-sisterly gesture between cousins as yet unaware of a stronger sentiment. Is she afraid of the physical?† Does she misunderstand it, or undervalue it, or sniff

---

*Elizabeth raises the question with Mrs. Gardiner: "Pray, my dear aunt, what is the difference in matrimonial affairs, between the mercenary and the prudent motive? Where does discretion end and avarice begin?"

†Here again, we must distinguish, between the physical and the sensual. Miss Austen's most restless loves—Marianne's, say, or Edmund Bertram's—are not, as she presents them, sensual, although they are heady, and in Marianne's case heedless. Even in the Henry Crawford-Maria Rushworth affair in *Mansfield Park* the motives on either side are not unambiguously sensual. Henry has snared himself into an adventure, and (it is no uncommon eighteenth-century reaction) seeks compensation for the discomfiture of his refusal by Fanny; and Maria is fed up by an unendurably stupid husband. Evidently Miss Austen did not feel that the case for prudence had to be argued against an abandoned sexuality. Of course her attitude makes good fun for those who think the prostratingly dull *Fanny Hill* a milestone in our intellectual liberation.

at it? Or is it that she herself, the anti-sentimentalist, has sentimentalized love to the point of trying to shield it from the profanation of the curious eye?

Marriage proposals, where love is truly and securely proved, are read into the record rather than acted out, although in *Mansfield Park,* in *Emma,* and in *Pride and Prejudice* she can elaborately dramatize a refusal. In *Sense and Sensibility* her avoidance of the spoken word may be excused, because a second choice, however satisfactory, scarcely invites exuberance. In *Pride and Prejudice* Darcy's second proposal is skillfully led up to by an opening, incautious but not bold, on Elizabeth's part, only to be snuffed out by Miss Austen's careful rhetoric. In *Mansfield Park* a profound affection, impending over the entire action, is dismissed in the end in three sentences of unimpassioned prose—and they are not the words of the lovers. In *Emma* the ritual of proposal is neglected, though Knightley's sentiments are clear. In *Persuasion* Miss Austen discovered an obligation to the reader after she had finished her story, and refashioned the first draft of the proposal scene, though still with reserve.

To say that Miss Austen does not over-dramatize affection is perhaps serious understatement. Take for example the first flowering (I believe that is the accepted phrase) of Elizabeth's conscious interest in Darcy, after she had met him again at Pemberley :

> She lay awake two whole hours endeavoring to make [her feelings] out. She certainly did not hate him. No; hatred had vanished long ago, and she had almost as long been ashamed of ever feeling a dislike against him, that could be so called. The respect created by the conviction of his valuable qualities, though at first unwillingly admitted, had for some time ceased to be repugnant to her feeling; and it was now heightened into somewhat of a friendlier nature by the testimony so highly in his favor, and bringing forward his disposition in so amiable a light, which yesterday had produced. But above all, above respect and esteem, there was a motive within her of good will which could not be overlooked. It was gratitude; gratitude not merely for having once loved her, but for loving her still well enough to forgive all the petulance and acrimony of her manner in rejecting him, and all the unjust accusations accompanying her rejection. He who, she had been persuaded, would avoid her as his greatest enemy, seemed, on this accidental meeting, most eager to preserve the acquaintance, and without any indelicate display of regard, or any peculiarity of manner, where their two selves only were concerned, was soliciting the good opinion of her friends, and bent on making her known to his sister. Such a change in a man of so much pride excited not only astonishment but gratitude—for to love, ardent love, it must be attributed; and as such, its impression on her was of a sort to be encouraged, as by no means unpleasing,

though it could not be exactly defined. She respected, she esteemed, she was grateful to him, she felt a real interest in his welfare; and she only wanted to know how far she wished that welfare to depend upon herself, and how far it would be for the happiness of both that she should employ the power, which her fancy told her she still possessed, of bringing on the renewal of his addresses.

The negatives have peculiar force in revealing what might be called the judicial approach to conscious affection : "She certainly did not hate him"; "the respect, though at first unwillingly admitted"; "its impression on her was of a sort to be encouraged, as by no means unpleasing." Elizabeth's ponderings embrace survey, analysis, recognition, a forward look, and finally a soupçon of strategy. These are bedtime reflections, but carefully laundered; so far as we can see without the faintest residual stain of physical consciousness. What would Byron have thought of them? Or Shelley? Yet for all its calculated reticences, the passage is not ineffectual. Beneath Elizabeth's "good will," her "gratitude," her "respect," her "real interest in his welfare," there is the clear dawn of affirmative love, however touched with gratitude and intensified by her sense of her earlier errors in misjudging Darcy. Rational and affective sentiment are ready to join for a result already clear to two thinking and feeling minds. This is Miss Austen's way, perhaps prissy, but it leaves us in no doubt as to just what she wishes to communicate. Elizabeth's meditation upon Darcy is as satisfactorily revealing as Mrs. Waters' less intellectual appraisal of Tom Jones—conceding the essential fact that Elizabeth Bennett is not a Mrs. Waters.

All of Miss Austen's novels, then, are studies in the subordination of passion to ultimate well-being. This had been, in one form or another, almost universally the theme of the women novelists from Mrs. Haywood, through Miss Burney, Mrs. Inchbald, Miss Edgeworth, and a host of less accomplished writers. When wedded to romantic incident in Charlotte Smith and Mrs. Radcliffe, it was still the salient theme for the woman novelist. But where Miss Austen's predecessors had often exploited the drama of self-extinction almost implicit in the more rational attitude, she refused to sentimentalize prudence by identifying it with martyrdom.

The women novelists (including Miss Austen) did not, as a rule, encourage revolt. Mary Wollstonecraft was the exception; and it might be noted that the direct answer to her radical teaching was also a woman's—the story of *Adeline Mowbray* (1805), written by Mrs. Amelia Opie, a friend of the Godwins before their marriage. Adeline learns the hard way that in spite of all that is unpredictable in conventional marriage, it offers its advantages to a sensible and adaptable wife. Miss Austen herself is without the makings of a rebel. She was, in fact, little interested in movements for reform—of anything—and she looked to personal wisdom and foresight to "place" her women.

It happened that her own solution of the woman's problem was not marriage, but too much may be inferred from that fact. She had, in the first place, through her family, a modest independence; so for her marriage was not a forced choice. In addition, from the very little that her sister Cassandra, the self-appointed protectresss of her memory, has permitted us to know of her inward life, and from scraps of knowledge from other sources, it seems clear that she was interested in young men, that she looked with encouragement, if not with hope, upon some of her earlier male acquaintances, that she had reached an understanding with a man to whom she felt she could give her heart, only to lose him through his early death, and that in her maturer years she had accepted a suitor for "prudent" reasons, but begged after a night of painful soul-searching, to be absolved of a decision in which her heart had not been sufficiently consulted. It is recounted further, though with apparent malice, that in her green years she had been thought a rather desperate flirt. And on the best of evidence we know that she was fond of dancing and parties and chat with men, and that within her family, when she was consulted upon problems of the heart, she could deal with them understandingly and with humor.

So she was no tabby. It was not incongruent with her personal experience that any of her novels might properly have been called "Getting Married." But a place in a good man's bed would probably not greatly have enlarged her understanding of the young lady's problem, which was planning the greater part of one's life with a partner who might or might not live up to romantic anticipations.

Her work, then, confronts us with a somewhat narrowly conditioned social outlook, and curious, though not for her time uncustomary, reticences. But her avoidance of topical and direct discussion of sex was no more, nor less, than her concession to good manners. The novels are silent upon matters which in her letters to her sister she discusses with interested and often laughable candor.

> We plan having a steady cook, and a young and giddy housemaid, with a sedate, middle-aged man who is to undertake the double office of husband to the former and sweetheart to the latter, no children of course to be allowed on either side.

These are not the words of a woman who over-valued propriety or blushed at broad humor. Nor are these which follow, her remarks on the decor of a select young lady's school :

The appearance of the drawing-room, so totally unschool-like, amused me very much. It was full of all the modern elegancies; and if it had not been for some naked Cupids over the mantelpiece which must have been a fine study for girls, one should never have smelt instruction.

And she credits herself with "a very good eye for an Adultress, for tho' repeatedly assured that another in the same party was the *She,* I fixed upon her right from the first."

At the same time, she was not blind to the fact that in her unsophisticated day sexual amusement, however proper and allowable, might carry with it embarrassments and even dangers for her sex. She counsels a niece thinking of early marriage to reflect—perhaps to wait.

Then, by not beginning the business of mothering quite so early in life, you will be young in constitution, spirits, figure, and countenance, while Mrs. Wm. Hammond is growing old by confinements and nursing.

That advice transcends the counsel of prudence; indeed, to many of her contemporaries it might have seemed frivolous or sinful. Marriage was in the current view a holy state, to be entered upon soberly, reverently, and in the fear of God. Ought prudence to embrace such worldly deterrents as the preservation of one's good looks, figure, and spirits? We tread new ground here. Miss Austen is questioning the brood-mare conception of marriage which was so important a part of the property and class philosophy of the time, and so casual a part of the unthinking fatalism (or the religious resignation) of the lower classes. In this friendly advice, reflected in many other passages in the letters, we confront the question of what Jane Austen thought of marriage itself. Her attitude was certainly in some degree the fruit of her sobering observation of what marriage then entailed for the married woman—in the example, let us say, of the young sister in law who died fulfilling her womanly duty in the birth of her eleventh child, physically wasted, as Jane was fully aware, by breeding. Of a niece, again pregnant, she says, "Poor Animal, she will be worn out before she is thirty—I am very sorry for her." But her reactions, we may be sure, were not merely sympathetic; they had a rational sanction in what was already being thought and said upon these matters.

In the novels themselves, Miss Austen shows the immemorial preference of writers of fiction for bringing a narrative only as far as the altar, if indeed quite as far as that august station. Yet her settled marriages, even where normal compatability and adaptiveness are to be assumed, are often doubtful recommendations of the holy state. The parents of her heroines, when we are permitted to meet them, are on the whole not much the better for years of marital give and take. Four functioning mothers are introduced in her novels, Lady Bertram, for purpose of comparison, standing *in loco parentis*. One of them is a woman of sense, one a featherbrain, and two of them mollusks. Fathers she has a penchant for presenting as somewhat imperfect examples of wisdom and responsibility. In most of the novels one or both parents of either hero or heroine have paid the debt of mortality, and while their deaths seem to have left behind an aura of conventional sentiment, there are generally scattered hints that the departed may not have been desperately unhappy at leaving their little world. The wives of General Tilney, Mr. Woodhouse, and Mr. Elliot must all have supplemented affection with singular endurance. Marriages of subsidiary characters—generally brothers or sisters or cousins—are as a rule strained or insipid. A number are conspiracies in selfishness or snobbery; in the case of the Eltons, in malice as well. Others, such as those of the Rushworths in *Mansfield Park* and the heir to the Elliot estate, have gone on the rocks of indifference or cruelty. The Prices in *Mansfield Park* are consigned to social outer darkness as examples of youthful unwisdom now bearing bitter fruit. There are three congenial and wholly satisfied couples—the Carpenters of *Pride and Prejudice,* the Westons of *Emma,* and the Crofts of *Persuasion,* one of them married late in life, the other two childless—both facts, perhaps, meant to carry significance.

Miss Austen's general view of marriage, then, seems not to have been recklessly sanguine; yet it was also not cynical. For the reasons for the failures go back invariably to the kind of motives in marriage that she deprecates. Wherever affection or freedom from exacerbating domestic cares is wanting, she sees lurking danger. But the central point of her doctrine can be summed up by rephrasing St. Paul's dictum—it is better to marry than to be economically helpless. The objection to the single state she sees is not its shame or its isolation, but its dependency. Harriet Smith says to Emma, "You will be an old maid—and that's so dreadful!" "Never mind, Harriet," Emma replies; "I shall not be a poor old maid." Yet there may be sacrifice and perhaps humiliation in accepting marriage without affection as a mere refuge from the distresses of spinsterhood. For the sensitive it implies risks to happiness calling for silent patience, or expressed in grudging subservience, or eruptive in mean and tiresome complaint.

We have dwelt upon Miss Austen's realistic attitude toward marriage; for her interest in what society offered the young woman of her time is taken up almost wholly with her philosophy of the prudent marriage. For some of the women novelists before her time—Mrs. Smith, notably, and Mrs. Inchbald—a better position for women had implied the enlargement

of her mental horizon as well as the improvement of her legal and social
status. But Miss Austen's liking for Miss Burney and Miss Edgeworth may
have had not a little to do with their freedom from contentiousness
upon questions of this nature. The good words she has for them touch exclusively their literary achievement : their "knowledge of human nature,"
and their ability to depict it "with wit and humor" and "in the best chosen
language." These qualities may be summed up as representational and
stylistic; they have little connection with ideation.

It is natural to attribute Miss Austen's detachment from social controversy to the religious, perhaps rather, the clerical, atmosphere of her
home. It would be helpful to know how far her views were determined,
particularly in her early years, by the make-up of her father's library and
the reading habits and preferences of her family. The intellectual life of
the family seems to have been taken for granted rather than proved; for in
the Austen correspondence there is little evidence of wide interests deeply
pondered. No one familiar with the letters of Jane herself fails to be struck
with their clinging to the material and the timely—dress goods, a visit from
cousins, expenses for hat trimmings, scraps of innocent scandal, who is
splendidly pregnant, meals, and domestic comings and goings. The environment provided neither the soil nor the climate for lush intellectual
growth.

We know little, except inferentially, of the quality of Miss Austen's own
intellectual life. We have that assurance that her family was generously fed
upon fiction; but did she do any serious reading to speak of—serious reading in her day being in large measure the literature of revolt? Would con-
troversial books have been among the five hundred volumes that were to
be sold from the Reverend George's library when the family removed
from Steventon? If so, would the two young ladies of the family have
been approved in the reading of Bage, Godwin, Miss Wollstonecraft, not
to speak of Voltaire, Rousseau, Hume, and Paine? In particular, did Jane
know Mary Wollstonecraft as anything more than a name spoken under a
proper young lady's breath?

The last question has peculiar interest. First, because a young woman of
Jane Austen's alertness should have been interested in what a free-minded
woman had to say about woman's social bondage. In the second place,
because there are some striking affinities between Mary Wollstonecraft's
early doctrine and Miss Austen's unimpassioned opinions. At the same
time, it must be stressed that Miss Wollstonecraft's attitude and contentions appear in two quite distinct phases : the first socially and politically
not greatly important, and never given factitious importance, because her
early and obscure years were free from any sort of public reproach. Her
second phase covers the larger part of her career, radical, aggressive, and

anathema to the proper-minded because she lived in open conformity with her professions.

The first phase produced only two published works at all memorable; the first for reasons we are to consider, the second for one already noted.* These were *Thoughts on the Education of Daughters* (1787) and *Original Stories from Real Life* (1788). Jane Austen could have read the *Thoughts* in her middle teens, at the impressionable age. The book could very well have been accessible to her, for it is so remote from impiety or even radicalism that it could not have disturbed the Archbishop of Canterbury. It is, in truth, so rich in good counsel that the Reverend George Austen might have been at pains to see that his growing daughters read it.

The *Thoughts* anticipates so explicitly the theme and temper of *Sense and Sensibility* that it might serve not only as the text but as a fair epitome of the sermon for young women to which Miss Austen gave that title. Its tenor may be judged from these few sentences, not too skillfully put together, but not too dim in intention.

> Feeling is ridiculous when affected, and even when felt, ought not to be displayed. It will appear if genuine, but when pushed forward to notice, it is obvious vanity that has rivaled sorrow, and that the prettiness of the thing is thought of. . . .
>
> It is too universal a maxim with novelists that love is felt but once; though it appears to me that the heart which is capable of receiving an impression at all, and can distinguish, will turn to a new object when the first is found unworthy. . . . When any sudden stroke of fate deprives us of those we love, we may not readily get the better of the blow, but when we find that we have been led astray by our passions, and that it was our own imaginations which gave the high coloring to the picture, we may be certain time will drive it out of our minds."†

Miss Wollstonecraft still thinks of a girl's education principally as preparation for marriage, yet maintains that the instrumentalities of education, both formal and informal, fail to serve a woman's capacities or interests—a point to be greatly elaborated five years later in her *Vindication of the Rights of Woman*. The detail of the *Thoughts* we can pass; it is probably sufficient to say that it is a modest plea for the revision of the accepted views of woman's mind, place, and opportunities. There is indignation, but not plied under the forced draft of the *Vindication*. Miss

---

*See page 310.

†Compare this suggestive amplification in the *Vindication of the Rights of Woman* (1792): Novels, music, poetry, and gallantry all tend to make women the creatures of sensation; and their character is thus formed in the mould of folly during the time they are acquiring accomplishments.

Wollstonecraft has, as yet, no quarrel with men, institutions, principles, or even privilege; and Miss Austen could have accepted without qualms all she had to propose in the *Thoughts*. It is equally certain that later she would have parted company with the "notorious" author of the two *Vindications* and of *Maria*.*

Both intrinsically and circumstantially, Miss Austen's views as to the proper mental and social aliment for young ladies may very well have come from Miss Wollstonecraft rather than from Rousseau. For the violent hatred of Rousseau in England during and after the French Revolution might have kept her from knowledge of the "Sophie" passages of *Emile*. And despite her feeling that woman's normal place in the society of her time was that of wife and mother, she would, if she had known *Emile,* have resented Rousseau's insistence that whatever a young woman's natural charm, it was to be cultivated for the attraction and service of men, and that upon "serious" matters her mind must be preserved in its juvenile vacuity. In the *Thoughts,* on the other hand, Miss Wollstonecraft's picture of the desirable woman as modest but self-reliant, cultivated beyond the requirements of wifehood, and religious-minded, all these graces and attainments to be worn without display or vulgarity, gives us the very pattern of the Austen heroine.

I expressly avoid the conclusion that *Thoughts on the Education of Daughters* must have been the determining influence, still less the source, of Miss Austen's opinions on this subject. The book is, however, a strong, quiet stream of refreshing ideas stirring the slow current of conventional and sentimental commitments. These ideas are the very ones that animate *Sense and Sensibility,* but they are clearly and trenchantly urged, therefore far more effectual than the whisperings of feminism which had already been breathed in *Emmeline* and *A Simple Story*. Whether Miss Austen knew the *Thoughts* at first hand is less important than her responsiveness, conscious or unconscious, to a new trend of opinion.

As to inferences of immediate influence, we are perhaps on safer ground with a book identified simply as "Gisborne" in a letter to Cassandra of August 30, 1805, Dr. Chapman identifies it (with a query) as the Reverend Thomas Gisborne's *Enquiry into the Duties of the Female Sex,* published in 1797 and reprinted frequently in the next few years. The identification seems to be confirmed by the fact that although other titles of Gisborne's might have fitted Jane's known interest in sermons and books of moral weight, she was pleased after reading it in spite of the fact that she had felt an initial prejudice—presumably against the surface implications of the title.

---

*For the earlier *Vindication of the Rights of Men* see page 310, *note.*

If the identification is correct, it is nevertheless hard to see what, apart from the sermonizing habit, could have "pleased" her in the work. It is heavily pious, and distrustful of human nature, particularly feminine nature, which Gisborne believes the Creator made vulnerable in order to deserve man's protection. His acceptance of feminine inferiority is bolstered by showy rhetoric :

> The female form, not commonly doomed, in countries where the progress of civilization is far advanced, to labors more severe than the offices of domestic life, He has cast in a smaller mould, and bound together by a looser texture. But, to protect weakness from the oppression of domineering superiority, those whom He has not qualified to contend he has enabled to fascinate. To me it appears that He has adopted, and that He has adopted with the most conspicuous wisdom, a corresponding plan of discrimination between the mental powers and dispositions of the two sexes. The science of legislation, of jurisprudence, of political economy; the conduct of government in all its executive functions; the abstruse researches of erudition; the inexhaustible depths of philosophy; the acquirements subordinate to navigation; the knowledge indispensable in the wide field of commercial enterprise; the arts of defence, and of attack, by land and by sea, which the violence or the fraud of unprincipled assailants render needful; these, and other studies, pursuits, and occupations, assigned chiefly or entirely to men, demand the efforts of a mind endued with the powers of close and comprehensive reasoning, and of intense and continued application, in a degree in which they are not requisite for the discharge of the customary offices of female duty. It would therefore seem natural to expect, and experience, I think, confirms the justice of the expectation, that the Giver of all good, after bestowing those powers on men with a liberality proportioned to the existing necessity, would impart them to the female mind with a more sparing hand.

What Gisborne has to say on "female education" is as vaguely focused as it could very well have been even for his obscurantist contemporaries. His views on balls and card-playing should have provoked Jane, who was fond of both. And his opinions on "novels and romances" run almost precisely counter to her own in *Northanger Abbey*. Yet there is a drift of good sense, even if rather narrowly clerical good sense. And his views on the judicious marriage Miss Austen might have borrowed from him if she had not already propounded them in the early novels.

But there is one arresting passage :

> For some years past the custom of acting plays in private theatres . . . has occasionally prevailed. It is a custom liable to this objection among

others : that it is almost certain to prove, in its effects, particularly injurious to the female performers. . . . Take the benefit of all these favorable circumstances; yet, what is even then the tendency of such amusements? To encourage vanity; to excite a thirst of applause and admiration on account of attainments which, if they are to be thus exhibited, it would commonly have been far better for the individual not to possess; to destroy diffidence by the unrestrained familiarity with persons of the other sex, which inevitably results from being joined with them in the drama; to create a general fondness for the perusal of plays, of which so many are improper to be read; and for attending dramatic representations, of which so many are unfit to be witnessed.

There has been no small amount of speculation as to why Jane Austen, who liked the theater and home theatricals, should have made so serious an issue of amateur performance in *Mansfield Park*. Have we the answer here?

On the whole, however, it must be said that Gisborne's *Enquiry* could have had little formative influence upon Jane Austen's mind, though that little could have been in some instances significant.

With Miss Austen it is rash to take for granted her reading acquaintance with things she does not clearly identify; for it is difficult to affirm that she was widely read in controversy, political, social, or economic—or, for that matter, that she was really a broadly cultivated woman. With Fanny Burney and Maria Edgeworth we are more confident of a background of effective culture, not only because of the more intellectual cast of their correspondence, but because the fathers of both had a firm footing in the intellectual world. So far as we can judge, the Reverend George Austen was not an unintelligent or unamiable parent; yet hints in the letters foster the notion that his home habits may have furnished the groundwork for his daughter's portrait of Mr. Bennet in *Pride and Prejudice,* who liked the quiet of his library—with the door closed—and left his daughters' mental growth largely to Providence, trusting they would learn no more than he thought would be good for them.

Before Miss Wollstonecraft's time the upper classes in England had expended little thought upon the education of anybody at any age. And what trickles there were of opinion and theory had little to do with the aims of education for women; for in general women were presumed to be unequal to, or unimportant for, the demands of thought. That view was not only a matter of unformulated every-day belief, it was inculcated by moralists, justified in the current theologies, and accepted by such well indoctrinated aristocratic-philosophic minds as Chesterfield's, Walpole's, and Gibbon's. Miss Austen herself was not, on the surface, greatly agitated by this question of how and how much a young woman should learn. She had ideas on the subject, but they seem to add up to no more than mildly indignant recognition of women's "agreeable ignorance."*

We have dwelt upon her kinship with the novelists, and in a more limited way with the thinkers, of her time. But while her important relationships seem clear, they were not broadly determinative. She picked up readily the shop-practices of an art in a fairly advanced state, though not in the work of her immediate precursors either lively or profound, and refashioned and vitalized them with her own originality. Conscious as she was of her schooling, she belonged to no school. What she in her turn contributed to the art of fiction was—beyond her skill in character-drawing—concentration and cohesiveness which it had previously lacked. In that sense she can be credited with having brought nearer realization a full maturity of form. Yet it can scarcely be said that she played a great part in perfecting the machinery of fiction; for the demands of form she took lightly. As she stands apart from her predecessors in the free-hand incisiveness of her work, she stands just as definitely apart from her successors; for her achievement was not of the easily imitable sort. When Meredith places her novels among the rare English examples of high comedy, it is with insistence upon his thesis that the comic genius is simply a miracle of artistic personality.

Her lack of palpable concern with efforts, violent, persuasive, or tactical, to remake the world has been from time to time urged against her. She was a small-minded woman, we have been told, in what was at least for the moment a great-minded world. Few, however, have attributed the confinement of her social horizon to ignorance of life. It is due rather to her quietism, which too often has been interpreted as apathy. But isn't her adherance to the society and environment she knew a matter of common sense? Without the passion of a Wollstonecraft or an Emily Brontë, she was not called upon to voice a resentment she did not feel or to nurse a flame of poetic fervor that was not in her nature. She demanded sincerity, and she dealt with herself and her art sincerely, setting a task which she knew she could perform intelligently and gracefully. At heart she was not democratic; that is sufficiently clear in the small place she has given the common man. At heart she was also not aristocratic; that is clear

---

*"The advantages of natural folly in a beautiful girl have been already set forth by the capital pen of a sister author; and to her treatment of the subject I will only add in justice to men, that though to the larger and more trifling part of the sex, imbecility in females is a great enhancement of their personal charms, there is a portion of them too reasonable and too well informed themselves to desire anything more in women than ignorance." (*Northanger Abbey*, Chapter XIV.)

"Men have every advantage of us in telling their own story. Education has been theirs in so much higher a degree; the pen has been in their hands. I will not allow books to prove anything." (*Pursuasion*, Chapter XL).

in her insistence that whatever the aristocratic virtues might be, they were virtues only when accompanied by intelligence and decency. She cherished respectability, but was quietly aware that it was not immune from canker. Working wholly within her true environment, she found ample material for judging and depicting human nature and social usage.

Miss Austen's intellectual growth has not been sufficiently insisted upon. Her emergence from adolescence was rapid. That is even more interestingly apparent, I believe, in her quick pick-up of the literary touch in her earliest letters than in the transition from juvenilia to novels. A letter to Cassandra of September 18, 1796, is full of unripe tomboy humor, with only now and then a phrase of undeniable rightness and niceness :

> What dreadful weather we have!—It keeps one in a continual state of Inelegance.—If Miss Pearson should return with me, pray be careful not to expect too much Beauty.

But two years later she is writing as the complete woman, the native art now become delicate and almost unconscious. Since we lack the first drafts of her early novels, we are without the same kind of before-the-eye evidence of how maturity grew upon her. But the gulf of difference between *Sense and Sensibility* or *Northanger Abbey* and the last three novels is everywhere recognized; and the superiority of *Pride and Prejudice* to the other novels of the earlier period is due, as we have seen, to the thoroughness of her revision. If it cannot be said that each of her novels was an improvement upon its predecessor, they do show from first to last a steady progress not only in insight but in firmness and finish.

She never achieved the range and diversity of interests of a George Eliot because her period and her family situation prevented it. Her perceptions, however, enlarged and ripened. Her first conscious purpose had been to make the young lady of her time more ladylike (as Miss Burney and Miss Edgeworth had meant to) but it quickly developed an added aim—to place the relations of men and women upon a more adult basis than gallantry and patronage. Her elders in the art of fiction had not succeeded in doing that.

Her awareness of the special nature of her own genius came late and slowly. Whether or not there were immediate causes for the long period of presumed inactivity, there were perhaps doubts of her own gift, or uncertainty as to whether she could reach the mass of not specially intellectual readers. It is not clear how her interest in writing revived, but once *Sense and Sensibility* and *Pride and Prejudice* had found their readers, she showed an almost incredibly rapid expansion of literary range and power. Of her artistic maturity she was certainly sure during the last three or four years. The firmness of the late novels is not accounted for by accelerated industry, but by her understanding of herself and her potential. Beginning as the admiring yet discriminating pupil of Miss Burney and Miss Edgeworth, she emerged as a novelist of almost unchallenged distinction.

In considering Miss Austen's place in the traditions of her art, I have neglected lip-service to some respected scholarly prepossessions. I have tried to avoid rash assumptions as to direct influences upon her work—for *Einfluss,* the darling of scholarship a generation ago, seems in my view too often a lurking-place for the *post hoc* fallacy. I have also spoken sparingly and cautiously of her part in the "development" or the "evolution" of the novel, simply because the scientific conception of evolution presents an imperfect analogy to what we find in the history of any aesthetic mode. The mechanistic process, still more, the trend to definitive form, are only dimly and uncertainly present in what we have so far seen in the writer's art. If we can isolate a survival factor in literary history, it would seem to be the infinite repetition of the human, which is after all the commonplace. Jane Austen's slowly enlarged but sustained reputation has accomplished as much as almost any other novelist's to prove the viability of that human-commonplace.

It is easier to avoid profundity than to affect it. But it is not altogether for that reason that I have taken the position, right or wrong, that Miss Austen's readableness lies on the surface of her fictions. Yet the delicacy of her ironic temper, her affirmative but undidactic morality, and perhaps the mystery of a virginal art, make her a peculiarly fascinating subject for interpretive and analytic scholarship—but scholarship which in some instances, I am afraid, may in its remoter paths prove for the common reader difficult or even thorny. I feel that I owe it to my reader, however, to supplement an admittedly limited treatment with a list of the more specialized, and in some cases, more recondite, studies of Miss Austen's art. So we end without dignity on a foot-note.*

---

*Familiar biographical and critical works I believe have been noticed in passing or foot-noted. Recent specialized studies include two volumes of "*Talks*" by Sheila Kaye-Smith and Gladys B. Stern on a variety of topics enjoyably handled. Mary Lascelles' *Jane Austen and Her Art* (1939) contains an admirable biographical-critical summary and has topical sections on the burlesque pattern in the novels, on style, and on narrative art. Marvin Mudrick's *Jane Austen: Irony as Defense and Discovery* (1952) and Andrew H. Wright's *Jane Austen's Novels, a Study in Structure* (1953) both indicate their special approach in their titles. Economic and sociological interpretations are found in papers or introductions by Leonard Woolf, Mark Schorer, and David Daiches which can be readily run down through the familiar reference media. Last, but not least stimulating, I suggest for anyone who has read enough of Miss Austen to know whether or not he admires her H. W. Garrod's *Jane Austen, a Depreciation,* an understanding and witty adverse judgment read in 1928 before the Royal Society of Literature and reprinted in William Heath's *Discussions of Jane Austen.*

A Note on the Illustrations

THE COMMON medium of book illustration in the eighteenth century was copperplate engraving—in Thomas Rowlandson's case, etching. Engraved plates were usually in line-engraving, rarely, and less effectively, mezzotint. Etched plates might be either in line or aquatint, sometimes the two in combination. All these processes called for handwork in the execution of the plate; for the mechanical processes (half tones and photo-engravings) were then unknown.

Customarily two artists were engaged in the making of an illustrative plate: the designer, who made the original picture in crayon, pen, charcoal, wash, water color, or perhaps oil; and the engraver, who with his engraving instruments copied the drawing as accurately as possible on the plate from which the printed impressions were to be taken.* The illustration itself was of course credited to the designer. The engraver might be regarded as an artisan rather than an artist; but he might also achieve a skill and refinement that could earn him the title of artist in his own right. Designer and engraver might also be combined in one person. Hogarth and Gravelot, for example, at various times in their lives engraved plates for other designers, engraved their own designs, or employed other engravers to work from their designs.

At the beginning of the eighteenth century George Vertue was the distinguished English engraver, working largely on portraiture. His hard line and strong masses were passed on to Hogarth. By the mid-century, French illustrative styling had already begun to displace the English. The French school included François Boucher, court painter to Louis XV, who became master in fact or in direct influence to Moreau le Jeune, Eisen, and most

---

*The names of both designer and engraver were generally given below the engraving; the designer's name on the left side (as printed) with *inv.* or *del.*, for *invenit* or *delineavit*, and the engraver's on the right side with *sc.* or *fec.* for *sculpsit* or *fecit*.

notably for our purpose, Hubert Gravelot. Gravelot lived and worked in London from 1730 to 1745, at one time conducting his own school, at which both Gainsborough the painter and Grignion the painter-engraver were his pupils. It was his influence rather than Hogarth's that determined in the main the character of English book illustration throughout the remainder of the century.

Gravelot had absorbed much of Boucher's delicate, even over-delicate, refinement and transparency. In his turn, as the master-illustrator of the mid-century, he strongly influenced the later work of Charles Grignion and Edward Francesco Burney, less markedly, the perhaps more English tone of Samuel Wale, Isaac Taylor the elder, and the distinguished Thomas Stothard, whose illustrations at the end of the century in the *Novelist's Magazine* were a lasting delight to Charles Lamb. In France, speaking broadly, book illustration was in the eighteenth century more common and more voguish than in England.

Throughout the century original issues ("first editions") of English fiction were almost never illustrated; that is, if by illustration we mean an artist's interpretation of the spirit and setting of a number of the incidents in a sizable narrative. When frontispieces were used, such as the plates in the first issues of Defoe's *Robinson Crusoe* (1719) and *The Fortunate Mistress* (1724), they merely added to the lure of an elaborately descriptive title page, rather than glossing the narrative. Frontispiece portraits of authors, not uncommon in the collected works of poets and dramatists as far back as the Elizabethan age, almost never appeared in the novels and romances of the eighteenth century. But from the middle of the century on, novels which had established their place and found a continuous market began to appear with true illustrations in reprints authorized or pirated.

The first example of true, or comprehensive, illustration for an English novel was Francis Hayman's and Hubert Gravelot's designs for the combined sixth edition of Part I of *Pamela*, and third edition of Part II, which together constituted the first illustrated edition of *Pamela,* in four volumes, 1742. Hayman designed twelve of the illustrations, Gravelot seventeen; but Gravelot engraved all the plates. Hayman used two of his designs in his decoration of the booths at Vauxhall; and these, no doubt, were the paintings (or among the paintings) which Mrs. Eliza Haywood tells us depicted the story of Pamela upon the walls of Vauxhall. Richardson himself commissioned Hayman's illustrations, and he presumably chose the incidents to be illustrated. The sensational incidents in the novel were not pictured—a fact which confirms the idea that Richardson was not blest with a sense of humor. The Hayman-Gravelot illustrations were not reproduced in the later editions of *Pamela.*

Joseph Highmore made on his own account twelve paintings of scenes from *Pamela* which were engraved by Antoine Benoist and published by Highmore in 1744-5. The work was apparently not done for Richardson's publishers, and was never used in any book form of *Pamela*.

The great William Hogarth did almost no book illustration in his ripe years, although his early illustrations to *Don Quixote* and Butler's *Hudibras* had much to do with the making of his reputation. It is known that Richardson negotiated with Hogarth for illustrations to *Pamela*. At least one plate was made—and rejected—because, we learn from one of his letters, the designs "fell short of the spirit of the passages they were intended to represent."

It is surprising that Hogarth illustrated no novel of Fielding's, for Fielding repeatedly expresses admiration of his work. The first illustrations to a novel by Fielding were sixteen plates designed by Gravelot, and executed by the Dutch engraver Van Punt, which appeared, rather curiously, not in an English edition, but in LaPlace's French translation of *Tom Jones,* published at "Londres" (but probably Paris) in 1750.

Gravelot's pupil, Grignion, engraved the earliest illustrations to *Roderick Random* and *Peregrine Pickle*. The frontispieces to the two volumes of the second edition of *Random* in 1748 were after Hayman, and those to the four volumes of the fourth edition of *Pickle*, 1769, are said to have been designed by Henry Fuseli, although Fuseli's name did not appear on the plates.

Hogarth's two illustrations to Tristram Shandy, done at Sterne's personal urging, are the only known work he did to illustrate a novel by a contemporary. *Tristram Shandy* was published in nine parts from 1760 [1759?] to 1767. The first of Hogarth's plates missed the first issue of Volume I, but appeared in the second edition of 1760, and the second plate in the first edition of Volume III, in 1761 Hogarth died before the succeeding volumes appeared.

The second edition, 1773, of Mackenzie's *Man of Feeling* is said to have had a frontispiece by Isaac Taylor, but I have been unable to see the volume. Stothard's illustrations to Strahan and Cadell's edition, London, 1800 (not the Chiswick edition of the same year), are among the most charming examples of his work.

Fanny Burney's *Evelina,* published in 1778, was followed in the next year by a three-volume edition (the fourth) with frontispieces by John Mortimer, who was not rated among the first illustrators of his time. However, his illustration of *Evelina* helping Mme. Duval out of the mire, from the second volume, is an interesting style-plate. In the following year, 1780, three colored illustrations of *Evelina* by Edward Francesco Burney, a favourite cousin, and a popular artist in the baroque fashion, were exhibited at the Royal Academy. These were not issued at the time in any published form, although Fanny herself greatly admired them.

A great fillip was given to the illustration of fiction when *The Novelist's Magazine* began in 1780 a series of reprints of both English and foreign fiction. In the twenty-three volumes put out from 1780 to 1788, the publisher, James Harrison, issued thirty-nine English novels, better or worse, with numerous copper-engravings, after drawings principally by Stothard, with a few from Edward F. Burney and Robert Smirke. They were agreeable and usually delightful work, from any of these hands, classically posed, sentimental, but faithful to the spirit of their text. All the illustrations for the ten or a dozen English novels of the first importance, with the exception of *Pamela* and *Humphry Clinker,* were after Stothard's originals. Burney, the champion of sentimentalism in art as Richardson was in fiction, designed those to *Pamela,* and also to *Humphry Clinker.*

Thomas Rowlandson's illustrations are in a class altogether their own, in their faultless discernment of the inevitable incident, in their vitality, and in their unquestionable artistic distinction. He shows two styles, both of which may appear in a single plate. One is highly exaggerative caricature, reminiscent of Hogarth and anticipatory of Daumier and Cruikshank; the other is suave, graceful, verging on the sentimental. Both are full of movement, with a characteristic Rubens-like exuberance in his drawing of women. These notable illustrations, to *Joseph Andrews, Tom Jones, Roderick Random, Peregrine Pickle, Humphry Clinker, The Sentimental Journey,* and *The Vicar of Wakefield,* were published and republished between 1790 and 1810.

The original of these Rowlandson plates was usually a water color, copied by his studio assistants in line-etching or aquatint, or both, and finished in either of two states, black and white, or hand colored after the original. The colored plates were necessarily expensive, and apparently issued in small number. The books containing them are rare in the extreme.

It may have been noticed that we have passed over the name of the English artist-engraver who is today, perhaps after Hogarth, the most highly regarded of his century. William Blake, poet, visionary, and painter, was trained and practised as an engraver. He did a series of drawings for Mary Wollstonecraft's *Original Stories from Real Life,* six of which were engraved for the second edition of the book in 1791. They were Blake's only work in illustration of a fiction, though he had engraved (without designing) some of the plates in *The Novelist's Magazine.*

The extravagantly popular Gothic romances of Ann Radcliffe and "Monk" Lewis were, like other fictions of their period, innocent of illustration in their original form, although their subject matter plainly invited it. In their later phase, at the very end of the century, when they had deteriorated into chap-book or "blue-wrapper" imitations of Mrs. Radcliffe, they frequently appeared with engraved frontispieces of the greatest naiveté. Mrs. Radcliffe's own romances were not illustrated until John Limbird produced cheap reprints of all five in 1824. These contained woodcuts printed in the text, incredibly awkward in figure drawing, but presentable in landscape recalling the Bewick manner. In the few instances in which these woodcuts are signed, they bear the name of one of three engravers, G. Watts, Mary Byfield, and M. Sears.

From the publication of *Pamela* on, practically all the notable designers and engravers of the period tried their hands, sooner or later, on the illustration of fiction. So the best of the illustrated novels are in reality an epitome of the best illustrative art of the period. Yet copies of these illustrated fictions are today in general extremely hard to find, for the original issue of a novel was at that time, we are told, customarily about five hundred copies, and wear and tear destroyed eventually a large portion of them. Our illustrations have been taken in every case from original copies of the first issues. It may be added that most of them have never been republished since their first appearance.

Four of our illustrations call for special comment. The frontispiece, Thomas Rowlandson's "Battle of Upton," was made as an illustration for *Tom Jones*; but we reproduce not the actual book illustration, but Rowlandson's original water color for it, now in the Yale University Library. This, it is believed, has never been reproduced.

The unsigned engraving attacking Sterne's immodesty is an entertaining bit of "curiosa," but not without interest in connection with the controversy. The "Tales of Wonder" of James Gilray is not an unfamiliar print, but probably the only piece from this celebrated political cartoonist which has literary bearing.

Sir Thomas Lawrence's crayon and pencil drawing of Holcroft and Godwin at the trial of their friend John Thelwall on a charge of treason in 1794 has had a curious history. From the time it was made, it was probably in the continuous possession of the Broderip family until 1872, when it was sold at Christie's. It again disappeared from general notice until 1961, when it was included in a Lawrence exhibition at the Royal Academy. In the interval, although it had passed through at least two dealers' hands, it had been thought by many students of the Revolutionary period to have been irretrievably lost. We reproduce it by courtesy of the owner, Dr. Kenneth Garlick, in the belief that it too has never been published.

Index

A Note about the Author

HARRISON R. STEEVES entered Columbia as a freshman in 1899 and retired from it a half-century later as Professor Emeritus. In the long interval he became known to thousands of students, helped in the making of eminent scholars and professional men, and entertained (so *they* say) some now distinguished entertainers. At eighty he emerged from rural retirement in New Hampshire to write this scholarly but graceful and charming account of popular taste in fiction during the eighteenth century.